LAW AND CONSTITUTIONAL CHANGE

A collection of some of the best papers presented at the 25th British Legal History Conference at Queen's University Belfast in July 2022, *Law and Constitutional Change* examines the role that law plays when countries experience a major constitutional upheaval. It examines the interaction of law and politics in history across different legal jurisdictions with different legal traditions. The theme of the conference was 'Law and Constitutional Change' and was inspired by the decade of anniversaries in Ireland (2012–23) commemorating events from a century ago that began with the Home Rule Crisis and ended with the partition of the country. It studies the changes that occurred at that time in a wider British and Irish as well as international context, with a view to deepening understanding of contemporary debates such as those surrounding Brexit and its longer-term implications.

This title is also available as open access on Cambridge Core.

DAVID CAPPER is Professor of Civil Procedure and Remedies at Queen's University Belfast and Joint Honorary Secretary of the Irish Legal History Society. He was co-convenor (with Professor Norma Dawson) of the 2022 British Legal History Conference. He has authored or co-authored four monographs on Civil Procedure and Remedies, as well as over seventy essays and law review articles in these fields.

CONOR McCORMICK is Senior Lecturer in the School of Law at Queen's University Belfast. He specialises in constitutional and administrative law, with a particular focus on the law and legal system of Northern Ireland. He has been elected to the Council of the Irish Legal History Society.

N. M. DAWSON is Professor Emeritus at Queen's University Belfast. A former President of the Irish Legal History Society, she is Honorary Professor at the University of Edinburgh. Her *Modern Legal History of Treasure Law* was published in 2023.

LAW AND
CONSTITUTIONAL CHANGE

Edited by

DAVID CAPPER
Queen's University Belfast

CONOR McCORMICK
Queen's University Belfast

N. M. DAWSON
Queen's University Belfast

CAMBRIDGE
UNIVERSITY PRESS

CAMBRIDGE
UNIVERSITY PRESS

Shaftesbury Road, Cambridge CB2 8EA, United Kingdom

One Liberty Plaza, 20th Floor, New York, NY 10006, USA

477 Williamstown Road, Port Melbourne, VIC 3207, Australia

314–321, 3rd Floor, Plot 3, Splendor Forum, Jasola District Centre, New Delhi – 110025, India

103 Penang Road, #05–06/07, Visioncrest Commercial, Singapore 238467

Cambridge University Press is part of Cambridge University Press & Assessment, a department of the University of Cambridge.

We share the University's mission to contribute to society through the pursuit of education, learning and research at the highest international levels of excellence.

www.cambridge.org
Information on this title: www.cambridge.org/9781009797740

DOI: 10.1017/9781009797733

First published 2025

A catalogue record for this publication is available from the British Library

A Cataloging-in-Publication data record for this book is available from the Library of Congress

ISBN 978-1-009-79774-0 Hardback

In Memoriam
Sir Anthony Hart
(1946–2019)

CONTENTS

CONTRIBUTORS

GABRIELLE APPLEBY, *University of New South Wales*

SIR JOHN BAKER, *University of Cambridge*

DAVID CAPPER, *Queen's University Belfast*

KEVIN COSTELLO, *University College Dublin*

PETER CROOKS, *Trinity College Dublin*

MEGAN DAVIS, *University of New South Wales*

N. M. DAWSON, *Queen's University Belfast*

STEPHANIE DROPULJIC, *University of Exeter*

LADY BRENDA HALE, *Rt. Hon. Baroness Hale of Richmond, Former President of the Supreme Court of the UK*

A. J. HANNAY, *University of Manchester*

JOEL HERMAN, *Trinity College Dublin*

COLUM KENNY, *Dublin City University*

KATRE LUHAMAA, *University of Tartu*

RICHARD McBRIDE, *Queen's University Belfast*

CONOR McCORMICK, *Queen's University Belfast*

THOMAS MOHR, *University College Dublin*

C. R. G. MURRAY, *University of Newcastle*

TIMOTHY MURTAGH, *Public Record Office of Northern Ireland*

MERIKE RISTIKIVI, *University of Tartu*

JULIA RUDOLPH, *North Carolina State University*

MAIKE SCHWIDDESSEN, *University of Würzburg*

GWEN SEABOURNE, *University of Bristol*

KARIN SEIN, *University of Tartu*

ROBERT BRETT TAYLOR, *University of Aberdeen*

CIARÁN WALLACE, *Trinity College Dublin*

IAN WARD, *University of Newcastle*

FOREWORD

Queen's University Belfast, together with the Irish Legal History Society, was privileged to host the 25th British Legal History Conference in Belfast in July 2022. Due to the pandemic, the conference had been postponed from 2021.

Since the success of the sixteenth conference held in Dublin in 2003 and the publication of the conference papers entitled 'Adventures and the Law', it was a burning ambition of the late Sir Anthony Hart to persuade the organising committee to allow Belfast to host the conference. This was achieved, and in 2018 a small organising committee was formed with Sir Anthony as chair.

Sir Anthony had attended quite a number of previous conferences, and his tactful diplomacy and commanding presence encouraged cooperation and indeed enthusiasm from a range of people and organisations, which ensured a well-organised event. Queen's agreed to provide the facilities for lectures, accommodation and entertainment.

Tragedy struck when Sir Anthony died suddenly on Tuesday, 9 July 2019. The legal history community was shocked and saddened at the loss of such a titan in legal history. The society was fortunate to have Emeritus Professor Norma Dawson take over as chair of the committee. Professor Dawson's tireless energy and management skills helped to formulate not only a programme of excellent speakers but a number of extra-curricular events such as a visit to Belfast City Hall and an excellent evening in Parliament Buildings, Stormont, generously sponsored by one of Ireland's leading law firms, Carson McDowell. The conference culminated in a gala event at Queen's which included a reception in the Graduate School building followed by dinner in the Great Hall.

Lady Hart was a constant source of tangible and moral support for the conference. This enabled us to establish the Sir Anthony Hart Memorial Prize competition for the best paper presented at the conference by a doctoral student, and to award prizes for those placed first and runner-up. Prizes were awarded to Ashley Hannay (University of Manchester) in first place, and to Stephanie Dropuljic (University of Exeter) in second place. We are delighted that both papers are published in this volume.

This publication is a testament to the high calibre of papers delivered at a deeply enriching conference. Our appreciation and thanks are extended to the editors – Professor David Capper, Dr Conor McCormick and Professor Norma Dawson – for their excellent work.

Patrick Geoghegan
President, ILHS, 2018–2021
John Gordon
President, ILHS, 2021–2024

ACKNOWLEDGEMENTS

We acknowledge the generous support of the Irish Legal History Society and the School of Law, Queen's University Belfast, which has made it possible for this volume to be published on an open-access basis. We also thank Marianne Nield, Biju Singh and their colleagues at Cambridge University Press for courteous assistance throughout the publishing process.

~

Editors' Introduction

DAVID CAPPER, CONOR McCORMICK AND N. M. DAWSON

This volume publishes selected papers from the 25th British Legal History Conference (BLHC), co-hosted by Queen's University Belfast and the Irish Legal History Society (ILHS) in 2022. That was the second occasion on which the ILHS co-hosted a BLHC, the first being in 2003 at University College Dublin, when the conference theme was 'Adventures of the Law', an echo of Judge William Johnston's suggestion that the Anglo-Norman invasion of Ireland in the twelfth century was 'the first adventure of the common law'.[1] Even as Judge Johnston's legal-historical paper was published in the *Law Quarterly Review* in 1920, events of immense constitutional significance for both Great Britain and Ireland were unfolding. Within two years, some of the public records on which he had relied were reduced to ashes in the fire at the Four Courts in Dublin, the opening engagement in the Civil War in Ireland (1922–23). The looming centenary of that tumultuous and testing time for the Union – the partition of Ireland, the creation of the Irish Free State, and the creation of Northern Ireland as a province within the United Kingdom – prompted the choice of theme for the 25th BLHC, 'Law and Constitutional Change', initially scheduled for July 2021. Although the Covid-19 pandemic necessitated postponement to July 2022, the conference theme lost none of its 'centenary' significance for British and Irish legal historians, as it still fell within the ambit of the so-called Decade of Centenaries in Ireland (2012–23).[2] At the same time, the organisers hoped that the conference theme was wide enough to be of international significance – and so it proved to be.

---

[1] W. J. Johnston, 'The First Adventure of the Common Law', *Law Quarterly Review*, 36 (1920), 9–30. Johnston was an Irish county court judge before and after partition, advancing to the Irish High Court in 1924 and to the Irish Supreme Court in 1939: see 'Johnston, William John (1863–1940), barrister and judge', by P. Gageby in *Dictionary of Irish Biography* (online, open access).

[2] https://decadeofcentenaries.com/about/ (accessed 27 February 2024).

For historians everywhere, the prospect of the loss of a national archive is a sobering thought. Before reconstruction could even be contemplated, it would be necessary first to audit the losses sustained, in itself a massive undertaking. The 'Virtual Record Treasury of Ireland' (VRTI) is a unique archives reconstruction project, established by Trinity College Dublin in collaboration with the National Archives of Ireland, the Public Record Office of Northern Ireland, The National Archives (UK) and the Irish Manuscripts Commission. The aim is to reconstruct, in virtual form, the 'Record Treasury' of the Public Record Office of Ireland, lost to the Four Courts fire in 1922. We invited the VRTI team (led by Dr Peter Crooks of Trinity College Dublin) to address the conference in plenary session, and were pleased to have a virtual presentation from Dr Tim Murtagh, a member of the team, heroically delivered while he was suffering from Covid-19. In this volume, we are delighted to showcase the VRTI project in a chapter prepared by Dr Crooks and Dr Murtagh, with their colleagues Ciarán Wallace and Joel Herman. Their chapter outlines the history of legal record-keeping in Ireland up to the establishment of the Public Records Office of Ireland in 1867, traces the events of 1922 and the destruction of most of a vast collection of legal records, and explains how it has been possible to ascertain the scale of the losses and to mitigate them by finding substitute records. The scale and extent of Anglo-Irish, then British–Irish relations, meant that duplicates of many records could be found in state repositories in London, while church and other semi-public or private collections have also facilitated substitution. Crooks, Murtagh and colleagues remind readers of the need to be aware of 'the archival turn', the process by which historical understanding may be influenced by the institutional nature and arrangement of state archives.

In providing this introductory digest of the chapters in this volume we take an essentially chronological approach, reflecting the main theme of the conference. The first five chapters address topics from the Middle Ages to the seventeenth century, the latter being a period of profound constitutional change in England and Scotland. The next four chapters are set in the eighteenth century, a period of great constitutional change. Themes connected to the tumultuous events in Ireland a century ago are the subject of the following four chapters as well as the final contribution to the volume by Crooks, Murtagh and colleagues, outlined above. Two contributions (Chapters 14 and 15) detail constitutional change in other parts of the world, and a plenary lecture by Lady Hale discusses a profound constitutional change in the United Kingdom in recent times, the 'bringing home' of the European Convention on Human Rights.

The Middle Ages to the Seventeenth Century

Constitutional change has not infrequently been viewed as treason by adherents of the regime *in situ* before the change occurred. Gwen Seabourne's chapter opens this volume by discussing treason of a different kind – wives killing their husbands. She begins by relating an early fifteenth-century case in which three persons were convicted of murder – the wife of the victim and her two male accomplices. The latter were hanged while the wife was burned, a feature of the case that raises interesting questions about the nature of the offence of husband-killing and the legal status of women at that time. The association of husband-killing with the offence of treason as well as murder gave rise to a highly nuanced legal position, the concept and terminology of treason playing differently across a range of scenarios and causing much complexity in matters of criminal procedure, sometimes involving other family members. The chapter explains how this complexity might even be exploited by wives who were 'both homicidal and canny', how it challenged the thinking of the common lawyers in the late medieval period, and how it informs our understanding of the status of women in both familial and legal contexts at that time.

Ashley Hannay's chapter discusses the processes of legislative drafting, political negotiation and litigation that culminated in the enactment of the Statute of Uses 1536 (transposed to Ireland in 1634). The Statute of Uses was the core stratagem in Henry VIII's policy of 'fiscal feudalism', which aimed to prevent landowner avoidance of feudal incidents, particularly those payable on death. Hannay's forensic examination of surviving bills and other contemporary documents advances an original account of the genesis of this legislation. Fresh light is shed on the relationship between the Crown, the legislature and the courts during the Reformation Parliament, a pivotal period in English constitutional and legal history.

Stephanie Dropuljic then takes us north to Scotland in a discussion of the Scots law doctrine of 'art and part'. This denotes a form of criminal liability that attaches to persons who collectively participate in an offence while sharing a common purpose. The chapter provides explanations of how this doctrine was understood in some early sources of Scots law, before assessing the extent of sixteenth-century legislative modifications. Dropuljic argues that, notwithstanding the ostensible intentions of Parliament represented in these provisions, the courts and the Privy Council seem to have been persuaded subsequently to recognise defences which knocked the hard edges off what would otherwise have been an unfairly wide and strict conception of criminal liability.

In one of the conference's plenary lectures Sir John Baker traces the roots of judicial review back to a set of fundamental constitutional principles that were revived in the late sixteenth century, namely that 'the king could do no wrong' and that 'the king could not acquire or part with property except by matter of record'. Sir John explains how these doctrines came to underpin what are now called the prerogative writs – principally habeas corpus, prohibition, mandamus and certiorari – each of which developed incrementally to form the collective basis of an extensive legal jurisdiction over executive actions. The King's Bench is credited, alongside the High Court of Parliament, with using these tools to shape the initial contours of judicial review and public law.

Chapter 5, Ian Ward's 'The Aspirations of James Stuart', brings us squarely into the revolutionary seventeenth century. This chapter, rich in seventeenth-century literary and cultural allusion, discusses the kingly and political hopes of James VI of Scotland and I of England. Three aspirations in particular are addressed. First is James's unshakeable belief in the divine right of kings to rule, unequivocally expressed in his political writings as king of Scotland, a belief that would eventually set him on a collision course with the common law judges of England. Second, James's aspirations for the Union of the Crowns in 1603 is explored. His hopes for an 'inner empire' of '*Great* Britain' were less widely shared in England than those for an 'outer empire' beyond the seas (including the Plantation of Ulster). Finally, Ward considers James's much narrower aspiration for Britain's relationship with continental European powers. The nature of monarchy and its role within the constitution; the political outworking of union within these islands; Europe and Britain's place within it – all these seventeenth-century constitutional concerns remain of vital interest today.

The Eighteenth Century

Robert Brett Taylor opens this group of chapters by interrogating the extent to which British constitutional law has been consonant with English constitutional law after the Acts of Union between England and Scotland in 1707. Taylor argues that the relevant provisions of the Acts of Union did not replace Scots public law with English public law. Nor was Scots law retained as an entirely distinct body of jurisprudence. Instead, it is argued that the Acts of Union created a unified British public law in respect of the Crown and Parliament, over which the UK Supreme Court (like its predecessor, the House of Lords) is the ultimate arbiter. As such, Taylor suggests there is nothing to stop Scots public law from having a greater influence over the content of British public law than it has done to date. Moreover, when viewed from this perspective, the author sees plenty of scope for the public laws of England and Scotland to diverge legitimately as regards everything but the Crown and Parliament.

Kevin Costello charts changes to the way in which judicial review by quo warranto was used to oversee parliamentary borough elections in the eighteenth century. His chapter explains the common law background to quo warranto before focusing on its operation after being placed on a statutory footing by the Municipal Corporations Act 1711. Costello demonstrates how, despite being preferred over a partisan parliamentary alternative, the quo warranto process under the 1711 Act became 'tainted by association' with a range of dishonourable electoral strategies. Nonetheless, he concludes that it should be recognised as an important turning point in the constitutional transition from parliamentary to judicial oversight of electoral malpractices.

Chapters 8 and 9 focus upon Ireland. Julia Rudolph discusses laws introduced in the eighteenth-century Irish Parliament regulating mortgage transactions. There were two significant contexts in which this legislation should be viewed. Legislation allowing Roman Catholics to lend on the security of a mortgage were viewed by proponents as a precursor to Catholic emancipation. Opponents were defenders of the Williamite settlement and its restrictions on Roman Catholics owning land. Enforcement of the security in the event of a debtor's default would lead to Catholics becoming landowners. The other context was as much, if not more, a reflection of developments in the United Kingdom and the wider British Empire. It concerned mortgage legislation, sometimes protective of the debtor and other times pro-creditor, that was a response to wider political and economic developments. One example of where the Irish Parliament was ahead of other jurisdictions in this regard concerned legislation passed in 1707 to set up a registry of deeds as protection against clandestine mortgages.

Maike Schwiddessen discusses the impact of the 'Constitution of 1782', under which the Irish Parliament acquired the right to initiate legislation. Previously, if the Irish Parliament wanted specific legislation enacted it had to propose a bill for the approval of the British Privy Council under the 'Heads of Bill' procedure. Schwiddessen acknowledges the symbolic significance of acquiring this power, but she is somewhat sceptical about its practical impact. The 'Constitution of 1782' lasted only until the coming into force of the Act of Union 1800. In that time the volume of legislation passed by Grattan's Parliament certainly increased but its quality was not significantly different from that which had been enacted using the 'Heads of Bill' procedure prior to 1782. Nor would it appear that the economic and social impact of the legislation passed was transformative. The Privy Council retained a right of veto over Irish legislation. It was rarely used, but the Catholic Relief Acts of 1792 and 1793 were pushed through against a reluctant Irish Parliament. Schwiddessen also acknowledges that had the Irish Parliament survived long after 1800 it might have further evolved, and the 'Constitution of 1782' might then have been viewed as a more significant milestone on that journey.

The Treaty

First, Richard McBride provides an account of the career of a significant legal personality of this time, Sir John Ross, the last Lord Chancellor of Ireland. Ross was an Ulsterman but for most of his legal career he was based in Dublin. He was a Unionist but of the Southern variety, decidedly unenthusiastic about partition. Ross served as a Chancery judge in Ireland from 1896 and lobbied for the position of Lord Chief Justice of Northern Ireland when the Northern Ireland state was established in 1921. McBride's view is that Sir James Craig, first Prime Minister of Northern Ireland, preferred Sir Denis Henry, a Catholic Unionist, as being more reliably disposed towards the Northern Ireland state. Not long after this disappointment Ross became the last Lord Chancellor of Ireland, but he was in truth Lord Chancellor in name only. The Government of Ireland Act 1920 provided for two 'Home Rule' Parliaments in Ireland, one for Southern Ireland and the other for Northern Ireland. There were two court systems with a Court of Appeal for each jurisdiction. Above these appellate courts was a High Court of Appeal for Ireland and Ross was the president of this court. His appointment was for life, unlike previous Lord Chancellors who had presided in court but left office when the government changed hands. McBride provides an account of the cases Ross judged in the High Court of Appeal from 1920 to 1922. When the settlement of the Irish conflict proposed by the Government of Ireland Act 1920 was rejected by Sinn Féin, the High Court of Appeal in Ireland ceased to exist and Ross's judicial career ended. His attempts to secure a judicial position in England came to nothing.

'The Treaty' refers to the ending of the British–Irish conflict a century ago. Two chapters consider the negotiations over the Treaty that established the basis for the founding of the Irish Free State and then the further negotiations over the constitution of the Free State.

Colum Kenny's chapter on 'Lord Birkenhead, Ambiguity and the Irish Border' is concerned with one particular aspect of the Anglo-Irish negotiations, namely how and where the border between Northern Ireland and the Irish Free State should be located. Kenny focuses on the disparity in legal expertise between the two negotiating teams. On the British side was F. E. Smith, Lord Birkenhead, then Lord Chancellor of the United Kingdom. Nobody on the Irish side matched his brilliance and experience. The Treaty provided for the establishment of a Boundary Commission to fix the border's location and until the time it reported in 1925 there was much speculation about how far its recommendations would depart from the border provisionally fixed in 1921/22. Hence the Treaty provisions relating to the Boundary Commission, its remit and modus operandi, were potentially crucial. Kenny considers who might have been suitable advisers to the Irish negotiating team who were labouring under great political pressure. Frank Russell (son of Lord Russell of Killowen), then a Chancery judge in England, was proposed by Lord Birkenhead as someone who might usefully advise the Irish team, and another potential candidate was Viscount Bryce, a noted constitutional law expert. Neither was consulted. As Kenny observes, the exploitation of legal ambiguity for political ends has clear contemporary resonance in the context of Brexit and its impact on Northern Ireland.

Thomas Mohr produces an account of the British–Irish negotiations on the drafting of the constitution of the Irish Free State. Michael Collins, Arthur Griffith and Hugh Kennedy were under huge pressure from the anti-Treaty wing of Sinn Féin, who had voted against the Treaty in the Dail debates of January 1922. In an attempt to bring Éamon de Valera and his anti-Treaty faction into coalition with supporters of the Treaty and avert civil war, Collins and his team drafted a constitution which significantly diluted the Irish Free State's Dominion status over issues like the oath of allegiance to the king and the Privy Council serving as the final court of appeal for law cases from Ireland. The British firmly rejected the draft constitution. Nevertheless, Mohr points out that the Irish delegation had more than modest negotiating successes of their own. It seems tolerably clear that had they not done so there was a severe risk hostilities would resume. This was averted but tragically the Civil War in Ireland commenced only two weeks after these negotiations concluded.

Colin Murray's chapter, 'No Way to Run a Railroad', is an account of the post-partition story of the Great Northern Railway of Ireland (GNRI). If a border is placed east–west across an island this is clearly going to present implications for any north–south transport network. In the immediate aftermath of partition, two governments somewhat reticent about engaging with each other were forced to do so to a minimal degree, dealing with customs at any rate. Murray's story is mostly focused upon the post-World War II experience of the GNRI. The railway's economic troubles forced a joint nationalisation by the governments of Ireland and Northern Ireland in 1953. Money problems persisted and the Northern Ireland government had difficulty in keeping its end up. Murray brings to light the toxic relationship between the governments of the United Kingdom and Northern Ireland and the inadequacy of the overall devolution funding system. Westminster believed the future lay with road transport and insisted on savings. These took the form of closing uneconomic lines, mostly west of the Bann. Murray places much of the blame for the eventual dissolution of the operating company on Westminster, one example of its tendency to engage in doublethink being the insistence on acquiring more expensive British locomotives in preference to cheaper and probably more efficient German models. At the same time Stormont does not emerge from this with its copybook entirely unblotted. The line running through the Unionist heartland of County Antrim to Coleraine and on to Derry did not suffer the fate of the lines west of the Bann. The Irish government certainly did not want to see the demise of the GNRI and the Belfast to Dublin Enterprise service was preserved. As anyone who travelled that route in the 1970s to 1990s can testify, the rolling stock was only slightly less ancient than that used by Northern Ireland Railways until the relaunch of the Enterprise service in 1997. Murray considers that the GNRI experience was a wasted opportunity for better North–South relations.

Contemporary Law and Constitutional Change Issues

Merike Ristikivi, Katre Luhamaa and Karin Sein's chapter tells the story of the wholesale reform of the Estonian legal system after Estonia ceased to be governed by Soviet-style Communism in 1991. It highlights how young lawyers were deliberately put at the forefront of this constitutional transformation because they were perceived to be more capable of innovative thinking. However, it also highlights that, over time, those young lawyers engaged in more collaborative projects which proactively involved established legal professionals 'who had received their education during Soviet times and brought experience of those times to the table'. Likewise, the authors emphasise the importance of non-intrusive support provided by foreign experts during Estonia's constitutional refurbishment. Their chapter exemplifies the importance of 'maintaining the delicate equilibrium between innovation and tradition' by reference to an empirical analysis of a unique but telling episode in modern European history.

Gabrielle Appleby and Megan Davis's chapter on 'First Nations Constitutional Recognition in Australia' contrasts the apparent embedding of the rule of law in the foundations of present-day Australian constitutional law with the 'weaponisation' of the rule of law in order to deny the *prior* sovereignty of Aboriginal and Torres Strait Islander people, present when the colonial settlement of Australia took place in the eighteenth century. They argue that Blackstonian justifications for British sovereignty following colonisation fall away when it is recognised that Australia was not in fact *terra nullius* but occupied – accepted in principle in *Mabo (No. 2)* in 2000 – and that settlement was not in fact peaceful. Appleby and Davis use this rule-of-law history to interrogate more recent developments in Australian political and constitutional thought, culminating in the Uluru Statement from the Heart to the Australian people (2017), which called for the embedding of a 'First Nations Voice' in the constitutional arrangements of Australia. As this was rejected in a referendum in 2021, the authors contend that the search for foundational coherence in Australian constitutional law continues.

Lady Brenda Hale's plenary lecture, 'The Rise and Fall of the UK Human Rights Act', explores some constitutional background to the Human Rights Act 1998 together with an examination of its impact on domestic law and policy in the United Kingdom. Lady Hale begins by explaining why the Act was enacted and how it was given effect in domestic law, before chronicling the extent to which various critiques of the Act have intensified since 2010. She comments, in particular, on several threats posed by a Bill of Rights Bill which would have repealed the 1998 Act, prior to its withdrawal from Parliament on 23 June 2023. Concluding that the future of the 1998 Act remains uncertain in the context of recent calls to withdraw from the European Convention on Human Rights altogether, as well as several instances of discrete disapplication by way of legislation in specific policy areas, Lady Hale reminds us of the conceptual tensions that have always been inherent in the goal of establishing a human rights culture.

There is a veritable feast in this collection. It is hoped that this Introduction will give those readers who want to read the book from cover to cover and those who want to 'dip in' to whatever appears to interest them a clear view of what they can expect.

1

'Another Sort of Treason'

The Troubled Home of Husband-Killing in Late Medieval Common Law

GWEN SEABOURNE

Two gaol delivery roll entries for a session at Leicester in 1419 deal with the death of a certain John Chaloner, said to have been killed in his bed one Saturday night in 1418.[1] Both record 'appeals' – that is, prosecutions initiated by an individual. The first appeal is by John's wife, Margery, against John Mathewe of Leicester, tailor, and Richard Bargeyn. The second sees a role reversal for Margery: now herself accused of participation in the killing. The roll notes that all three accused were found guilty, and were sentenced to death, but there is a striking difference in the method of despatch: the two male defendants were to be hanged, in accordance with the usual form of capital punishment for felony, but Margery was to be burned. This mode of execution set husband-killing apart from most other homicides, including other homicides within the family.[2] This setting apart survived until 1828, when the legal differences between husband-killing and 'ordinary' homicide were removed,[3] and it came with procedural and doctrinal implications which were of interest and concern to common lawyers, in Margery Chaloner's era and for several centuries thereafter. Much scholarly attention has been paid to ideas about husband-killing and literary representations of it, especially in the early modern period,[4] but there is also much here for the legal historian, including the medieval legal historian, to consider. Two

---

[1] TNA, JUST 3/195 m. 72d (AALT IMG 0414).
[2] G. Seabourne, *Women in the Medieval Common Law c.1200–1500* (Milton, 2021), 145–8.
[3] Offences Against the Person Act 1828: 9 Geo. IV, c. 31, s. 2. The penalty of burning was removed in An Act for Discontinuing the Judgement which has been required by Law to be given against Women convicted of certain Crimes, and substituting another Judgement in lieu thereof, 1790: 30 Geo. III, c. 48.
[4] See, in particular, the copious scholarship on the Elizabethan play, *Arden of Faversham*: e.g. D. Berg, ""'Tis Fearful Sleeping in a Serpent's Bed": Arden of Faversham and the

important aspects of the English common law's distinct and distinguishing response to husband-killing are evident in *Chaloner* and will be discussed here: on the one hand, the English association of this offence with treason,[5] and, on the other hand, the particular struggle to fit some husband-killing cases within the common law's pre-existing procedural frameworks. As will be seen, husband-killing caused intellectual and practical legal problems, as intense, in their own way, as the better-known fears it aroused in the breasts of patriarchal elites and the plot ideas it placed in the minds of writers.

Treason, Homicide, Husband-Killing: Complicated Relationships

By the time of *Chaloner*, there had been an explicit association between husband-killing and treason for more than six decades, and some degree of connection for considerably longer. The nature of the association, however, was not straightforward. If we examine the entry relating to the prosecution of Margery Chaloner, we will note that this contains different descriptions of her offence. As well as the appeal against Margery, the entry mentions proceedings initiated by indictment, and, in the latter context, describes her offence as *proditio*, a word which had come to be associated with treason directed at the king.[6] *Proditio* is not used throughout, however: where the entry is concerned with the appeal against her, it uses only the language of felony, as in any other homicide case. This inconsistency of terminology highlights an important truth about the common law's response to husband-killing: its dual and shifting nature. Throughout the centuries of its formally separate treatment, husband-killing sat between the two categories, felony and treason, and, while lawyers might push it somewhat towards one or the other, with their choices about rules and procedure and their theoretical

---

Threat of the Petty Traitor', in L. Tracy (ed.), *Treason: Medieval and Early Modern Adultery, Betrayal, and Shame* (Leiden, 2019), 340–55, and works cited there.

[5] Not all jurisdictions marked out husband-killing from other close-family homicides and associated it with treason: see e.g. S. H. Cuttler, *The Law of Treason and Treason Trials in Later Medieval France* (Cambridge, 1981), 16; G. Mackenzie, *The Laws and Customes of Scotland, in Matters Criminal* (Edinburgh, 1678) I, tit. VIII, XIV; D. Hume, *Commentaries on the Law of Scotland Respecting Crimes*, 2 vols. (Edinburgh, 1844), vol. 1, cc. VI, XXVI; W. K. Dickson, 'Scots Law of Treason', *Juridical Review*, 10 (1898), 243–56, 249.

[6] See e.g. YB Pasch. 1 Hen. VII f. 22b pl. 15; J. G. Bellamy, *The Law of Treason in England in the Later Middle Ages* (Cambridge, 1970), 7.

constructions, its association with treason was always a somewhat troubling complexity: neither an inevitable, nor a perfect, nor a stable, union. This section of the chapter will explore the nature of the association in the later medieval period.

A preliminary complication for such an exploration is that neither 'felony' nor 'treason' can be pinned down to one straightforward concept, and there is a degree of overlap: treason had 'more than one centre', focusing in part on lord–vassal relationships and in part on king–subject relationships as something special and distinct, and felony seems to have imported an idea of betrayal.[7] In addition, the definition and content of the offences themselves had not reached a fixed state in the later medieval period, with treason in particular being pushed to respond to political crises and developments in constitutional thought.[8] Nevertheless, by the later medieval period, a tolerably clear conceptual distinction was in place, with felony representing a more general class of serious wrong, regarded as disrupting the king's peace, and treason becoming primarily the 'place where law and politics meet',[9] comprising offences against the king's person, royal government or the constitution.[10]

Another relationship which should not be oversimplified is that between the penalty of burning, women and treason. The sentence of death by burning in husband-killing cases, as seen in *Chaloner*, can be traced back to the thirteenth century at least.[11] While this served to single

---

[7] F. Pollock and F. W. Maitland, *History of English Law before the Time of Edward I*, 2 vols. (Cambridge, 1895), vol. II, 501; E. P. Kamali, '*Felonia Felonice Facta*: Felony and Intentionality in Medieval England', *Criminal Law and Philosophy*, 9 (2015), 397–421, at 400–3; S. D. White, 'The Ambiguity of Treason in Anglo-Norman-French Law c. 1150–c. 1250', in R. Mazo Karras et al. (eds.), *Law and the Illicit in Medieval Society* (Philadelphia, PA, 2008), 89–102.

[8] See e.g. Bellamy, *Treason*; Pollock and Maitland, *History*, II, 498–508; E. A. McVitty, *Treason and Masculinity in Medieval England: Gender, Law and Political Culture* (Woodbridge, 2020). For statutory extensions of 'treason', see W. S. Holdsworth, *A History of English Law*, 13 vols. (London, 1903–72), vol. II, 450; J. G. Bellamy, *The Tudor Law of Treason: An Introduction* (London, 1979).

[9] J. H. Baker, *The Oxford History of the Laws of England. Vol. VI, 1483–1558* (Oxford, 2003), 581 (hereafter Baker, *OHLE*).

[10] Note the additional complication of another duality, that of the king and crown: E. Kantorowicz, *The King's Two Bodies: A Study in Medieval Political Theology*, with Introduction by C. Leyser and Preface by W. C. Jordan (Princeton, NJ, 2016).

[11] See Seabourne, *Women*, 149. Some doubt is cast on the inevitability of burning in documents relating to Juliana Murdak, convicted in 1316 of involvement in her husband's killing. She was ordered to be burned but some records state that she was hanged 'for felony': P. R. Coss, *The Lady in Medieval England 1000–1500* (Stroud, 1998), 131–8, 134; *Calendar of Inquisitions Miscellaneous Vol. II: 1307–1349* (London, 1916), no. 657;

it out from most other homicides, it is not a clear sign that the offence was regarded as treason, or as having a relationship to king- or government-centred treason, as opposed to a wider idea of an offence against one's lord,[12] or even a manifestation of a deeper, older, vaguer association between women and death by fire.[13] An explicit conceptual association between husband-killing and king- or government-centred treason was made only in the Statute of Treasons 1352. Having listed treason offences against the king, his family, the realm and the coinage, this measure designated husband-killing (and two other non-royal homicide scenarios: servant kills master and prelate is killed by one owing him faith and obedience) as *autre manere de treson*: 'another sort of treason'.[14]

The association was not a complete absorption of the three 'other' scenarios into the treason category, nor can it quite be mapped onto later constructions of the relationship as one of parallel offences against hierarchies, with 'petty treason' offences representing a scaled down version of 'high treason' offences. A complete assimilation of husband-killing to the treason category was put forward in a case of the 1540s,[15] but no such statements would have been found in the later medieval period. Distance is maintained in the 1352 statute: the three 'other' scenarios are explicitly differentiated from those treasons listed beforehand, in terms of the forfeiture consequences which would follow conviction. Later accounts, including those of and concerning early modern literature, and those located in the era of moves towards ending the

---

Calendar of Close Rolls 1318–23 (London, 1895), 471 (hereafter *CCR*); *CCR 1323–7*, 304; TNA, JUST 1/635 mm. 19d, 34, 54 (AALT IMG 0905, 0732, 0779); KB 27/282 m. 96 (IMG 0193); KB 27/242 mm. 4, 31 (AALT IMG 0322, 0278) KB 27/243 m. 7 (AALT IMG 0262). Blackstone connects burning to the 'laws of the antient Druids': 4 Bl. Comm., c. 14, 204.

[12] For the link between offences against a lord and burning, see F. M. Nichols (ed.), *Britton*, 2 vols. (Oxford, 1865), vol. I, 40–1. It seems to have been understood in the early fifteenth century that a woman convicted of 'high' treason would be burned: E. Hutchison, 'Treason in France and England in the Later Middle Ages', in H. Skoda (ed.), *A Companion to Crime and Deviance in the Middle Ages* (Leeds, 2023), 173–95, 183. See also J. H. Baker and A. Taussig (eds.), *A Catalogue of the Manuscripts of Anthony Taussig* (Selden Society Supplementary Series 15, London, 2007), 63, no. 168.

[13] Seabourne, *Women*, 147; Bellamy, *Treason*, 225; Henry de Bracton et al., *Bracton on the Laws and Customs of England* (Cambridge, MA, 2020), vol. 2, 299; Nichols, *Britton*, I, 40–1.

[14] 25 Edw. III, stat. 5 c. 2 (*Statutes of the Realm*, vol. I, 320) (1352).

[15] J. H. Baker (ed.), *Reports of William Dalison* (124 Selden Society, London, 2007), 61, no. 13, and 69, no. 26.

penalty of burning for women and the special treatment of husband-killers, emphasise a parallel between king-killing and husband-killing in particular, but care is needed here when considering the medieval position.[16] We should note that husband-killing was not, in fact, foremost amongst the three 'other sorts of treason' listed in the statute. The first of these, servant kills master, seems likely to have been the main concern at this time of government fear of the power of labourers.[17] I would conjecture that the inclusion of the husband- and prelate-killing scenarios was not particularly indicative of a concern with the incidence of these offences at that time, but a noting of situations which seemed analogous – in the case of husband-killing, tidying up and making explicit a vaguer prior connection to vaguer prior ideas of treason, and in the case of prelate-killing, in a rather more intellectual than practical manner (since one who stood in the right relationship to a prelate to commit this offence would be likely to have been able to avail himself of benefit of clergy, and might well not have had property to forfeit).[18] It has the look of legislation being created using the sort of running through of analogies familiar from accounts of common lawyers' reasoning in Year Books and readings, a reconstruction which seems plausible given the strong case made by Bertha Putnam for the influence of a leading common lawyer, Sir William Shareshull, chief justice of the King's Bench, on its drafting.[19] The 1352 statute was certainly important in the development of husband-killing as an offence associated with treason, but evidence from practice following the statute suggests that the link remained relatively loose in the medieval period.[20]

[16] See e.g. A. Rackham Cleveland, *Woman under the English Law from the Landing of the Saxons to the Present Time* (London, 1896), 95; M. Lockwood, 'From Treason to Homicide: Changing Conceptions of the Law of Petty Treason in Early Modern England', *Journal of Legal History*, 34 (2013): 31–49, 34; F. E. Dolan, 'Battered Women, Petty Traitors, and the Legacy of Coverture', *Feminist Studies*, 29 (2003), 249–77, 261; Berg, ''Tis Fearful', 341.

[17] See e.g. R. C. Palmer, *English Law in the Age of the Black Death, 1348–1381: A Transformation of Governance and Law* (Chapel Hill, NC, 1993).

[18] 25 Edw. III, c. 6, s. 4 (1352); stat. 12 Hen. VII c. 7 (1496).

[19] B. H. Putnam, *The Place in Legal History of Sir William Shareshull: Chief Justice of the King's Bench 1350–1361* (Cambridge, 2013), 52. We might note that, given his Staffordshire connection, Shareshull is likely to have been particularly alive to the issue of husband-killing, not as a result of problems in the 1350s, but because of the older case of Juliana Murdak, convicted of involvement in the killing of her husband at Stourton Castle, near Stourbridge, in 1316: Coss, *The Lady*, 131–8.

[20] Note, also, the general absence of treason terminology in medieval accounts of the action of Isabella of France in relation to her husband, Edward II's, death: S. Menache, 'Isabella

The link's relatively loose nature can be seen in the language in husband-killing records. I have mentioned the use of *proditio*, a term associated with treason, in *Chaloner*. A reading from the late fifteenth century, however, denied that the offence was to be called treason at all,[21] and the language seen in other entries also suggests a degree of indecision as to whether to follow the linguistic conventions associated with treason, or to use regular 'felony' language. It is not unusual for early records to note a penalty of burning, but otherwise to use language indistinguishable from that seen in 'ordinary' homicides.[22] Sometimes they use an additional, condemnatory, term, most frequently something in the *seditio* or *seductio* field, and occasionally *traditio*, rather than *proditio*.[23] The use of 'treason terms' increases during the reign of Richard II, a period which saw special attention to, and moves towards definition of, treason,[24] and the 'treason term' used becomes increasingly likely to be *proditio*.[25] This seems to bring husband-killing closer to treason, in which a similar movement to *proditio* can be seen,[26] but there still does not seem to be an absolute necessity to include 'treason terms' in general, or *proditio* terms in particular, in husband-killing accusations at this time.[27] A husband-killing case from a 1390 gaol delivery roll, for example, classes the deed as having been done feloniously and *traditorie*, elsewhere says that the victim was murdered *horribiliter*, and the verdict is simply in

of France, Queen of England: A Postscript', *Revue Belge de Philologie et d'Histoire*, 90 (2012), 493–512, especially at 506–8. Laura Slater, 'Rumour and Reputation Management in Fourteenth-Century England: Isabella of France in Text and Image', *Journal of Medieval History*, 47 (2021), 257–92. We might note that Isabella was still alive in 1352.

[21] J. H. Baker (ed.), *Select Readings and Commentaries on Magna Carta 1400–1604* (132 Selden Society, London, 2015), 359; Cambridge University Library, MS Ee 5.22 ff. 371–5.

[22] See e.g. TNA, JUST 1/538 m. 13 (AALT IMG 3188), 1274; JUST 3/139 m. 4d (AALT IMG 0082), 1357.

[23] Pollock and Maitland, *History*, II, 500. For use of *seductiose* and *seductiue*, apparently interchangeable terms, see e.g. TNA, JUST 3/35B m.53d (AALT IMG 0217); KB 27/243 m. 7 (AALT IMG 0261).

[24] Bellamy, *Treason*, 111–16 and 229; Hutchison, 'Treason', 180–1.

[25] For use of *proditio*, see TNA, JUST 3/178 m. 9b (AALT IMG 0040) (1391); JUST 3/186 m. 4d (AALT IMG 0027) (1401).

[26] A close association between trials for 'higher' treason and for husband-killing has been noted in one section of a monastic chronicle from this reign: P. Strohm, 'Treason in the Household', in *Hochon's Arrow: The Social Imagination of Fourteenth-Century Texts* (Princeton, NJ, 1992), 121–44, at 121; L. C. Hector and B. F. Harvey (eds.), *The Westminster Chronicle, 1381–1394* (Oxford, 1981), 322.

[27] No treason terms, 1380s: TNA, JUST 3/163 m.10 (AALT IMG 0021); 1390s: JUST 3/179 m. 17d (AALT IMG 138).

terms of felony and murder (though the wife is ordered to be burned).[28] The coroner's roll, with a record of the appeal, has no treason words, but describes the accused having 'horribly murdered and feloniously killed' the victim.[29] Even in the later fifteenth century, there are some entries which do not use special vocabulary beyond felony, including those relating to what would appear highly transgressive episodes, such as a wife alleged to have killed her husband by dragging him by the 'secret members' and a poisoning case in which the devil's instigation was invoked, but not the treacherous adverb *proditorie*.[30] In *Chaloner*, as noted above, the section of the entry recording the appeal against Margery uses only felony language, whereas that noting the indictment also classes her offence as *proditio*.[31] This should remind us of the need to take seriously the fact that the 'rules of the game', including what seem to us important differences of terminology or classification, could be different, depending on the form of prosecution employed. The occasional 'exaggerated' use of treason words, such as the use in *Chaloner* of the language of *proditio* in relation to one of the male defendants, who is neither identified, nor punished, as a servant, should also urge us to caution in assuming there to have been settled vocabulary in this area.

Indicative of an evolving relationship between husband-killing and other treason offences in later medieval legal thought is the move, around the time of *Chaloner*, to a new conceptual structure. Husband-killing (along with master-killing and prelate-killing) came to be described not as a 'sort of treason', but as 'petty treason', contrasted with 'high' treason. This move, though often backdated to the 1352 statute, was an independent development.[32] The high treason/petty treason binary had rivals well

---

[28] TNA, JUST 3/177 m. 27 (AALT IMG 0058).

[29] TNA, JUST 2/58 (AALT IMG 0046). For *seductio/seditio* as well as felony in this reign, see e.g. TNA, KB 27/476 m. 19 (AALT IMG 0521). For a 1390 instance in which an offence is recorded in felony language, until the jury verdict introduces *proditio*, see TNA, JUST 3/181 m. 16d (AALT IMG 0033).

[30] TNA, KB 9/308 m. 37 (AALT IMG 71); KB 9/317 m. 6 (AALT IMG 12); KB 9/358 m. 3 (AALT IMG 6). The *Chaworth* case, TNA, JUST 3/105 m.9 (AALT IMG 0018), dealt with below, also left out treason language. For a reading, probably from the 1460s, which holds it unnecessary to include *proditorie* in a husband-killing indictment, see Baker (ed.), *Selected Readings and Commentaries on Magna Carta*, 359.

[31] TNA, JUST 3/195 m. 72d (AALT IMG 1414).

[32] Bellamy, *Treason*, 229; C. Given-Wilson et al. (eds.), *Parliament Rolls of Medieval England* (Leicester, 2005), Parliament of October 1423, no. 60; Dolan, 'Battered Women', 261; W. S. Holdsworth, *History of English Law*, 3rd ed., 17 vols. (London, 1922–66), vol. 3, 449.

into the fifteenth century, in classifications splitting treason into that which touched the king directly and that which did not, and in the great/petty, as opposed to high/petty, distinction seen in some statutes, and arguably importing different nuances of constitutional thought.[33] The inclusion of offences relating to the coinage militated against a neat two-level structure for treason, for these were offences against the king/realm, treated severely and yet not fully assimilated to 'high treason',[34] and the parallel between treasons closely involving the king or realm and those against superiors at a lower level was not complete, since a number of different 'higher' offences amounted to treason, whereas only killing a master, husband or prelate, and not lesser transgressions against such a superior, was singled out for special treatment in the 1352 statute.[35] The prominence of the high treason/petty treason binary increased and became conventional in legal texts from the sixteenth century to 1828, shaping accounts of the law and its history which placed in the fore-ground ideas of a neat parallel between 'high' and 'petty' offences, a neat, logical, perhaps natural, relationship of derivation of the lesser from the greater offence.[36] The medieval evidence suggests a less straightforward association of the different offences and less of an ambition to create an exhaustive list of 'other sorts of treason'. Later lawyers looking at the 1352 statute, with its three 'other sort of treason' scenarios, were not infrequently rather uncomfortable with the fact that its 'petty treason' scenarios did not cover all of the offences against hierarchical relation-ships which would fit their interpretation of that class, in particular

---

[33] The great/little treason distinction in Nichols, *Britton*, I, 40–1 focuses on directness, rather than whether the offence was against lord or king. See also Statute of Westminster I (1275) c. 15; 5 Ric. II st. 1 c. 6 (1381) (*Statutes of the Realm*, vol. 1, 30; vol. 2, 20). For *haute treson*, see e.g. stat. 11 Ric. II c. 1 (1387–8); 21 Ric. II c. 3 (1397–8); 2 Hen. V stat. 1, c. 6 (1414) (*Statutes of the Realm*, vol. 2, pp. 47, 98–9, 178); though note the undifferen-tiated *traison* of 4 Hen. V stat. 2, c. 6 (1415–16) (*Statutes of the Realm*, vol. 2, 195), and *graund treson/petit traison* divide in stat. 2 Hen. VI, c. 21 (1423) (*Statutes of the Realm*, vol. 2, 226–7). There is fluctuation between *haut* and *graunt* in the reign of Henry VI: stat. 8 Hen. VI, c. 6 (1429); stat. 20 Hen. VI c. 3 (1441–2) (*Statutes of the Realm*, vol. 2, 242, 318, 541).

[34] See e.g. *Boke of Justices of Peas* (London, 1521), f. 2; TNA, JUST 3/41/1 m. 17 (AALT IMG 0040); JUST 3/127A m. 23 (AALT IMG 0049).

[35] The parallel was, however, inexact, given that 'high' treason would cover more than killing the king, but 'petty' treason was confined to killing the superior: Pollock and Maitland, *History*, II, 503. Public/private: see Strohm, 'Treason in the Household', 125.

[36] See e.g. W. Staunford, *Les Plees del Coron* (London, 1557), Lib. I, c. 2, fols. 1 and 10 (*graund* or *haut* and *petit* treason); 3 Co. Inst., cc. 1, 2; W. Hawkins, *Treatise of the Pleas of the Crown*, 8th ed., 2 vols. (London, 1824), cc. 2, 14.

making no mention of patricide (or matricide).[37] We may regard this as illustrative of differing ideas of the nature and purpose of legislation: the 1352 statute clearly did not set out to be exhaustive in terms of situations covered, and makes it clear that extensions were envisaged. Some later accounts, however, treated the statute as if it was an exhaustive list and felt compelled to force the 'petty treason' category to cover children who killed a parent, either by classing them as servants, or else by misreading a medieval report of a master–servant case as if it was about the killing of a mother.[38]

Equally important to recognise, in exploring the medieval common law response to husband-killing, is that, while it is tempting to see it as more-or-less homicide or more-or-less treason,[39] the better view is that it was not clearly seen as one or the other. While the inclusion of husband-killing in the 1352 statute, the 'petty treason' label and the burning penalty for husband-killing all signalled an affinity with non-husband-killing treason, husband-killing did not always follow the treason pattern. It followed the homicide pattern in some respects, and elsewhere it sat between the two poles. In the 'like homicide' column, we can place the fact that suspects were always tried in the same way as 'normal' suspected killers: on appeal or indictment, rather than using the special modes devised for 'high' treason, and the fact that forfeitures followed the felony, not the treason, pattern.[40] In other areas of theory and practice, there was some uncertainty, or change over time, with regard to the position of the offence vis-à-vis treason and homicide. We can see change with regard to the relevance of benefit of clergy for males accused or convicted of petty treason, and in treatment of degrees of participation.

---

[37] On intellectual links between family and state in the early modern period, see e.g. S. Amussen, *An Ordered Society: Gender and Class in Early Modern England* (Oxford, 1988), 1; G. J. Schochet, *Patriarchalism in Political Thought* (New York, 1975); Su Fang Ng, *Literature and the Politics of the Family in Seventeenth-Century England* (Cambridge, 2007); C. Jordan, 'The Household and the State: Transformations in the Representation of an Analogy from Aristotle to James I', *Modern Language Quarterly*, 54 (1993), 307–26; Lockwood, 'From Treason to Homicide', 35.

[38] YB 21 Edw III f. 17: W. Lambarde, *Eirenarcha* (London, 1599), c. 7, 241; 3 Co. Inst., c. 2; M. Dalton, *The Countrey Justice* (London, 1619), 213–14; Baker, *Reports of William Dalison*, 59, no. 8; Holdsworth, *History of English Law*, II, 449–50; Pollock and Maitland, *History*, II, 503.

[39] See e.g. Bellamy, *Treason*, 87; Lockwood, 'From Treason to Homicide', 42.

[40] This was so well before 1352: see D. W. Sutherland, *The Eyre of Northamptonshire 1329–30* (97 Selden Society, 1981) 216–17; TNA, JUST 1/635 mm. 19d, 34, 54 (AALT IMG 0905, 0732, 0779); KB 27/282 m. 96 (IMG 0193).

In the early fifteenth century, as with homicide (or indeed any felony) benefit of clergy was available to males but not females.[41] This, however, was changed by statute in the late fifteenth century.[42] Probably better classed as somewhat uncertain are the questions of principal and accessory, and of attempts. The treason pattern of liability did not rank participants as principal and accessory, and punished attempts as well as completed actions, while the homicide pattern distinguished principal and accessory and, aside, perhaps, from a brief period in the early fourteenth century, generally did not punish attempts.[43] To some extent, petty treason followed the homicide pattern with regard to principal and accessory. Thus, the liability of a woman who was an accessory in the killing of her husband was dependent upon that of the principal in so far as, if the principal succeeded in trial by battle in an approver appeal, or died, for example, she would be acquitted.[44] An issue which was not covered by the homicide rules but with which petty treason cases had to contend was whether it was possible to convict a (non-servant) principal of ordinary homicide, and a wife, described in terms which seem to position her as an accessory, of petty treason, hanging the one and burning the other. There are occasional cases which seem to suggest this,[45] but we may also detect some discomfort as to how to describe the wife's actions in an 'accessory' situation. There is a slightly odd description in the appeal against Margery Chaloner, for example, suggesting that she, as well as her co-accused, broke into her husband's house at night. While it is possible that Margery was not living with John, it is, perhaps, more likely that this tying of Margery to the break-in is an attempt to play up her active role in the whole enterprise, rather than casting her as an accessory to a man who does not seem to have been treated as a servant. At least as odd is the description of a man and a woman using one knife to kill her husband, which we see in a case of 1424, again

---

[41] This could result in a wife 'accessory', not present at the killing, being burned while the man who had actually struck down her husband obtained benefit of clergy and lived. See e.g. TNA, KB 27/690 m. 3 (AALT IMG 218) and JUST 3/202 m. 4 (AALT IMG 0826).

[42] Stat. 12 Hen. VII c. 7 (1496); Baker, *OHLE*, 537.

[43] John Baker, *Introduction to English Legal History*, 5th ed. (Oxford, 2019), 570; Baker, *OHLE*, 574–9; E. P. Kamali, *Felony and the Guilty Mind in Medieval England* (Cambridge, 2019), 79–82.

[44] See e.g. TNA, KB 27/394 m. 16 (AALT IMG 2822) (1359); JUST 3/167 m. 28 (AALT IMG 0066) (1381). For later developments with group killings of a husband, see Baker, *OHLE*, 558; Baker, *Reports of William Dalison*, 68, no. 25.

[45] See e.g. TNA, JUST 3/164 m.23 (AALT IMG 0047), JUST 3/189 m. 5 (AALT IMG 13).

involving a non-servant male.[46] It may be that one of the jobs done by the inclusion in indictments of allegations of a wife's alleged adultery with her husband's killer, seen in a number of cases, and in addition, no doubt, to acting as a general smear on her character and credibility, was tying her to the act as firmly as possible, to get around uncertainty about the rules on accessories in petty treason in general, or the particular issue of finding principal and accessory guilty of different offences in these cases.[47]

As far as attempted husband-killing is concerned, the situation in the medieval period is somewhat unclear. Later commentary suggests that an attempt to kill one's husband would be prosecuted and punished as petty treason, but all who say so cite for this proposition one somewhat ambiguous, and as yet unverified, source: a short account, ascribed to Spigurnel J, contained in an early fourteenth-century Year Book report of a case on a different topic (receiving stolen goods).[48]

There was much for medieval lawyers to discuss with regard to the appropriate rules and procedure for petty treason in general, and its husband-killing species in particular. Their idea of husband-killing as treason was not sufficiently absolute as to constrain them to treat it identically to the 'higher' forms of treason, and they elected to follow treason jurisprudence and procedures or those of homicide, as seemed appropriate. In some cases, however, accommodating husband-killing within the common law brought with it additional difficulties which led to explorations of possibilities beyond either the treason or the homicide pattern. One scenario which caused particular concern to medieval lawyers and those wishing to use the law, arose in *Chaloner* and some other fifteenth-century cases, and it is this matter to which I now turn.

[46] TNA, JUST 3/202 m. 4 (AALT IMG 0827), in which the wife was said to have been the victim of *raptus* by the man with whom she plotted her husband's death.
[47] For later routes to ensuring that an 'accessory' wife was a 'petty traitor', when somebody else struck down her husband, through doctrines based on presence or proximity, see Baker, *OHLE*, 558.
[48] A. Kiralfy, 'Taking the Will for the Deed: The Mediaeval Criminal Attempt', *Journal of Legal History*, 13 (1992), 95–100, 95; A. Kiralfy, *A Source Book of English Law* (London, 1957), 42; YB Pasch. 15 Edw. II, pl. 4, f. 463 (1322). Debates on whether to follow treason or homicide patterns continued, and different answers were given in different areas. On witnesses, see stat. 1 Edw. 6, c. 12, s. 22; 5 & 6 Edw. 6, c. 11, s. 12; 1 & 2 Phil. and Mary, c. 10; Baker, *Reports of William Dalison*, 119; Bellamy, *Treason*, 153; *R v. Henrietta Radbourne* 1 Leach 456; 168 ER 330 (1787). For increasing availability of 'homicide-like' defences for husband-killers, see Lockwood, 'From Treason to Homicide'; Baker, *Introduction*, 567; Kamali, *Felony and the Guilty Mind*, 79–82.

Prosecuting Problems

A perceived problem which was present in *Chaloner* was how to prosecute when it was alleged that a wife had participated with others in
killing her husband. This could present a difficulty in such cases as a
result of the existence of different methods of starting a criminal prosecution and the rules for their interaction, and the role given to wives in
bringing an appeal.

The alleged husband-killer could be prosecuted by a group or an
individual, by way of presentment/indictment or appeal, and sometimes,
as in *Chaloner*, both were brought in respect of the same alleged
offence.[49] A difficulty arose, however, when the wife herself also brought
an appeal. A widow's right to bring an appeal when her husband had
been slain was accepted, justified in the legal formula, until the later
fourteenth century, through a claim of physical proximity, if not unity,
between husband and wife: he had to be said to have died 'within her
arms'.[50] The need to repeat this metaphorical tag disappeared well before
Chaloner, but the strength of the wife's right to bring an appeal remained
sufficient to cause complications since her appeal was given priority over
appeals by others, including heirs and blood relations, and over indictments.[51] A wife who was both homicidal and canny could, therefore,
bring an appeal to delay any prosecution of herself by others, and give
herself a chance to find some means of legal escape, or to flee. She could
delay the passing of property to the family of the deceased.[52] Further

---

[49] On the wife's right to appeal, see Seabourne, *Women*, 95. For other examples of overlapping prosecutions in this context, see *Handes* (1407): TNA, JUST 3/189 m. 5 (AALT IMG
13); KB 27/589 m. 38 (AALT IMG 0086): *CPR 1405–8*, pp. 371, 470 (1427–8).
An approver appeal, as well as the appeal of an heir, can be seen in *Handes* (1407). For
fourteenth-century approver appeals for husband-killing, see SS 97, 217 (1317): JUST 1/
635 m. 19d, 34, 54 and KB 27/282 m. 96. See also JUST 3/167 m. 28 (AALT IMG 0066).

[50] See S. Jenks, '*Occidit ... inter brachia sua*: Change in a Woman's Appeal of Murder',
Journal of Legal History, 21 (2000), 119–22; S. M. Butler, 'Discourse on the Nature of
Coverture in the Later Medieval Courtroom', in T. Stretton and K. J Kesselring (eds.),
Married Women and the Law: Coverture in England and the Common Law World
(Montreal, 2013), 24–44.

[51] See e.g. TNA, KB 27/669 m. 81 (AALT IMG 206). D. R. Ernst, 'The Moribund Appeal of
Death: Compensating Survivors and Controlling Jurors in Early Modern England',
American Journal of Legal History, 28 (1984), 164–88, 173; YB Hil. 21 Hen. 6, f. 28,
pl. 12 (1443). For later doubt that an heir should be able to appeal a woman of killing his
father, her husband, see Baker, *Reports of William Dalison*, 61, no. 13, and 69, no. 26.

[52] See also an appeal against a widow by the deceased's sons, perhaps attempting to avoid
her dower entitlement: *Curia Regis Rolls vol. 13: 1227–30* (London, 1959), no. 2091. There

complications in prosecuting a husband-slaying wife in such a situation might also be caused when an heir did not want to, or could not, bring an appeal.

Chaloner gives an example of one way of minimising delay, by what seems to have been a relatively new adjustment of procedure. A 1421 law report, probably influenced by the judicial experiences of William Babington in *Chaloner*, puts an interesting remark into Babington's mouth, having him comment that a woman could appeal X for her husband's death, even when she herself had (allegedly) been involved in that death, and she could be appealed afterwards.[53] *Chaloner* shows that 'afterwards' meant *immediately* afterwards: the two cases could be heard in the same session, thus avoiding some chances for delay or flight. This case may also have involved manoeuvring to get around the problem of an heir unwilling or unable to bring an appeal against the allegedly murderous wife, for reasons of his youth or incapacity, or reluctance to act against a defendant who might, of course, be his own mother.[54] Some aspects of the record of the appeals in *Chaloner* suggest that such a problem had materialised there. Margery was appealed by a certain John Smyth of Moreton, who declared himself to be John Chaloner's brother and heir. Questions are raised by the fact that his name is not Chaloner, but the entries indicate the involvement of somebody who *is* called Chaloner: Robert Chaloner, one of Smyth's pledges for prosecution. Was John Smyth not actually heir to John Chaloner, but something of a device to ensure Margery's prosecution in a situation in which none of the Chaloners wanted to bring an appeal? Divergent surnames are not necessarily a clear indication of a lack of relationship, and while 'John Smyth' might strike a modern reader as suspiciously generic, and while there are entirely fake people to be found in the historical records of common law, this was not a conventional fake name in medieval proceedings.[55] Although it would be quite a leap to imagine that the appeal

is no information about any land Margery Chaloner might have held, and the entry notes that she had no chattels.

[53] YB Mich 9 Henry V f. 125r pl. 15. For a 1420 petty treason case with appeal by a wife, and then indictment, conviction and sentence to burn of the wife, in which Babington had some involvement, see TNA, KB 27/638 m. 20d (AALT IMG 0583); KB 9/216/2 m. 20 (AALT IMG 42); KB 29/63 m. 14d (AALT IMG 108); KB 29/63 m. 30d (AALT IMG 0142); JUST 3/195 m. 91 (AALT IMG 0223).

[54] For this issue in the earlier case of Juliana Murdak, see Coss, *The Lady*, 31–2.

[55] On occupation-based surnames at this time, see R. A. McKinley, *A History of British Surnames* (London, 1990), 28–34. Note the divergence between the names of the deceased

was a complete fabrication, 'covenous' appeals of other sorts have been noted and a degree of fiction is a possibility.[56]

It is not inconceivable that John Smyth was a real person but not actually the brother and heir. The fact that John Smyth and Robert Chaloner are both listed as Margery's pledges for prosecution of her appeal tends to suggest that the two cases were not simply proximate in time but co-ordinated. Quite what was the aim is unclear, however: was this a strategy to expedite the matter so that Margery could be removed from the scene, or a strategy intended to help her by giving her an escape route, through a challenge to John Smyth's right to appeal? We can see, however, that Margery did not avail herself of any such plea, trusting instead to the favour of the jury, and perhaps (despite the weight of scholarship which shows that this was not a wise strategy) the plea of pregnancy which she tried but failed to make out?[57] There is no basis upon which to offer more than speculation, but the evidence does seem to suggest a strategy to deal with a perceived problem.

Similarly, perceived problems relating to the use of appeals in such scenarios were brought out in the documentation relating to the later-fifteenth-century case of *Chaworth*.[58] John Chaworth had died in 1464, killed, so his family said, by men hired by Robert Marshall, allegedly the lover of his wife, Margaret. Margaret was also implicated. The Chaworths expressed concern that she could delay the prosecution by bringing an appeal against the actual killers, and that they would have problems bringing an appeal against her. Their particular difficulty was that the heir was only eight and the next choice, the deceased's brother, was

---

and a 'brother and heir' in TNA, JUST 3/177 m. 27 (AALT IMG 0058); JUST 2/58 m. 13 (AALT IMG 46). John Chaloner's surname is not an occupational name, as he is given a separate 'job description': '*taillour*'. Neither John Smyth nor Robert Chaloner has a separate employment appellation. W. Sayers, 'The Ancestry of John Doe: A Squib', *Eolas: Journal of the American Society of Irish Medieval Studies*, 5 (2011), 193–8; YB 9 Edw. IV (1469) f. 26 pl. 36.

[56] See Ernst, 'Moribund Appeal', 175, on later 'covenous appeals' to delay prosecution.

[57] See e.g. S. M. Butler, 'Pleading the Belly: A Sparing Plea? Pregnant Convicts and the Court in Medieval England', in S. M. Butler and K. J. Kesselring, *Crossing Borders: Boundaries and Margins in Medieval and Early Modern Britain* (Leiden, 2018), 131–53. For a successful plea of pregnancy, and a pardon, achieved in a comparable earlier case, see *Handes* (above, n. 49).

[58] TNA, KB 27/816 m.70 (IMG 0147); KB 27/817 mm. 105–7 (IMG 0237-0241); KB 9/308 m. 82 (IMG 0162); KB 9/318 m. 59 (IMG 0118); S. J. Payling, 'Murder, Motive and Punishment in Fifteenth-Century England: Two Gentry Case-Studies', *English Historical Review*, 113 (1998), 1–17.

sickly.[59] Rather than employing a double prosecution and (perhaps) a questionable appellant, the family opted to step outside common law processes and petition for a derogation from the usual rules. The request was that Margaret be excluded from appeal, and a special scheme directing an entail-like path for appeal right should be set up. The right would pass over the child and instead go to William Chaworth, (sickly) eldest brother of the deceased, then another brother, and then the king. This suggests that families who wished to prosecute a woman in this scenario had still not hit upon a secure and straightforward means to do so within the ordinary processes of the common law.

Some limitation of the ease with which a woman could be prosecuted for the death of her husband might not be antithetical to justice, of course, since apparently tenuous prosecutions, including one in which it became apparent that the husband in question was not dead at all, do provide evidence that suspicion against a wife was relatively easy to kindle or to affect.[60] Nevertheless, families of deceased men seem to have seen a problem with bringing prosecutions of women in this area. Cases like *Chaloner* and *Chaworth*, with their multiple interested parties and their overlapping methods of prosecution, highlight the fact that the husband–wife relationship was interwoven with other family links, and, indeed, had an impact upon the local community beyond the family. We draw an incomplete picture of law and practice if we portray the offence simply as relating to one hierarchical relationship, a parallel with the king–subject relationship. Husband-killing presented genuine challenges to the existing legal categories and procedures which common lawyers had devised and into which it had to be fitted. The attempt to accommodate it within those patterns gave rise to considerable mental effort and creativity.

Conclusion

Once husband-killing had been reabsorbed, doctrinally, into the mainstream of homicide, common lawyers, even those with historical interests, might treat its encounter with treason dismissively, as a rather embarrassing byway in legal thought, best passed over in short order. 'The use of this subdivision of murder I do not understand', was the

---

[59] For an earlier example of petitions for underage heirs in a similar context, see TNA, SC 8/261/13005; SC 8/170/8483; SC 8/170/8434.
[60] Seabourne, *Women*, 152–3; TNA, JUST 3/105 m. 9 (AALT IMG 0018).

exasperated verdict of one historically inclined legal luminary.[61] The English legal response to husband-killing, or the perceived threat of it, as developed over a prolonged period, is, however, worth the attention of legal historians, whether of a social or doctrinal bent. As well as its great interest and importance in terms of gender relations and marriage, it was a matter of concern and keen interest to common lawyers throughout its existence as something separate from 'ordinary' homicide. In examining a body of law which developed over several centuries, we should, of course, be careful not to assume consistency of concepts and rules, or of relationships between legal categories. As this chapter has argued, the evidence from the medieval period shows that the relationship between husband-killing and 'higher' forms of treason, though evidenced by the words of the 1352 statute, was looser than the relationship drawn in later legal texts, and was not as neat, or at any rate not the same, as some of relationships between husband-killing and high treason in the scholarship on early modern literature. Husband-killing was not the only, perhaps not the most concerning, 'other sort of treason' in the 1352 statute. Medieval records of practice show that treason terms did not always have to be mentioned in husband-killing cases, and the law on treason did not straightforwardly dictate rules and procedures for these cases, which might be drawn from treason or homicide jurisprudence, or, as in the case of the scenario in *Chaloner* and *Chaworth*, be found in other ways.

At the heart of the husband-killing allegations in cases such as that of Margery Chaloner lay, we may conjecture, the story of a troubled relationship between two people. There were, however, additional dimensions of concern, and there are other relationships with which we must reckon. First of all, people beyond the spousal unit felt that they had a stake in the way in which these cases were handled: the wider family in particular might push to be involved in legal action concerning a suspected wife. Secondly, other, more metaphorical, 'troubled relationships' are highlighted by this material: those between different modes of criminal prosecution, between husband-killing, homicide and treason, and, ultimately, between women and the common law.

---

[61] J. F. Stephen, *History of the Criminal Law of England*, 3 vols. (London, 1883), vol. 3, 35.

2

The Origins of the Statute of Uses

A. J. HANNAY

The Reformation Parliament which sat from 1529 to 1536 was one of the most constitutionally significant assemblies in the history of these islands.[1] Moreover, with the passing of the Statute of Uses 1536 it was also one of the most significant in the history of English (and Irish) private law.[2] The importance of the Statute of Uses has long been recognised and should not be understated.[3] The statute enacted the most radical reform of English landholding since at least *Quia Emptores* (1290), and perhaps even the Conquest. This chapter explores the statute's origins and its passage through Parliament: from its earliest drafts, to the Commons rejection of proposed reform, then through the courts, to its eventual enactment in 1536. It will be argued that orthodox accounts of the statute's passage are inadequate, and an alternative view is proposed.

The mischief that the Crown sought to remedy with the passage of the Statute of Uses was the avoidance of feudal incidents caused by feoffments to uses. A use of freehold land would be created when a landholder enfeoffed feoffees to uses for the benefit of *cestui que use*.[4] It was

I am grateful to Professor Neil Jones, Professor David Ibbetson and Dr Ian Williams for their insight and helpful comments.

[1] S. E. Lehmberg, *The Reformation Parliament 1529–1536* (Cambridge, 1970).
[2] Note that the Statute of Uses was not enacted in Ireland until 1634, when it was passed, alongside the Statute of Wills, by the Irish Parliament: Statute of Uses, 27 Hen. VIII, c. 10 (1536); Statute of Uses (Ireland), 10 Chas. I, sess. 2, c. 1 (1634); Statute of Wills (Ireland), 10 Chas. I, sess. 2, c. 2 (1634).
[3] See J. H. Baker, *Oxford History of the Laws of England, 1483–1553*, vol. 6 (Oxford, 2003) (hereafter Baker, *OHLE*), 672–86; N. G. Jones, 'Trusts in England after the Statute of Uses: A View from the 16th Century', in R. Helmholz and R. Zimmerman (eds.), *Itinera Fiduciae: Trust and Treuhand in Historical Perspective* (Berlin, 1998), 173; and N. G. Jones, 'The Authority of Parliament and the Scope of the Statute of Uses 1536', in M. Godfrey (ed.), *Law and Authority in British Legal History 1200–1900* (Cambridge, 2016), 13–32.
[4] *Cestui que use* is a shortened version of *cestui a que use le feoffment fuit fait* (he to whose benefit the feoffment was made). A feoffment with livery of seisin was 'the classic medieval

common practice by the fifteenth century for landholders to seek to avoid the common law rule prohibiting the devise of land by last will by enfeoffing feoffees to their own use and to perform the feoffor's last will.[5] One effect of feoffments to uses to perform last wills was that the land would not be inherited and therefore the feoffor's feudal lord would be deprived of incidents arising from inheritance.[6] From the fourteenth century, the Crown had sought to protect itself from the avoidance of incidents, with varying degrees of success, through the provisions of the Statute of Marlborough, c. 6, and from the mid-1520s there was a renewed focus on the avoidance of incidents,[7] which culminated in the passage of the Statute of Uses. The effect of the Statute of Uses was to annex legal title to the use, that is to say, following the creation of a use the feoffees would no longer stand seised of the land but, by operation of the statute, legal title would follow the use and *cestui que use* would be seised.

The passage of the Statute of Uses through the Reformation Parliament was difficult, with the Crown facing significant opposition from the Commons. Our understanding of the statute's passage is shaped by a number of draft bills, and other documents related to the statute which came to the attention of historians following the late nineteenth-century publication of volumes five to eleven of the *Letters and Papers of Henry VIII*.[8] Reconstructing the passage of the statute through Parliament has, however, proved particularly challenging.[9] It has been

---

conveyance' made by a feoffor with seisin and usually accompanied by a charter or deed. For more detail, see A. W. B. Simpson, *A History of the Land Law*, 2nd ed. (Oxford, 1986), 119–21.

[5] J. L. Barton, 'The Medieval Use', *Law Quarterly Review*, 81 (1965), 562–77; J. Biancalana, 'Medieval Uses', in R. Helmholz and R. Zimmerman (eds.), *Itinera Fiduciae: Trust and Treuhand in Historical Perspective* (Berlin, 1998), 111–52; J. M. W. Bean, *Decline of English Feudalism* (Manchester, 1968), 104–79.

[6] H. E. Bell, *An Introduction to the History and Records of the Court of Wards and Liveries* (Cambridge, 1953), 1; Simpson, *History of Land Law*, 16–19. The most notable feudal incidents were wardship and relief, with the Crown also benefitting from prerogative wardship and primer seisin.

[7] 52 Hen. III, c. 6 (1267). I have addressed the avoidance of feudal incidents through feoffments to uses in the period up to 1529 elsewhere: A. J. Hannay, '"By Fraud and Collusion": Feudal Revenue and Enforcement of the Statute of Marlborough, 1267–1526', *Journal of Legal History*, 42 (2021), 65.

[8] J. S. Brewer et al. (eds.), *Letters and Papers of Henry VIII*, 21 vols. (London, 1862–1932) (hereafter *LP*). Vols. 5–13, which cover the period between 1531 and 1538, were published between 1880 and 1893.

[9] Baker, *OHLE*, 664–5; Bean, *Decline*, 258–70; W. S. Holdsworth, *A History of English Law*, 16 vols. (London, 1922–66) (hereafter Holdsworth, *HEL*), vol. 4, 95–6; E. W. Ives, 'The Genesis of the Statute of Uses', *English Historical Review*, 82 (1967), 673; Lehmberg,

generally thought that following a compromise with a number of peers a bill was put before the Commons which was then rejected in 1532, leading King Henry VIII to turn to the courts. This led to the litigation in *Dacre's Case* (1533–35), following which the Commons position was untenable, and they were forced to capitulate by passing the eventual Statute of Uses, a defect in which was remedied by the swift passage of the Statute of Enrolments.[10]

Through detailed analysis of surviving draft bills, this chapter will argue that the traditional interpretation of the passage of the Statute of Uses and the Statute of Enrolments is incorrect. We will consider six earlier draft proposals, four of which were rejected, to present a more complete picture of the origins of both statutes.[11] Consideration will first be given to the drafts leading up to the Commons rejection of the Crown's proposal in 1532, before turning to the litigation in *Dacre's Case* and the later drafts. Reconstructing the passage of the statutes and presenting a more accurate and complete account allows for more detailed consideration of both difficult doctrinal questions relating to the Statute of Uses and important constitutional issues relating to the relationship between the Crown, Parliament and the courts in the mid-sixteenth century.

* * *

Understanding the progress of early drafts of the Statute of Uses has not proved to be straightforward. The publication of *Letters and Papers of Henry VIII* brought to our attention a number of documents relating to the Act. Of these, two in particular have shaped our understanding of the passage of the statute: the text of a draft bill, and an agreement between

---

 Reformation Parliament, 94–5; T. F. T. Plucknett, 'Some Proposed Legislation of Henry VIII', *Transactions of Royal Historical Society*, 19 (1936), 119.

[10] Statute of Enrolments, 27 Hen. VIII, c. 16 (1536). For a more detailed summary, see Baker, *OHLE*, 664–5.

[11] The four which were rejected are: The National Archives Public Record Office (TNA PRO) SP 1/56, ff. 36–9; *LP*, vol. 4, no. 6043, printed in: Holdsworth, *HEL*, vol. 4, 572–4; BL, MS Cotton Titus B.I, f. 486; *LP*, vol. 5, no. 396; TNA PRO SP 1/101, ff. 286–91; *LP*, vol. 10, no. 246, printed in: Holdsworth, *HEL*, vol. 4, 580–1; TNA PRO SP 1/101, ff. 303–21; *LP*, vol. 10, no. 246 (6), printed in Holdsworth, *HEL*, vol. 4, 582–6. The final two are the drafts of the Statute of Uses which are almost identical to the eventual statute: TNA PRO SP 1/101 ff. 252–60; *LP*, vol. 10, no. 246 (1) (incomplete draft of the Statute of Uses, c. 1535/6); TNA PRO SP 1/101, ff. 261–81; *LP*, vol. 10, no. 246 (2) (complete draft of the Statute of Uses, c. 1535).

Henry and a number of peers on the feudal incidents of primer seisin and wardship. Both are dated in *Letters and Papers* to 1529; however, as we shall see, the agreement with the peers appears to have been later.[12]

Furthermore, we know from Thomas Cromwell's remembrances that Henry instructed him to prepare a 'bill of primer seisin' to be presented in the third session of Parliament, which ran from 15 January to 28 March 1532.[13] We also learn from Edward Hall, who was sitting in the Commons at the time, that on 18 March 1532 Henry confronted the Commons, lamenting their lack of progress on his 'bill concerning wards and primer seisin' and saying that he already had the agreement of the peers to limit the avoidance of feudal incidents.[14] After their rejection in March 1532 of Henry's 'bill of primer seisin', the king turned to the courts in *Dacre's Case* (1533–35), following which three further drafts of the Statute of Uses and one of the Statute of Enrolments were calendared in *Letters and Papers*.

It seems clear that the bill presented to the Commons in 1532, as reported by Hall, was the one drafted by Cromwell. Furthermore, the agreement with the peers in *Letters and Papers* must be what Hall reported the king as relying on in his confrontation with the Commons in March 1532. However, understanding the draft bill in *Letters and Papers* has proved more difficult. It is unlikely that this draft bill was the one prepared by Cromwell in 1532; as we shall see, it is more likely that it was a separate draft prepared and rejected earlier in the Parliament.

As noted, the editor of *Letters and Papers* calendared the earlier draft bill immediately before the agreement with the peers and dated both to 1529.[15] This approach was followed by Holdsworth but is likely to reflect no more than the date for the beginning of the Reformation Parliament.[16] For the draft bill, a date of 1529 seems likely but for a number of reasons it is unconvincing for the agreement with the peers.[17]

---

[12] Draft bill: TNA PRO SP 1/56, ff. 36–9; *LP*, vol. 4, no. 6043; printed in Holdsworth, *HEL*, vol. 4, 572–4. Agreement with the peers: BL, MS Cotton Titus B.IV, ff. 114–18; *LP*, IV, no. 6044; printed in Holdsworth, *HEL*, vol. 4, 574–7. The agreement with the peers was signed by thirty of the fifty-six lords temporal. For the composition of the Lords: see Lehmberg, *Reformation Parliament*, 36–7.

[13] BL, MS Cotton Titus B.I, f. 486; *LP*, vol. 5, no. 396.

[14] E. Hall, *Henry VIII*, ed. by C. Whibley, 2 vols. (London, 1904), vol. 2, 203.

[15] *LP*, vol. 4, nos. 6043, 6044.

[16] Holdsworth, *HEL*, vol. 4, 572–7.

[17] Bean, *Decline*, 265–7.

Of the peers who signed the agreement, five were ennobled on 1–2 December 1529, after Parliament had been summoned: Barons Bray, Burgh, Hussey, Wentworth and Windsor. Indeed, of those five, three had sat in the Commons at the opening in August.[18] The first session concluded on 17 December, and with only a very short period between their ennoblement and the end of the session, it seems unlikely that the agreement can be dated to 1529.

Although it seems clear that a date of 1529 can be dismissed, settling on a more accurate date is difficult. The agreement must have been concluded before 18 March 1532, when the king referred to it when lamenting apparent lack of progress in the Commons for his 'bill concerning wards and primer seisin'.[19] However, the task is complicated by the presence of two other signatories: Thomas Grey, marquis of Dorset, and Edward Stanley, earl of Derby. The negotiations with the peers must have begun, and been at an advanced stage, before 10 October 1530, the date of Dorset's death. In addition, the negotiations are unlikely to have concluded much before 24 January 1531 when Derby, following his maturity, sued his livery and entered into his inheritance.[20] The earl's date of birth is uncertain: it was most likely late 1509 or 1510,[21] which would make him around twenty-one in January 1531. It is possible that the king allowed Derby to enter into his inheritance early on condition of his agreement, which could suggest a late 1530 date for the agreement.

Ascertaining the connection, if any, between the draft bill and the agreement with the peers has proved difficult. The main provisions of the bill were radical and proposed wholesale reform of landholding. First, the bill proposed the abolition of all entails, so that upon enactment all lands, tenements and other hereditaments would be held in fee simple.[22] A later clause would have excluded the nobility from this abolition while providing that any alienation by a nobleman must be licensed by the king. Second, the bill would have rendered all uses invalid unless enrolled in the Court of Common Pleas. Third, it provided that, immediately

---

[18] Lords Hussey, Wentworth and Windsor: Bean, *Decline*, 260.

[19] Hall, *Henry VIII*, vol. 2, 203.

[20] TNA PRO C 66/656, m. 24 (*LP*, vol. 5, no. 119 (22)). Livery was performed at York Place on 22 January and confirmed by privy seal at Westminster on 8 February. Bean gives a date of 31 January, but it is not clear why: Bean, *Decline*, 266.

[21] L. A. Knafla, 'Stanley, Edward, Third Earl of Derby (1509–1572), magnate', *Oxford Dictionary of National Biography* (online), 23 September 2004.

[22] Holdsworth, *HEL*, vol. 4, 572. Note that this appears to be solely addressing estates in fee tail and would not affect a life estate granted out of the fee simple.

following the sale of any land, tenement, or other hereditament, the deed was to be read out in the parish or parishes in which the land lay and was then to be registered in the shire town. The remaining provisions concerned limitation and should be viewed very much as measures to simplify landholding. A limitation period of five years following a fine or recovery was proposed, after which the land was to be treated as held in fee simple. A further limitation period of forty years was outlined in the final provision, within which any claims against title must be made.[23]

It has been suggested that this earlier draft bill was designed to effect a degree of social engineering by reasserting the social and economic privileges of the nobility under the king,[24] but as Bean has argued, 'such an imaginative scheme' seems very unlikely.[25] The proposed abolition of entails in the draft bill is perhaps better seen as symbolic, the real focus of the bill being elsewhere. Following the decision in *Taltarum's Case* (1472), entails could be broken by common recovery.[26] Although the abolition of entails would have removed the need to effect a common recovery, and indeed the expense of doing so, it is likely that the concession to the peers was 'intended as a sop to the pride of the nobility',[27] as opposed to being of any tangible benefit. It has been argued that the concession to the peers in the draft bill persuaded them to support Henry's efforts to limit loss of feudal revenue through uses in his agreement with the peers.[28] This position is untenable: whilst there was some advantage to the peers in the provisions of the draft bill, it is difficult to suggest that this was enough to justify a quid pro quo in relation to incidents. Furthermore, a textual analysis of the draft bill renders it very unlikely to have been the same as Cromwell's 'bill concerning wards and primer seisin' which was rejected in 1532.[29]

---

[23] It is worth noting that forty years was not one of the periods set out in the Statute of Limitation of Prescriptions, 32 Hen. VIII, c. 2 (1540), although it was a canon law period, and appeared in Chancery in the later sixteenth century, which may suggest a canonist, or at the very least Chancery, influence on the draft. For further detail on limitation periods more generally, see H. Dondorp, D. J. Ibbetson and E. J. H. Schrage (eds.), *Limitation and Prescription: A Comparative Legal History* (Berlin, 2019).

[24] Plucknett, 'Some Proposed Legislation of Henry VIII', 121–4.

[25] Bean, *Decline*, 260–1.

[26] *Taltarum's Case (Hunt v. Smyth)* (1472): TNA PRO CP 40/844, m. 631; YB Mich., 12 Edw. IV, f. 14, pl. 16; f. 19, pl 25; YB Mich., 123 Edw. IV, f. 1, pl. 1; J. H. Baker (ed.), *The Reports of Sir John Spelman*, 2 vols. (93–4 Selden Society, London, 1976–77), vol. 2, 204.

[27] Bean, *Decline*, 260.

[28] Baker, *OHLE*, 664–5; Bean, *Decline*, 259–61; Holdsworth, *HEL*, vol. 4, 450–1.

[29] Hall, *Henry VIII*, vol. 2, 203.

An alternative explanation has been offered by Ives, who argues that the earlier draft bill and the agreement with the peers were unrelated as the draft bill, rather than being an official proposal, was in fact written by a 'well-intentioned but inexperienced' amateur.[30] To support his position, Ives advances two arguments. He contends firstly that the impractical nature of several of the provisions, particularly in relation to registration, suggest that it was ill-conceived and not an official proposal, and secondly, that the draft bill focused on general reform, rather than being specifically aimed at the avoidance of feudal incidents through uses.[31]

The first of Ives' arguments is not wholly compelling. As he himself accepts, '[t]he fact that suggested legislation is ill-conceived does not, of course, establish that it is unofficial in origin'.[32] Furthermore, that a radical proposal to completely overhaul late medieval English landholding would create difficulties is not merely unsurprising, it is to be expected. The second limb of Ives' argument is more interesting. He argues that the draft bill was unlikely to be official as it was not focused on the avoidance of feudal incidents. However, this is a somewhat anachronistic observation, as contemporary critiques of uses also considered wider issues.[33] Furthermore, the registration requirement for uses would have addressed concerns relating to certainty and permitted the pre-existing legislation concerning incidents (the Statute of Marlborough, c. 6 (1267) and 4 Henry VII, c. 17 (1490)) to be more easily enforced.[34]

---

[30] Ives, 'Genesis of the Statute of Uses', 677–9. Lehmberg agreed with Ives that the content of the bill indicates that it was unofficial before going on to suggest that the bill was likely connected to the Statute of Enrolments: Lehmberg, *Reformation Parliament*, 94–5. Cf. G. R. Elton, 'Parliamentary Drafts, 1529–1540', *Bulletin of the Institute of Historical Research*, 25 (1952), 117, 132.

[31] In contrast to the agreement with the peers in which incidents were central. Clauses 1 and 2 outlined the king's prerogative right to wardship. Clauses 3, 4 and 5 stipulated the amount of military tenure land that could be devised by last will to two-thirds, leaving the king with wardship of one-third. For more detail, see Bean, *Decline*, 261–3.

[32] Ives, 'Genesis of the Statute of Uses', 679.

[33] Note in particular the *Damna Usuum*: TNA PRO SP 1/101, f. 282 (*LP*, vol. 10, no. 246), printed in Holdsworth, *HEL*, vol. 4, 577–80. See also Thomas Audley's reading at the Inner Temple: BL, MS Hargrave 87, ff. 427–55; CUL, MS Ee. 5. 19, ff. 1–17; Duke of Northumberland MS 475, f. 187v; University of Illinois at Urbana-Champaign MS 27, ff. 69–95v. The anonymous *Replication of a Serjeant at the Laws of England*: J. Guy (ed.), *The Replication of a Serjeant at the Laws of England*, in *Christopher St German on Chancery and Statute* (6 Selden Society Supplementary Series, London, 1985), 99–105.

[34] For the continuing importance of Marlborough, see Hannay, 'By Fraud and Collusion'.

The most plausible explanation is that the draft was official but did not directly correspond to the agreement with the peers in the manner that has been suggested. The evidence connecting them is shaky at best. Indeed, when the contents of the two are considered side-by-side, it appears to be far more persuasive that they were unrelated; the contents of the draft bill and of the agreement with the peers are manifestly different. It seems that the early draft bill received a cold reception in the first session of Parliament and the Crown changed tack, likely reaching an agreement with the peers by January 1531.

The agreement with the peers was likely concluded ahead of the second session of Parliament, 16 January to 31 March 1531. In his chronicle, Hall makes no reference to a bill being presented to the Commons in the second session,[35] and Cromwell's 'bill concerning wards and primer seisin' was prepared for the third session, 15 January to 28 March 1532. The Imperial ambassador to England, Eustace Chapuys, reported to Charles V, Holy Roman Emperor, in March 1531 that '[t]he Parliament continues, but has done nothing, as I am told, and it is supposed the King keeps it sitting for some mysterious purpose'.[36] It seems likely that following the agreement with the peers, the king entered into a period of negotiations with the Commons over feudal incidents which may have been the 'mysterious purpose'. In another letter, dated 30 January 1532, Chapuys reported that Parliament was debating feudal incidents,[37] and on 14 February 1532, Chapuys wrote that the king was seeking to obtain one-third part of feudal property.[38] This corresponds with the agreement for one-third with the peers and the date fits with the Commons' subsequent rejection of the proposal on 18 March 1532, reported by Hall. In other respects, however, Hall's account appears, at least initially, somewhat difficult to reconcile with Chapuys.

Following on from his recounting of Henry's speech to the Commons, Hall explained that the king's proposal was for half of military tenure land to be devisable by last will,[39] as opposed to the two-thirds in the agreement with the peers and outlined by Chapuys. He then goes on to declare that the Commons erred in either not accepting this proposal or at least

[35] Hall, *Henry VIII*, vol. 2, 203; Bean, *Decline*, 267.
[36] *LP*, vol. 5, no. 120.
[37] Ibid., no. 762.
[38] Ibid., no. 805.
[39] Hall, *Henry VIII*, vol. 2, 203–4.

not pushing back against the king to negotiate him down to a third or a quarter, 'which offer [Hall] was credibly informed the king would have taken'.[40] As he was a lawyer and an MP sitting in the Commons at the time, it is tempting to defer to Hall. For Bean, Hall was more reliable than Chapuys, and he argued that Hall's assertion suggests that Henry had in fact reached a second agreement with the peers for one-half, which was rejected by the Commons. This is rather tenuous and not an especially convincing reading of the evidence. As the Imperial ambassador resident in England, Chapuys had good access to information and was writing contemporaneously; his accuracy is too readily doubted by Bean. Although Hall had better information – he was very possibly in the room throughout – he was likely writing much later.[41]

It is possible to reconcile the accounts of Hall and Chapuys. It is more likely that Hall, writing at least a decade later, misremembered the order of the king's proposals, than that Chapuys, writing contemporaneously, was wrong in February 1532. The most plausible explanation appears to be that, rather than Henry increasing his demands after the agreement with the peers, there was a significant period of negotiation, initially with the peers, in which Henry started at half and was negotiated down to a third. Negotiations then continued with the Commons and Henry instructed Cromwell to prepare a bill of wardship and primer seisin', based on the agreement with the peers, ahead of the third session. This bill was eventually rejected by the Commons in March 1532, prompting Henry's strikingly ominous foreshadowing that he would 'search out the extremity of the law'.[42]

> ⋆ ⋆ ⋆

Following the failed attempt to legislate, Henry then turned to the courts. The first peer to die, having enfeoffed feoffees to perform his will, following the Commons' rejection of the bill in March 1532 was Thomas Fiennes, Baron Dacre of the South (died 9 September 1533): *Dacre's Case* was to be the king's test case.[43] The case began with an

---

[40] Ibid., 204.

[41] The first edition covering the period up to 1532 was not printed until 1548, a year after Hall's death, and revised edition to the end of the reign, based on Hall's notes, was published posthumously in 1550.

[42] Hall, *Henry VIII*, vol. 2, 203.

[43] *Re Lord Dacre of the South* (1533–35), TNA PRO C 142/80/24–5 (inquisition); C 42/2/32 (traverse); YB Pasch. 27 Hen. VIII. f. 7, pl. 22.

inquisition post-mortem in Chancery, before being referred to the Exchequer Chamber. Following the exertion of significant pressure on behalf of the Crown, the king prevailed and it was held that uses of freehold land were incapable of being devised by will.[44] Furthermore, not only were future wills devising land considered to be invalid, but any title that was traced through a will at any point in the past was now vulnerable.[45] The king's threat to 'search out the extremity of the law' had been realised beyond the Commons' worst imaginings. The situation was untenable, and legislation required. The only real question was how the Crown would approach a remedy.

Surviving documents calendared in *Letters and Papers* give important insight into the Crown's approach. Three drafts of the Statute of Uses and one of the Statute of Enrolments have survived which enable us to trace the development of the Crown's thinking in light of the litigation in *Dacre's Case*.[46] Turning first to the Statute of Uses, it is clear that two separate approaches to legislation were considered. The first proposed a scheme which was to apply common law rules for legal title to uses but this was not pursued beyond an initial draft.[47] The second proposed to annex the legal estate to the use and would become the Statute of Uses. Two drafts have survived, the first an early draft and a second which was the same in substantive content but was in a more formal and parliamentary style[48]; indeed, it is almost identical to the Statute of Uses itself.

The first draft was clearly an early version. It is more concise and without the style or character expected of a formal bill but is nonetheless interesting and informative. The comparatively short document begins by declaring that the common law had been subverted by uses. The remedy proposed, as noted, was, in effect, to apply the common law of real property to uses.[49] As Baker notes, the bill sought to effect an extension of the provision in 4 Henry VII, c. 17 (1490), which treated

---

[44] Baker, *OHLE*, 671.

[45] Ibid., 672.

[46] TNA PRO SP 1/101, ff. 286–91; *LP*, vol. 10, no. 246 (4). Printed in Holdsworth, *HEL*, vol. 4, 580–81; TNA PRO SP 1/101 ff. 252–60; *LP*, vol. 10, no. 246 (1); TNA PRO SP 1/101, ff. 261–81; *LP*, vol. 10, no. 246 (2); TNA PRO SP 1/101, ff. 303–21; *LP*, vol. 10, no. 246 (6). Printed in Holdsworth, *HEL*, vol. 4, 582–6.

[47] TNA PRO SP 1/101, ff. 286–91; *LP*, vol. 10, no. 246 (4). Printed in Holdsworth, *HEL*, vol. 4, 580–1.

[48] TNA PRO SP 1/101 ff. 252–60; *LP*, vol. 10, no. 246 (1); TNA PRO SP 1/101, ff. 261–81; *LP*, vol. 10, no. 246 (2).

[49] Holdsworth, *HEL*, vol. 4, 457.

the heir of *cestui que use* who died intestate as if his ancestor had died seised.[50] It was viewed by Holdsworth as being 'useless, or almost useless, to the king',[51] and by Lehmberg as 'not very advantageous to the Crown financially'.[52] The central point to this argument is that the draft would not prevent the devise of land. However, as noted by Bean, this is a misreading of the text. Whilst certainly 'clumsy', the effect of the provision was to treat the *cestui que use* as if he had been in possession at common law, which would include preventing the devise of land by last will.[53]

It has been presupposed that this initial draft, like the later drafts beside which it is calendared, was prepared after the decision in *Dacre's Case*.[54] However, this is almost certainly not the case. If the decision in *Dacre's Case* was as fundamental and substantively damaging to the security of title as it appears to have been, then the Commons was in no position to object to anything Henry's government put forward. There was no need in 1535–36 for subtle negotiation or compromise; following *Dacre's Case*, the Commons had lost. Furthermore, the draft did nothing to remedy the vulnerability that landholders faced in the decision in *Dacre's Case*. It is much more likely that the initial draft can be dated to the period before the decision in *Dacre's Case*.[55]

It has been suggested that a memorandum of October 1533 demonstrates that Cromwell was contemplating further legislation at this point.[56] This relies on reading two consecutive notes on instructions to the Crown's lawyers – the first relating to the order of the king's wards and the second to investigate Lord Dacre's will – as being connected. The inquisition following Dacre's death was not held until January 1534. Although possible, it therefore seems unlikely that Cromwell was considering legislation before the inquisition, and the reference to 'order of the king's wards' is rather too vague to support a conclusion that Cromwell was considering legislation. However, later in 1534, the inquisition had been traversed by Dacre's feoffees, and it appears that

---

[50] Baker, *OHLE*, 672,n. 127.
[51] Ibid.
[52] Lehmberg, *Reformation Parliament*, 236.
[53] Bean, *Decline*, 288.
[54] Parliament was scheduled to meet in November 1535, however, due to plague in London this was delayed until February 1536: Lehmberg, *Reformation Parliament*, 217 (nn. 1–2).
[55] Baker, *OHLE*, 672, n. 126; Ives, 'Genesis of the Statute of Uses', 692.
[56] Ives, 'Genesis of the Statute of Uses', 690; BL, MS Cotton Titus B. I., ff. 453, 478; *LP*, vol. 6, no. 1381.

Cromwell was less than confident of a positive outcome. In autumn 1534 he sought the advice of the judges,[57] and a memorandum noting the need for Cromwell to find 'some reasonable way to be devised for the king's wards and primer seisin' could suggest that he was considering legislation.[58] Although the Dacre litigation had begun, the outcome was far from certain. It can be suggested that the 'reasonable way to be devised' in the memorandum was the draft bill,[59] but that it was not pursued beyond this initial draft. The memorandum suggests that the bill may have been prepared ahead of the sixth session, 3 November to 18 December 1534.[60] The content of the draft, particularly the preamble, strongly resembles the complaints raised in the *Damna Usuum*, a contemporary list of complaints on the 'mischiefs, wrongs and inconveniences' which were caused by the employment of uses.[61]

Parliament was set to return in November 1535, following the decision in *Dacre's Case* in Easter Term, but due to plague it did not return until February 1536.[62] There is some evidence of very minor negotiation over the precise form of the eventual Statute of Uses. This can be seen in two further drafts: the first an early draft which was subject to slight amendments before a second in formal parliamentary style which was almost identical to the eventual Statute of Uses, with only some minor deletions to clause 10.[63] The main provision was for the legal estate to be annexed to the use. Where previously, following a feoffment to feoffees to the use of *cestui que use* the feoffees would stand seised with the *cestui que use* merely having the use of the land, by operation of the Statute of Uses, following such a feoffment legal title would cease to be vested in the feoffees and would automatically vest in the *cestui que use*. The solution enacted by the Statute of Uses was remarkably simple yet there were significant oversights.

[57] Ives, 'Genesis of the Statute of Uses', 691.
[58] BL, MS Cotton Titus B. I, f. 159v; *LP*, vol. 9, no. 725. For the date, see Ives, 'Genesis of the Statute of Uses', 692, n. 2. The memorandum states that it was to be prepared 'for the next session', which was planned be in November 1535.
[59] TNA PRO SP 1/101, ff. 286–91; *LP*, vol. 10, no. 246 (4). Printed in Holdsworth, *HEL*, vol. 4, 580–1.
[60] Lehmberg, *Reformation Parliament*, 216, n. 3.
[61] See above, n. 33.
[62] TNA PRO SP 1/101, ff. 282–5; *LP*, vol. 10, no. 246 (3). The text is printed in Holdsworth, *HEL*, vol. 4, 577–80. For more detail on the *Damna Usuum*, see A. J. Hannay, 'Damna Usuum: Common Law, Conscience and the "Sufferance of Uses"', *Cambridge Law Journal* 84 (in press).
[63] Ives, 'Genesis of the Statute of Uses', 693.

As well as express and resulting uses, the statute also executed implied uses that arose to the benefit of the purchaser on a bargain and sale. Following the Statute of Uses, the purchaser would stand seised by virtue of the statute, thus removing the time to make enquiries.[64] Before the Statute of Uses this was common practice and would have caused significant difficulties for conveyancers. Unlike issues relating to dower and jointure, which were addressed in the Statute of Uses itself,[65] it appears that the drafters did not recognise the problem with implied uses until a relatively late stage. This was addressed by the passing of the Statute of Enrolments later in the seventh session.[66]

The Statute of Enrolments has long been recognised as part of the same scheme as the Statute of Uses. Indeed, Francis Bacon, in his 1600 reading at Gray's Inn, stated that it was 'but a proviso' to the Statute of Uses.[67] The eventual Statute of Enrolments was short and contained no preamble. It prevented the automatic execution of implied uses by providing that no estate or inheritance or freehold would pass by virtue only of a bargain and sale unless the bargain and sale was 'indented, sealed and enrolled' within six months at a court of record in Westminster or in the county in which the land was situated.[68]

Like the Statute of Uses itself, we are assisted in understanding the origins of the Statute of Enrolments by the survival of an earlier draft bill.[69] The draft bill is a great deal more ambitious and sophisticated than that which was eventually passed. An initial point to make is that the draft bill is far longer than the eventual Statute of Enrolments. In addition, unlike the statute itself, the draft contains a broad preamble in the conventional style.[70] Following the preamble, the substance of the draft begins by providing that after the last day of July 1536 the use of any

---

[64] Baker, *OHLE*, 677.

[65] 27 Hen. VIII, c. 10, clauses 4–7.

[66] 27 Hen. VIII, c. 16; J. M. Kaye, 'A Note on the Statute of Enrolments 1536', *Law Quarterly Review*, 104 (1988), 617.

[67] F. Bacon, *The Learned Reading of Sir Francis Bacon upon the Statute of Uses* (1642), 46; Bean, *Decline*, 291; Holdsworth, *HEL*, vol. 4, 462–3; Simpson, *History of Land Law*, 188.

[68] To be enrolled in the county or counties in which the land was held it must have been enrolled before 'the *Custos Rotulorum* and [two] Justices of the peace and the Clerk of the Peace of the same County or Counties or [two] of them at least whereof the Clerk of the Peace to be one'. *SR*, vol. 3, 549; J. H. Baker, *Baker and Milsom Sources of Legal History: Private Law to 1790*, 2nd ed. (Oxford, 2019), 135.

[69] TNA PRO SP 1/101, ff. 303–21; *LP*, vol. 10, no. 246 (6). Printed in Holdsworth, *HEL*, vol. 4, 582–6.

[70] Lehmberg, *Reformation Parliament*, 238.

lands, tenements and hereditaments should not pass unless agreed in writing, made under seal and enrolled.[71] The remaining clauses outline a series of administrative reforms empowering the king to appoint officers in each shire who would be responsible for recording and entering the same writing within forty days on to a roll to be deposited in the Chancery which could be inspected by interested parties. Failure to enrol within the specified forty days would result in the disposition being void.

The content of the draft bill is interesting. The draft speaks of declared uses, proposing that all uses would be invalid unless they were declared in writing and enrolled. That is to say, it applied to express uses, and resulting uses arising from a feoffment or other form of conveyance, for no express use or consideration, but not uses implied into a bargain and sale. The Statute of Enrolments that was eventually enacted was far more limited and addressed only implied uses. The inclusion of other uses in the draft bill and not in the eventual Act itself may explain Lehmberg's apparent confusion in arguing that the Statute of Enrolments was specifically addressed to 'secret conveyances',[72] which are generally understood to have been resulting uses, such as in 1 Richard III, c. 1.[73]

The fact that the draft gives a date of the end of July 1536 after which uses were to be invalid unless they were in sealed writing and enrolled is interesting. The seventh session of Parliament ended on 14 April 1536, so the draft must have been completed before then – indeed completed with time to change tack and pass the subsequent Statute of Enrolments. It is likely that the draft's July date was proposed to allow time to implement the administrative bureaucracy that the king was empowered to establish, the scale of which was substantial, and is suggestive of a date far in advance of the end of parliamentary session in April. The Statute of Uses itself was to take effect from 1 May 1536. As this draft of the Statute of Enrolments would have taken effect, had it been enacted, almost three months after the Statute of Uses, it appears unlikely that it was prepared after the Statute of Uses.

That the draft required the enrolment of all declared uses appears to suggest a number of things in relation to the drafting of the Statute of

---

[71] TNA PRO SP 1/101, ff. 303–21; *LP*, vol. 10, no. 246 (6). Printed in Holdsworth, *HEL*, vol. 4, 582 (numbered by Holdsworth as clause 1).

[72] Lehmberg, *Reformation Parliament*, 238.

[73] Baker, *OHLE*, 655–60, 675; A. J. Hannay, 'The Statute of Richard III (1484) and the Emergence of Beneficial Ownership in Freehold Land', in C. Mitchell and D. Foster (eds.), *Essays in the History of English Equity* (London, in press).

Uses. The draft bears a striking similarity to the first draft bill dated to 1529 in *Letters and Papers*, which required all declared uses to be enrolled with the Common Pleas.[74] Indeed, it may be that this draft of the Statute of Enrolments is a more developed, and narrower, version of the 1529 draft bill. The 1529 draft was quickly rejected in favour of a more direct approach focused on feudal incidents, but it may be that those who prepared it continued to propose a much broader reform to the law of real property. With regard to the draft's purpose, and its relationship to the Statute of Uses, two alternative explanations can be suggested.

The first is that it was an alternative to the Statute of Uses in which, rather than attaching legal title to the use, the Crown could seek to protect itself from loss of feudal revenue by requiring all declared uses to be enrolled. As we have noted in relation to the 1529 draft bill, it is possible that this would have provided a greater protection to the Crown from loss of feudal incidents, but only to a limited extent in allowing easier enforcement of earlier legislation. If the draft was prepared before the decision in *Dacre's Case*, this understanding of the draft of the Statute of Enrolments may be more plausible, as a creative means of providing some protection to the Crown, but it seems unlikely. A more probable explanation for the draft is that it was prepared alongside the Statute of Uses and was intended to apply to those uses of land which were not caught by the Statute of Uses, that is to say, uses of non-freehold land and those with active duties.[75] This could therefore represent a more holistic reform to the law of uses generally, and one which sought to reconcile uses with the broader law of real property. However, it is likely that as a result of practical and administrative difficulties it was ultimately not pursued, only for the idea of enrolment to be quickly resurrected in a hasty reassembling of the initial draft directed solely at implied uses to address the flaw in the Statute of Uses.[76]

> * *

---

[74] TNA PRO SP 1/56, ff. 36–9; *LP*, vol. 4 no. 6043, printed in Holdsworth, *HEL*, vol. 4, 572–4.

[75] This assumes that the Statute of Uses was not intended to apply to uses with active duties and of non-freehold land, which seems likely. For the intended scope of the statute, see Jones, 'Authority of Parliament', 13.

[76] For the haste in which the statute was passed, see G. R. Elton, *Reform and Reformation: England 1509–1558* (London, 1977), 146–7, although, as Baker notes, Elton misunderstood the purpose of the Statute of Enrolments: Baker, *OHLE*, 678, n. 149.

Ascertaining the precise path through the Reformation Parliament of Henry VIII's attempts to address the uncertainty caused by uses, including the loss of revenue from the avoidance of feudal incidents, is far from straightforward. Previous historians have suggested that an initial bill, linked to an agreement with the peers, was rejected by the Commons in 1532 before the litigation in *Dacre's Case* led to the Crown prevailing and the enactment of the Statute of Uses. In this chapter, we have seen that close evaluation of the evidence supports a re-evaluation of this orthodoxy, particularly in the period before *Dacre's Case*.

A textual analysis of the 1529 draft Commons bill and the agreement with the peers demonstrates that they are manifestly different schemes and suggestions of a close connection between them is unconvincing. It is much more probable that rather than one Commons draft bill we have two: the 1529 bill,[77] which was quickly abandoned, and, following a period of sustained negotiations and subsequent agreement with the peers,[78] Cromwell's 'bill of wardship and primer seisin', which was rejected by the Commons in March 1532.[79]

At this point, the Crown changed tack and sought to pursue the avoidance of incidents in the courts in *Dacre's Case*. Likely doubting the outcome in *Dacre's Case*, it seems that Cromwell prepared a compromise bill for the sixth session of Parliament, in late 1534, but it was not presented.[80] Following this, substantial pressure was applied to the judges, ensuring the Crown's success in *Dacre's Case*, and the Commons were undone. At this point it appears that two schemes were considered. Firstly, one which would require the enrolment of all uses, evidenced in what has become known as the draft of the Statute of Enrolments,[81] and a second which became the Statute of Uses, and for which two drafts survive.[82] The first scheme likely faltered due to administrative unworkability; however, following the eventual passage of the Statute of Uses, a

[77] TNA PRO SP 1/56, ff. 36–9; *LP*, vol. 4, no. 6043 (1529 draft bill), printed in Holdsworth, *HEL*, vol. 4, 572–4.
[78] BL, MS Cotton Titus B.IV, ff. 114–18 (*LP*, IV, no. 6044), printed in Holdsworth, *HEL*, vol. 4, 574–7 (agreement with the peers).
[79] BL, MS Cotton Titus B.I, f. 486; *LP*, vol. 5, no. 396.
[80] TNA PRO SP 1/101, ff. 286–91; *LP*, vol. 10, no. 246 (1534 draft bill), printed in Holdsworth, *HEL*, vol. 4, 580–1.
[81] TNA PRO SP 1/101, ff. 303–21; *LP*, vol. 10, no. 246 (6), printed in Holdsworth, *HEL*, vol. 4, 582–8.
[82] TNA PRO SP 1/101 ff. 252–60; *LP*, vol. 10, no. 246 (1); TNA PRO SP 1/101, ff. 261–81; *LP*, vol. 10, no. 246 (2).

scheme of enrolment was resurrected to prevent the automatic execution of implied uses.

In his 1600 reading, Francis Bacon described the Statute of Uses as 'the most perfectly and exactly conceived and penned of any law in the book'.[83] As we have seen, its origins and drafting are rather more complex than Bacon allowed. The statute that was enacted in 1536, and transplanted to Ireland in 1634, was the result of sustained negotiations and significant intellectual, parliamentary and judicial scrutiny. As well as providing a far clearer understanding of technical questions relating to uses and trusts, the passage of the Statute of Uses and the Statute of Enrolments elucidates important features of the relationship between the Crown, the peers, the commons and the judiciary in this fundamentally important period in our history.

---

[83] Bacon, *Bacon upon the Statute of Uses*, 25.

3

Examining the Doctrine of Art and Part in Early Modern Scotland

STEPHANIE DROPULJIC

Introduction

In 1586, James Findlay, his son John, wife Janet, and sister Elspeth, along with Tibble Smart, were accused of the art and part cruel slaughter, or killing, of Peter, David, and William Reid and their mother Christina Maher by using witchcraft and enchantment.[1] The case of *James Findlay and others* (1586) was a typical example of the way in which art and part liability operated: to demonstrate that all those within the dwelling house, by implication, were equally culpable of the resulting death. The defence of James, John, Janet, and Elspeth was that Tibble was the principal accused and the death was a direct result of his actions. These four accused were continued to another day, and Tibble proceeded to a trial. He was subsequently acquitted by an assize (jury). This construction of art and part in the early modern period is a significant departure from its modern form.

Art and part is a term of art used in Scots law to denote a form of derivative liability, namely, persons who collectively participated in some way (regardless of the role they played) in an offence and shared a common criminal purpose with the primary actor(s). This doctrine operates to extend criminal liability to a person who did not have the *actus reus* of the offence in question and may not have, in some circumstances, had the *mens rea*. In the modern context, art and part has been the subject of criticism and controversy, particularly in respect to homicide offences.[2] This is because an accused who neither inflicted nor anticipated the deceased's death could be convicted of murder.[3]

---

[1] National Records of Scotland (NRS) MSS JC2 vol. 2 High Court Book of Adjournal (1 December 1584–20 October 1591) f46v (88).

[2] F. Leverick, 'The (Art and) Parting of the Ways: Joint Criminal Liability for Homicide', *Scots Law Times (SLT)*, 37 (2012), 227.

[3] Ibid., 227.

There is currently no academic literature which considers the development of art and part liability. There have been modern cases heard by the High Court of Justiciary (Scotland's highest criminal court) which have considered the nuances involved in applying the doctrine to primary and co-accused individuals,[4] and Fiona Leverick has considered various issues associated with applying the principles of art and part.[5] The scholarship on criminal liability has tended to focus on the doctrinal developments associated with attributing responsibility.[6] Whilst some of it has considered the intersection of history, law, and criminal responsibility,[7] its primary focus has been on modern issues and developments. However, Nicola Lacey's study of criminal responsibility demonstrated that legal concepts connected to responsibility were intrinsically linked to the legal and cultural environments which influenced their development,[8] and Michele Pifferi has shown that the early modern period was significant because of the development in theoretical definitions and concepts.[9] This chapter builds on these insights to consider how the legal environment of the early modern period influenced the development of art and part liability before the justiciary court.

The sixteenth and seventeenth centuries witnessed important developments in the legal and political institutions in Scotland.[10] The complexities associated with applying the doctrine of art and part in the early

---

[4] *Docherty v. HM Advocate* 2003 SLT 1337; *Socratous v. HM Advocate* 1987 SLT 244; *McKinnon v. HM Advocate* 2003 JC 29. *Brown (Lilian Hazel Carr) v. HM Advocate* 1993 SCCR 382; *Robert Kidd, John Tifforey v. HM Advocate* [2010] HCJAC 98, 2010 WL 3975644; *Ann Gorman v. HM Advocate* [2010] HCJAC 9, 2011 WL 398152; *John Crawford v. HM Advocate* [2012] HCJAC 40, 2012 WL 1015834.

[5] Leverick, 'The (Art and) Parting', 227.

[6] N. Lacey, *In Search of Criminal Responsibility: Ideas, Interests, and Institutions* (Oxford, 2016), 10–11; H. L. A. Hart, *Punishment and Responsibility: Essays in the Philosophy of Law*, 2nd ed. (Oxford, 2008); J. Forder, *Excusing Crime* (Oxford, 2007); V. Tadros, *Criminal Responsibility* (Oxford, 2007).

[7] L. Farmer, *Criminal Law, Tradition and Legal Order: Crime and the Genius of Scots Law* (Cambridge, 1996); A. Norrie, *Crime, Reason and History*, 3rd ed. (Cambridge, 2014); R. A. Duff, L. Farmer, S. E. Marshall, M. Renzo and V. Tadros (eds.), *The Boundaries of Criminal Law* (Oxford, 2010).

[8] Lacey, *Criminal Responsibility*, 176–179.

[9] M. Pifferi, 'Criminal Responsibility and Its Histories: New Perspectives for Comparative Legal History', *Critical Analysis of Law: An International and Interdisciplinary Law Review* 4 (2017), 222, 225.

[10] W. C. Dickinson, 'The High Court of Justiciary', in *An Introduction to Scottish Legal History* (20 Stair Society, Edinburgh, 1958), 410–411; A. M. Godfrey, *Civil Justice in Renaissance Scotland: The Origins of a Central Court* (Leiden, 2009); J. D. Ford, *Law and Opinion in Scotland during the Seventeenth Century* (Oxford, 2007); J. Goodare, *State and*

modern period have important implications for our understanding of its modern form. The aim of this chapter is to consider the historical development of the concept of art and part, seeking to trace the rule through selected early sources of Scots law and, for comparison, early sources of English law. It will explore the extent to which the concept was reformed by legislative provision in the sixteenth century, and will assess, through the examination of selected homicide prosecutions from 1580 to 1650, how far initiatives for enhancing the administration of justice impacted on the prosecution of art and part. The conclusions drawn about the law in practice will go beyond the law as recorded in the parliamentary legislation and key legal books to consider how concepts such as culpability, intention, and knowledge contributed to wider understandings of criminal liability.

Earlier Sources of Scots Law: *Regiam Majestatem* and *Quoniam Attachiamenta*

To investigate the historical development and textual analysis of art and part, a wide construction of the concept and terminological usage(s) was required when examining the earlier sources of law. These sections, and indeed the chapter more broadly, will not speak to the learned authority or discuss the authoritative sources of legal learning.

The medieval law book known as *Regiam Majestatem* is one of the earliest sources of Scots law. Several manuscript editions exist of this treatise.[11] There were two printed texts available in the seventeenth century and these were published in 1609 by Sir John Skene of Curriehill. These editions have been preferred here because of the date of publication and Skene's role as a jurist in the sixteenth century.[12]

Society in Early Modern Scotland (Oxford, 1999); J. Goodare, *The Government of Scotland: 1550–1625* (Oxford, 2004).

[11] A modern critical edition of *Regiam* and an in-depth study of the text can be found in J. R. Davies (ed.) with A. Taylor, *Regiam Maiestatem – The Earliest Known Version* (68 Stair Society, Edinburgh, 2022).

[12] The printed editions of this sources have been preferred, as the use of manuscript sources is problematic given their moveability in the period under review and the scope of this chapter. See: A. L. M. Wilson, 'The Transmission and Use of the Legal Decisions of Sir Richard Maitland of Lethington in Sixteenth- and Seventeenth-Century Scotland', *The Library* 19 (2018), 325, 328; A. L. M. Wilson, 'The Textual Tradition of Stair's Institutions, with Reference to the Title "of Liberty and Servitude"', in H. L. MacQueen (ed.), *Miscellany VII* (62 Stair Society, Edinburgh, 2014), 2–4; J. W. Cairns, 'The Moveable Text of Mackenzie: Bibliographical Problems for the Scottish Concept of

Skene translated and edited two versions of the text, one of which was printed in Latin and the other in Scots.[13] The Latin version of *Regiam* was then transcribed (into modern English) and edited by Lord Cooper for the Stair Society[14] in 1947.[15] The text, *Regiam*, is divided into four books, with corresponding chapters within each.[16]

An initial appraisal of the Stair Society's edition of *Regiam* demonstrates that art and part was in operation, or at least that the terminology was in use.[17] The rule can be found in book IV, chapter twenty-six, titled 'actor and art and part'.[18] The body of the text reads '*de ordine cognitionis in criminus*', which has been translated by Cooper as 'the order in which crimes should be prosecuted'.[19] It notes that if two are accused (one of theft and the other of instigating it) then the person who is accused of theft should be tried first and the other thereafter. The same, it is argued, would apply to theft and reset (handling of stolen goods). Procedurally, this is a rule regarding the prosecuting of actors for two different, if linked, crimes.

If the principal (in this case the person who stole the goods) is acquitted then it follows that the person who instigated it, or who handled stolen goods, would also be acquitted. There appears to be no difference between the actor who carries out the offence and someone who acts on behalf of another. The rule articulated in *Regiam* is in fact a rule that uses one crime (theft) to establish or corroborate the other (reset or instigating the crime). Presumably, the individual accused of theft would be tried, convicted, and punished first, so that this could be used to establish that the goods were stolen and thus the crime of reset had occurred. This, in its very basic form, is an evidential principle. This rule is very different to imposing liability for an offence on actors, regardless of their individual actions.

The other medieval source contained in the Stair Society volume prepared by Cooper from Skene's 1609 version is the text known as

---

Institutional Writing', in J. W. Cairns (ed.), *Law, Lawyers and Humanism* (Edinburgh, 2015), 500–505.

[13] J. Skene (ed.), *Regiam Majestatem: The Auld Lawes and Constitutions of Scotland* (1609).

[14] 'The Stair Society: Scotland's Leading Society' (Stair Society, 2023), www.stairsociety.org.

[15] Lord Cooper (ed.), *Regiam Majestatem and Quoniam Attachiamenta Based on the Text of Sir John Skene* (11 Stair Society, Edinburgh, 1947).

[16] Ibid., 20.

[17] Ibid., 247, 270–271; Davies with Taylor. *Regiam*, 437.

[18] Cooper, *Regiam*, 247.

[19] Ibid., 270.

Quoniam Attachiamentia.[20] *Quoniam* was the name given to the work of Scots law which dealt with the procedure of the baronial courts and has been attributed to the fourteenth century.[21] *Quoniam* is similarly split into chapters, each on a different matter concerning procedure. Chapter 83 discusses how those who have been accused of reset should only be punished after the thief has been convicted.[22] This concerns the same principle articulated above about summoning of individuals in the appropriate order to essentially corroborate another offence. *Quoniam* develops this further by arguing that 'when this has been done the rule should be applied that actor and art and part should be punished alike'.[23] This is a development to the rule as formulated in *Regiam* and demonstrates that both those who participated in the theft and those who are in possession of the stolen goods are equally liable for the purposes of punishment, regardless of their respective parts.

Additionally, it is not clear if the rule contained in *Quoniam* relates *only* to the punishment of thieves and resetters, or *more generally* to those accused art and part of other offences. Based on the above reading, if the rule were to be applied to all offences, then there would be no assessment of the actor's culpability. Likewise, mitigating factors which could excuse (or qualify) degrees of wrongdoing would not be considered. Both *Regiam* and *Quoniam* are silent on how varying levels of liability might be dealt with, for example, aiding, abetting, and accomplice. Indeed, given the above reading, it is submitted that these various forms of liability would be treated as equally liable. The construction of art and part liability in these two earlier sources demonstrates a strict application with respect to the punishment of participants involved, without regard to the degrees of responsibility. It is not clear how knowledge, intention, and capacity would have interacted with art and part liability, which could bring about unfair applications before the court.

A final note should be made regarding a discrepancy found between the text of *Quoniam* that Cooper translated for the Stair Society and the edition prepared by T. D. Fergus in 1996 for the Stair Society.[24] The

---

[20] See Skene, *Regiam*; Cooper, *Regiam*.
[21] See the introductory comments by Cooper, *Regiam*, 1–55.
[22] Ibid., 371.
[23] Ibid..
[24] T. D. Fergus (ed. and trans.), *Quoniam Attachiamenta* (44 Stair Society, Edinburgh, 1996).

version Fergus prepared does not contain the chapter discussed above regarding reset.[25] It is thus plausible that the section which appeared in Skene's edition of *Quoniam* (and prepared by Cooper) was a fragment from the chapter which appears in *Regiam* with additional material from other sources of law. If indeed this is the case, this would indicate that *Quoniam*, which is regarded as belonging to the fourteenth century and as exclusively Scottish, did not contain provisions which could be regarded as art and part.

Conversely, the aim of the compilers differed between the two texts. The text which Skene prepared was used by Scottish lawyers for centuries, as a text for legal practice. This is different from an edition which is produced as a surviving textual edition for evidence of its history.[26] Additionally, *Regiam* was a text which sought to cover both civil and criminal law, more consistent with the approach found before the royal courts,[27] whereas *Quoniam* was a manual concerned with procedure before the baronial courts.[28] This could explain why the chapter concerning art and part liability is not included in Fergus's edition. Indeed, a closer examination of the textual history of both *Regiam* and *Quoniam* may reveal whether the change in scope of this provision was made by its original compiler or at a later point in its transmission.

Reference to English Legal Authority: *Glanvill* and *Bracton*

Scholars have drawn comparisons between the text of *Regiam* and that of the English medieval law book that became known as *Glanvill*.[29] Traditionally, these considerations have looked at the composition of the two treatises.[30] The following textual analysis will, for the first time,

---

[25] Ibid., 387–388.

[26] Ibid., 8.

[27] Cooper, *Regiam*, 48.

[28] See ibid., 48.

[29] G. D. G. Hall (ed. and trans.), *Tractatus de legibus et consuetudinibus regni Anglie qui Glanvilla vocatur: The Treatise on the Laws and Customs of the Realm of England Commonly Called Glanvill* (Nelson with Seldon Society, London, 1965).

[30] H. MacQueen, 'Regiam Majestatem, Scots Law, and National Identity', *Scottish Historical Review* LXXIV (1995), 1; A. A. M. Duncan, 'Regiam Majestatem: A Re-consideration', *Juridical Review* 6 (1961), 199; A. Harding, 'Regiam Majestatem amongst Medieval Law Books', *Juridical Review* 29 (1984), 97; H. L. MacQueen, 'Glanvill Resarcinate: Sir John Skene and Regiam Majestatem', in A. A MacDonald, M. Lynch and I. B. Cowan (eds.), *The Renaissance in Scotland: Studies in Literature, Religion, History and Culture Offered to John Durkan* (Leiden, 1994), 385–403; A. Taylor, 'What Does Regiam Maiestatem

consider how the legal text construed art and part and how this informs discussions on criminal liability.

Glanvill book XIV deals explicitly with criminal pleas. This book is short, separated into various sections concerning the different crimes of homicide, arson, robbery, rape, and falsifying. It briefly excludes theft and other offences, as those crimes were not heard before the King's Court.[31] Within the section on homicide, the text refers to the two common types of homicide.[32] The first type is murder, which is done 'secretly, out of sight and knowledge of all but the killer and his accomplices'.[33] This hints at a principal killer with accomplices, but no clear conclusions can be drawn regarding liability.

The Stair Society volume of *Regiam* and *Quoniam* prepared by Lord Cooper notes that the sections discussed above were similar to the rules formulated in Henry de Bracton, *De legibus et consuetudinibus Angliae* (hereafter, *Bracton*).[34] The rule contained in *Bracton* reiterates that the principal accused should be prosecuted first and the accessories thereafter. Further sections articulate a more thorough understanding of criminal liability. The text makes it clear that if the principal is convicted it may also be presumed that those listed as accused and instigators are also guilty, and they are to appear that same day.[35] This would have created a presumption against the remaining accused. The text also outlines that the accessory must come before the instigator, as 'giving assistance in whatever way involves an act which instigating does not'.[36] This reinforces an awareness and focus on criminal acts which directly result in an outcome.

The text of *Bracton* questions why it should be that the principal, accomplices, and instigators are to be joined in such a way.[37] The text states that all parties involved (principal, accomplices, and instigators) are linked because they are considered equally liable; regardless of the

---

actually Say (and What Does It Mean)?', in W. Eves, J. Hudson, I. Ivarsen and S. B. White (eds.), *Common Law, Civil Law, and Colonial Law: Essays in Comparative Legal History from the Twelfth to the Twentieth Centuries* (Cambridge, 2021), 47–85.

[31] *Glanvill*, 177.

[32] Ibid., 174.

[33] Ibid.

[34] G. E. Woodbine (ed.) and S. E. Thorne (trans.), *Bracton on the Laws and Customs of England*, 4 vols. (Cambridge, MA, 1968–77), vol. 2, 389.

[35] *De legibus* vol. 2, 392.

[36] Ibid.

[37] Ibid.

individual actions, each single action is regarded as a collective forming a single deed or joint perpetration. These discussions are far more developed than those in *Regiam* and *Quoniam*. The discussions contained in *Bracton* are, conversely, more closely aligned with the doctrine of art and part: that the natural and probable consequences of shared perpetration is to be treated as jointly liable, regardless of individual actions. The above four legal treatises differ on how those, once found guilty, should be punished. The changes in the formulation of art and part require a closer examination of the law in practice, to consider how courts dealt with more complex cases which involved taking into account principles of culpability in fairly attributing responsibility.

Legal Treatises: *Balfour's Practicks* and *Hope's Major Practicks*

Balfour's Practicks, compiled in the sixteenth century, treats the matter of liability in a comment within a section titled 'summonding of partakaris and complices'.[38] The treatise argues that the parties who are accused of a crime must appear before the summoning justice, and this applies to any persons who are named as accomplices or suspected as art and part of the alleged offence.[39] Balfour does not elaborate further, nor is it clear from the treatise how art and part liability is constituted. The only citation attributed to this section is a single case dated from 1535.

Hope's *Major Practicks* develops this further. In his title on criminal causes, he notes that all crimes must be charged in the criminal indictment as art and part.[40] This tract cites an Act of 1592, which stipulates that exemptions may not be raised in respect to whether art and part is relevant.[41] Hope further develops this by citing another Act of 1600, which concerns the 'guiltiness of crimes'.[42] He notes, with respect to the guiltiness of crime, that it is not only those who are the actual committers, but also those who were involved as 'actitors, causers and movers of the samen to be committed', as they all should be held as art and part of the said act.[43] This is a similar rule to that which is set out in *Bracton* and

---

[38] *Balfour's Practicks*, vol. 2, 307.
[39] Ibid.
[40] *Hope's Major Practicks*, vol. 2, 285.
[41] Ibid., 287–288.
[42] Ibid., 288 (para. 36). The corresponding citation is listed as 1600 c. 25. *Records of the Parliaments of Scotland to 1707* (RPS) and the record edition of *The Acts of the Parliaments of Scotland* (APS) produce no corresponding match.
[43] *Hope's Major Practicks*, vol. 2, 288.

confirms the rule as contained in *Quoniam* applying to all crimes: that is, regardless of the level of involvement (committing the act or causing it to come about), each are art and part of the crime and equally guilty of the resulting act. This raises a key issue: if early modern Scotland was treating actors in a crime equally, regardless of individual participation or contribution, this could result in unfair practices. If a defendant had contributed in a minor way to the offence, could it be said that they were as culpable as those who undertook the substantive act? There was very little discussion of intentionality or knowledge in Hope's *Major Practicks*, which would become significant in regulating art and part liability.[44]

These two sources demonstrate that by the sixteenth century art and part had retained its usage as a mechanism which regulated the procedural order of summoning individuals involved in the offence. However, a more developed understanding was articulated in Hope's *Major Practicks*. These developments were attributed to Parliament through legislative initiative. A closer consideration of the legislative sources is therefore necessary as these changes to art and part indicate a substantial change in practice.

The Scottish Parliament and Legislation

The Records of the Parliaments of Scotland provide further insight into the nature of art and part liability. Two fifteenth-century Acts demonstrate that liability need not be a physical act or deed in which the actor(s) participated; if someone counsels, fortifies, supplies, or offers assistance they could be held art and part of the crime.[45] Similarly, the doctrine is applied to a wide range of criminal activity from treason, homicide, theft, to the taking of salmon in 'time forbidden'.[46] Liability for art and part was not therefore confined to any one form of criminal activity and there was little difference between the ways in which this doctrine was applied to these different offences.

The phrase art and part was in use from at least the late fifteenth century.[47] The wording contained in the various Acts indicated that art and part involved extending liability to any person who participated in

---

[44] See section below on 'The Use of Art and Part in Practice before the Justiciary Court'.
[45] *RPS*, 1484/2/7 and 1484/2/10.
[46] Ibid.
[47] *RPS*, 1450/1/2; 1484/2/6; 1484/2/7; 1484/2/10; 1505/1/24; 1506/2/6; 1526/6/18; 1526/6/19; 1535/52; 1546/7/9; 1568/4/33; 1579/10/66.

the offence, in any way, and if this were alleged, they were treated as the principal.[48] This suggests that there would *not* be a differentiation between the principal and the secondary actors, at least where punishment might be considered. This is, again, a much wider understanding of the doctrine than was postulated in *Regiam* and *Glanvill*, which demonstrates that there was a substantive change over time to the development of extending liability.

The Act of 1592

In 1592, the Scottish Parliament enacted a piece of legislation titled *Concerning the Relevancy of Libels in Causes Criminal.*[49] The use of libel in this context refers to the formal statement of the complaints or grounds of the charge(s) in a criminal prosecution, similar to an indictment.[50] This Act stipulated:

> seeing that diverse exceptions and objections rise [raised] upon criminal libels and parties frustrated of justice, that in time coming all criminal libels shall contain that the persons complained [of are] art and part of the crime libelled, which shall be relevant to accuse them thereof so that no exception or objection takes away that part of the libel in time coming.[51]

There are three particularly noteworthy elements in this Act. The first element is that no exceptions (or defence) can be established on the basis that either party was *not* art and part of the crime. This appears to be a legislative initiative to change the confines of art and part liability as well as augmenting procedure. It would have significantly increased the number of prosecutions for those who were deemed to be art and part. The second notable feature of this piece of legislation was its implementation following concerns regarding the administration of justice. This indicates that Parliament is responding with legislation to combat a perceived issue. The third and final notable feature is that art and part was a doctrine that extended to all criminal actions, as this legislative initiative was not confined to a specific criminal activity. Here the language of the statute becomes important for our understanding of

---

[48] See e.g. *RPS*, 1450/1/2.
[49] *RPS*, 1592/4/95.
[50] Scottish Language Dictionaries, *Dictionary of the Scots Language*, www.dsl.ac.uk/. Hereafter referred to as *DSL*. For more on the context of this word see https://dsl.ac .uk/entry/snd/libel.
[51] *RPS*, 1592/4/95.

parliamentary reform in this area – was this strictly procedural or administrative in nature, or did it make substantive changes to the law?

Procedural or Administrative Reform?

The 1592 Act specifically called attention to the dissatisfaction and frustration of justice in respect to this aspect of the criminal process. In this context, the 1592 Act appears to be a legislative mechanism to ensure expediency in the execution of criminal justice and thereby avoid high costs and lengthy delays. It is difficult to state empirically that Scotland experienced an increase in criminal actions prosecuted before the Royal Courts. Scholars have drawn attention to the greater number of cases that were handled by the English courts during this period, which in turn increased business, put greater pressure on the courts, and created longer delays.[52] In the present state of scholarship, any suggestions as to whether these trends also occurred in Scotland can only be tentative.

The 1592 Act does not indicate an administrative change when compared to similar statutes which regulated the Scottish civil court, the Court of Session. Administrative changes before the Court of Session generally concerned 'regulating the number required for a quorum, the order for hearing actions (i.e., "tabling"), other matters associated with tabling, calling and continuations, the roles of procurators, clerks and macers, and the fees they might charge'.[53] The changes enacted by the 1592 Act do not alter the administrative processes of the court. The Act does however alter the use of exceptions (defences) relating to art and part.

Exceptions were regulated under the Romano-canonical procedure according to type. Mark Godfrey has noted that Scotland was a 'notable instance of embedding the procedural law of the *ius commune* within a distinctive native tradition'.[54] The procedural tradition of the *ius commune* was not static and there was variation among the courts – the so-called *stylus curiea*.[55] There were however 'procedural items characteristic of a Romano-canonical approach . . . in which certain types

---

[52] B. J. Shapiro, *Law Reform in Early Modern England 1500–1740: Crown, Parliament and the Press* (Oxford, 2019), 43; S. Hindle, *The State and Social Change in Early Modern England 1550–1640* (Basingstoke, 2000); M. Braddock, *State Formation in Early Modern England 1550–1700* (Cambridge, 2000).

[53] Godfrey, *Civil Justice in Renaissance Scotland*, 170.

[54] Ibid., 170.

[55] R. H. Helmholz, *The Oxford History of the Laws of England Volume I: The Canon Law and Ecclesiastical Jurisdiction from 597 to the 1640s* (Oxford, 2004), 313.

of defences to claims would be categorised in terms of the Romano-canonical taxonomy of "exceptions".[56] There were three main categories of exceptions recognised in the *ius commune*. These were dilatory, peremptory, and those which were difficult to classify and have been referred to as 'mixed'.[57] The various types of exceptions had to be raised at certain *stages* of the proceedings, as they either prevented further process of the action or excluded the plaintiff's actions altogether. If the defendant failed to raise the exception(s) at the appropriate stage, they lost their right to do so.

The order in which the exceptions were listed was prescribed by law, to ensure a procedural framework in which all parties and the court operated.[58] This phenomenon was also used in common law jurisdictions.[59] Before the justiciary court, the so-called *stages* of the trial were somewhat different, generally all evidence and/or arguments that related to any matter had to be raised prior to the case being put to the assize (the jury).[60]

The 1592 Act therefore explicitly regulates exceptions which relate to the part of the criminal indictment that accused *the parties as art and part of the crime*. There does not appear to be a temporal limit, and therefore it can be concluded that exceptions raised at any point in the trial which related to whether the defendant(s) were art and part would not be heard. This would not have barred the defendant from raising *other* defences. Critically, the changes enacted by the 1592 Act were not only a change to the procedure before the justiciary court but also to the substantive operation of this device

Substantive Law Reform?

The Act of 1592 expressly stated that *all criminal libels* should include that the persons complained of *are art and part of the crime*.[61] A moderate reading of this indicates a substantive change to the confines

---

[56] Godfrey, *Civil Justice in Renaissance Scotland*, 170.

[57] Helmholz, *Oxford History*, 323; Godfrey, *Civil Justice in Renaissance Scotland*, 171.

[58] C. H. Van Rhee, 'The Role of Exceptions in Continental Civil Procedure', in P. Brand, K. Costello and W. N. Osborough (eds.), *Adventures of the Law: Proceedings of the Sixteenth British Legal History Conference, Dublin, 2003* (Dublin, 2005).

[59] Ibid.

[60] S. Dropuljic, 'The Justiciary Court and Criminal Law in Early Modern Scotland from 1580 to 1650, with Special Reference to Actions for Homicide' (unpublished PhD thesis, University of Aberdeen, 2023), 55–57, 63–75, ch. 5.

[61] RPS, 1592/4/95.

of art and part liability. It was no longer a device used to regulate the procedural summoning of parties, nor was it a form of derivative criminal liability. Art and part was no longer a doctrine that *extended* criminal liability. Rather, it was a doctrine to *inculpate* (incriminate) those who were complained of as art and part of the crime. This would have created an irrefutable presumption against any person who acted with others in joint preparation of an offence (especially as the Act expressly prohibited any defence to that point of the charge). Therefore, presumably, proof (or evidence) would not be required to establish that the parties acted in joint preparation of the offence as there was an express requirement to charge all persons complained of in any criminal cause as art and part. This would be a substantive change to the raising and prosecuting of offences before the court, in respect to the confines of criminal liability and in core requirements of proof. In addition, the Act is silent regarding how those who were found guilty would be treated (or punished) by the law. It can only be presumed that regardless of the role each actor played in the activity, they were equally liable for the resulting act. Importantly, all these changes would have altered the substantive operation of the device, as the nature of criminal liability was widened, and core requirements of proof would have been removed (so far as they related to this specific aspect of the criminal libel).

Did the 1592 Act Reform the Administration of Justice?

Early modern law reform in Scotland typically involved revisiting or codifying the existing law rather than superseding or revising it.[62] In the sixteenth century, commissioners were tasked with making the existing law more accessible.[63] For example, the terms of reform for the 1575 and 1592 commission were to consider and draw together the law from the various law books, Acts of Parliament, and the decisions before the Court of Session.[64] The 1575 commission resulted in *Balfour's Practicks* and the 1592 commission resulted in the volume titled *The Lawes and Actes of Parliament*, Skene's *De Verborum Significatioune* (an account of the difficult and technical words found in the old laws), as well

---

[62] Goodare, *Government of Scotland*, 74.
[63] Ibid., 76–77.
[64] RPS, 1592/4/67; J. W. Cairns, 'Historical Introduction', in K. Reid and Zimmermann (eds.), *A History of Private Law in Scotland*, 2 vols. (Oxford, 2000), 96–97.

as Skene's edition of *Regiam Majestatem*.[65] These publications meant that a considerable amount of legislative material was available in print for the first time, with regular printing of Acts of Parliament thereafter.[66]

Likewise, the decades following the 1580s and 1590s witnessed the Scottish Parliament becoming a legislature which reformed the law rather than merely debating it.[67] Successive parliaments would go on to pass more new legislation than previous parliaments.[68] Goodare notes that the legislation of two parliaments 'in particular – those of 1584 and 1587 – can be seen as an absolutist manifesto [of James VI and I]'.[69] Following on from 1587, a significant amount of new legislation as well as reforming legislation was enacted.[70]

It is within this reform environment that the 1592 Act needs to be considered. On the one hand, commissioners were undertaking a consolidation exercise to examine existing laws and make them more accessible. On the other, there appears to be a legislative initiative to reform, specifically ensuring the efficient administration of criminal justice. The evidence from this examination indicates that the 1592 Act would have, whether purposely or incidentally, increased the remit of art and part liability and the criminal law.

The Use of Art and Part in Practice before the Justiciary Court

The analysis of the catalogue of homicide hearings from 1580 to 1650 revealed that 82 per cent of such hearings brought before the court were charged as art and part.[71] From a purely numerical perspective, this indicates that the 1592 Act was being respected. There was, however, a fluctuation in the use of art and part throughout the period under review. During the first decade (1580–1590), 86 per cent were indicted as art and part. Thereafter the use of art and part remained significantly high, with 92 per cent indicted from 1600 to 1609; and 90 per cent from 1610 to 1619. There was a drop in its use from 1640 to 1650, with 66 per cent

---

[65] Cairns, 'Historical Introduction', 96–97.
[66] Ibid., 97.
[67] A. R. C. Simpson and A. L. M. Wilson, *Scottish Legal History: 1000–1707* (Edinburgh, 2017), vol. 1, 224.
[68] Goodare, *Government of Scotland*, 72–73.
[69] Goodare, *State and Society*, 73.
[70] Simpson and Wilson, *Scottish Legal History*, vol. 1, 225.
[71] The methodology of that study can be found at Dropuljic, 'The Justiciary Court and Criminal Law', 60–74.

indicted as art and part. This could be attributed to the overall decrease in actions before the court because of the political and religious turbulence of the wider historical environment.[72] Conversely, it could be attributed to a change in practice. This section will examine the complexities encountered in practice by practitioners when advancing their clients' defences, and how key legal concepts evolved through adaptation in the court.

The Law in Practice: Prosecuting Art and Part

The case of *James Findlay and others* (1586), discussed in the introduction, illustrates art and part in operation. The five individuals were accused as art and part because they were all within the dwelling house and therefore equally culpable of the resulting deaths which occurred therein.[73] However, the advocate for the first four accused (Mr Thomas Craig) argued that they should not be put to a trial because the death was the direct result of Tibble Smart's actions, and he was the principal accused. Craig contended that the principal accused should be tried first. The trial of the principal accused would, once found guilty, corroborate the trial of the remaining co-accused. The justice agreed and the first four accused were continued to a later date and Smart was then put before the assize and acquitted of the slaughter. It is not clear what happened to the other accused persons, but it is presumed that no trial took place following the acquittal of Smart. The procedural regulation of the principal accused and the remaining actors demonstrates the rules as evidenced above in practice before the court. Importantly, this demonstrates that the law regarded at least one person as the principal accused, which became an important development and distinction before the court.

As a matter of course, the focus during the prosecution of homicide was on the common activity which the accused persons undertook and/ or were involved in.[74] Art and part were not the only words invoked during the prosecution. For example, the phrasing 'art, part, redd and

---

[72] D. Stevenson, 'The Covenanters and the Court of Session, 1637–1650', *Juridical Review* (1972), 227; A. MacDonald, *The Jacobean Kirk, 1567–1625: Sovereignty, Polity and Liturgy* (London, 1998), ch. 4; Ford, *Law and Opinion*, ch. 2.

[73] NRS MSS JC2/2, f46v.

[74] NRS MSS JC2 vol. 3 High Court of Adjournal (15 May 1596–26 June 1604) f1063r (1063)–f1065r (1065); JC2 vol. 4 High Court of Adjournal (25 July 1604–19 July 1611) 807.

counsel' of the crime was included in the indictment.[75] The counsel aspect retained its mundane meaning of giving guidance – specifically when certain individuals were evidenced to have 'communed' in the perpetration of the offence.[76] The 'redd' aspect is ambiguous. Given the context in which it was used, it appears to have invoked a similar meaning to guidance, a form of advising as to a certain course of action.[77] Individuals therefore invoked liability, not only from participating in the physical acts of the offence, but also in the counselling and preparatory stages of the offence. This, importantly, did not substantially change the liability that was imposed. Therefore, in attributing criminal liability, the law did not regard those who planned the crime (perhaps a more active role) and those who were incidentally involved (perhaps a more passive role) as any different. This reiterates the rules as discussed above, that all those who participated in the joint perpetration of an offence were equally liable.

In summary, the activity involved in art and part liability included physical acts as well as counselling, aiding, or advising as to a certain course of action. Art and part had a wide remit in the early modern period and conveyed derivative liability from different forms of participation. Practitioners before the court encountered issues in practice when advancing defences for their clients. Advocates before the court had to raise defences against establishing core requirements of the liability, predominantly this involved an argument that evidence of intentionality and knowledge were lacking.

The Use of Exceptions (Defences) in Practice

The case of *William Jameson and another* (1632) demonstrates the practical developments of art and part liability.[78] This case accused two persons, William and Walter Jameson, as art and part of the killing of Harry Hamilton. It was alleged that they were on the public highway between Leith and Edinburgh and committed a deadly strike, under the silence of night, upon the victim who died two days later.[79]

---

[75] NRS MSS JC2/2, f139r (273); JC2/3, f1005r (1005)–f1005v (1007).

[76] NRS MSS JC2/2, f139r (273).

[77] DSL, https://dsl.ac.uk/entry/dost/rede_r._1.

[78] NRS MSS JC2 vol. 7 High Court Book of Adjournal (26 March 1631–15 November 1637) f052r; Stair A. Gillon, *Selected Justiciary Cases 1624–1650*, vol. 1 (16 Stair Society, Edinburgh, 1953), 201–204.

[79] NRS MSS JC2/7, f052r.

The principal dispute before the court was whether William Jameson, who was the son of Walter, *could be held to be art and part for the killing by being in the company of his father whilst the deadly strike was given.*[80] The emphasis has been added to demonstrate that, although expressly prohibited by the 1592 Act, this action involved the use of a defence which pertained to the part of the libel that charged both defendants as art and part. Therefore, whilst the 1592 Act was an effort to introduce reform, there were exceptions in practice to the implementation by the courts.

The advocate for the defendant (Mr Robert Craig) advanced an argument before the court that William had no previous knowledge of a plan to undertake the killing, he had no weapon upon his person, and what had occurred between his father and the victim was on the spur of the moment, proceeded upon randomly.[81] This indicates that lack of knowledge meant that he could not have intended to participate in the joint perpetration of the offence. The focus on lack of intention and knowledge of a common purpose demonstrates that this was a key component of art and part liability. This also highlights concerns that can arise when transposing knowledge of the offence from one accused to the other.

If considered purely on the facts, William (regardless of his involvement in the physical act) was present when a lethal act took place. A strict reading is that he was art and part liable for the offence, regardless of the role he played. This is how most instances before the court were tried. The allegation that William had no prior knowledge and was merely an innocent bystander contributes to our understanding of the doctrine in practice. If a person, by their act, was closely associated with or involved in the activity, they could be charged art and part. Therefore, an evidential presumption of art and part liability was created by the collective involvement in the circumstances accompanying the fatal act. Additionally, it was the accused who would have to disprove the allegations brought forward and demonstrate that they were not privy to the planning, nor had they willingly entered into a joint venture – as evident from the argument by the advocate. Although no evidence was supplied to support the claim that William was not involved the argument put forward seems to have been persuasive, as William was acquitted by the assize.

[80] Ibid.
[81] Ibid.

Interestingly, the courts would hear arguments about the respective roles of the defendants to differentiate their punishments.[82] This is despite the Act of 1450 which stipulated that those alleged art and part were to be punished equally to the principal doer. For example, in the case of *Patrick McGregor and others* (1636), several persons were charged with multiple offences including slaughter. The verdict was culpable and convict; however, the court differentiated the accused based on culpability. Two of the accused (Allister and Callum Forbes) would be referred to the Privy Council for their punishment to be considered in light of their judicial confession, indicating their marginal contribution to the crimes.[83] This is a significant development. It demonstrates that a practice developed before the court to refer marginal cases to the Privy Council so that punishment could be reflective of their individual contribution and therefore their respective culpability in the offence.

Conclusions and Reflections

This chapter has begun the task of re-examining a key criminal law doctrine, art and part liability, to understand its development. In the earlier sources (*Regiam* and *Quoniam*), art and part liability had retained a narrow application, as it was a procedural mechanism to regulate the summoning of individuals for offences. There was some indication that this device regulated derivative liability, but the extent and scope was obscured in the law books and practicks.

An examination of the legislative sources revealed a much wider understanding of art and part liability. The Acts of Parliament demonstrated the extent to which this device applied to all offences and included physical acts as well as deeds such as counselling, fortifying, supplying, or offering assistance. The 1592 Act made significant changes to this device and reformed the raising of exceptions. The wider legal environment demonstrated that royal justice was under scrutiny, by both Parliament and the King. The 1592 Act changed the substantive operation of the device, as the nature of criminal liability was widened and core requirements of proof relating to establishing liability were removed.

The law in practice before the court challenged the rules expressed in the earlier written sources, practicks, and legislation. The practice before the court confirmed elements of art and part liability as a summoning

---

[82] *RPS*, 1450/1/2.
[83] NRS MSS JC2/7, f333v.

device to prosecute those involved in committing an offence. There were, conversely, actions which challenged the scope and impact of the legislation. Practice developed not only to challenge aspects of the libel (indictment) which alleged art and part liability, but also to differentiate art and part actors as to their involvement in carrying out the offence. The latter allowed the court (and privy council) to mitigate punishments according to the respective actor's level of culpability.

The developments before the court demonstrate two points. The first concerns legal reform in the early modern period. A numerical analysis showed an appreciable change to the use of this mechanism. Combined with the legislative initiatives and reformulating of the law, this indicated that the 1592 Act was a successful attempt to regulate criminal procedure. That said, the wider practice of the court was not reflective of this legislative turning point for art and part liability. There was a continued use of exceptions to differentiate involvement of actors, to ensure broader principles and core constituent elements of the offence (such as knowledge and intention) were satisfied.

The second point relates to refinement of sentencing procedures before the court. The doctrine of art and part treated those who participated in the offence, regardless of their role, equally before the law. However, the practice of referring punishments to the Privy Council demonstrates that the court was circumventing this approach by considering an individual's degree of involvement. These wider practices demonstrate the contentious use of the doctrine and the unfair outcomes which could result from an expansion in the scope of criminal liability. This is significant because this differs substantially to the modern form.

These changes in the legal landscape illustrate that the early modern period is an important historical period, understandings of which can contribute to discussions on criminal lability and how notions of culpability manifested over time. Importantly, the law of art and part liability required the raising of exceptions to ensure against any injustices. This is significant as it forms part of a wider picture in the historical foundation of art and part liability. Returning to the early modern period and the various sources of law therefore contributes to an important but under-researched area of Scottish criminal law.

The Beginnings of Judicial Review

SIR JOHN BAKER

This volume bears witness to an encouraging growth of interest in the history of public law.[1] Decades ago I was asked to teach legal history at the Inns of Court School of Law, and Lord Justice Scarman (as he then was) complained that my draft syllabus did not include the prerogative writs. My first reaction was to reply, 'Of course not, that isn't what we do'. The legal history courses which I had studied and taught, inherited from generations before me, concentrated on land law, contract and tort. However, after a few moments' thought, I saw how right Sir Leslie was. Here was a fundamental piece of the common law which legal historians had treated as somehow off limits. And it was not only lawyer-historians who were narrowly focused. In 1991 I took part in a conference on the 'history of freedom in the West'. It was, no doubt, progressive of political historians to think of inviting a lawyer. The obvious English topics to deal with seemed to me to be the ending of villeinage and the rise of habeas corpus; but I had the sense that this was regarded as a weird aberration by an interloper. No one else at the conference thought it relevant to consider how personal liberty was protected in real life: how, where or when people could escape from being locked up or enslaved. Constitutional historians, likewise, steered clear of practical law. They used the terminology 'constitutional history' rather than the history of constitutional *law*, and they focused on the growth of Parliament and governmental institutions rather than on legal debates, judicial decisions and real people. Even Maitland's lectures on constitutional history, published posthumously in 1908,[2] had nothing to say about the judicial

---

[1] I was invited to speak on the same topic at two different conferences in the same week, and with the agreement of the organisers gave a similar lecture at both. A slightly extended version of the lecture presented in Dublin will appear in J. Varuhas (ed.), *The Making (and Re-Making) of Public Law* (in press).

[2] F. W. Maitland, *Lectures on Constitutional History: A Course of Lectures* (H. A. L. Fisher ed., Cambridge, 1908).

origins of the prerogative writs. Maitland was immersed in the year books of Edward II and what went before; but his kind of research was not bestowed on the early modern period until much later.[3]

The year books were not the place to start anyway, because there is little or nothing in them about personal liberty. According to Sir John Dodderidge, speaking in the House of Commons in 1610, only private law was to be found in the law reports, whereas public law had to be sought in records – meaning principally the formal records of Parliament, Chancery and Exchequer. The law reports, he said, were 'nothing else for the most part but the reports of private suits'.[4] That had in fact begun to change in the time of Elizabeth I, as we shall see, though it is not much evident from the printed books. Most reporters were students or barristers educated in a tradition which omitted public law from the curriculum, and they put down their pens when such cases began to come before the courts. There was therefore a self-perpetuating convention of exclusion, not unlike that which has prevailed among English legal historians since Maitland's day. But the subject was of practical importance to judges and law officers, and it is chiefly from their long-unpublished notebooks that we are able to trace the beginnings. There were some significant public law cases in Dyer's reports, but they were cut out by the editors of 1585 and not printed until 1993.[5] Coke's notebooks, likewise, contained a good deal of public law which he did not feel able to publish. Some found its way into print in the 1650s, but the rest is only just going to press.[6] The dearth of readily accessible information explains why historians' books of constitutional sources – beginning with Bishop Stubbs's influential *Select Charters*[7] and continued

---

[3] The important pioneering work of Stanley de Smith (see n. 47, below) and Edith Henderson (see n. 39, below) made no use of manuscript law reports.

[4] E. R. Foster (ed.), *Proceedings in the Parliament of 1610*, 2 vols. (New Haven, CT, 1966), vol. II, 205. It is notable that Sir Matthew Hale's *The Prerogatives of the King* (D. E. C. Yale ed., 92 Selden Society (hereafter SS), London, 1976), which was the first major treatise on English constitutional law (c. 1660), made extensive use of records but none at all of unpublished case law.

[5] J. H. Baker (ed.), *Reports from the Lost Notebooks of Sir James Dyer* (110–11 SS, London, 1994–95).

[6] J. Baker (ed.), *Reports from the Notebooks of Edward Coke* (136–40 SS, London, 2022–23). These five volumes cover the period 1572–1600. Three further volumes (141–3 SS, London, 2025) will complete the edition, with reports from 1601 to 1616.

[7] W. Stubbs (ed.), *Select Charters and Other Illustrations of English Constitutional History ... to the Reign of Edward I* (Oxford, 1870). This was a standard text for a century and was reprinted as recently as 2012.

forward in time by others – were filled with bare documents, such as statutes, rather than arguments and judgments.[8]

The story of public law in the year-book period has yet to be told. The author of *Bracton* used the term 'public law', but it was a learned term borrowed ultimately from Ulpian and did not creep into the year books. He had some useful things to say about the king being under the law, but that did not mean the king could be sued or prosecuted in his own courts.[9] Lawyers knew about chapter 29 of Magna Carta (1225) and the restraints which it seemed to place on the king's power, but it mentioned no remedies and it left open the question of what absolute prerogatives were allowed to the king by the *lex terrae*. To a fifteenth-century lawyer, Magna Carta was chiefly about wardship and dower, and other matters of private law, mixed with a lot of spent and obsolete material. The potentiality of chapter 29 was missed by the lecturers in the inns of court, who were content to explain it with breath-taking literalism as being mainly about trial by peers in Parliament and not charging fees for writs of right or *justicies*. Selling justice, on this interpretation, was forbidden only in the case of manorial and county courts. The great charter of liberties would only acquire – or retrieve – its importance in constitutional law when it was revived in the 1570s and invested with a new potency.[10]

Since actions could not be brought against the king for acting unconstitutionally, any legal protection had to work differently. The key to this was the principle – seldom spelt out explicitly – that the king could do no wrong. It is an idea which often causes mystification and misunderstanding. I remember an external examination candidate in the 1960s writing: 'The queen can do no wrong. That is why she has ministers, to do the wrong for her.' I suppose the candidate was grasping at an underlying truth. Of course, kings were better placed to do wrong de facto than anyone else; but the principle meant that kings were incapable de jure of

---

[8] A selection of the legal sources, some of which have not been printed before, has been published in translation in J. Baker (ed.) *Sources of English Legal History: Public Law to 1750* (Oxford, 2024) (hereafter SPL).

[9] *On the Laws and Customs of England*, 4 vols. (S. E. Thorne ed., Cambridge, MA, 1968), vol. II, 25–6, 33. The possibility of suing the king was accepted in *Corbet's Case* (1307) Year Books 35 Edw. I (Rolls Series), 467, at 469 (and see the editor's note at xv). But during the fourteenth century it became orthodox learning that one could only sue *to* the king, by petition of right.

[10] See J. Baker, *The Reinvention of Magna Carta 1216–1616* (Cambridge, 2017). For the readings see J. Baker (ed.), *Selected Readings and Commentaries on Magna Carta 1400–1604* (132 SS, London, 2015).

authorising wrong, and therefore a commission, patent or executive decision which harmed a subject contrary to law was simply void. That gave the courts a limited power of judicial review. In a famous case of 1368, the chief justices sitting at Chelmsford expressed indignation at a Chancery commission authorising an arrest without due process of law, and complained about it to the king's council.[11] In 1406 the King's Bench struck down a royal charter authorising the chancellor's court of Oxford University to proceed according to the civil law, since it infringed the right of every subject to be governed by the common law.[12] And in 1461 the Common Pleas rejected a writ of protection whereby a party on royal service at the Roman Curia was placed outside the reach of the law for three years – the legal limit for a protection being one year. As Moyle J observed, the king was bound by law to do right to all his subjects, and he was unable to do that if someone was granted exemption from legal proceedings for a lengthy period.[13] That was another way of saying that the king could do no wrong. If something wrong was done or attempted in his name, it would be quashed.

A supporting principle of some importance was that the king could not acquire or part with property except by matter of record. The courts could therefore, by reviewing the relevant record, strike down grants of things to which the crown was not entitled. The courts could even grant relief, by petition of right, in respect of property in the king's hands. No doubt property claims in general should be considered outside the scope of public law, even when the king was a party. But when property included jurisdictional and administrative franchises, the boundary seems less sharp, especially since such franchises could be taken away (by *quo warranto*) for misuse, disuse or abuse: another kind of judicial review.

These, in outline, were the roots from which public law grew; but they were a far cry from judicial review as we know it today. The administrative functions of central and local government, in so far as they were off the record, were largely beyond reach. If on the record, it was mainly in the labyrinthine Exchequer, not in the two common-law benches.

---

[11] *Sir John atte Lee's Case* (1368) Lib. Ass. 42 Edw. III, pl. 5; Baker, *SPL*, 67. For the context see Baker, *Magna Carta*, 58–60.

[12] *Pedyngton v. Otteworth* (1406) 88 SS 166; Baker, *SPL*, 412. This was known to Coke: Baker, *Magna Carta*, 385. The same principle later prevented Oxford University claiming a jurisdiction in equity: *Perrot v. Mathew* (1588) *Coke's Notebooks*, 137 SS 372; Baker, *SPL*, 382.

[13] *Abbot of Glastonbury v. Lax* (1461) YB Hil. 39 Hen. VI, fo. 38, pl. 3; Baker, *SPL*, 83.

In the last resort, the coercive power of government was enforced by imprisonment. But imprisonment by the king or his ministers was hardly ever questioned before the sixteenth century, and we do not even know how common it was. Decisions by the king and his council were mysteries of state, beyond the jurisdiction of the courts. They would be classified by Tudor jurists as absolute prerogatives.

Even so, the absolute prerogatives were never as extensive as is often supposed. When Coke listed them around 1600, he could only find nine, most of which are still with us today.[14] Coke's list was admittedly incomplete, because it omitted the power to imprison people without showing any reason, to which we shall return. It also omitted torture, about which Coke was ambivalent until the judges declared it to be unlawful in 1628.[15] But there was not the vast range of unlimited prerogative which is sometimes imagined. The essential feature of the absolute prerogatives was that the manner of their exercise was outside the jurisdiction of the courts. However, it was the prerogative of the common law judges to define and confine them. Coke was fond of the expression found in Plowden's *Commentaries* that the common law 'admeasured' the king's prerogative; in other words, it set and controlled the boundaries.[16]

How far this admeasurement could be achieved depended on remedies, and there were not many relevant remedies to be found in the old register of writs. Although it had been enacted in 1267 that actions for damages could be founded on Magna Carta, this did not bear much fruit.[17] The earliest known example of an action on Magna Carta was in 1501, when there began a number of challenges to the coercive jurisdiction of the new Court of Requests: not exactly actions against the central government, but nevertheless challenges to the prerogative power with

---

[14] *Coke's Notebooks*,138 SS 589; Baker, *SPL*, 11–13.

[15] R. v. Felton (1628), *Howell's Complete Collection of State Trials*, vol. III (London, 1809) (hereafter 3 St. Tr.), 371. This was the first case in which the judges were formally asked to pronounce on it. For Coke's contemporary approval see 3 Co. Inst. 48. But see Baker, *Magna Carta*, 170–2.

[15] *Willyon v. Lord Berkeley* (1561) Plowd. 227 at 236; Baker, *SPL*, 9 at 10; 3 Co. Inst. 84. It was quoted four times in Coke's commonplace books before 1600: *Coke's Notebooks*, 136 SS cxli n. 9. Cf. *Case of Proclamations* (1610) 12 Co. Rep. 74 at 76 ('The king hath no prerogative but that which the law of the land allows him'); Baker, *SPL*, 186 (slightly different translation from the French).

[17] Statute of Marlborough 1267 (52 Hen. III), c. 5; Baker, *SPL*, 53. Although actions could not be brought against the king, they could in principle be brought against officials acting in the king's name.

respect to the erection of new jurisdictions outside the common law. Few of these actions resulted in judgment, and the formula devised in 1501 was not a vehicle for later development.[18] An attempted revival in 1595, also aimed against the Requests, was stamped on by the Privy Council.[19] It was not a promising route to follow. In any case, as with the action of trespass for false imprisonment, such actions lay only for damages after the event; and it was not always obvious who to name as defendants. It was hardly politic in Tudor times to sue officers of state and ministers of the government, and it did not happen.

The difficulties were brought home in 1532 when a serjeant at law was committed to prison by order of Henry VIII without a criminal charge. He was soon released, but he complained to the Privy Council, and all the judges were summoned to give their advice. The question was evidently embarrassing, even though no remedy was being sought. They pointed out that it was against Magna Carta for the king to treat his subjects contrary to law. But they also pointed to a statute of 1275 which provided that a person committed by the king was not bailable: so that was *lex terrae*. They concluded that, if the king sent someone to prison, his discretion was not to be disputed. The case was reported by one of the judges, Sir John Spelman, but was not printed until 1976.[20]

A new chapter in public law began thirty years later with the development of the prerogative writs. The first was habeas corpus, followed by mandamus and certiorari. Unlike ordinary original writs, they were returnable immediately in the court which issued them, and they were not brought against defendants. They could therefore be used to challenge coercive measures by the government or by the new prerogative jurisdictions, tacitly applying the old idea that the king could do no wrong. As far as we know, they were not called 'prerogative writs' until the early seventeenth century. But it was a cleverly chosen name, contrived to reinforce the delicate principle which underlay them. In practice, the writs were often used to challenge exercises of prerogative jurisdiction or authority. Yet they were represented as defending a higher prerogative, that of keeping all ministers, institutions and jurisdictions within the law. It was the practical mechanism whereby the king, through

---

[18] Baker, *Magna Carta*, 97–9, 456–62. The 1501 case is translated in Baker, *SPL*, 273.

[19] *Parsons v. Locke* (1595), Baker, *SPL*, 275; Baker, *Magna Carta*, 277–8, 484–7.

[20] *Serjeant Browne's Case* (1532) *Spelman's Reports*, 93 SS 183 (misdated 1540); Baker, *SPL*, 418; Baker, *Magna Carta*, 100–1. The statute was Westminster I (3 Edw. I), c. 15; Baker, *SPL*, 627.

his own court, discharged the duty of his coronation oath to uphold the law.[21] Prerogative writs were brought on behalf of the king, not against him. They came to fulfil the prerogative, not to destroy it. Even Stuart kings could accept the underlying principle.[22]

The main prototype was the medieval writ of prohibition, which was designed to keep ecclesiastical courts within their bounds. In the context of jurisdictional disputes with the Church, seen as a competing authority, it made sense for the writ to recite that excesses of jurisdiction were 'against the king's crown and dignity'. It was also used against admiralty courts, which were likewise seen as competitors. Another prototype was *quo warranto*, initiated by the Attorney General to challenge encroachments on royal authority by those claiming franchises. But those writs were brought against defendants and were therefore not available to challenge the government directly. The furthest reach, perhaps, was of the kind discovered by Coke as Attorney General, when he used *quo warranto* to strike down exorbitant patents of monopoly – treating them, in effect, as franchises. However, the vehicle for most of the new development in the second half of the sixteenth century was the writ of habeas corpus.[23]

It is difficult to attribute the innovation to a single cause. No doubt Elizabeth I's relative tolerance helped create a receptive atmosphere, as did the sympathetic legal mindset of her enlightened chief minister William Cecil, Lord Burghley, who was educated in the common law. We know from Coke's private notes that the queen explicitly instructed her law officers, on appointment, not to stretch her prerogative beyond its legal bounds.[24] It is difficult to imagine her father doing the like. But the story of habeas corpus unfolded in Westminster Hall, not in the corridors of power. The beginnings, in the 1560s, are revealed in the long-unpublished notes of the three chiefs at the beginning of the reign: Sir Robert Catlyn, Chief Justice of the King's Bench, Sir James Dyer, Chief Justice of the Common Pleas, and Sir Edward Saunders, Chief Baron of the Exchequer. It may not be a coincidence that they were all alumni of the Middle Temple, where William Fleetwood played a role in

[21] Hale, *Prerogatives of the King*, 14–15.
[22] Baker, *Magna Carta*, 310–11, 485, 512–13.
[23] The important study by P. D. Halliday, *Habeas Corpus from England to Empire* (Cambridge, MA, 2010) makes full use of the records but begins the story later, with an important case of 1605 (see n. 32, below).
[24] *Coke's Notebooks*, 138 SS 474, 573; 3 Co. Inst. 79; 2 Bulst. 44. See also Baker, *Magna Carta*, 149.

reawakening Magna Carta from centuries of slumber, where Edmund
Plowden wrote of admeasuring the prerogative, and where (a few years
later) Robert Snagge and James Morice would give lectures reintroducing
Magna Carta and constitutional monarchy into legal discourse.[25]

Both Dyer and Saunders made detailed notes of a case in 1560 which
set the judges thinking seriously about habeas corpus.[26] Mary I had
unlawfully granted an office in the Common Pleas, while the chief
justiceship was vacant, to a young courtier who lacked the requisite
technical knowledge. Dyer CJ rejected the grantee and nominated a
qualified attorney instead. The earl of Bedford and Lord Dudley then
used improper influence at court to procure a special commission to
determine the title to the office, which was a freehold, with power to
commit Dyer's nominee if he refused to answer. He did refuse to answer
and was committed for contempt. This was a newly invented, ad hoc,
power of imprisonment. But what could be done? The chief justice
considered using a general habeas corpus, which he thought could be
issued under the inherent jurisdiction of the court, and a writ was
actually prepared but not sealed. However, it was decided to rely instead
on the prisoner's status as an attorney and release him on a writ of
privilege, a long-established special form of habeas corpus. He was
immediately rearrested by the commissioners and remained in prison
for over five weeks before a settlement was reached. The judges were
deeply affronted by this 'check to the law' (as Dyer called it), and Dyer
began collecting precedents of general writs of habeas corpus from the
King's Bench rolls, showing how judges earlier in the century had
discharged or bailed prisoners committed by statesmen such as Wolsey
and Cromwell. His colleague Catlyn CJ joined in the search. These were
not law reports, just records; but the bare record was enough to show
what the court could do.

Two important cases of habeas corpus occurred in 1565. The first
concerned an imprisonment by the Council in the North at York.[27] The

---

[25] For Fleetwood see Baker, *Magna Carta*, ch. 6. Robert Snagge gave the first known reading
devoted entirely to Magna Carta, c. 29, in 1581: ibid., 251–5. James Morice had prepared
the way with an important reading on the prerogative in 1578. For Morice and the
'Puritan' lawyers serving in Parliament, see ibid., 255–61. For Plowden see n. 16, above.

[26] *Scrogges' Case* (1559–60) Dyer 175; 109 SS 34, 54–7; Baker, *SPL*, 224; Baker, *Magna
Carta*, 156–7. Scrogges relied explicitly on Magna Carta, c. 29.

[27] *John Lamburne's* (alias *Lambert's*) *Case* (1565), Baker, *SPL*, 284; Baker, *Magna Carta*,
158–9. The case was noted as a precedent by Coke (ibid., 506) and Christopher Yelverton
(British Library [hereafter BL] MS. Hargrave 430, fo. 181).

prisoner's body was not produced in obedience to the writ, because (as appeared from the return) the archbishop had ordered his gaoler to disobey it. The archbishop, as president of the Council in the North, was apparently awaiting instructions from the Privy Council. The King's Bench was greatly affronted by this. Catlyn CJ protested:[28]

> In this court we hold we hold pleas before the queen herself, inasmuch as it is the queen's highest court ... [and] this court is of such dignity that, in whatever prison someone is, we may command the officer to bring him here. Even if someone is in the Tower by command of the Council, we may send for him here by writ of *corpus cum causa* directed to the constable of the Tower.

The court not only ordered an alias habeas corpus but an attachment against both the archbishop and the gaoler. We know that Lamburne was in fact a criminal who had turned queen's evidence against some robbers.[29] But that was not the point. The King's Bench had no judicial notice of the surrounding facts. It was for the court to decide on the lawfulness of an imprisonment, and without a proper return they could not do so.

The other case in 1565 concerned the ecclesiastical High Commission, which was established in 1559. A gentleman who had been imprisoned for hearing mass (an indictable misdemeanour) was released by the King's Bench on the grounds that the commissioners had no power to imprison, especially without bail. He was promptly rearrested – yet another example of high-handedness which was 'much debated' by the judges, but again (as in 1560) without a satisfactory resolution.[30] Three years later the Common Pleas, using a writ of privilege, released a prisoner of the High Commission who had refused to incriminate himself upon the oath *ex officio* concerning his alleged attendance at mass. Though not reported in print, it was the first clear decision affirming the privilege against self-incrimination.[31] It is noteworthy that both these

---

[28] R. Crompton, *L'Authoritie et Jurisdiction des Courts* (1594), ff. 78v–79; translated in Baker, *SPL*, 284. He cited the case of the imprisonment by Cardinal Wolsey, identifiable as *Ex parte Apryse* (1518): Baker, *Magna Carta*, 157–8. He had also found precedents from the 1520s: Catlyn's commonplace book, Alnwick Castle MS. 475, fo. 95.

[29] See the archbishop's letter in M. A. E. Green (ed.), *Calendar of State Papers Domestic (Elizabeth): Addenda*, vol. 12 (1870), 554.

[30] *Mytton's Case* (1565) *Dyer's Notebooks* 109 SS lxxix, 107. Mytton was subsequently indicted at common law, but died in 1568 before trial.

[31] *Thomas Lee's Case* (1568) *Dyer's Notebooks*, 109 SS 143; Baker, *SPL*, 343; copy of the habeas corpus in BL MS. Harley 7648, fo. 267v; Coke's memorandum on c. 29 of Magna

decisions were in favour of Roman Catholics; there were other contemporary decisions in favour of Puritan ministers.

During the same period, the King's Bench discharged or bailed persons imprisoned by the Court of Requests, the Council in the Marches, and even the Chancery. These were prerogative courts, but the remedy was given in the name of a superior prerogative and was supported by the queen's law officers. In a habeas corpus case of 1605, Coke (still Attorney General) explained[32]:

> Even if the king gives authority by his commission to some persons to execute justice, or the law does so by Act of Parliament, nevertheless the examination thereof – as to what may be done by such authority – must remain in the absolute and supreme power of the king, that is, in his Bench, which is the proper seat of justice. And although there are no law reports to be found to prove this, yet he said that he had by search found infinite precedents to prove the continual use of it.

He was referring to the precedents, such as those collected by Dyer and Catlyn, in the rolls of the clerk of the crown. But the great question was, how far habeas corpus could reach towards the centre of government, the Privy Council. In 1577 Dyer CJ conceded that a general or unspecific return could not be reviewed in the case of a committal by the whole Privy Council, because there might be secret reasons which it would not be appropriate to make public.[33] Nevertheless, the King's Bench in 1567 and again in 1578 granted bail to prisoners sent to the Tower by the Privy Council without any cause shown,[34] and in 1587 it declared that those imprisoned by the Council were in all cases entitled to be brought before the court so that the lawfulness of their imprisonment could be examined.[35] Thus, as Catlyn CJ had asserted in 1565, even the Privy Council could not place someone completely beyond the reach of the law. It was, however, an empty remedy, since all the judges

---

Carta (1604) 132 SS 399; Baker, *Magna Carta*, 506; abridged, Baker, *SPL*, 438. It was frequently cited by Coke as chief justice.

[32] *Honnyng's Case*, arising from *Whetherley v. Whetherley* (1605) BL MS. Lansdowne 1075, ff. 101v–103v, translated in Baker, *Magna Carta*, 512; Baker, *SPL*, 290 at 292. The remark was in response to Francis Bacon's assertion that proceeding in this way would damage the royal prerogative.

[33] *Hynde's Case* (1576–77), Baker, *SPL*, 343; 109 SS lxxx n. 61. Cf. the report in 4 Leon. 21 ('because it may concern the state of the realm, which ought not to be published').

[34] *Robert Constable's Case* (1567) KB 29/201, m. 68; *John Brownyng's Case* (1578) KB 29/213, m. 73d.

[35] *John Howell's Case* (1587) 1 Leon. 70; Baker, *SPL*, 420.

collectively conceded in 1592 (albeit tacitly) that they could not go behind a general return by the queen or the whole Council.[36] Despite a lone protest from Walmsley J in 1601, this remained the position until the Petition of Right 1628.[37] The initial victory, in the Elizabethan period, was the ending of arbitrary imprisonment by individual ministers or courtiers and excesses of jurisdiction by newly created tribunals.

Habeas corpus was, obviously, limited to restraints on bodily liberty. But there were other kinds of liberty which were not adequately protected (if at all) by actions for damages.[38] The two further media of judicial review, mandamus and certiorari, were developed in the seventeenth century to fill some of the gaps.[39] They were originally aimed at local government: mandamus against municipal authorities, certiorari against county magistrates and other commissioners. The first of them, chrono-logically, was mandamus. Fractious behaviour in urban government was commonplace by 1600 and sometimes resulted in arbitrary abuses of position by those in authority. A freeman might be disenfranchised, which would deprive him of a vote; an alderman, town clerk or recorder might be removed on trumped-up or exaggerated charges of misconduct; an elected mayor might be kept out of office. Mandamus ('we command') is a word which occurred in various earlier writs. But a new version, known initially as a 'writ of restitution', was nurtured in the early 1600s.[40] It worked by ordering the municipal corporation to restore the applicant, whereupon the corporation could make a return justifying its conduct so that the court could review the stated reasons. The earliest reported case in the King's Bench, brought against the mayor of

---

[36] *Memorial from the Judges* (1592) 1 And. 297; Baker, *SPL*, 143; Baker, *Magna Carta*, 166–9, 496–8. An earlier version, signed in autograph by all the judges on 9 June 1591, is in the Burghley Papers, BL MS. Lansdowne 67(87).

[37] *John Bate's Case* (1601), Baker, *SPL*, 423; first noted in J. Baker, *English Law Under Two Elizabeths: The Late Tudor Legal World and the Present* (Cambridge, 2021), 49–50. Walmsley J had signed the memorials of 1591–92.

[38] E.g. it was not decided until *Ashby v. White* (1702) 2 Ld Raym. 938 (Baker, *SPL*, 143), after much debate and dissension, that an action on the case lay against a returning officer for rejecting a valid vote in a parliamentary election.

[39] The story below is told mainly from the reported cases. The full story lies in the records. The original returns are in the King's Bench *recorda* files (KB 145 to the year 1689, then KB 16) and the proceedings in court may be followed in the controlment rolls (KB 29) and the rule books (KB 21). The pioneering study by E. G. Henderson, *Foundations of English Administrative Law* (Cambridge, MA, 1963), made good use of the controlment rolls but did not use the files, which were not then available, or the manuscript reports.

[40] Baker, *Magna Carta*, 203–6. Here again the roots of the remedy had been discovered by Dyer (in 1574).

Cambridge in 1606, involved an element of habeas corpus as well as restitution, since the complainant bailiff had been imprisoned after an altercation with the mayor[41]; but mandamus rapidly became an independent procedure in regular use, and there were several reported cases (mostly not in print) testing its limits.[42] Although it was a judicial invention, Coke CJ attributed it in 1615 to chapter 29 of Magna Carta – not as a matter of history, of course, but of legal doctrine – and went so far as to assert that[43]:

> To this court of King's Bench belongs authority not only to correct errors in judicial proceedings, but other errors and misdemeanours extra-judicial tending to the breach of peace or oppression of the subjects, or to the raising of faction, controversy, debate or any manner of misgovernment; so that no wrong or injury, either public or private, can be done but that it shall be reformed or punished by the due course of the law.

That sweeping restatement of the rule of law drew an indignant rebuke from Lord Ellesmere LC prior to Coke's downfall the following year[44]:

> In giving excess of authority to the King's Bench, [Coke CJ] doth as much as insinuate that this court is all sufficient in itself to manage the state. For if the King's Bench may reform 'any manner of misgovernment' (as the words are), it seemeth that there is little or no use either of the king's royal care and authority exercised in his person … nor of the Council Table, which under the king is the chief watch-tower for all points of misgovernment, nor of the Star Chamber, which hath ever been esteemed the highest court for extinguishment of all riots and public disorders and enormities.

He went on to accuse Coke of claiming for the King's Bench 'a superintendency over the government itself, and to judge wherein any of them

---

[41] R. v. Mayor of Cambridge, ex parte Tompson (1606) KB 29/246, m. 125 (translated in Henderson, Foundations of English Administrative Law, 163–7); judgment in KB 21/3, fo. 72; reported in BL MS. Lansdowne 1075, fo. 189v; MS. Add 35954, fo. 444v; 1 Rolle Abr. 456; Baker, SPL, 392.

[42] Notably R. v. Burgesses of Stamford, ex parte Loveday (1609) KB 29/249, m. 138d; reported in Cambridge Univ. Lib. MS. Mm. 6.69, ff. 113, 117v; Baker, SPL, 392; R. v. Mayor of Lincoln, ex parte Shuttleworth (1613) KB 29/255, m. 23; Calthorpe's reports, BL MS. Hargrave 385, fo. 115; R. v. Mayor of Boston, ex parte Midlecott (1615) KB 29/257, m. 103; Calthorpe's reports, fo. 353v.

[43] R. v. Mayor of Plymouth, ex parte Bagg (1615) 11 Co. Rep. 98; also reported in 1 Rolle Rep. 224; Baker, SPL, 393; record in KB 29/259, m. 76; Baker, Magna Carta, 396–8.

[44] Lord Ellesmere, 'Observations on Coke's Reports', printed in L. A. Knafla (ed.), Law and Politics in Jacobean England: The Tracts of Lord Chancellor Ellesmere (Cambridge, 1977), 297–318, at 307 (here modernised); Baker, SPL, 398.

do misgovern'. That was, indeed, exactly what Coke was claiming. And it has been the foundation of English administrative law ever since. It may have seemed preposterous to the lord chancellor in 1616; but leaving the review of misgovernment to the government itself, whether in the person of the king or through the Privy Council or Star Chamber, was hardly satisfactory to an aggrieved subject. In any case, in his exasperation with Coke's sweeping assertions, and in his desire to be rid of him, Ellesmere had exaggerated the potential scope of mandamus. The writ did not lie against the crown, or against a minister of the crown, and therefore was not (until 1968) available to challenge misgovernment at the highest level.[45] Moreover, it was still a writ of restitution, limited to public offices and positions, or freehold offices which existed 'for the common weal'.[46] It did not lie to enforce private contracts of employment or even (at first) the performance of official duties.

The last of the prerogative writs, certiorari, is briefly noticed in manuscript law reports in the 1640s, though it only rose to importance in the Restoration period. The formula had long been used for removing indictments and other records into the King's Bench from lower courts of record,[47] and Coke found a year-book case in which something similar was used to review a decision by justices of the forest.[48] Like prohibition, it lay only to control courts; but there were several courts in the seventeenth century which exercised governmental functions. In the first half of that century it began to be used to review fines imposed by commissioners of sewers or convictions by justices of the peace exercising summary jurisdiction.[49] On the surface, it operated formally in the same way as in the past: the writ merely ordered that the record be sent up to the King's Bench, and the bare record was all that the return contained. But when the return contained a judgment or order, it operated as an informal counterpart to the writ of error as a way of obtaining a judicial review. More or less

---

[45] The position was changed by *Padfield v. Ministry of Agriculture* [1968] AC 997.

[46] *Cock's Case* (1658) 2 Sid. 112; Baker, *SPL*, 398.

[47] For earlier uses see S. A. De Smith, 'The Judicial Writs' (1951) 11 *Cambridge Law Journal* 40, 45–8. For its use in Chancery see W. J. Jones, *The Elizabethan Court of Chancery* (Oxford, 1969), 187–9.

[48] *Case of the Forest of Pickering* (1347) YB Mich. 21 Edw. III, fo. 48, pl. 70; 4 Co. Inst. 294. It was not called certiorari: Coke called it a *venire facias recordum*.

[49] See K. Costello, 'The Writ of Certiorari and Review of Summary Criminal Convictions 1600–1848' (2012) 128 *Law Quarterly Review* 443–65. It was presumably this use of the writ which occasioned complaints in 1621 that it was issued too frequently, resulting in judges' rules to regulate it: J. F. Larkin and P. L. Hughes (eds.), *Stuart Royal Proclamations* (Oxford, 1973), vol. I, 513, no. 217.

invisible before the 1640s, it became a standard procedure during the later seventeenth century for challenging orders made by quarter sessions – in effect, the county local government – such as the assessment of rates, the settlement of paupers, and affiliation orders.[50]

The development may have been connected with the abandonment of oversight of local government by the assize judges in the middle of the seventeenth century, though that cannot be the full explanation.[51] The first reported debate about the extension of the remedy occurred in 1642, when certiorari was used successfully to remove and quash an order made by commissioners of sewers. Although it was resisted as a new departure, once again the principle which prevailed was that no inferior authority was beyond the scope of judicial review by the King's Bench.[52] Bramston CJ remarked that he did not think the writ would be much used,[53] though in that prediction he was much deceived. The procedure rapidly gained a foothold because it suited all parties not to challenge it.[54] It relieved complainants from having to wait for an unlawful order to be enforced against them so that they could bring a civil action for damages or a replevin,[55] and it settled the status of the order itself rather than just the issue between particular parties. Yet these were purely public law remedies, in that they lay only in respect of public authorities or courts.[56]

---

[50] See K. Costello, 'The King's Bench and the Poor Law 1630–1800' (2014) 35 *Journal of Legal History* 3–26.

[51] See J. Baker, 'Equity and Public Law in England' in J. Baker, *Collected Papers on English Legal History* (Cambridge, 2013), vol. II, at 956–60. The Star Chamber also exercised some control over local government before its abolition in 1640, but it was chiefly concerned with criminal misconduct.

[52] *Comyns v. Masham* (1642) March N.R. 196 (Baker, *SPL*, 408); Harvard Law School MS. 113, 170–5; KB 29/291, m. 39 (writ and return); KB 21/13, fo. 14 (decree affirmed); followed in *Re Newton and Tydd St Giles* (1648) Style 178, 184, 191; KB 29/297, m. 33 (writ); KB 21/13, ff. 120v–127v (rules). The 1642 case is discussed in Henderson, *Foundations of English Administrative Law*, 101–6; and for earlier but unreported precedents see ibid., 93–101. I am grateful to Dr Paul Warchuk of St John's College, Cambridge, author of a recent PhD dissertation on the history of certiorari (1600–1800), for a helpful discussion of the subject.

[53] From the citation of *Comyns v. Masham* in *Re Newton*, as reported in Barnard's reports, BL MS. Add 25222, fo. 166 (reversing).

[54] This was emphasised in *Comyns v. Masham* (n. 52, above), Baker, *SPL*, 409.

[55] E.g. *Wythers v. Rookes* (1598) Coke's Notebooks, 139 SS 844, 5 Co. Rep. 99 (replevin); Baker, *SPL*, 405; *Keighley's Case* (1609) 10 Co. Rep. 139 (action on the case); *Hetly v. Carryer* (1614) 2 Bulst. 197 (replevin). These were all brought in respect of distraints to enforce the orders of commissioners of sewers.

[56] This was also at first true de facto of habeas corpus. No examples have been found of habeas corpus against private individuals before the time of Charles II, but it was then

There was one remaining obstacle to treating the King's Bench as judicially supreme. The power of the Privy Council to imprison people without giving reasons was usually defended with reference to treasonous plots, and it was certainly one of the proper functions of the Council to authorise and make preparations for state trials. Even Coke, both as law officer and as lord chief justice, accepted that such pre-trial proceedings were beyond review.[57] But imprisonment could potentially be used in connection with politically controversial ends, such as the enforcement of monopolies[58] and extra-parliamentary taxation. The most hotly contested aspect of this in the early modern period was prerogative taxation by means of impositions. In *Customer Smyth's Case* (1598), concerning an imposition on alum, and in *Bate's Case* (1606), concerning an imposition on currants, the Court of Exchequer held that the king had an absolute prerogative power to lay impositions on imported merchandise.[59] Fleming CB wryly observed in *Bate's Case* that the only losers were wealthy epicures who had to pay a little more for their currants; but the constitutional principle at stake was widely considered to be fundamental. The decision caused a major stir and was frequently debated in the Commons, where it was the subject of lengthy historical and legal discourses. Coke and Popham CJJ were of the view that import duties could be imposed for the public good – for instance, in order to achieve parity with duties imposed by foreign governments – but that there was no general prerogative power of taxation.[60] That came to be tested with the even more controversial forced loan of 1626, which caused a furore in Parliament but was not ruled upon decisively,[61] and with the ship-money levy imposed in 1636, which was upheld by only a bare majority of the

---

used (e.g.) to liberate children from would-be guardians: Baker, *SPL*, 446–7. For an unsuccessful attempt to use it for an accused wife see *R. v. Lord Leigh* (1675) ibid., 445–6. For an inconclusive attempt to use the analogous writ *de homine replegiando* for a slave see *Sir Thomas Grantham's Case* (1687) ibid., 453.

[57] *Ruswell's (alias Rosewell's) Case* (1615) 118 SS 453; *Saltonstall's Case* (1615) 1 Rolle Rep. 219; Baker, *Magna Carta*, 401, n. 342. For the first case see also Baker, *SPL*, 260.

[58] *Leathersellers' Company v. Darcy* (1598) Baker, *Magna Carta*, 168, 196.

[59] *Att.-Gen. v. Smyth* (1598) *Coke's Notebooks*, 139 SS 873; Baker, *SPL*, 469; *Att.-Gen. v. Bate* (1606) Lane 22; extracts in Baker, *SPL*, 471. The imposition on alum was effected by letters under the privy signet. That on currants was effected by letters patent addressed to the lord treasurer.

[60] *Case of Impositions* (1606) 12 Co. Rep. 33; Baker, *SPL*, 478.

[61] Its enforcement by imprisonment was contested in *The Five Knights' Case* (1627) 3 St. Tr. 1 (extracts in Baker, *SPL*, 426), but the returns to the writs of habeas corpus deliberately did not disclose the reason for the imprisonment, and therefore the only issue was whether the king could commit people to prison without giving reasons.

judiciary in 1638.[62] By that time the judicial robustness of Coke's day had waned, and public confidence in the judges was reaching a low point. Coke had been dismissed in 1616, and his successor Sir Randall Crewe was removed in 1626 for opposing the loan. These were heroic moments, but they fostered a sense that the judges who managed to remain in office might no longer be as independent as in the past.

The control of local government by means of mandamus and certiorari was to become a major part of King's Bench business by 1700. However, after the failure of the King's Bench judges effectively to oppose the forced loan, the protection of the subject from unconstitutional taxation and arbitrary imprisonment passed for a time to the High Court of Parliament, where the advocacy of the lawyer members – some of whom had represented the loan refusers in 1627 – stood a better chance of success. Coke was among them. Having himself been imprisoned without cause shown, in 1621 and again in 1622, he now recanted his former opinion about imprisonment by the king or the Privy Council.[63] In 1628 he was the chief promoter of the Petition of Right, which (with the king's grudging assent) guaranteed that 'that no man hereafter be compelled to make or yield any gift, loan, benevolence, tax, or such like charge without common consent by Act of Parliament' or be imprisoned without cause shown. That did not avail the defendant in the ship-money case, but in 1640 Parliament reversed the judgment in that case and guaranteed the availability of habeas corpus in all cases of committal by the king or the Privy Council.[64]

The role of the House of Commons in establishing such basic principles of public law is well known and beyond the scope of the present discussion. It is enough to observe that it was a very different body from its successor today. It was not tied by party politics to do the government's bidding. Its members came (in Selden's words) 'bound by the trust reposed in them by their country that sent them' to defend their freedoms.[65] Most importantly, the House was full of barristers, always chaired by a prominent lawyer, and frequently resounded with legal arguments of the highest quality, replete with legal and historical

---

[62] R. v. Hampden (1638) 3 St. Tr. 1127 (Exchequer Chamber); extracts in Baker, *SPL*, 482. Five judges supported Hampden, who had declined to pay a tax of £1 for the construction of warships, but seven voted for the crown.

[63] He excused his former opinion on the grounds that 1615 was 'an ill time': 3 St. Tr. 81–2 (1628).

[64] Ship Money Act 1640 (16 Car. I), cc. 10, 14.

[65] Debate on the liberty of the subject (1628) 3 St. Tr. 145.

citations. Legal history had become both a vocational subject and a force in politics. The lawyers in the Commons thought they were defending an ancient inheritance represented by Magna Carta. They did their utmost to ensure that the king (and Parliament itself) stayed within the rule of law. It is perhaps unsurprising that kings saw Parliament as troublesome, and sought to manage without it. As it turned out, that was a serious miscalculation. Constitutional monarchy had already been firmly implanted in the legal and political mind by the decisions of the courts in Westminster Hall, and by their inspired notion that the king's prerogatives in executive action could legitimately be controlled by the king's higher prerogative in judicature.

5

The Aspirations of James Stuart

IAN WARD

In 1636, a set of nine paintings was installed on the ceiling of the Banqueting Hall in Whitehall Palace. Three central and six side panels. They had arrived a year earlier, but installation was delayed on discovery that an English inch was different from a Flemish one. So there needed to be some trimming first. The set had arrived from the studio of Peter Paul Rubens in Antwerp. Quite how much Rubens was involved remains uncertain. The relatively modest cost, at £3,000, suggests that much of the work might have been completed by students.[1] The original contract lost, we can only surmise the various terms of the commission. It is generally agreed that the contract was probably drafted during Rubens's visit to London over the winter of 1628–1629; though it is possible that the idea was originally negotiated with a young Antony van Dyck, who had visited in 1621.[2] The subject of the commission, who died midway between these dates in early March 1625, was James Stuart, King of England, Scotland and, in his own mind at least, 'greater' Britain.

Having not met James in the flesh, Rubens was dependent on other artists for a likeness of the recently deceased king. Comparison of facial features suggests that Paul van Somers's 1618 portrait was the most likely source.[3] Fifty-two years old in the moment, van Somers's James looks as 'weary' as he commonly liked to complain.[4] The James that Rubens and

---

[1] For this surmise, and a broader account of the composition and installation of the set, see O. Millar, 'Rubens' Whitehall Ceiling', *The Burlington Magazine*, 147 (2007), 101–4.

[2] Van Dyck was at that time serving an informal apprenticeship at Rubens's studio, working more particularly on the decoration of the Jesuit Church of Saint Ignatius Loyola, the so-called 'Marble Temple'. Rubens had been commissioned by the order in 1620 to provide thirty-nine paintings for the church at a cost of 7,000 guilders. Amongst van Dyck's contributions was the beautiful *Coronation of Saint Rosalie*.

[3] It was apparently the portrait which Charles favoured, for reason of likeness. At James's insistence, van Somers painted him standing in front of the still half-built Banqueting Hall.

[4] Having, as one historian has suggested, a 'crusty weariness' about him: see W. Jones, *Politics and the Bench: The Judges and the Origins of the English Civil War* (London, 1971), 26.

his students conceived is spectacularly different. Still greying, still middle-aged, but otherwise every contested inch majestic, set against a predictably Rubensian backdrop of classical and Christian imagery. The themes for the three central canvasses were, of course, determined by the man who commissioned the set, James's son and heir, King Charles I. So, we have *The Apotheosis of King James*, *The Peaceful Reign of King James*, and *The Union of Crowns*. It may be as James wished to be remembered. It is certainly how Charles wished his father to be remembered. Our contention is that these three canvasses describe the associated kingly aspirations of James Stuart. And that, furthermore, each speaks to the matter of constitutional crisis; then, and now.

Apotheosis

The Apotheosis of King James I is the centrepiece. James is seated in the middle, glancing up towards a laurel wreath held by the figure of Mercury. It will replace the symbols of his earthly authority, the crown and sceptre. His feet are planted on an eagle and an imperial globe, ready to be raised by Justice, escorted by Religion and Scriptural Truth. A slightly detached Victory flutters a nearby approval. James would have been flattered for sure. In part because he always fancied himself in the guise of a 'deified' Roman emperor, Augustus most particularly. His coronation pageant, back in 1604, had been soaked in Augustan imagery, his coronation medal bearing the inscription, in translation, 'James I, Caesar Augustus of Britain, Caesar heir of Caesars'.[5] All the best *princeps* are raised to the gods. But flattered also because the imagery chimes so obviously with the collateral, and defining, tenet of James's idea of kingship: that he ruled by divine right.

James had already ventured the idea in three treatises on kingship composed in the late 1590s, most obviously perhaps in *The Trew Law of Free Monarchies*, first published in Scotland in 1598, which opened in vaunting terms. Monarchy, 'as resembling Divinitie, approcheth nearest to perfection'.[6] In refining his thesis, James sought recourse to a mixture of scriptural and classical authority.[7] Thus the bold, and bald, statement,

[5] A. Kernan, *Shakespeare, the King's Playwright: Theatre in the Stuart Court* (New Haven, CT, 1995), 12.

[6] King James, *Political Writings*, ed. J. Sommerville (Cambridge, 1994), 63.

[7] See P. Monateri, *Dominus Mundi: Political Sublime and the World Order* (Oxford, 2018), 87–8.

reworked from *Psalms* 82:6 and 101: 'Kings are called Gods by the propheticall King David, because they sit upon God his Throne in the earth'.[8] Repeated invocations of patriarchy too: 'By the Law of Nature the King becomes a natural Father to all his Lieges at his Coronation' and 'the stile of *Pater patriae* was ever, and is commonly used to Kings'.[9] Classical authority in the shape of Ulpian's affirmation, written into Justinian's *Digest*, *princeps legibus solutus est*; 'the Emperor is not bound by law' (Digest 1.3.31). And again, *Quod principi placuit, legis habet vigorem*; 'what pleases the prince has the force of law' (Digest 1.4.1). The congruence between 'divine right' and the species of absolutism discovered in the writings of Bodin and other continental classicists may not be exact,[10] but it comes close.

The narrower juridical implication was spelled out in James's account of the 'law of equitie', which 'so mixeth Mercy with Justice, as it preserves men from destruction'. And 'thus (as I before told you) is the King's Throne established by Mercy and Justice'.[11] The logic is simple enough: to secure the law, a king must be above it. This does not mean that a 'good king' will do other than 'frame all his actions to be according to the Law'. But it does mean that, being 'above the law', he is not 'bound thereunto'.[12] James Cowell, Regius Professor of Civil Law at Cambridge, was moved to clarify the situation, for any of James's new subjects unfamiliar with the *Trew Law*. The king ruled *supra legem*, 'by his absolute power', in both his realms.[13]

A fresh reprint of the *Trew Law*, within months of James arriving in London, was evidently purposed to lend further clarity, at least regarding the kind of kingship James preferred.[14] How apposite it might be was

---

[8] King James, *Political Writings*, 64.
[9] Ibid., 65, 76. James made similar recourse to the patriarchal analogy in his 1610 address to Parliament: ibid., 182–3.
[10] See here C. Russell, *The Causes of the English Civil War* (Oxford, 1990), 147, thinking the term 'absolutism' rather too encompassing, and G. Burgess, *Absolute Monarchy and the Stuart Constitution* (New Haven, CT, 1996), 17–21, 31–3, 63–6, 93–6.
[11] King James, *Political Writings*, 214.
[12] Ibid., 75. For a commentary, see I. Evrigenis, 'Sovereignty, Mercy, and Natural Law: James VI/I and Jean Bodin', *History of European Ideas*, 45 (2019), 1073–88, at 1082.
[13] Cowell was the author of a best-selling primer for law students, civil and common, entitled *The Interpreter*, wherein could be discovered numerous similar assertions. For commentaries on Cowell and his *Interpreter*, see J. Sommerville, *Politics and Ideology in England 1603-1640* (London, 1986), 121–2; and Monateri, *Dominus Mundi*, 90.
[14] The spring 1603 republication 'flooded the market', according to J. Wormald, *James VI and I: Collected Essays by Jenny Wormald* (Edinburgh, 2021), 36.

another matter. The spring 1603 reprint of the *Trew Law* was also accompanied by a first look, for some, at a second of James's treatises. This was a *specula* piece entitled *Basilicon Doron*, within which could be found similar commentary regarding James's idea of kingship – not least in the opening sonnet which advised the 'argument' of the essay: 'God giues not Kings the stile of Gods in vaine, / For on his Throne his Scepter doe they sway'.[15] We will return to the *Basilicon* shortly.

The third of the treatises, which James had completed a couple of years before, was entitled *Daemonology*. Inspired by his personal involvement in the 'discovery' of a coven in North Berwick in 1590, *Daemonology* was written as contribution to a burgeoning genre of witch-hunting manuals. Alongside various bits of practical advice on how to spot a witch, James thought fit to reaffirm the existence of certain 'mysterious' prerogatives which he enjoyed by reason of his divine appointment.[16] All part, as James later affirmed in his 1608 *Apologie for the Oath of Allegiance*, of being 'The Lords anoynted, Sitting in God's throne', and doing His work[17] – a belief from which he never wavered. 'The mysteries of the Kings power is not lawfully to be disputed', he reminded Star Chamber in 1616, for it 'would be to take away' the 'mystical reverence that belongs unto them that sit in the Throne of God'. To do so, indeed, was a form of 'atheisme and blasphemy'.[18] Put simply, the 'presence of the Devil' legitimates a prince's 'occult' prerogatives.[19]

James's new subjects did not dispute much of what could be read in *Daemonology*, or the urgency of the situation. After all, England was a 'land full of witches', as Lord Chief Justice Anderson had soberly observed just a year before James's succession.[20] For which reason, England was lucky to acquire a king like James, so evidently skilled in the matter of 'discovering' witches. Rather less settling was the collateral

---

[15] King James, *Political Writings*, 1.

[16] See Wormald, *James VI and I*, 27–8; and P. Elmer, *Witchcraft, Witch-Hunting and Politics in Early Modern England* (Oxford, 2016), 64–5.

[17] King James, *Political Writings*, 128. The *Apologie* was written in rebuttal of a 'letter' sent by Cardinal Bellarmine which advised English Catholics to nominally subscribe to a fresh oath of allegiance imposed following the discovery of the Gunpowder Plot. Precisely how much of the *Apologie* was James's work remains a matter of conjecture.

[18] King James, *Political Writings*, 213.

[19] Monateri, *Dominus Mundi*, 98–9, 138.

[20] J. Sharpe, *Instruments of Darkness: Witchcraft in Early Modern England* (Philadelphia, PA, 1997), 216.

insinuation, that the 'occult' prerogatives necessarily lay beyond the margins of the common law. But again hardly unfamiliar, at least to readers of the *Trew Law* and the *Basilicon Doron*. Particularly disconcerted were all the common lawyers, whose serried ranks dominated the House of Commons. And for good reason, as it transpired, since much of the first part of James's reign would be consumed by an enervating squabble between King James and Sir Edward Coke, chief justice of Common Pleas (1606–1613), then lord chief justice of King's Bench (1613–1616), over the reach of Crown prerogative. Culminating in the 'year to consecrate justice', as Francis Bacon famously termed it[21] – that year being 1616. As for the consecration, Bacon was alluding to the famed *Case of Commendams*.

Not, at first glance, a case which intimated constitutional crisis, *Commendams* moved around the capacity of the king to intervene in a dispute regarding tithing arrangements in a vacant 'living'. But a crisis it became, ultimately leading an exasperated king to descend on his judges, much as Shakespeare imagined his Jupiter descending from Olympus to sort out the 'mangled' laws of *Cymbeline*'s Britain, 'thunderbolt' at the ready[22]:

> And as no King can discharge his accompt to God, unlesse he make conscience not to alter, but to declare and establish the will of God: So Judges cannot discharge their accompts to Kings, unlesse they take the like care, not to take upon them to make the Law, but joyned together after a deliberate consultation, to declare what the Law is. For as Kings are subject unto God's Law, so they to mans Law. It is the Kings Office to protect and settle the trew interpretation of the Law of God within his Dominions: And it is the Judges Office to interpret the Law of the King, whereto themselves are also subject.[23]

The admonishment was targeted particularly at his lord chief justice, Sir Edward Coke, and was the product of a long imagining.

It was portended a decade earlier in the famous *Case of Prohibitions*, in which a barrister of 'schismatical and factious humour' named Nicholas Fuller challenged his detention by order of the High Commission, a

---

[21] For a compelling account of the case, see J. H. Baker, *The Reinvention of Magna Carta 1216–1616* (Cambridge, 2017), chapter 10.

[22] *Cymbeline*, Act 5, Scene 4, stage direction at lines 92–3. For a commentary on the jurisprudential significance of the direction, see P. Raffield, *The Art of Law in Shakespeare* (Oxford, 2017), 188–9.

[23] King James, *Political Writings*, 206.

prerogative court established to govern Church discipline.[24] Fuller had compared the Commission to the Jesuit Inquisition. Coke, then chief justice of Common Pleas, had closed his judgment in support of Fuller with a judicious bit of Bracton: 'The king ought not to be under any man but under God and the law'. A principle which, Coke added, surely 'delights the honour of the king, whose person they represent as they sit in justice'.[25] Not that James seemed particularly delighted, muttering darkly that his chief justice was too 'full of craturity'.[26] And he was probably not much surprised either, especially if he had noted Coke's opinion in *Roper's Case* a few months earlier: An 'ecclesiastical court is like a fountain of sweet water to refresh all the earth, but if that fountain does not contain itself within its banks it will flood the lower lands'. For which reason it is an incumbent duty of the common law to 'reduce it within its channel when it runs over'.[27]

Battle continued in a series of high-profile 'constitutional' cases, including the *Case of Proclamations* in 1608, *Bonham's Case* in 1610, and the *Earl of Oxford's Case* and *Glanvil's Case*, both in 1615. Each tested the jurisdictional reach of the prerogative and its 'grinding courts', as John Milton termed them.[28] In *Proclamations*, it was the legal status of certain royal proclamations which were purposed to replenish the Exchequer. This was an opportunity for Coke to remind James that a 'King cannot change any part of the common law, nor create any offence by his proclamations, which was not an offence before, without Parliament'. It was, he affirmed, 'resolved that the King hath no Prerogative, but that which the Law of the Land allows him'.[29] In *Bonham's Case* it was the authority granted by royal charter to the College of Physicians to award licences.[30] In the *Earl of Oxford's Case*, it was the role of Chancery in adjudging the enforceability of an order

---

[24] See S. Wright, 'Nicholas Fuller and the Liberties of the Subject', *Parliamentary History*, 25 (2006), 176–213 at 192–3; D. Smith, *Sir Edward Coke and the Reformation of the Laws: Religion, Politics and Jurisprudence* (Cambridge, 2014), 194f.

[25] *Case of Prohibitions* (1607) 12 Co. Rep. 63; 77 E.R. 1342. See also Smith, *Sir Edward Coke*, 249; Baker, *Reinvention of Magna Carta*, 367–8.

[26] I. Ward, *The Trials of Charles I* (London, 2023), 18.

[27] *Roper's Case* (1607) 12 Co. Rep. 45; 77 E.R. 1327.

[28] In *Of Reformation*: see J. Milton, *Complete Prose Works*, ed. D. Wolfe (New Haven, CT, 1953–62), 1.520–3.

[29] *Case of Proclamations* (1610) 12 Co. Rep. 74; 77 E.R. 1352.

[30] *Bonham's Case* (1610) 8 Co Rep. 113b; 77 E.R. 638. The licensing power granted by statute in 1540, and then reaffirmed in 1553, touched a collateral common law nerve, that of prospective Crown monopolies.

regarding the conveyance of former Crown property.[31] That was a moment for Lord Chancellor Ellesmere to articulate a pointed defence of his office, as a place where 'any error or defect in judgment' might be corrected 'for the hard conscience of the party';[32] and an inspiration for Bacon, as Attorney General, who was invited to draft a royal declaration on the subject, published amidst the fall-out from the *Commendams* in July 1616: 'For inasmuch as Mercy and Justice be the true Supporters of our Royal Throne, and that it properly belongeth unto us in our Princely Office to take care and provide, that our Subjects... should not be abandoned and exposed to perish under the Rigor and Extremity of our Laws.'[33]

Glanvil's Case was different again. A conman tried to avoid gaol by convincing the now lord chief justice that his detention would threaten the very future of the English Reformation, as well as the common law.[34] And he succeeded, a splenetic Coke berating a disobliging jury as a bunch of 'varletts and knaves' and giving 'faire warning' that his hand would 'fall heavy' on any who attempted to interfere with the run of a King's Bench writ. 'We must looke about or the common lawe of England will be overthrown', he screeched to a close.[35] How startled everyone was, is a matter of conjecture. Coke was commonly furious. But it is fair to say that as the year 'to consecrate justice' dawned there was not much of the *pax Jacobus* about Westminster Hall.

A Peaceful Reign

The *pax* is the theme of the second of our Rubens canvasses, *The Peaceful Reign of James I*, in which James again takes centre-stage. He is seated, shielding Peace and Plenty, whilst Minerva casts down Mars, the god of war. The goddess of wisdom, Minerva was the obvious support for a king

---

[31] *Earl of Oxford's Case* (1615) 1 Ch. Rep. 1; 21 E.R. 485. For an interesting contextual account of the case, see G. Watt, *Equity Stirring: The Story of Justice Beyond the Law* (Oxford, 2009), 67–72.

[32] (1615) 1 Ch. Rep. 1, 6–7, 10.

[33] *Case of Commendams* (1616) 1 Ch. Rep. 49; 21 E.R. 65.

[34] The facts of the case involved the sale of paste jewellery, and the attempt of the gulled purchaser to secure rescission of contract in Chancery. Glanvil was attached by Chancery order for his refusal to repay the money and sent to the Fleet. Coke, in King's Bench, ordered his release. The lord chancellor then ordered his rearrest. And so it went on. For an account, see Ward, *Trials of Charles I*, 23–4.

[35] *Glanvil's Case* (1615) Cro. Jac. 343; 79 E.R. 294.

who so prided himself on his intellect. And it was an abiding cultural motif, the aligned supposition being that it was James's wisdom which elevated him above princes of a more martial inclination. Shakespeare dressed his wizard-king Prospero in this guise in *The Tempest*. Thomas Middleton imagined similarly in his play *The Peace-Maker*: James as Solomon, the 'great' king to whom all the bickering princes of Europe would come for counsel and conciliation.[36] Daniel Mytens's portrait of James, completed in 1621, works the same theme, placing his subject before a tapestry embossed by the Tudor rose with the words *beati pacifici*, 'blessed are the peacemakers'. At pretty much the same moment Bacon was conceiving his *New Atlantis*, and its brilliant founder, King Solamona: A man of 'large heart, inscrutable for good', and 'wholly bent' to 'make his kingdom and people happy'; a 'lawgiver' too, who designed his laws so that they 'preserved all points of humanity'.[37] Atlantis had not needed to fight anyone for as long as memory served.

The *Trew Law* and the *Basilicon Doron* were testament to James's intellectual vanity. The latter, as already noted, was written as a contribution to the presently fashionable *specula* genre, intended to provide a 'mirror viue and faire' of good kingship.[38] Thus all the advice on dressing sensibly, eating a balanced diet, and learning to write good poetry, meaning 'rich in quicke inventions', rather than merely rhyming 'right'.[39] Not everyone was sure of the 'wisest fool in Christendom', as the Duc de Sully famously disparaged the new King of England.[40] Certainly not the diplomat Antony Weldon, whose physical description of James is notorious: Thin of beard, thick of speech, a man 'naturally of timorous disposition', his 'eyes large, ever rolling after any stranger that came into his presence', forever 'fiddling about his cod-piece'.[41] Nor Lady Anne Clifford, who famously railed against a court 'grown scandalous'. Nor

---

[36] The authorship of the play, which first appeared in 1618, is generally ascribed to Middleton. There were plenty more flattering references to James's 'union', as an exemplar of how peace might be secured between nations, along with a sub-text on the dangers of alcohol-induced disorder at home.

[37] F. Bacon, *The Advancement of Learning and New Atlantis*, ed. A. Johnston (Oxford, 1974), 228 (first published in 1605).

[38] King James, *Political Writings*, 1.

[39] Ibid., 55.

[40] The precise derivation of the quote is contested. An alternative suggests that it might have been Sully's king, Henry IV of France.

[41] A French ambassador attested to similar, during a visit to Edinburgh in 1584; 'his gait is bad, composed of erratic steps': see A. Stewart, *The Cradle King: A Life of James VI and I* (London, 2003), 75, 270.

Sir James Harington, who left a withering description of the Bacchanalian festivities which greeted the visiting King Christian of Denmark in 1606 – an inspiration for Shakespeare's *Antony and Cleopatra* perhaps. Sir James imagined himself in 'Mahomet's paradise', rather than the court of a Christian prince.[42]

But there was more to it than rolling eyes and drunken orgies. James disappointed because he was not Elizabeth. Solomon replacing Gloriana was always going to be a tough sell. His predecessor was no less keen to display her princely wisdom but had always taken care to decorate herself in a variety of martial poses. Thus the 'valiant' Britomart, the Redcrosse Knight's Amazonian bodyguard, who bestrides the third book of Spenser's *Faerie Queene*; and the renowned speech given at Tilbury as the Spanish Armada hove into view in August 1588: 'I know I have the body but of a weak, feeble woman; but I have the heart and stomach of a king, and a king of England too'. Affirming her trust 'under God' and having placed 'my chiefest strength and safeguard in the loyal hearts and good-will of my subjects', the armoured Elizabeth is ready for battle.[43] James never had to give a speech like this, and that was the problem. In his *Inquiry into the Literary and Political Character of James I*, published in 1816, Isaac D'Israeli supposed that it was the *pax Jacobus* that did for James Stuart. Lacking 'military character', too determinedly unheroic, too dull.[44]

Instead of joining in the murderous 'wars of religion' that were presently raging across the continent, James aspired to be their honest broker. An idea that impelled him towards seeking a *rapprochement* with Catholic Spain; another hard sell. More so still when details of Prince Charles's bizarre attempt to press the so-called Spanish 'match' became popular knowledge in 1623. Donning false beards, Charles and his best

---

[42] Letter to Secretary Barlow, in *Nugae Antiquae, being a collection of original papers in prose and verse, written in the reigns of Henry VIII, etc., by Sir J. Harrington and others*, selected by H.H., 2 vols. (1779), 2.126–30. For accounts of the event, see G. Blakemore Evans, *Elizabethan-Jacobean Theatre: The Theatre in Its Time* (London, 1988), 201–2, and Stewart, *The Cradle King*, 236–7.

[43] A horse-backed Elizabeth was reported to have been wearing a shiny cuirass and waving a sword about. There are various accounts of the speech, the original version of which appears to have been recorded by a subaltern attached to the camp of the Earl of Leicester. The possibility that Elizabeth wrote the speech herself is considered in J. Green, '"I My Self": Queen Elizabeth I's Oratory at Tilbury Camp', *The Sixteenth Century*, 28 (1997), 421–45.

[44] See I. Ferris, 'The "Character" of James the First and Antiquarian Secret History', *The Wordsworth Circle*, 37 (2006), 73–6.

mate, George Villiers, prospective Duke of Buckingham, had travelled incognito to Madrid to see the Infanta dance. She had not disappointed, at least not in her footwork. But Charles did.[45] A collateral casualty of the fated 'match' was Sir Walter Raleigh. Released from the Tower, where he had been held since 1603 on suspicion of treason, Raleigh had set off on an expedition of the Orinoco, with his king's grudging approval and on one condition, that he must not attack any Spanish colonies. Which was ignored. On arriving back in summer 1618, Raleigh was promptly returned to the Tower and a couple of months later executed at the behest of the Spanish ambassador, Count Gondomar.

By this time, James had eagerly taken up an invitation, conveyed by the same Count, to 'interpose himself for the accommodating of the business on Bohemia'. The 'business' related to an incident during which a couple of imperial officials had been defenestrated in Prague. The consequence was a stand-off between imperial forces and those of the protestant Duke of Savoy. At first glance this was a highpoint in the *pax Jacobus*, except that James was being played. His 'vanity', as Gondomar confirmed to his king, was 'so great'. This was something the Venetian ambassador appreciated too, noting how much James liked to pass himself off as 'the chief of a great union in Europe'. But also how the English invariably 'resolve upon nothing', never seeming sure whether they want to be in Europe, or out.[46]

James's endeavours, such as they were, were anyway overtaken by events, as the Bohemians chose to 'elect' a new king. Their choice, Frederick, already Elector Palatine, was James's son-in-law. Not that James was impressed; kings were chosen by God, not by electorates. The event threatened 'to set all Christendom by the ears'.[47] Worse still, Frederick promptly started negotiating an alliance with the Ottoman empire. Meanwhile the rest of Europe cogitated on the possibility that James was a Machiavellian mastermind, who had used Frederick as a guise for inviting the Turkish hoard to ransack Rome. A year later, Frederick was ousted, following defeat at the battle of the White Mountain. A 'sad and grieved' James did have a prospective military

---

[45] Maria Anna was reputed to be the finest dancer in Europe. But she had no intention of marrying outside the faith, and her father King Philip IV was not much enamoured of the idea either. In the end, she married King Ferdinand of Hungary-Bohemia. Charles meanwhile travelled back via Paris, where he spied a consolation prize, Princess Henrietta Maria.

[46] For an account of the affair, and James's naivety, see Stewart, *The Cradle King*, 297–300.

[47] In the person of Frederick, already Elector Palatine.

intervention in Bohemia priced up, but the sum was prohibitive.[48] The king, it was reported, was disinclined to 'meddle' further in 'the affairs of Bohemia'.[49]

Union of Crowns

The final canvas is *The Union of Crowns*. It depicts Mars ushering two female figures into James's presence. Representing England and Scotland, they hold two crowns above the head of an infant, there in turn to represent the nascent 'union'[50]; the *dominus* of James Stuart and his progeny. James's imperial aspiration was layered. There was the 'inner' empire already carved out in the Reformation settlement. The Act in Restraint of Appeals 1532 had confirmed that 'whereas by divers sundry and authentic histories and chronicles it is manifestly declared that this realm of England is an empire, and so hath been accepted in the world, governed by one supreme head and king, having the dignity and royal estate of the imperial crown the same'.[51] Only a proper empire, the inference ran, could extricate itself from Rome.

And then there was an 'outer' empire still being sketched by an assortment of early-day global entrepreneurs and obliging pirates.[52] All part of the same ambition of course: to make Britain 'world-beating'. As Bacon confirmed, in 'the great frame of kingdoms and common-wealths, it is in the power of princes or estates to add amplitude and greatness to their kingdoms'.[53] Better still to establish 'plantations' – in Ireland, the Bermudas, wherever. Not just an 'heroical' and godly enter-prise, but also profitable.[54] James, invariably short of money, cleaved to profit. The various constitutional cases in which he became embroiled were commonly about it. *Proclamations* moved around 'fines' levied for

---

[48] £200,000 to raise, £1 million a year to keep an army in the field. Parliament offered a one-off subsidy of £160,000.

[49] Stewart, *The Cradle King*, 308–10.

[50] It has been speculated that the baby is modelled on the future Charles II. See Millar, 'Rubens' Whitehall Ceiling', 103.

[51] 24 Henry VIII, c. 12. A statement reaffirmed, the following year, in the Act of Supremacy 1534: 26 Henry VIII, c. 1. For a comment on the significance of Henry's imperial assertion, and the extent to which it served to develop a more conscious, and confident, 'England', see L. Greenfield, *Nationalism: Five Roads to Modernity* (Cambridge, MA, 1992), 30–5, 50–1.

[52] Or privateers as they were called, operating under Crown licence, or 'letters of marque'.

[53] F. Bacon, *The Essays* (London, 1985), 155.

[54] Ibid., 162.

building regulation and starch manufacture, *Bonham's Case* around licensing regimes for physicians, the *Commendams* around tithe income. Regardless of what legal nicety his chief justice dreamt up, James wanted his cut. The idea of a global empire was born of the same venality. Along, of course, with the collateral assurance that 'discovering' faraway lands, and then taking them over, was doing God's work.

James's most cherished concern, however, was discovered in sealing the 'inner' empire, more especially the union of his two crowns. An aspiration which Jonson had carefully flattered in the coronation pageant back in summer 1604. The very first 'triumphal' arch, at Fenchurch, was precisely on message. '*Orbis Britannicus, Divisus ab orbe*', to 'shew that this empire is a world divided from the world'.[55] James had already assured his Scottish Privy Council that the case for a 'perfect and sincere union' was now unarguable.[56] On arriving in England, he had established a Commission on Union, headed by Bacon and Ellesmere, to look into the practicalities of union.[57] It had returned three recommendations: abrogate 'hostile lawes', create a uniform commercial law, and establish a kind of common citizenship. At the same time, James issued a *Proclamation on the Post-Nati*. A *post-nati* was someone born in Scotland after James had succeeded to the English throne. Such a person, the proclamation confirmed, should acquire rights in English, as well as Scots, law, by virtue of their birth. James also asked Parliament to approve a statutory change of title, so that he might restyle himself King of 'Great Britain'.

To which the answer was no. England was a name of 'ancient reverence', as opposed to the dark age murkiness of 'Briton'. Undaunted, James issued a proclamation declaring himself King of 'Great' Britain and citing, by way of reason, cultural and religious commonality: 'A communitie of language, the principall meanes of civil societie. An unitie of Religion, the chiefest band of heartie Union, and the surest knot of lasting Peace.'[58] The proclamation had also confirmed that there would be some shiny new coins celebrating the new 'union', starting with a twenty-shilling piece, called the 'Unite'. 'James by grace of God King of Great Britain, France and Ireland', the obverse read. The reverse was inscribed with a no less hopeful bit of scripture. From *Ezekiel* 37:22, 'I will make them one nation'.

---

[55] Wormald, *James VI and I*, 355.
[56] Stewart, *The Cradle King*, 209.
[57] The Commission comprised forty-eight Englishmen and thirty-one Scots.
[58] In Wormald, *James VI and I*, 244.

Parliament retaliated by rejecting two bills proposed by the Commission. A first would have added statutory heft to the *Proclamation on the Post-Nati*. The second was intended to naturalise the *ante-nati*. By way of compensation, it would agree to a new flag; to become known as the 'Union Jack'.[59] But that was all Parliament was prepared to concede. The mood was uncompromising. Gervase Holles bemoaned a London full of swaggering Scotsmen sporting 'beggarly bluecaps'.[60] John Hoskyns regretted the £100,000 that James had gifted the same. No wonder the new King was broke.[61] Sir Christopher Pegge managed to get himself suspended from the House for claiming that there 'was as much difference between an English and a Scots man as between a judge and a thief'.[62]

James kept trying. The 'union' as an 'eternal agreement' between the two 'crowns' would seal the security of the realm, he advised Parliament in March 1607, and its prosperity in 'perpetuitie'. It would also help to further the cause of a broader legal 'reformation'.[63] Bacon advised his fellow members to reread their Livy. Was it not the case that classical Rome was 'best state of the world', and the happiest? 'Posterity' supposes that 'greatness' is scaled.[64] Shakespeare conceived *King Lear* in poetic support. At a mild tangent, James recommended that his critics peruse the 'mappes' of 'great Antiquitie', where the isle of 'greater' Britain was clearly 'described'.[65] All well and good. Ultimately, though, the fate of the prospective union would depend on politics not poetry. And by now attention was anyway turning to the courts, and more particularly a case involving a deracinated infant named Robert Colville.

Robert was just three years old, the grandson of an otherwise much more interesting man, James Colville, the famed 'Laird of Wemyss', mercenary, privateer, diplomat, and prime mover in helping to secure the succession of James Stuart. Robert's life was nothing like as exciting.

---

[59] Jack after *Jacobus*.
[60] Meaning woollen bonnets. The occupants of the Bedchamber were always a matter of peculiar concern, in every sense of the word.
[61] The King's 'cistern has sprung a leak', as Hoskyns put it to fellow Members of Parliament. Around £90,000 in gifts and a further £10,000 in pensions. Not to be repeated, James tried to assure Parliament. See Wormald, *James VI and I*, 47.
[62] Stewart, *The Cradle King*, 215.
[63] King James, *Political Writings*, 164.
[64] See Bacon, *Essays*, 3.94–6, making pointed comparison with Sparta, and its reluctance to extend rights of naturalisation, and also 3.313.
[65] In Wormald, *James VI and I*, 381.

Except, perhaps, to legal historians, for it was in Robert's name that the legal action was launched which would become known as *Calvin's Case*.[66] Little Robert was a *post-nati*, and the legal contention moved around whether, by reason of birth, he might thereby enjoy the legal rights of an Englishman. This was the precise issue which James had treated in his *Proclamation on the Post-Nati*. The converse argument supposed that he was an 'alien', whose status in English law would be dependent on some other form of naturalisation. This mattered, because if an 'alien' did not acquire this 'personality', Robert could not by right own or inherit property in England.

It was, Coke opined, the 'greatest' case 'that ever was argued in the hall of Westminster'.[67] And, for once, he was in obliging mood, agreeing with Attorney General Bacon that the 'law of nature is that which God at the time of creation of the nature of man infused into his heart, for his preservation and direction; and this is *lex aeterna*, the moral law, called also the law of nature', and it is by this law that the 'faith, ligeance, and obedience of the subject is due to his Sovereign or superior'.[68] Regardless of the disparity between respective legal systems, James embodied the supervening unity of his two crowns.[69] In his 1610 address to Parliament, an approving James revisited the same reasoning, to confirm that a 'generall union' of laws would not infringe the authority of English common law.[70] The applause was presumably polite. But there was no give. A decade on, James would write a *Meditation upon the 27, 28, 29 Verses of the xxvii Chapter of St Matthew*. Predictably doleful, the 'epistle dedicatory' confirmed that he was by now 'weary of controversies'.[71] And no controversy had been more wearying than that which attended the proposed union of crowns.

Resonances

History is always tempted by resonance. It may not repeat, as Mark Twain is said to have said. but it commonly rhymes. Four centuries have

---

[66] Calvin being an English-ised corruption of Colville.
[67] Preface to volume 7 of *Coke's Reports*, at iii.
[68] (1608) 7 Co. Rep. 1b–28a; 77 E.R. 377, 392.
[69] See here P. Price, 'Natural Law and Birthright Citizenship in *Calvin's Case*', *Yale Journal of Law and Humanities*, 96 (1997), 100–2, 123–8, gesturing towards a species of 'general' jurisprudence.
[70] King James, *Political Writings*, 173–4.
[71] In Wormald, *James VI and I*, 66.

passed since James Stuart died, in March 1625. It might be reasonably supposed that much has changed since then, and it has. There again we might also recall another aphorism, more familiar still: *Plus ça change, plus c'est la même chose*; the more things change, the more they stay the same. These were the words of Jean-Baptiste Alphonse Karr, minor French novelist of the nineteenth century, and renowned dahlia cultivator. Karr would not have been surprised to discover that pretty much the same constitutional stresses which agitated Jacobean England are those which agitate us today.

Starting with the idea of kingship. Successions tend to unsettle, so it is an apposite moment to contemplate, once again, the institution of monarchy; as the most recent King Charles settles into his role. Following a Queen Elizabeth, as we have already supposed, is never easy. At least James could fall back on the idea of 'divine right'. The idea of a God-given king is less credible today, in a godless age. So what are the alternatives? At his trial in January 1649, the last King Charles demolished the idea that his crown was 'elective'.[72] No one had elected him king. And no one has elected Charles III king either. The idea that the crown is legitimated by the constitution is plainly circular and gets us nowhere. At which point we are obliged to fall back on more prosaic possibilities, chiefly functional.

Walter Bagehot famously spotted an oddly consonant couple, apathy and entertainment. So long as the 'charmed spectacle' of the monarchy keeps us entertained, we will put up with it.[73] This is a rationale which intimates how we might spot the end of the British monarchy. Whilst astrologers of old would peer at the sky in the hope of spotting an ominous meteor, or pore over the entrails of slaughtered poultry, all we need to do is read the papers. We will know the end of the monarchy has finally arrived the first week that passes without a picture of Princess Kate adorning the front-pages of the tabloids, or the second week that we have lost track of what Harry and Meghan are doing – the measure of our 'childish' fascination with all things royal, as Bagehot put it.[74]

The second theme painted by Rubens was the 'peaceful reign'. Britain's place in Europe, or maybe just outside. James sensed the need to improve relations with his European neighbours because of the difficulties which had attended England's attempt to break with Rome seventy years earlier.

---

[72] See Ward, *Trials of Charles I*, 104–5.
[73] W. Bagehot, *The English Constitution*, ed. P. Smith (Cambridge, 2001), 30–1.
[74] Bagehot, *English Constitution*, 37.

The English Reformation had proved strangely hard to get 'done'. Or maybe not that strange, according to Bacon. In his *History of the Reign of King Henry VII*, Bacon supposed that the Henrician Reformation did 'so much busy the world' because nobody had thought through its consequences.[75] But then Henry VIII was not, by nature, a planner. His Brexit was a vanity project, necessitated by the fact that he wanted rid of his first wife, and was short of cash. And there was no surprise in discovering that when the difficulties became starkly apparent, Henry cast around for someone else to blame: all the 'remainers', as he tearfully asserted in his last speech to Parliament in 1547.[76] They had messed up England's Reformation, not him.

Not, of course, that James wanted to rejoin Catholic Europe, or at least he was not going to say as much. So instead, as we have noted, he decided to hover around the edges, offering himself up as an honest broker. This was the role that attracted Winston Churchill three and a half centuries later in recommending the formation of a European 'united states' after the Second World War. Britain would not join this incipient union of course; far too many foreigners. But it would lend a hand where it could. It took a generation to appreciate Churchill's misperception. The economic imperatives were unarguable, and Britain would have to join the 'common market'. Much as it took a generation for Stuart England to appreciate the futility of James's aspiration. Being on the edge of something means that you are part of it, not outside it. England's 'war of religion' finally broke out in spring 1640.[77]

Shakespeare's John of Gaunt famously declared England to be:

> This fortress built by Nature for herself
> Against infection and the hand of war . . .
> This precious stone set in a silver sea,
> Which serves it in the office of a wall,
> Or as a moat defensive to a house,
> Against the envy of less happier lands.
>
> (*Richard II*, Act 2, scene 1:43–4, 46–9)

But it is not. The English are just as likely to be visited by plague as anyone else, bubonic or coronaviral. And nor are they much 'happier'; certainly not now. Brexit Britain is a consummately poorer place, as well

---

[75] Bacon, *Essays*, 171.

[76] For commentaries here, see D. MacCulloch, *Thomas Cranmer* (New Haven, CT, 1996), 348; and J. Scarisbrick, *Henry VIII* (New Haven, CT, 1997), 471.

[77] J. Morrill, *The Nature of the English Revolution* (London, 1993), ch. 3.

as more fractious; its economy has sustained a 4 per cent retraction in GDP since exiting the Union, including an estimated £40 billion a year loss in tax take. It will probably rejoin the European Union at some point, for financial reasons if no other. Not yet though. It is the fate of a 'chosen' people to suffer, for a while at least.

And so to the third of Rubens's painterly themes, the 'union' of crowns. Not readily extricable, of course, from the first two. The rationale for a 'union' was, in considerable part, to make England more secure, or so James liked to counsel his critics. The building of an 'inner' empire providing the foundation, hindsight supposes, for an 'outer'. It would also serve to refurbish the idea of monarchy. Whilst there would be Acts of Union in 1707 and then again in 1800, the constitutional realisation of empire would have to wait until the passage of the Royal Titles Act in 1876, a sop intended to cheer up Queen Victoria and entice her to assume a more active role in public life.[78] It was in the same year that the Indian National Association was founded, the first step in a journey to independence which was realised in 1947. Most of the rest of Britain's 'outer' empire has gone the same way over the last century, leaving just a few scattered colonial outposts, alongside a loose confederation of 'commonwealth' countries, lots of nostalgia, and a fair bit of xenophobia.

And the 'inner' empire? Time will tell if Brexit strengthens the still-just-about United Kingdom, or conversely accelerates its fragmentation. Only the English voted to leave the Union, and the enactment of the European Union (Withdrawal) Act 2018 prompted motions of censure in each of the devolved assemblies. It is possible to discern the first signs of a prospective break-up of modern Britain, even before Brexit, in the passage of the 1998 devolution statutes. There again it is equally possible to argue that the same statutes are designed to stabilise the union. As James Stuart supposed, the entire point of a statutory 'union' of crowns was to secure the *imperium* of 'greater' Britain. It was not in the moment especially prescient, since the 'war of three nations' began when a Scottish army crossed the Tweed in summer 1640.

Arguments for independence continue in each of the constituent parts of the United Kingdom. But whilst they remain essentially sentimental in Scotland and Wales, Brexit has added a further, barely tractable,

---

[78] 39 & 40 Vict., c. 10. After an extended retirement following the death of Prince Albert in 1860. Amongst those concerned that the retirement might result in the end of the British monarchy was Walter Bagehot. The chapters on monarchy in his *English Constitution* were written as a caution: see Bagehot, *English Constitution*.

dimension in Northern Ireland; working out a way of securing an 'internal' market within the United Kingdom, whilst respecting the *acquis communitaire* of the European single market, and not compromising the terms of the 1998 Good Friday Agreement. The original withdrawal treaty included a specific protocol purposed to facilitate trade across the Irish 'border' with minimal customs intervention. Which the UK government almost immediately sought to renegotiate, along the way threatening an 'internal markets' bill designed to force the issue. The situation remains fluid, a newly devised 'Windsor framework agreement' only eventually helping to facilitate the reopening of the Northern Ireland Assembly in Stormont.

Brexit is not, of course, the sole cause of our present constitutional crisis. The role of the Crown, questions of executive accountability, the state of the 'union', each has a critical life aside from Britain's latest attempt to break with Rome. But Brexit is an accelerator, a constitutional Hadron collider. And it is at such moments that we incline to question the integrity of our constitution, and indeed our public life, more closely. Hindsight supposes that this was the case in 1616 when James fired his lord chief justice and set his nascent 'union' on the road to civil war – a Whiggish hindsight, of course. If we like our history to have an ironic twist, we might just project forward to the early afternoon of 30 January 1649, and imagine James's second son, Charles, taking a last glance at Rubens's ceiling before stepping through a Banqueting Hall window, and onto a specially constructed scaffold, to greet his executioner, and his own apotheosis.

6

A British Common Law?

Public Law after the 1707 Union between England and Scotland

ROBERT BRETT TAYLOR

Introduction

In the 1953 Scottish case of *MacCormick v. Lord Advocate*,[1] John MacCormick and Ian Hamilton sought to challenge the publication of a proclamation pursuant to the Royal Titles Act 1953 designating the new Queen's royal title as 'Elizabeth the Second of the United Kingdom of Great Britain'. Although there had previously been a Queen Elizabeth, she had reigned only in England, never in Scotland, and crucially before the creation of the Kingdom of Great Britain in 1707 in accordance with the Treaty of Union. According to MacCormick and Hamilton, therefore, the adoption of the numerals 'the Second' was contrary to Article I of the Treaty of Union which, being a fundamental condition of the Treaty, was *ultra vires* of the powers of the Westminster Parliament.[2] The case was dismissed by both the Outer House and Inner House of the Court of Session, albeit on different grounds,[3] with the Lord President (Lord Cooper) in the latter doing so in part on the basis that the Court of

The research underpinning this project was conducted by the author when he was undertaking a Visiting Scholarship at Edinburgh Law School, University of Edinburgh. The author is grateful to Edinburgh Law School for its support, in particular Professor John Cairns. He is also grateful to the Aberdeen Humanities Fund (AHF), the Society of Legal Scholars (SLS), and the Scottish Universities Law Institute (SULI) for supporting this research financially. The author would like to thank the organisers of the 2022 British Legal History Conference hosted at Queen's University Belfast for the opportunity to present an earlier version of this work, as well as to the participants for their constructive feedback. He would also like to thank Professor Adelyn Wilson for her helpful and supportive comments on an early draft.

[1] *MacCormick v. Lord Advocate* 1953 SC 396.
[2] Ibid., 401; 405–409.
[3] Ibid., 402–405 (Outer House Decision); 409–418 (Inner House Decision).

Session lacked the competence necessary to determine whether or not any governmental acts conform with the terms of the Treaty of Union.[4]

Despite this, however, the Lord President made a number of *obiter* remarks regarding parliamentary sovereignty which stood, and indeed still stand, in stark contrast to constitutional orthodoxy. Parliamentary sovereignty, he argued, 'is a distinctly English principle which has no counterpart in Scottish constitutional law', and he therefore found it difficult to understand 'why it should have been supposed that the new Parliament of Great Britain must inherit all the peculiar characteristics of the English Parliament but none of the Scottish Parliament'.[5] The Lord President also expressed strong support for the claim that some, but not all, provisions of the Treaty of Union are unalterable by Parliament, as well as dismay at 'English constitutional theorists' for viewing all provisions of the Treaty in the same way (and thus presumably alterable) despite some of them expressly stating that they are 'fundamental and unalterable in all time coming'.[6]

The Lord President's remarks regarding the fundamental nature of the Treaty of Union are significant, and as a result will be explored elsewhere. However, this chapter is concerned with what it views as the Lord President's underlying criticism of the post-Union constitution: the apparent conflation of English constitutionalism with British constitutionalism. The thrust of this argument was captured by MacCormick in his subsequent book, where he noted that '[t]hroughout the writings of all the English constitutional lawyers, and particularly those of Professor Dicey, there runs the arrogant assumption that the history of the Kingdom of England has been continuous from the Norman Conquest until the present day.'[7]

The Treaty of Union, which was given effect in both England and Scotland by legislation known as the Acts of Union,[8] was incorporating rather than federal in nature. The Kingdoms of England and Scotland were accordingly unified into the new Kingdom of Great Britain, which was to be governed by a unified Crown and Parliament.[9] Therefore, as a fusion of both England and Scotland, one might legitimately expect to see traces of

---

[4] Ibid., 413.
[5] Ibid., 411.
[6] Ibid.
[7] J. M. MacCormick, *The Flag in the Wind: The Story of the National Movement in Scotland* (London, 1955), 188.
[8] Union with Scotland Act 1707, 6 Anne, c. 11 (Parliament of England); Union with England Act 1707, *APS* xi 406, c. 7; 1706/10/ (Parliament of Scotland).
[9] Articles I–III.

both legal traditions reflected in Great Britain's constitutional arrangements. However, instead we find the predominance of the English tradition
of public law and, at the very least, the marginalisation of the Scottish.

Some scholars have attributed this predominance of English public law
to Article XVIII of the Acts of Union, which they argue preserved Scots
private law, but replaced Scots public law with English public law. W. L.
Mathieson, for instance, claimed that 'the public law of Scotland was to
be assimilated to that of England, but the law as to private right was not
to be altered except for the evident utility of Scotsmen'.[10] Andrew
Simpson and Adelyn Wilson have also argued the following:

> This new unified state would require a system of public law. This was set
> down in article eighteen. This new public law would need to apply not just
> within the borders of the two kingdoms but also in the various colonies.
> England's colonies already applied English law. In part that contributed to
> the decision that the public law of the new state would be English law.[11]

Although not explicit, A. J. MacLean's leading work on Scottish appeals
to the House of Lords post-Union was similarly concerned only with
Scots private law; the work's underlying assumption being that public law
posed no difficulties because it had been incorporated.[12]

However, other scholars have outright rejected this reading of Article
XVIII, arguing instead that it preserved not just Scots private law but
Scots public law also. J. D. B. Mitchell, for instance, argued that the Act of
Union 'did not unify even public law, it merely purported to place public
law more readily at the disposal of Parliament than private law'.[13] The
predominance of English public law is accordingly explained by a desire
for uniformity with English law.[14] Aileen McHarg has similarly argued
that Article XVIII 'did not actually require assimilation of Scots and
English public law, and in fact [the Act of Union] guaranteed the
continued existence of certain important Scottish institutions'.[15] As a

---

[10] W. L. Mathieson, *Scotland and the Union: A History of Scotland from 1695–1747*
(Glasgow, 1905), 116.

[11] A. R. C. Simpson and A. L. M. Wilson, *Scottish Legal History Volume One: 1000–1707*
(Edinburgh, 2017), 377. See also 381.

[12] A. J. MacLean, 'The 1707 Union: Scots Law and the House of Lords', *Journal of Legal
History*, 4(3) (1983) 50, 51.

[13] J. D. B. Mitchell, 'The Royal Prerogative in Modern Scots Law', *Public Law* (Spring 1957)
304, 319.

[14] Ibid., 319.

[15] A. McHarg, 'Public Law in Scotland: Difference and Distinction' in A. McHarg and T.
Mullen (eds.), *Public Law in Scotland* (Edinburgh, 2006), 3.

result, notwithstanding the 'considerable doctrinal assimilation' post-Union by Scottish judges,[16] '[e]lements of a distinct body of Scots public law have persisted ever since the Union with England in 1707'.[17]

Proponents of both accounts seldom, if ever, engage in debate with one another on this important matter. However, taking into account both positions, one would appear to be faced with a stark choice: either Scots public law remains separate and distinct post-Union, or it was replaced with English law. However, it is submitted that neither position alone is satisfactory in explaining the predominance of English public law post-Union. Instead, this chapter will seek to reconcile these opposing positions by presenting a new and original hypothesis of the Acts of Union which, it is submitted, provides a more coherent understanding of the post-Union constitution and the role of both English and Scots public law within it.

It will be shown that, upon the proper construction of its provisions, the Acts of Union, by necessary implication, created a unified British public law, which finds expression in the form of a unified British common law. Crucially, this unified British public law is only partial in nature, applying only to British-wide institutions, namely the Crown and Parliament, thus leaving other areas of public law open to variation between England and Scotland. Although the Acts of Union did not create a unified court system, the retention of the House of Lords (now the UK Supreme Court) as the highest appellate court on public law matters for England and Scotland, nevertheless enabled it to emerge as a de facto constitutional court for Britain, the decisions from which should be understood as binding in both jurisdictions. The content of this partially unified British public law is unquestionably English in nature, the result of a variety of factors, none of which entirely preclude the influence of Scots public law on its continuing development.

A Unified British Public Law?

The starting point for determining the extent to which the Acts of Union sought to unify public law across England and Scotland is Article XVIII, which stipulates the following:

> That the laws concerning regulation of trade, Customs, and such Excises to which Scotland is by virtue of this treaty to be liable, be the same in

---

[16] Ibid., 4.
[17] Ibid., 3.

Scotland from and after the union as in England, and that all other laws in
use within the kingdom of Scotland do after the union and notwithstanding thereof remain in the same force as before (except such as are
contrary to or inconsistent with this treaty), but alterable by the
Parliament of Great Britain, with this difference betwixt the Laws concerning public right, policy and civil government, and those which concern private right, that the laws which concern public right, policy and
civil government may be made the same throughout the whole united
kingdom, but that no alteration be made in laws which concern private
right except for evident utility of the subjects within Scotland.[18]

As noted above, Article XVIII is frequently credited by scholars for
preserving Scots private law whilst unifying the public law of Great
Britain by replacing Scots law with English law. Although it is clear that,
by using the term 'public right', '[t]he commissioners were clearly thinking of what would now be called constitutional law',[19] contemporary
sources nevertheless provide little insight into how Article XVIII and its
impact on public law was understood at the time of Union.[20] Daniel
Defoe, a prominent pamphleteer and spy at the time, in his assessment of
the alterations made to Scotland by Union, seems to suggest that the
effect of Articles XVIII and XIX was to preserve the private law of
Scotland whilst replacing its public law with that of England. As he
observed:

These clauses preserved the ordinary process of law, in case of private
right, in the same course and condition as before; but all pleas to the
Crown, matters of dispute between the Queen and subject, relating to the
revenue and trade, being to be the same as in England; for that reason,
there were necessary alterations to be made to the methods, and even new
models of proceedings to be formed, special to Scotland.[21]

---

[18] Act of Union 1707 (*Statutes of the Realm*, VIII, 566–577) as transcribed in D. Douglas
and A. Browning (eds.), *English Historical Documents Volume VIII 1660–1714* (London,
1953), 685.

[19] J. D. Ford, 'The Legal Provisions in the Acts of Union', *Cambridge Law Journal* 66(1)
(2007), 106, 108.

[20] Scottish parliamentarians were seemingly concerned with other matters, such as tax and
the legislative powers of the new British Parliament in relation to changing Scots private
law. See Sir John Clerk of Penicuik, *History of the Union of Scotland and England,
Extracts from His MS 'De Imperio Britannico' Translated and Edited by Douglas
Duncan* (Edinburgh, 1993), 101, 155–156 and 195.

[21] D. Defoe, *The History of the Union between England and Scotland, by Daniel De-Foe: with
an Appendix of Original Papers to Which Is Now Added a Copious Index* (London, 1786),
592.

However, Defoe's interpretation of public law in the context of Article XVIII appears broad, mostly concerned with commercial matters.[22] Furthermore, Defoe draws a distinction between Scotland's constitution and its laws,[23] and argues that Scotland's constitution was not dissolved by Union but only altered,[24] and even then seemingly only in relation to its institutions rather than in the substance of its laws.[25]

It is submitted that, upon close examination of the wording, Article XVIII did anything but create a unified body of British public law by extending English law to Scotland. Under Article XVIII, England's existing laws on trade, customs and excises were to apply to Scotland, thus unifying the law in these areas. However, it appears that the crucial trade-off for the Scottish commissioners in accepting this was that all other existing Scots law was to be preserved post-Union subject only to this difference between public and private law: (1) that public law – 'the laws which concern public right, policy and civil government' – may be made the same throughout the United Kingdom by the Parliament; and (2) that Scots private law was alterable only by the Parliament of Great Britain where for the 'evident utility of the subjects within Scotland'.[26] The Scottish commissioners also required that the Scottish court system be preserved post-Union.[27]

Far from imposing complete legal uniformity, therefore, the Acts of Union in fact secured legal pluralism: Scots private law, and by necessary implication English private law, were to remain separate and distinct. This was further reinforced by Article XIX which expressly preserved the Scottish court system and, again by necessary implication, the English court system also. Only the British Parliament could make any changes to Scots private law, and even then not without limitation – there is a clear threshold test for any such legislative alterations under Article XVIII. The same is not true for Scots public law.

---

[22] Ibid., 602.
[23] Ibid., 600–602.
[24] Ibid., 600.
[25] Ibid., 600–602.
[26] Act of Union 1707 (*Statutes of the Realm*, VIII, 566–577) as transcribed in Douglas and Browning (eds.), *English Historical Documents Volume VIII 1660–1714*, 685.
[27] Indeed, it was the Scottish commissioners who proposed much of the wording of what became Articles XVIII and XIX, both of which were accepted by the English commissioners. See *The Journal of the Proceedings of the Lds Commissioners of Both Nations in the Treaty of Union, Which began on 15th of April 1706, and was concluded on the 22d of July following. With the Articles then Agreed on* (Edinburgh, 1706), 26–27. See also Defoe, *The History of the Union between England and Scotland*, 148–152.

Article XVIII, except where 'contrary to or inconsistent with' the Treaty of Union,[28] expressly preserves Scots law in its entirety, including not only private law but also public law. However, in stark contrast to Scots private law, it is clear from the wording of Article XVIII that the new British Parliament has the power to make uniform all of public law, including therefore alterations to Scots public law, without limitation. Had it been the purpose of the Acts of Union to extend English public law to Scotland – an assimilation of a new body of British public law with English law – Article XVIII would likely have said so explicitly. The first part of Article XVIII, for instance, states that 'the laws concerning regulation of trade, Customs, and such Excises to which Scotland is by virtue of this treaty to be liable, *be the same in Scotland from and after the union as in England*'.[29] In stark contrast to public law, therefore, this wording shows a clear extension of England's laws on trade, customs and excises to Scotland, in effect transforming English law into British law.

Crucially, therefore, Article XVIII does not mandate that public law in the new Kingdom of Great Britain is to be made uniform, only that it is capable of being made so. This is further reinforced by the fact that Article XVIII is silent on the nature and content of any such unified British public law.

Furthermore, the continuation of English constitutionalism as British constitutionalism cannot be attributed to the unlimited power of the British Parliament to legislate on public law matters under Article XVIII. According to A. V. Dicey and R. S. Rait, for instance, Parliament, in accordance with the terms of Articles XVIII and XIX, seldom legislated to change Scots law post-Union, noting that 'Scottish opinion condemned the extension of English law to Scotland'.[30] Indeed, very few statutes have ever been passed imposing English law on Scotland generally, with the most notable example being the extension of the English law of treason to Scotland in 1708.[31]

Although certainly not precluded by the wording of Article XVIII, there is accordingly nothing within that Article which necessitates

---

[28] Act of Union 1707 (*Statutes of the Realm*, VIII, 566–577) as transcribed in Douglas and Browning (eds.), *English Historical Documents Volume VIII 1660–1714*, 685.

[29] Ibid. (emphasis added).

[30] A. V. Dicey and R. S. Rait, *Thoughts on the Union between England and Scotland* (London, 1920), 284.

[31] An Act for Improving the Union of the Two Kingdoms 1708 (The Treason Act 1708), 7 Anne c. 21. See also W. I. R. Fraser, *An Outline of Constitutional Law*, 2nd ed. (London, 1948), 330.

English public law becoming British public law. The inherently English nature of British public law, therefore, cannot be directly attributed to the wording of Article XVIII. We must accordingly look elsewhere for an explanation.

Partial Unification by Necessary Implication

It is submitted that any uniformity of public law post-Union arose by necessary implication from other provisions of the Acts of Union, specifically those provisions related to the creation of British-wide institutions, and was accordingly only partial in nature.

Article I declares '[t]hat the two Kingdoms of England and Scotland shall upon the first day of May ... and for ever after, be united into one kingdom by the name of Great Britain'.[32] Furthermore, Article III states '[t]hat the United Kingdom of Great Britain be represented by one and the same Parliament to be stiled [sic] The Parliament of Great Britain'.[33] Both of these provisions created British-wide institutions of government which replaced the pre-existing English and Scottish equivalents, namely the Crown and Parliament. As MacLean observes:

> In 1603 James VI of Scotland succeeded to the English throne. Constitutionally this Union of the Crowns was dynastic only. The crowns of Scotland and England remained separate and sovereign (with the national parliaments) in their respective countries ... This position was to change in 1707 because by it the sovereign powers of the two nations would be united into a common sovereignty. There would be one Monarchy, one imperial Crown and one parliament of Great Britain which would be the only sovereign power in Great Britain.[34]

The creation of a new Crown of Great Britain was, admittedly, implicit rather than explicit: the unification of the two Crowns of England and Scotland arises by necessary implication from the unification of the two kingdoms under Article I. This certainly appears to be the assumption under Article II, which settled the succession of 'the monarchy of the united kingdom of Great Britain'.[35] Furthermore, following the initial

---

[32] Act of Union 1707 (*Statutes of the Realm*, VIII, 566–577) as transcribed in Douglas and Browning (eds.), *English Historical Documents Volume VIII 1660–1714*, 680.
[33] Ibid., 681.
[34] MacLean, 'The 1707 Union', 60.
[35] Act of Union 1707 (*Statutes of the Realm*, VIII, 566–577) as transcribed in Douglas and Browning (eds.), *English Historical Documents Volume VIII 1660–1714*, 681.

approval of Article I by the Parliament of Scotland, George Lockhart, a Scottish commissioner but opponent of Union, noted criticism of what was described as 'an incorporating Union of the Crown and Kingdom of *Scotland* with the Crown and Kingdom of *England*'.[36]

Additional evidence of this unification can also be found with the abolition of the Scottish Privy Council in 1708. Article XIX stated that, 'after the Union, the Queen's Majesty and her royal successors, may continue a Privy Council in Scotland for preserving of public peace and order until the Parliament of Great Britain shall think fit to alter it or establish any other effectual method for that end'.[37] At the meeting of the first British Parliament in 1707, a Bill was accordingly passed abolishing the Scottish Privy Council and replacing it with the Privy Council of Great Britain, a rebranded and expanded English Privy Council,[38] on 1 May 1708.[39]

By contrast, the creation of a new British Parliament was considerably more explicit. For instance, Queen Anne's proclamation for the summoning of the first Parliament of Great Britain in June 1707 declared the following:

> [W]e, for many weighty reasons, have thought fit to declare by our royal proclamation ... that it was expedient that the Lords of Parliament of England, and Commons of the Parliament of England ... should be members of the respective Houses of the first Parliament of Great Britain for and on the part of England; and whereas in pursuance of an Act passed in the Parliament of Scotland ... sixteen peers and forty-five commissioners for shires and burghs, have been chosen to be the members of the respective Houses of the said first Parliament of Great Britain for and on the part of Scotland; we do by this our royal proclamation under the great seal of Great Britain ... declare and publish our will

---

[36] [G. Lockhart], *Memoirs Concerning the Affairs of Scotland from Queen Anne's Accession to the Throne, to the Commencement of the Union of the Two Kingdoms of Scotland and England, In May, 1707. With an Account of the Origine and Progress of the Design'd Invasion from France, in March, 1708. And some Reflections on the Ancient State of Scotland* (London, 1714), 253. In support, see also Defoe, *The History of the Union between England and Scotland*, 600.

[37] Act of Union 1707 (*Statutes of the Realm*, VIII, 566–577) as transcribed in Douglas and Browning (eds.), *English Historical Documents Volume VIII 1660–1714*, 687.

[38] P. W. J. Riley, *The English Ministers and Scotland 1707–1727* (London, 1964), 28.

[39] An Act for Rendering the Union of the Two Kingdoms more Intire and Complete 1707 (Union with Scotland (Amendment) Act 1707), 6 Anne c. 40. On the passage of the Bill in Parliament, see Clerk, *History of the Union of Scotland and England*, 204–205; and Riley, *The English Ministers and Scotland 1707–1727*, Chapter VII.

and pleasure to be, and do hereby appoint, that our first Parliament of Great Britain shall meet.[40]

Correspondence between Sidney, first Earl of Godolphin, and John, first Duke of Marlborough, the leaders of the English Ministry at the time of Union, reinforces this position, with Godolphin noting that: 'Tomorrow, the Queen declares in Counsell [sic] that this present Parliament, shall be the first Parliament of Great Britain which it's generally thought will have the construction of a new Parliament'.[41] Furthermore, it is clear from the Acts of Union that the British Parliament was not only a new institution, but one which was, at least in part, a hybrid Parliament of both its Scottish and English forebears. This is evident from the composition of the British Parliament and the election of its Scottish members.

Under Article XXII, as noted by Queen Anne in her proclamation above, Scotland was to be represented in the Parliament of Great Britain by sixteen peers in the House of Lords and by forty-five representatives in the House of Commons; determining the selection of these representatives was to be left to the Scottish Parliament. Subsequent legislation was accordingly passed which stipulated that the sixteen peers were to be elected from amongst the Scottish peers to represent Scotland in the House of Lords (which persisted until the Peerage Act 1963, section 4); and of the forty-five representatives of the House of Commons, thirty were to be selected from the shires and stewartries, with the remaining fifteen being selected from the royal burghs.[42] Furthermore, the pre-Union system for electing commissioners for the royal burghs largely continued post-Union until the Scottish Reform Act 1832.[43] Crucially, the wording of Article XXII reveals

---

[40] Proclamation summoning the first Parliament of Great Britain, 1707 (*London Gazette*, 5–9 June 1707) as transcribed in Douglas and Browning (eds.), *English Historical Documents Volume VIII 1660–1714*, 222.

[41] Godolphin to Marlborough [28 April 1707] Blenheim MSS. A2–23. as transcribed in H. L. Snyder (ed.), *The Marlborough-Godolphin Correspondence* (Oxford, 1975), 756–757.

[42] Election Act 1707, *APS* xi 425, c. 8; 1706/10/293. Restated under Article XXV of the Union with Scotland Act 1707, 6 Anne, c. 11 (Parliament of England). See Article XXV(VI) of the Act of Union 1707 (*Statutes of the Realm*, VIII, 566–577) as transcribed in Douglas and Browning (eds.), *English Historical Documents Volume VIII 1660–1714*, 693–695.

[43] Representation of the People (Scotland) Act 1832 (2 & 3 Will. 4), c. 65, s. X, printed under the original title of An Act to Amend the Representation of the People in Scotland 1832 available in *The Statutes of The United Kingdom of Great Britain and Ireland, 2 & 3 William IV 1832* (London, 1832), 387–388. See Dicey and Rait, *Thoughts on the Union between England and Scotland*, 49 and 246. See also R. Sutherland, 'Aspects of the Scottish Constitution Prior to 1707' in J. P. Grant (ed.), *Independence and Devolution: The Legal Implications for Scotland* (Edinburgh, 1976), 20–21.

another key characteristics of the new British Parliament inherited from its English predecessor: bicameralism. The Acts of Union do not explicitly say that the new British Parliament was to have two houses modelled on the English Parliament, but the reference to both the House of Commons and the House of Lords in Article XXII puts this beyond doubt. Structurally, therefore, the new British Parliament that emerged from the 1707 union between England and Scotland had characteristics of both of its predecessors, albeit to varying degrees.

Legally, therefore, neither the British Parliament nor the British Crown was a mere continuation of their English or Scottish predecessors, but were instead a unification of them resulting in the creation of entirely new institutions. These new institutions, in particular the scope of their powers, would need to be governed, as they always had been, by law. However, it is submitted that, by necessary implication, the creation of new British institutions under the Acts of Union would necessitate the unification of the law relating to them, thus constituting a partial unification of public law post-Union in the form of a new body of British public law. It is through this new body of public law that Britain's new institutions, the Crown and Parliament, would acquire additional characteristics, such as parliamentary sovereignty. It is further submitted that this new British public law would take the form of common law, thus creating a British common law.

A British Common Law

The common law – or judge-made law – is a source of law in all three legal jurisdictions of the United Kingdom. The jurisdiction of England and Wales, which applies English law, is undisputedly a common law system, as is Northern Ireland. Scotland, although a common law system since the twelfth century, is nevertheless considered to be a 'mixed' legal system due to the influence of Roman law, principally from the sixteenth century onwards.[44] Common law in turn is seen as a major source of law for the UK Constitution,[45] including, it is submitted, those laws governing its institutions, namely the Crown and Parliament.

The courts have routinely determined the existence and extent of the prerogative powers of the Crown, from the *Case of Proclamations*[46] in the

---

[44] See generally Simpson and Wilson, *Scottish Legal History Volume One: 1000–1707*.

[45] P. Leyland, *The Constitution of the United Kingdom: A Contextual Analysis*, 3rd ed. (Oxford, 2016), 27–28.

[46] *Case of Proclamations* (1610) 12 Co. Rep. 74.

seventeenth century to *Miller (No. 2)/Cherry*[47] in the twenty-first century. It is submitted that, because the Acts of Union unified the Crowns of England and Scotland into a single British Crown, there would have been by necessary implication a partial unification of the prerogative powers of both Crowns, at least in so far as they extended to matters related to the unified Kingdom of Great Britain and its Parliament. Consequently, although it is widely accepted that the law between England and Scotland is now post-1707 mostly the same on the prerogative,[48] minor variations remain possible,[49] especially so in relation to any private law application of the prerogative.[50]

The courts are capable of determining the powers of the British Parliament, most notably the doctrine of parliamentary sovereignty. This major constitutional principle has no statutory basis whatsoever, meaning that its legal basis as a feature of the British Parliament, at least in a formal sense, can only be attributed to the common law: the courts recognise and enforce parliamentary sovereignty, thus giving it its legal force.[51] Indeed, notwithstanding the above observations of the Lord President in *MacCormick v. Lord Advocate*, parliamentary sovereignty has been upheld consistently by both the English and Scottish courts alike.[52] Parliamentary sovereignty, although by no means the exclusive creation of the common law,[53] is nevertheless capable of modification by the courts.[54]

---

[47] *R (Miller) v. The Prime Minister; Cherry v. Advocate General for Scotland* [2019] UKSC 41, [2020] AC 373.

[48] See A. Tomkins, 'The Crown in Scots Law' in A. McHarg and T. Mullen (eds.), *Public Law in Scotland* (Edinburgh, 2006), especially 278–280.

[49] See in particular *Glasgow Corporation v. Central Land Board* 1956 SC (HL) 1, at 16. On this case, see Mitchell, 'The Royal Prerogative in Modern Scots Law', 305; T. B. Smith, *The British Commonwealth: The Development of Its Laws and Constitutions Volume I: The United Kingdom (Scotland)* (London, 1955), 658–659; and Tomkins, 'The Crown in Scots Law', especially 269–270.

[50] See Fraser, *An Outline of Constitutional Law*, 149: 'In so far as the prerogative concerns the public rights and positions of the Crown, it is probably identical in England and Scotland, although in the realm of private law it is not always the same'.

[51] See R. B. Taylor, 'The Contested Constitution: An Analysis of the Competing Models of British Constitutionalism', *Public Law* (July 2018) 500, 519.

[52] See A. Tomkins, 'The Constitutional Law in *MacCormick v. Lord Advocate*', *Juridical Review* 3 (2004) 213, 216–220.

[53] See J. Goldsworthy, 'Abdicating and Limiting Parliament's Sovereignty', *King's College Law Journal* 17(2) (2006) 255, 261. See also Taylor, 'The Contested Constitution', 519–520.

[54] See Taylor, 'The Contested Constitution', 520–521. See also Tomkins, 'The Constitutional Law in *MacCormick v. Lord Advocate*', 216–217.

Ideally, any such judicial pronouncements on the powers of these British institutions would need to be British-wide in order to ensure uniformity throughout the Kingdom, accordingly producing a new British common law in the field of public law. Otherwise, Britain would risk internal constitutional divergence.

However, there are two potential problems with this hypothesis which need to be addressed if it is to succeed: (1) the absence of a unified court system for Britain following the 1707 Union; and (2) the application of English common law to these British institutions by English and Scottish judges. Both of these issues will be addressed in turn.

No Unified Court System

Article XIX declares the following:

> That the Court of Session or College of Justice do after the Union and notwithstanding thereof remain in all time coming within Scotland as it is now constituted by the laws of that kingdom, and with the same authority and privileges as before the Union, subject nevertheless to such regulations for the better administration of justice as shall be made by the Parliament of Great Britain.[55]

By virtue of this provision, therefore, there is no unified British court system post-Union. Instead, the Scottish court system is expressly preserved, along with the English court system by implication. As a result of the separate court systems post-Union, courts in Scotland do not have to follow decisions of courts in England and vice versa, they are merely persuasive. As Robert Sutherland noted, '[t]he legislative and the executive functions of government may have been substantially merged by the Acts of Union but not the judicial'.[56] Taken in conjunction with Article XVIII, which preserved much of Scots law, the preservation of the Scottish court system makes apt sense: English law and Scots law are separate and distinct, thus necessitating equally separate and distinct enforcement mechanisms. It would make little sense for an English court, with little knowledge or experience of Scots law, to decide a matter of Scots law and vice versa.

However, although particularly applicable to private law, the same cannot be said of public law where the lack of a unified British court

---

[55] Act of Union 1707 (*Statutes of the Realm*, VIII, 566–577) as transcribed in Douglas and Browning (eds.), *English Historical Documents Volume VIII 1660–1714*, 686.
[56] Sutherland, 'Aspects of the Scottish Constitution Prior to 1707', 19. See also 18–19.

system risks constitutional divergence, thus undermining the case for a British common law. For this reason, Mitchell has in fact pointed to the lack of a unified court system under the Articles of Union as evidence of the absence of any such unified British public law. As he noted:

> [I]t is ... true that judicial precedent is of considerable importance, either as an original source of principle or as a secondary source, when the courts are interpreting a statute. Here again problems arise from the fact that the Union of 1707 was in some sense incomplete. Separate systems of courts were then preserved, and thus English decisions (outside revenue matters) are not binding upon Scottish courts, and it is possible for conflicting decisions to be arrived at in the different jurisdictions.[57]

However, it is submitted that Mitchell is mistaken in this view. Despite the Acts of Union not introducing a unified court system for Great Britain, they nevertheless made provision for – or at least did not expressly prohibit – the creation of an apex court for both England and Scotland post-Union: the House of Lords.

Article XIX, in addition to preserving the Scottish court system, also states that 'no causes in Scotland be cognoscible by the Courts of Chancery, Queen's Bench, Common Pleas or any other Court in Westminster Hall'.[58] This crucial element of Article XIX is sadly ambiguous: it is unclear what was intended by the words 'Westminster Hall'. One might conclude that, because it is not mentioned otherwise, it is referring to House of Lords, at the time the highest court in England, which of course sat in Parliament.

However, Dicey and Rait argued that this was not so. Whilst acknowledging that the words of Article XIX 'look full enough to exclude every possible intervention by any English court in any cause tried in Scotland',[59] they have nevertheless argued that the prohibition on appeals from Scotland to Westminster Hall cannot possibly be construed so as to include the House of Lords. As they observed:

> [T]he House of Lords neither was nor indeed is, a Court in Westminster Hall. It is a Court which exists wherever Parliament happens to be sitting, and the men living in 1706 and 1707, could, many of them, remember the meeting of an English Parliament, and a very notable

---

[57] J. D. B. Mitchell, *Constitutional Law*, 2nd ed. (Edinburgh, 1968), 23.

[58] Act of Union 1707 (*Statutes of the Realm*, VIII, 566–577) as transcribed in Douglas and Browning (eds.), *English Historical Documents Volume VIII 1660–1714*, 686.

[59] Dicey and Rait, *Thoughts on the Union between England and Scotland*, 192.

English Parliament, during the reign of Charles II, held not at
Westminster but at Oxford.[60]

Dicey and Rait, therefore, concluded that the commissioners had been
intentionally ambiguous in their wording, leaving open the question for
future generations, in order to ensure the passage of the Act of Union in
Scotland.[61] As they noted:

> For on the one hand it would probably be a benefit to Great Britain that it
> should possess one Court of Appeal to which important cases might be
> brought from every part of the British Kingdom for decision, whilst on the
> other hand it must have seemed highly imprudent, while the carrying of
> the Act of Union was in doubt, to raise a most irritating, though some-
> what speculative, question about appeals to the House of Lords.[62]

Dicey and Rait's reasoning seems to be that the Acts of Union, because
they did not explicitly preclude appeals from the Scottish courts to the
House of Lords, allowed the House of Lords to emerge as Britain's apex
court through subsequent practice.

MacLean, however, argues that it would have been 'obvious' to both
the Scottish and the English commissioners at the time that the House of
Lords would have the jurisdiction to hear appeals from the Court of
Session. Had this not been intended, the Scottish commissioners could
have remedied the matter during the passage of the Act of Union in the
Scottish Parliament of which they were members.[63] According to
MacLean, the post-Union writings of Sir John Clerk of Penicuik, one of
the Scottish commissioners for Union and later Baron of the Exchequer,
also imply that he supported the House of Lords being Britain's highest
civil and criminal court.[64] Indeed, the work of Defoe likewise suggests
that the House of Lords, as the 'the sovereign judicature of Great
Britain'[65] capable of hearing appeals from Scotland, was both discussed
and accepted by the English and Scottish commissioners for Union.[66]

Whatever the case may be, it is clear that Article XIX posed no real
obstacle to the granting of appeals from the Scottish courts to the House
of Lords post-Union.

---

[60] Ibid., 192.
[61] Ibid., 192–193.
[62] Ibid., 193. See also MacLean, 'The 1707 Union', 52.
[63] MacLean, 'The 1707 Union', 63.
[64] Ibid., 57.
[65] Defoe, *The History of the Union between England and Scotland*, 159.
[66] Ibid., 158–161.

In the case of civil appeals, and thus private law matters, the House of Lords started hearing appeals from the Court of Session – Scotland's highest civil court – shortly after union in 1707[67] and this has remained the case to this day, albeit now with the House of Lords successor the UK Supreme Court. This seemingly proved uncontroversial as the appeals from the Court of Session to the Scottish Parliament were possible pre-Union.[68]

In the case of criminal appeals, despite early indications to the contrary, the House of Lords by the end of the nineteenth century had established that they did not have the jurisdiction to hear appeals from the Court of Justiciary (this was later put on a statutory footing under the Criminal Procedure (Scotland) Act 1887).[69] This had been decided on the basis that there were no appeals from the Court of Justiciary to the Scottish Parliament in the immediate pre-Union period.[70] The decision was not taken, therefore, on the basis of the wording of Article XIX.

Intriguingly, therefore, the House of Lords quickly emerged as Britain's apex court on civil matters, although not for criminal matters, on the basis of continuity of practice pre-Union to post-Union.

However, the impact of permitting Scottish appeals to the House of Lords is largely unclear. Dicey and Rait, for instance, do not comment on the extent of any changes to Scots law as a result, but were of the view that '[s]uch assimilation as has arisen is one of the beneficial effects of the House of Lords being a final Court of Appeal from decisions both of the Scottish Court of Session and of the English Courts of Common Law and of Equity'.[71] By contrast, T. B. Smith noted that, '[t]hough the House of Lords was almost overwhelmed in the late eighteenth century and early nineteenth century with Scottish appeals, the Lords' decisions had little impact on the content of the law itself'.[72] Whatever the truth, both of these assessments appear restricted to the impact of the House of Lords on private law appeals from Scotland. What then of public law?

---

[67] See generally MacLean, 'The 1707 Union'

[68] See Fraser, *An Outline of Constitutional Law*, 223.

[69] See A. J. MacLean, 'The House of Lords and Appeals from the High Court of Justiciary, 1707–1887', *Juridical Review* (1985) 192.

[70] See N. Walker, *Final Appellate Jurisdiction in the Scottish Legal System* (Scottish Government, Edinburgh, 2010), 22–23. For contemporary arguments for and against this position see generally MacLean, 'The House of Lords and Appeals from the High Court of Justiciary, 1707–1887'.

[71] Dicey and Rait, *Thoughts on the Union between England and Scotland*, 330.

[72] T. B. Smith, 'Scottish Nationalism, Law, and Self-Government' in N. MacCormick (ed.), *The Scottish Debate: Essays on Scottish Nationalism* (London, 1970), 40.

Constitutional matters tend to be discussed as part of judicial review (although they are certainly not limited to this court action). Judicial review is a civil court matter and thus subject to appeal to the UK Supreme Court (formerly the House of Lords) in both England and Scotland. On matters of public law, therefore, the UK Supreme Court is the highest court for both jurisdictions. As argued above, the Acts of Union, in creating British institutions, by necessary implication unified the law governing such institutions, thus creating a British common law. Accepting this, it logically follows that the post-1707 decisions of the House of Lords (and later the UK Supreme Court) on such public law matters should be treated as equally binding in both England and Scotland, no matter which jurisdiction the action originates from. This suggests, it is argued, that the House of Lords, now the UK Supreme Court, has in fact been a de facto constitutional court for Britain since 1707.

However, Neil Walker has argued that 'in formal terms, even the Supreme Court itself, like the predecessor House of Lords, is not one court but many, its umbrella status speaking not only to its functional versatility but to its variety of formal identities as an English, Scottish and Northern Irish court'.[73] In reaching this conclusion, he relies on section 41(2) of the Constitutional Reform Act 2005, which states that '[a] decision of the Supreme Court on appeal from a court of any part of the United Kingdom, other than a decision on a devolution matter, is to be regarded as the decision of a court of that part of the United Kingdom'.[74] According to Walker, '[t]his suggests that, when read properly, the section provides that the new Supreme Court should be seen as a Scottish court applying Scottish law'.[75] However, although section 41(2), along with the recognition of a distinct devolution jurisdiction for the UK Supreme Court,[76] might appear to support such a conclusion, it is submitted that this is not the case.

Section 41(1) states that '[n]othing in this Part is to affect the distinction between the separate legal systems of the parts of the United Kingdom'. Walker has noted that this provision 'can be interpreted differently',[77] meaning that, whilst it is clear the UK Supreme Court sits

[73] Walker, *Final Appellate Jurisdiction in the Scottish Legal System*, 19.
[74] Ibid., 23–24.
[75] Ibid., 24.
[76] Constitutional Reform Act 2005, s. 41(3).
[77] Walker, *Final Appellate Jurisdiction in the Scottish Legal System*, 25.

as a Scottish court in cases brought from Scotland, 'what is less clear is the extent to which and the circumstances under which it will apply Scottish law as a distinct body of law'.[78] According to Walker, this is due to the considerable similarities in substantive law between Scotland and the rest of the United Kingdom, whether by the influence of English common law on Scottish cases, or through imposition by UK-wide statute.[79] Following this, it is submitted that the same would naturally be true of any unified British public law arising by virtue of the Acts of Union: the UK Supreme Court sitting as the highest Scottish court in civil matters, applying not Scots public law but British public law. It is nevertheless conceded that any such determinations by the UK Supreme Court would not, under Walker's reading of section 41(2) at least, make them binding precedent in the United Kingdom's other jurisdictions, although it is submitted that they would likely be so persuasive as to make the distinction largely academic.

However, as confirmed by the Explanatory Notes, it is important to stress that section 41 is concerned primarily with ensuring that the decisions of the UK Supreme Court have the same effect within the different legal jurisdictions of the United Kingdom as the previous decisions of the House of Lords and the Judicial Committee of the Privy Council.[80] Section 41(2) achieves this with regard to the House of Lords by stating that decisions of the UK Supreme Court on appeal are 'to be regarded as the decision of a court of that part of the United Kingdom'. However, although this guarantees that decisions of the UK Supreme Court appealed from Scotland are binding in Scotland, they are crucially not jurisdictionally limited; section 41(2) is silent on whether the UK Supreme Court in making such a decision is sitting as a Scottish court only, or as a UK-wide court with jurisdiction in Scotland. This will vary, it is submitted, depending on the area of law being determined.[81]

When determining a matter of either private law or public law, as per Articles XVIII and XIX of the Acts of Union, the UK Supreme Court's jurisdiction will rightly be restricted to the place from which the case was

---

[78] Ibid., 24–25.

[79] Ibid., 24.

[80] Constitutional Reform Act 2005, Explanatory Notes, para. 162.

[81] See Walker, *Final Appellate Jurisdiction in the Scottish Legal System*, Appendix III, especially 67–68. Walker acknowledges that s. 41(2) is vague on whether the UK Supreme Court sits as a Scottish court or a UK Court but leaves open the question of what impact either interpretation could have on precedent.

appealed.[82] However, when determining a matter of public law which relates to the Crown and Parliament, by necessary implication from Articles I and III of the Treaty of Union, the UK Supreme Court's jurisdiction will be wider, meaning that the decision should be binding in the other jurisdiction also.

Consequently, because section 41 is concerned with preserving the pre-UK Supreme Court jurisdiction of the House of Lords, and in the absence of any express or implied intention to the contrary, it is submitted that section 41 likewise preserves, as part of the UK Supreme Court, the constitutional jurisdiction of the House of Lords arising from the Acts of Union. For these reasons, therefore, section 41 of the Constitutional Reform Act 2005 is no barrier to either the existence of British public law or indeed to the role of the UK Supreme Court as a de facto constitutional court.

Indeed, the UK Supreme Court has certainly in recent times increasingly found itself making decisions about the constitutional arrangements of the United Kingdom regardless of which jurisdiction the case originated from. For instance, in *Miller (No. 1)*, concerning an appeal from England and a referral from Northern Ireland, the UK Supreme Court held that the UK government could not trigger Article 50 of the Treaty on European Union (TEU) using the royal prerogative without first receiving authorisation from Parliament in the form of an Act of Parliament.[83] In so doing, the Court noted that '[s]ome of the most important issues of law which judges have to decide concern questions relating to the constitutional arrangements of the United Kingdom'.[84] Likewise, in *Miller (No. 2)/Cherry*, on appeal from both England and Scotland, the UK Supreme Court held that the Prime Minister's prorogation of Parliament was unlawful, with the Court stating the following:

> Although the United Kingdom does not have a single document entitled 'The Constitution', it nevertheless possesses a Constitution, established over the course of our history by common law, statutes, conventions and practice. Since it has not been codified, it has developed pragmatically, and remains sufficiently flexible to be capable of further development. Nevertheless, it includes numerous principles of law, which are

---

[82] Constitutional Reform Act 2005, Explanatory Notes, para. 164. The example given here to illustrate the effect of s. 41(2) is clearly one of a purely private law nature.

[83] *R (Miller) v. Secretary of State for Exiting the European Union* [2017] UKSC 5, [2018] AC 61.

[84] Ibid., at [4].

enforceable by the courts in the same way as other legal principles. In giving them effect, the courts have the responsibility of upholding the values and principles of our constitution and making them effective. It is their particular responsibility to determine the legal limits of the powers conferred on each branch of government, and to decide whether any exercise of power has transgressed those limits.[85]

It therefore seems likely that, by virtue of the Acts of Union, the House of Lords (now the UK Supreme Court) has become a de facto constitutional court, creating binding precedent for both England and Scotland. Despite this, the arrangement is still not without its challenges. Crucially, the UK Supreme Court can only determine matters which are appealed to it, and not every constitutional case brought in either England or Scotland is appealed to the UK Supreme Court for final determination.[86] This means that variations in the application of British public law between England and Scotland remains possible.

English Public Law as British Public Law

Accepting that a body of British common law on public law matters emerged post-Union, and that the House of Lords (now the UK Supreme Court) emerged as Britain's apex court capable of ruling on this body of public law for the whole country, we must now seek to understand why this new body of British law is seemingly indistinguishable from English law, accepted and applied by English and Scottish courts alike.

It is submitted that there would have been a strong compulsion towards uniformity of public law post-Union. Although Mitchell attributed much of the adoption of English rules in Scotland to a 'desire for uniformity',[87] he was nevertheless of the view that this went beyond the terms of the Acts of Union themselves. As he noted: '[T]here has been some readiness to concede too great a scope to the Act of Union ... It is certainly not possible to regard that Act as compelling uniformity though clearly the circumstances which resulted from it would tend to induce that result'.[88] Indeed, although the terms of Article XVIII did not unify

---

[85] *R (Miller) v. The Prime Minister; Cherry v. Advocate General for Scotland* [2019] UKSC 41, [2018] AC 61 at [39].

[86] See for example *Wightman v. Secretary of State for Exiting the European Union* [2018] CSIH 62.

[87] Mitchell, 'The Royal Prerogative in Modern Scots Law', 319.

[88] Ibid., 319. See also 308: 'It is ... arguable that the effect of this legislation [Act of Union] has been greater than its terms warrant'.

public law, some have suggested that the provision was nevertheless relied upon by Scottish judges to extend English public law to Scotland.[89]

However, as demonstrated above, the Acts of Union by necessary implication unified public law in relation to Britain's shared institutions. As a consequence of this, and contrary to the view taken by Mitchell, it is submitted that the Acts of Union themselves would have compelled greater uniformity of law in relation to those shared institutions. This, it is argued, is precisely what occurred in the case of *Macgregor v. Lord Advocate* in relation to the Crown, where Lord Justice-Clerk stated the following:

> We have had no argument as to what was the effect of the Union of the two Kingdoms in 1707; but it seems to me that the legislation that then took place almost necessarily resulted in this, that the position of the Crown in such matters must be the same on both sides of the Border. Accordingly, although few questions have arisen, the English decisions have been accepted as correctly expressing the law of Scotland.[90]

The consequence of this uniformity was predominantly the extension of English rules to Scotland. Smith, for instance, argued that English law had a major impact on the development of constitutional law in Scotland since Union,[91] 'especially in questions which affect the United Kingdom as a whole'.[92]

Although a compulsion towards partial uniformity of public law can be attributed to the Acts of Union, uniformity of this law along English lines cannot be. Why then did both English and Scottish judges, in a desire for uniformity, adopt English rules in relation to Britan's shared institutions?

England was, and indeed remains, a bigger legal jurisdiction to that of Scotland. It seems likely, therefore, that England, as the larger of the two legal systems, on matters of shared interest such as the British Crown and Parliament, would exert the greatest influence on the development of British public law.

Smith has argued that the influence of English law on Scots law has been both direct and indirect.[93] The House of Lords, he argues, where

---

[89] See A. O'Neill, 'Parliamentary Sovereignty and the Judicial Review of Legislation' in A. McHarg and T. Mullen (eds.), *Public Law in Scotland* (Edinburgh, 2006), 197.

[90] *Macgregor v. Lord Advocate* 1921 SC 847, at 851–852. See also 852–853 per Lord Salvesen.

[91] T. B. Smith, *Studies Critical and Comparative* (Edinburgh, 1962), 129–130.

[92] Ibid., 129.

[93] Ibid., 116–136.

English peers greatly outnumbered Scottish peers, would have exerted a direct influence over the law of Scotland in those cases brought before it.[94] Indeed, it was not until the nineteenth century that lay peers were prohibited from hearing appeals to the House of Lords,[95] with expertise in Scots law prior to this also lacking.[96] As a result, it is perhaps unsurprising that such a historically English-dominated court would apply English public law on British matters, in turn creating binding precedent for England and Scotland which is English in nature.

By contrast, Smith argues that the use of English precedent in Scottish courts post-Union will have given English law an indirect influence over the law of Scotland also.[97] It is submitted that, in a public law context, this should only have been the case in relation to decisions not originating from the House of Lords; decisions from the House of Lords, as argued above, should be treated as binding in both England and Scotland, although it is conceded that Scottish judges may not have been conscious of this, instead treating such authority as highly persuasive. As Smith argued: 'Since there is a common court of appeal from the civil courts of England and of Scotland to the House of Lords, it is natural enough that, when the English courts have pronounced upon a problem which later arises in Scotland, the English solution will in many cases be listened to with respect'.[98]

However, it is submitted that the adoption of English public law by both English and Scottish judges would have been the natural choice based, at least for a time, on its merits. Unlike Scotland, which is a mixed legal system, England is a purely common law one, which even by 1707 was stable and well-established. English constitutional principles were likewise well-established both politically and legally, including, for instance, the doctrine of parliamentary sovereignty, which also had no clear Scottish alternative.[99] This was in large part due to the fact that it was the English courts rather than the Scottish courts which, before Union, had the opportunity to hear and decide such matters. This was due to the Union of the Crowns in 1603, whereby King James VI of Scotland, in also becoming King James I of England, moved from

[94] Ibid., 122–125. See also MacLean, 'The 1707 Union', 68.
[95] Fraser, An Outline of Constitutional Law, 223–224.
[96] Smith, Studies Critical and Comparative, 122–123.
[97] Ibid., 125–127.
[98] Ibid., 126.
[99] See C. Kidd, 'Sovereignty and the Scottish Constitution before 1707', Juridical Review 3 (2004) 225.

Edinburgh to London. James, and his successors, remained in England thereafter, and as a result had questions over the scope of the Crown's prerogative powers determined by English rather than by Scottish courts. As Mitchell has noted: 'Differences in history have meant that the general issues of prerogative did not come before the courts in Scotland in the same way and at the same time as they did in England, and the conflicts of opinion were resolved by other means and in other places'.[100] The net result of this, it is submitted, was that English law had answers to constitutional questions which Scots law did not, hence their adoption post-Union by both English and Scottish courts in response to questions concerning the British Crown and Parliament.

However, it must be stressed that the adoption of English constitutionalism as British constitutionalism is neither permanent nor indicative of the demise of Scottish constitutionalism. Any British common law is in effect a shared legal space where its content could, and indeed should, be shaped by the legal traditions of its constituent jurisdictions. There is accordingly nothing preventing the Scottish courts from contributing to the continuing evolution of the law governing Britain's shared institutions. As demonstrated above, Scots public law, so far as it was not inconsistent with any of the terms of the Acts of Union, survived post-Union. Although it will ultimately be up to the UK Supreme Court to make the final determination, there is nothing preventing the Scottish courts from revisiting such law, or indeed from developing new law post-Union.

Furthermore, it should be stressed that the body of British common law advanced here, although dealing with constitutional matters of fundamental importance, is nevertheless limited in scope to the law governing Britain's shared institutions only. Scots public law can therefore develop differently to that of English public law in all other matters, and indeed already has.

Judicial review, for instance, is the most notable area of divergence between England and Scotland in the field of public law. Historically, the test for standing in Scotland had been title and interest rather than sufficient interest as in England; sufficient interest only became the test in Scotland following the 2011 decision of the UK Supreme Court in *Axa General Insurance v. Lord Advocate*,[101] which was subsequently put on a statutory footing in the Courts Reform (Scotland) Act 2014. Although the test under English law and Scots law is now sufficient interest, and

---

[100] Mitchell, 'The Royal Prerogative in Modern Scots Law', 307.
[101] *Axa General Insurance v. Lord Advocate* [2011] UKSC 46, [2012] 1 AC 868.

both are focused on interests rather than rights, each are capable of independent development, and thus divergence. In stark contrast to England, Lord Hope's tripartite test in *West v. Secretary of State for Scotland*[102] also means that private bodies, and not just public bodies, can fall under the supervisory jurisdiction of the courts in Scotland. Furthermore, the Scottish courts have also recently developed a new and distinct public law action of declarator.[103]

It is submitted that the reasons for this divergence between English law and Scots law can be clearly attributed to the Acts of Union. As argued above, Scots public law was explicitly preserved post-Union by Article XVIII. Because the courts were also preserved and not unified under Article XIX, they could still develop their own rules, both private and public, post-Union. Consequently, this divergence provides clear evidence of there being a distinct body of Scots public law post-Union, but one which crucially does not extend to Britain's shared institutions, thus also providing further evidence, it is submitted, of a unified body of British public law.

Conclusion

The above analysis has shown that, upon the proper construction of the Acts of Union, public law after 1707 was partially unified under a British common law in relation to the Crown and Parliament, which the House of Lords (now the UK Supreme Court) was empowered to make determinations on for the whole of Britain; public law was otherwise kept separate and distinct in England and Scotland, subject only to the sovereignty of Parliament. In so doing, this chapter has presented a more coherent understanding of the post-Union constitution and the role of both English and Scots public law within it. This in turn provides a clearer framework from which Scots public law may continue to develop independently of English public law, but where it may also contribute to the continuing development of British common law which, although traditionally influenced by English public law, is nevertheless a shared legal space which can be shaped by both legal traditions.

---

[102] *West v. Secretary of State for Scotland* 1953 SC 396.

[103] See R. B. Taylor, 'Preserving the Rule of Law in Public Law Cases: *Keatings v Advocate General for Scotland and the Lord Advocate*', *Edinburgh Law Review* 25 (2021) 231 and R. B. Taylor, 'Public Law Declarators, the Jurisdiction of the Court, and Scottish Independence: *Keatings v Advocate General*', *Edinburgh Law Review* 25 (2021) 362.

7

Quo Warranto and the Borough Office Holder, 1700–1792

KEVIN COSTELLO

In 1713, members of the Whig faction in the Wiltshire borough of Calne, who had been denied a seat by reason of the presence of fifteen ineligible burgesses on the electoral roll, considered their next move. They decided against using the conventional process of a petition to the partisan House of Commons Committee on Privileges and Elections, 'despairing of relief from that Parliament'.[1] Instead, they decided on the more novel course of taking their case to the Court of Queen's Bench by way of a prosecution for quo warranto under the recently enacted Municipal Corporations Act 1711[2] – where they ultimately managed to disqualify the illegally appointed burgesses.

Prosecutions by way of quo warranto under the Municipal Corporations Act 1711[3] became a regular feature of the eighteenth-century English parliamentary electoral cycle. The common resort to the 1711 Act was related to three features of the unreformed electoral system. First, eligibility to vote in the parliamentary boroughs was often confined to a small group of office holders: aldermen, common councillors, capital burgesses, or common freemen. In small boroughs with very few voters and very small majorities, the elimination of even a small number of office holders could affect the outcome of a parliamentary election. Second, litigation was encouraged by the lack of a centralised legal framework regulating eligibility to office (and the derivative title to vote in parliamentary elections). The law regulating election to borough offices was usually local and customary and, as a result, often uncertain.

The author gratefully acknowledges the financial assistance provided by the University College Dublin, College of Social Sciences and Law Research Funding Scheme.
[1] S. Handley, 'Calne 1690–1715' in D. Hayton and E. Cruickshanks (eds.), *History of Parliament: The House of Commons, 1690–1715, Vol. II* (Cambridge, 2002), 651, n. 9.
[2] 9 Anne c. 20.
[3] Ibid.

The quo warranto information provided a means of determining these controversies over the exact content of these customs. Third, the pre-existing means of challenging the title to vote was by means of a post-election petition to the House of Commons Committee of Privileges and Elections. However, the Committee was notoriously partisan.[4] Petitioners who were affiliated with the majority party in Parliament would likely prevail; petitioners attached to the opposition were likely to lose.[5] The quo warranto information provided those who, like the candidates from Calne, '[despaired] of relief' from Parliament with a means of independent judicial review of eligibility overseen by the Court of King's Bench.

The Criminal Information and Admission to Borough Office, 1690–1711

Between 1690 and 1711, two types of criminal prosecution, initiated by an information in the Court of King's Bench, had been deployed against disqualified officers, and against those who had admitted them to office: (i) an ordinary criminal information and (ii) an information by way of quo warranto. Ordinary prosecution by way of criminal information lay, according to the rather open-ended test, 'wherever a matter concern[ed] the public government'.[6] In 1697, a criminal prosecution was taken against a member of the Council of Six of Nottingham for presiding without having taken the oath prescribed by the Corporation Act 1661.[7] In 1699, burgesses from Maldon and Malmsbury were prosecuted for failing to take the oaths of office and for participation in an illegal assembly at which alderman and burgesses were elected.[8] In Hilary term 1703, Edward Northey initiated criminal prosecutions against Richard Vavasor for taking office in Totnes[9] without observing the Toleration

---

[4] W. A. Speck, '"The Most Corrupt Council in Christendom": Decisions in Controverted Elections 1702–1742' in C. Jones (ed.), *Party and Management in Parliament* (Leicester, 1984), 107, 108.

[5] Ibid.

[6] *Mr Prynn's Case* (1690) 5 Mod. 459.

[7] *R v. Cooke* (1699) (PRO, KB 11/18); 13 Car. II, c. 1.

[8] *R v. Bartlett* (1699) and *R v. Abraham Huggins* (1699) (PRO, KB 11/18 (Box 1 (Trin 1699)).

[9] (1703) (PRO, KB 28/4, no. 16); Privy Council Register, 11 May 1704 (PRO, PC 2/80, f. 112).

Act 1688,[10] and against Edward Seabrooke for, as mayor, illegally creating freemen in the town of St Albans.[11]

The criminal information by way of quo warranto had developed in the early sixteenth century[12] as a mechanism for dealing with the abuse of franchises by the grantees of franchises devolved to local entities by the crown. There was a legal condition that 'annexed to, and grew upon all franchises, that they be not abused'.[13] Exercising 'liberties privileges and franchises' beyond that granted by the charter was one form of abuse and a criminal offence. The penalties included exclusion from the franchise.[14] The sanction of permanent removal from the franchise could be more effective than the simple fine which might be imposed following an ordinary criminal information.[15] In 1546, a quo warranto information was taken against the borough of Reading for admitting ineligible persons as burgesses.[16] In 1699, a quo warranto information was taken against the mayor of Holt in Denbigh for illegally admitting non-resident freemen.[17] The previous year, the borough of Hertford had illegally created honorary freemen to vote in the interest of the Tory faction and to outvote the non-conformist Whig resident freemen. The Attorney General, Sir Edward Northey, explained that a prosecution by way of information in the nature of quo warranto could be used to restrict the corporation from continuing the practice:

> if an information be exhibited against the corporation in the nature of a quo warranto for claiming a right to make persons not inhabiting within the borough free of that corporation, the corporation must either disclaim such right or set out a title to it on which a judgment will be given, to allow the claim, or to oust them from such right, if the matter shown in the plea shall be adjudged sufficient.[18]

[10] (1688) 1 Wil. & Mar., c. 18.
[11] (1703) (PRO, KB 28/4, no. 18).
[12] H. Garrett-Goodyear, 'The Tudor Revival of *Quo Warranto* and Local Contributions to State Building' in *On the Laws and Customs of England; Essays in Honour of Samuel E. Thorne* (Chapel Hill, NC, 2011), 231, 232; C. Patterson, 'Quo Warranto and Borough Corporations in Early Stuart England' *English Historical Review*, 120 (2005), 879.
[13] *R v. City of London* (1682) 8 Howell State Trials 1039, 1087.
[14] See the text at n. 23 below.
[15] See the text at nn. 6–11 above.
[16] (1546) (PRO, KB 29/178, 34d); Garrett-Goodyear, 'The Tudor Revival', 294.
[17] (1699) (PRO, KB 11/19 (Box 1/Trin 1699). In 1705, a quo warranto information issued against the parish of Chard for purporting to act as a corporation: *R v. Donne* (1705) (PRO, KB 28/14, no. 7).
[18] Opinion of Edward Northey, 29 December 1698 (Hertford Record Office, Hertford Borough Records, Vol. 25, f. 26).

A second strain of quo warranto information, of which there were instances in the late seventeenth century,[19] was revived in a series of prosecutions initiated by Edward Northey in the middle of the first decade of the eighteenth century. A wider understanding of the idea of a franchise underlay this form of quo warranto prosecution. On a narrower view, a franchise was understood as a right that might be directly conferred on the borough by the Crown by a grant: for instance, the right of a borough to elect a mayor or the right to admit burgesses. On a wider view, the notion of a franchise also included the electoral offices derived from the greater franchise: the franchise of being a mayor or being a burgess. This theory of a derivative franchise enabled the institution of the second variety of quo warranto information: for exercising the 'liberty, privilege and franchise' of being a borough officer without having been lawfully appointed. In Easter 1705, Northey laid an information charging Daniel Whidby with exercising the 'liberty privilege and franchises' of acting as mayor of Orford without lawful authority.[20] In 1706, quo warranto informations were initiated against Henry Cocksedge for exercising, without being lawfully elected, the franchise of capital burgess of Thetford,[21] and against Peter Clarke for assuming the office of capital burgess of Devizes.[22] Being a lawfully entitled capital burgess was, according to the charge in these cases, a 'liberty franchise and privilege'. It followed that exercising that borough officer franchise without 'any warrant or royal grant' was amenable to criminal prosecution. As the range of defendants amenable to the quo warranto information was extended – from the immediate franchisee to those who purported to be appointed by that franchisee – so too was the remedy. Corporate officers who asserted the liberty privilege and

---

[19] In proceedings lasting between 1680 and 1683, the defendants were prosecuted for illegally exercising the office of alderman in Winchester. *R v. Higgins* (1682) 1 Vent. 366. The link between the Winchester case and the early eighteenth-century prosecutions was identified by Paul Halliday in *Dismembering the Body Politic* (Cambridge, 1998), 201–204.

[20] (1705) (PRO, KB 28/13, no. 25).

[21] (1706) (PRO, KB 28/19, no. 29). The process was also used against individuals illegally claiming to be members of craft guilds. In *R v. Critchlow* a quo warranto was issued against a defendant claiming to be member of the Coventry Drapers' Company (1706) (KB 21/27, f. 70).

[22] (1706) PRO KB 28/20, no. 18 *R v. Clarke* (1706) Wiltshire Records Office (G 20/1/90 (7)). In *R v. Foley* the defendant was prosecuted for claiming the right to vote for the bailiff in Bewdley (1706) (PRO, KB 28/18). See Halliday, *Dismembering the Body Politic*, ch. 9.

franchise of being a corporate officer without lawful authority now became liable to the traditional quo warranto penalty of exclusion from office.[23] Henry Cocksedge, a Thetford burgess, was fined 40 shillings and was, in addition, ousted from the office of burgess of Thetford.[24] The effect of the notion of the secondary franchise was that constituency managers could now use the criminal information, and its sanction of exclusion, as a voter suppression strategy in parliamentary elections.

In 1711, the new process was given a legislative basis: the Municipal Offices Act 1711.[25] In *R v. Taylor*,[26] more than twenty years later, the origins of the 1711 Act were explained as related to doubts about the capacity at common law of the Court of Queen's Bench, when processing a quo warranto information, to issue a judgment of ouster. The process by information was criminal. The defendant might be fined; but, it was said, a criminal court, trying an information, had no power to impose the civil sanction of excluding a defendant from office. According to Barnardiston's report, the barrister John Willes recollected that '[b]efore the Statute of 9 Ann[e] ... it was far from being a clear point, that judgments of ouster could ever be entered up in informations in the nature of a quo warranto. Lord Chief Justice Holt declared his doubts of it often'.[27] The suggestion that Holt CJ should have 'declared his doubts ... often' about the jurisdiction to order ouster is difficult to reconcile with contemporary legal practice or with Holt CJ's own rulings. Since the early seventeenth century, judgments of ouster or ('excludatur') had been inserted when individuals or corporations were prosecuted by way of quo warranto for illegally asserting privileges and franchises.[28] In 1709, Holt CJ ordered that a burgess from Thetford 'should be ousted of his office'.[29] A decade earlier, Holt CJ actually declared that a judgment in an information in the nature of quo warranto would be positively irregular without 'an ouster of the particular franchise'[30] – an

---

[23] *R v. Helden* (1610) Edward Coke, *Book of Entries* (London 1614), 527; *R v. Fitzwater* (1676) John Tremayne, *Pleas of the Crown* (London, 1773), 446.

[24] (1706) (PRO, KB 28/19, no. 29); *R v. Turner* (PRO, KB 28/21, no. 11); *R v. Sharpe* (PRO, KB 28/23, no. 45).

[25] 9 Anne c. 20.

[26] (1733) 2 Barn. KB 280.

[27] Ibid. 281.

[28] See *R v. Helden*; Coke, *Book of Entries*; *R v. Fitzwater*; Tremayne, *Pleas of the Crown*.

[29] *R v. Tyrrill and Barber* (1709) 11 Mod. 235 referred to in *R v. Bennett* (1717) 1 Strange 101.

[30] *Banbury's Case* (1695) 3 Salk. 213.

assertion which was virtually the opposite of Holt CJ doubting the jurisdiction to order ouster.

Parliament's claim of exclusive jurisdiction in electoral matters may have provided a more urgent need to underpin the process with a legislative foundation. In *Goodwin v. Fortescue*,[31] in 1604, the Court of Chancery had annulled the election of Sir Francis Goodwin (on the ground of his being an outlaw). The House of Commons protested against the interference of the Court of Chancery, arguing that Parliament had 'ever used to appoint special committees ... for examining controversies concerning elections'.[32] Parliament's objection was conceded by James I. The problem was that the quo warranto information against voters appeared to offend this injunction: the information was being used to determine the right of electors other than in the Commons. The principle in *Goodwin's* case was then underscored by Parliament's response to the decision of the Court of Queen's Bench in *Ashby v. White*.[33] In *Ashby*, the Court of Queen's Bench had resolved that a returning officer who illegally denied the right to vote to an eligible voter could be sued by the elector in a civil action. The House of Commons, in turn, denounced the decision of the Court of Queen's Bench as an infringement of its privileges to determine electoral disputes, and condemned prosecutions which brought the 'right of electors to the determination of any other jurisdiction'.[34] The language used by the Commons in January 1704 could be seen as a direct repudiation of the quo warranto information, about the admission of non-resident freemen, which was being prosecuted in the Court of Queen's Bench against the corporation of Hertford;[35] by that information, the Court of Queen's Bench was 'determining' the right of a group of 'electors' (non-resident freemen). The Commons statement went on to threaten consequences for lawyers who, by prosecuting an information, infringed the resolution. Lawyers, it declared, who 'shall commence or prosecute any information, which shall bring the right of electors to the determination of any other jurisdiction' were to be regarded as 'guilty of a high breach of the privilege of this House'.[36]

---

[31] (1604) 2 St Tr. 91.
[32] Ibid. 104.
[33] (1703) 2 Ld Raym. 938.
[34] 26 January 1704, 14 *Commons Journals* 308 (26 January 1704).
[35] (1703) 12 Mod. 224. See Opinion of Edward Northey, above.
[36] 26 January 1704, 14 *Commons Journals* 308 (26 January 1704).

The 1704 resolutions contained a proviso: electoral disputes could be determined elsewhere 'in cases especially provided for by act of parliament'. The House of Commons could agree to cede by legislation part of its own exclusive right to determine 'the qualification of any elector'. This was precisely what Parliament did when in 1711 it enacted the Municipal Offices Act.[37] In 1711 leave was given to Sir Gilbert Dolben, Serjeant Webb, and Sir Robert Eyre, the Solicitor General, to prepare a bill for 'the more easy trying and determining the rights of officers in corporations'.[38] The 1711 Act provided parliamentary authority for the common law process and removed the conflict with Parliament. Section 4 provided that after the first day of Trinity term 1711, 'in case any person or persons shall usurp, intrude into, or unlawfully hold and execute any of offices or franchises' within boroughs or towns corporate 'it shall and may be lawful' for the court to 'proceed therein in such manner as is usual in cases of information in the nature of a quo warranto'.

The House of Commons and the Quo Warranto Information, 1708–1735

After 1711, the two processes of the petition to the House of Commons Committee of Privileges and Elections[39] and the quo warranto information operated concurrently. Occasionally, the two processes came into conflict. A direct conflict could arise where the Committee's determination on voter eligibility contradicted an earlier quo warranto judgment. In the first of these conflicts, the Commons chose to ignore a prior King's Bench judgment. The borough of Bewdley had split; it was reported that the factions attached to two rival bailiffs were acting 'like rival popes'.[40] The question as to which of the mayors had a legal title to act depended, in turn, on the question of which of two charters (one of 1605 or a later charter) governed the borough; that question had been determined in quo warranto proceedings in 1708 in Smith's Case[41] in favour of the

---

[37] 9 Anne c. 20.

[38] 16 *Commons Journals* 450 (9 January 1710/11). Serjeant Webb was the MP and Recorder for Devizes and had been implicated in quo warranto proceedings in 1706 (*R v. Clarke* (1706) Wiltshire Records Office (G 20/1/90 (7)). In *R v. Williams* (1757) 1 Wm Bl. 93. Foster noted that the Act had been drafted by Justice Powell.

[39] Speck, 'The Most Corrupt Council in Christendom', 107, 108.

[40] J. Burton, *A History of Bewdley* (London, 1883), 45.

[41] (1708) (PRO, KB 28/26, no. 1).

older 1605 charter.[42] The Committee on Privileges, however, refused to abide by the judgment in the quo warranto case, finding that the bailiff elected under the subsequent charter was lawfully elected.[43]

Parliament again pushed its superior claim to determine the legality of elections in 1729 in a case from Queenborough.[44] The validity of the election of the (Tory) MP, Richard Evans, depended on the votes of newly admitted burgesses. Those burgesses had been admitted at a meeting of the mayor, jurats and bailiffs, but without the concurrence of the existing free burgesses. On an information in the nature of quo warranto in 1728,[45] it had been held that the election was invalid because it did not have the concurrence of the free burgesses. Counsel for the petitioner opened the judgments entered up in the King's Bench in 1728. As it had done twenty-one years earlier, the Commons refused to be bound by the King's Bench and, notwithstanding the verdict on the quo warranto, ruled the election valid.

Eventually, in the Marlborough election dispute of 1735, the House of Commons conceded the superior validity of the quo warranto judgment. By 1735, Sir Robert Walpole's majority had been cut by thirty-four seats. The government was anxious to reverse its defeat at Marlborough. It could do this if it could disqualify ten of the burgesses who had voted for the Tories. The validity of the admission of those ten burgesses depended, in turn, on the validity of the election of a capital burgess named Bell.[46] The problem for the government was that the matter had already been tried by quo warranto and a jury had found that Bell had been properly admitted. Although the jury in quo warranto proceedings had found that Bell had been properly elected, the committee, urged on by Sir Robert Walpole, ruled that it could admit evidence in contradiction of the verdict.[47] The 1708 Bewdley precedent and the 1729 Queenborough petition were produced. The diarist William Hay MP set out the Committee's reasoning:

> The sole right of judging and determining their own elections is one of their most essential privileges and it would be highly imprudent to suffer themselves to be precluded from determining the merits of the election by

[42] 'Anthony Lechmere and Salvey Winnington ... The Case' (London, 1710), 1.
[43] 8 February 1709, Orders Determinations and Resolutions of the House of Commons (London, 1741), 11.
[44] 21 *Commons Journals* 325, 326, 327 16 & 17 April 1729.
[45] (1728) PRO, KB 21/33, ff. 61, 85.
[46] Edward Harley's Journal, 28 March 1735 in *Tory and Whig: The Parliamentary Papers of Edward Harley* (Martlesham, 1998), 7.
[47] 22 *Commons Journals* 435, 28 March 1735.

verdicts and judgments in inferior courts which are in the last resort to be
decided by the House of Lords.[48]

Walpole's behaviour appalled a number of the more senior lawyers in the
Commons. The Solicitor General, Dudley Ryder, deliberately withdrew
from the House rather than be seen to be associated with Walpole.[49]
A last moment intervention by the elderly Master of the Rolls, Sir Joseph
Jekyll, against his own government, persuaded the House of Commons to
dis-continue its conflict with the Court of King's Bench. Edward Harley
reported that the seventy-three-year-old Jekyll 'spoke so very strong of
the consequences of hearing evidence at the bar contrary to a verdict on
quo warranto'.[50] The effect was decisive. In deference to the verdict in the
quo warranto, the Commons voted, in line with the verdict at Wiltshire
Assizes, to sustain the qualification of the Tory burgesses at
Marlborough. Jeckyll's intervention in favour of the superiority of the
Court of King's Bench upset both the Prime Minister and Queen
Caroline.[51] Edward Harley recorded that 'this was a great blow upon
the court'.[52] Following the 1735 ruling, decisions in quo warranto proceedings began to be admitted as evidence in committee petition hear-
ings. In January 1769, counsel in a petition against William Strode (the
MP for Yarmouth Isle of Wight) produced records of the Court of King's
Bench on quo warranto prosecutions tried at the previous Lent Assizes in
Winchester. These judgments established that twenty of the burgesses
who had voted for Strode had been illegally admitted.[53] The evidence was
admitted and Strode was unseated.[54]

The 1711 Act and Its Prosecutors

Prior to 1711 the decision to allow an information to be exhibited was
entirely at the discretion of the Crown. In 1703, the Queen's Bench
advised a petitioner that 'your way will be to petition the Queen, and
she perhaps will order the Attorney General to bring a quo warranto

---

[48] C. Jones, 'Lord Bruce and the Marlborough Election Petition of 1735', *Parliamentary History* 38 (2019), 362; Speck, 'The Most Corrupt Council in Christendom', 107–21.
[49] Speck, 'The Most Corrupt Council in Christendom', 107, 116.
[50] Edward Harley's Journal, 28 March 1735, 7.
[51] John Lord Hervey, *Some Materials towards the Reign of George II, Vol. 1* (London, 1931), 418.
[52] Edward Harley's Journal, 28 March 1735, 7.
[53] 32 *Commons Journals* 122, 19 January 1769.
[54] Ibid.

against them'.[55] One of the objects of the 1711 Act was to avoid the informer's dependence on the government. Section 4 of the Act broke the prerogative by authorising the master of the King's Bench to exhibit a quo warranto information 'at the relation of any person or persons desiring to sue or prosecute'. The phrase 'any person' was, in practice, interpreted as allowing an application to be made by 'any person' acting on behalf of the actual prosecutor. The actual prosecutor, 'on behalf' of whom the application was made, was usually concealed behind the name of an attorney. James Clear of Gray's Inn fronted an Ipswich-related case in 1773,[56] while all of the challenges made against Portsmouth burgesses in the 1770s were submitted by Peter Taylor of Pall Mall.[57] In 1785, Mansfield CJ, noticing how the real prosecutor had concealed himself behind the relator, teased the prosecutor: 'who are you? What concern have you with the corporation?'[58] The usual answer to the question 'who are you?' was, of course, parliamentary candidates and their managers. A series of quo warranto applications in Droitwich in 1747 were reported to have been taken by Thomas Foley MP and his friends on the one side and Lord Sandys and Mr Winnington on the other.[59] In 1758, the Poole MP Sir Richard Lyttleton was alleged to have secretly funded a series of quo warranto prosecutions.[60] 'Partisans' of the unsuccessful parliamentary candidate, Alexander Fordyce, lay behind several quo warranto challenges in Colchester in the late 1760s.[61] Some quo warranto prosecutions were financed by the government. In the 1740s, Sir Robert Walpole's administration financed quo warranto campaigns aimed at eliminating opposition influence in the boroughs of Orford and Romney.[62] An attorney, Leonard Martin, the son-in-law of the Treasury Solicitor, usually acted as relator in these government-backed quo warranto applications.[63] In the early 1770s, it was alleged that Frederick Rogers, the prosecutor in a case involving the borough of Saltash, was acting under 'the direction and at the expense of the Treasury'.[64]

[55] *Vaughan v. Company of Gunmakers* (1703) 6 Mod. 82.
[56] (1773) (PRO, KB 28/286, no. 9).
[57] (1774) (PRO, KB 28/290, nos. 5 to 7).
[58] *R v. Stacey* (1785) 1 Term Reports 1, 3.
[59] Re Borough of Droitwich, William Penrice, 27 January 1749/50 (PRO, KB 1/10/2).
[60] Re Borough of Poole, John Mansfield, 22 November 1758 (PRO, KB 1/13/5).
[61] *Oxford Journal*, 30 July 1768.
[62] *Cobbett's Parliamentary History of England*, Vol. 12 (London, 1812), 631, 633.
[63] (1741) (PRO, KB 28/156, rot. 4).
[64] Re Borough of Saltash, Affidavit of John Hill 16 January 1772 (PRO, KB 1/18/4).

The Quo Warranto Process and the Electoral Cycle

From the early 1720s onwards, the eighteenth-century English general election was usually held in the spring. As the date of the election drew nearer, it was essential to the effectiveness of the electoral quo warranto information that it work with dispatch. The mayor, who would serve as the returning officer on election day, had usually been elected the previous autumn, typically on St Michaelmas day.[65] The prosecutor needed to be able to remove the illegally appointed mayor between Michaelmas and the election in the late spring. Under the pre-statutory version of quo warranto, the defendant had been able to retard the process by a delay in entering an appearance. In Hertford-based litigation in 1699, the defendants had avoided entering an appearance for a year; Holt CJ described the common law process as like 'church-work, very slow in its progress'.[66] The 1711 Act was designed to work at a more accelerated pace than the common law remedy: Mansfield CJ described the 1711 Act as the statute 'for quickening the amotion of usurpers'.[67] Under the pre-statutory form of the prosecution, the prosecutor would have to obtain writs of *capias* and of *distringas* to compel the defendant's appearance.[68] The 1711 Act cut out this requirement and substituted a condition that the defendant 'shall appear and plead as of the same term in which the ... information ... shall be filed'. It did not specify what was to happen if the defendant did not plead within the term. The Court of King's Bench remedied that omission by interpreting the 1711 Act as allowing the court to give judgment in default where a defendant failed to appear and plead after four rules.[69] If the prosecutor managed to have the case ready for trial at the spring assizes, the officer, whose title was disputed, might possibly be removed in time for the general election later that spring. In Hilary 1734, an information was laid against an Oxford burgess, Benjamin Beart. Pleadings were exchanged and the case tried at Easter assizes, where the defendant was fined and ousted.[70] Of course, most

---

[65] Worcestershire: *R v. Higgins* (1681) T. Raym. 484; Carlisle: *Haddock's Case* (1680) T. Raym. 435; Orford: *R v. Goodwyn* (1694) Comb. 269; Guildford: *Mayor of Guildford v. Clarke* (1690) 2 Vent. 247.

[66] *R v. The Town of Hertford* (1704) Carth. 503.

[67] *R v. Dawes* (1767) 1 Wm. Bl. 634, 635.

[68] *R v. Compson* (1707) (PRO, KB 28/21, no. 36); *R v. Cocksedge* (1707) (PRO, KB 28/23).

[69] *R v. Stephens* (1734) (PRO, KB 28/128, no. 26); *R v. Fussell* (1734) (PRO, KB 28/129, no. 7). A 1722 Crown Office note of the practice is set out *R v. Ginever* (1796) Term Rep. 594 (n. 2).

[70] (1734) (PRO, KB 28/128, no. 4).

cases were still determined outside four months; prosecutions were invariably delayed by adjournments, references by the judges of assize to the Court of King's Bench and by writs of error.[71] Borough officers with dubious titles were aware of the danger of being ousted by the accelerated procedure under the 1711 Act and took steps to evade the process. The mayor elected for Scarborough in the autumn of 1738 refused to appear in his robes in public during the Michaelmas term in order 'to prevent informations being brought against [him] in time for trial at lent assize'.[72]

The Grounds of Review by Quo Warranto

While the borough charter established the basic constitutional framework of the borough, key legal issues about the legal conditions of eligibility to borough office (and thereby to vote in parliamentary elections) often remained unaddressed in the charter. The charter of the borough of Southwold was 'silent' as to who was to administer the oath of office to a newly elected burgess.[73] In a 1733 case from Walsall, it was noted that no provision was made by the charter as to what period of notice of the holding of a borough election was necessary.[74] Aston J noted that most charters 'unhelpfully' failed to set out the conditions for election as a burgess or freeman.[75] A dispute in Maidstone over the method of election of the jurats was caused, the Solicitor General explained, by the fact that the 'penning of the charter of Elizabeth leaves it uncertain'.[76] In a case involving the conditions to be elected chamberlain for the borough of Nottingham, Mansfield CJ complained that 'the charters are totally silent'.[77]

To fill the silences in charters, boroughs resorted to custom. In 1742, Lord Romney said that the political community in the boroughs never read the charters but simply relied upon what their predecessors did in similar cases in the past.[78] The grounds of judicial review by way of quo

---

[71] *R v. Trew* (1734) (KB 28/128. no. 2) (adjournment); *R v. Seward* (1734) (KB 28/128, no. 9) (delay by writ of error).

[72] Benjamin Fowler, 27 October 1739 (PRO, KB 1/6/3).

[73] *R v. Wake* (1728) 1 Barn. KB 30.

[74] *R v. Corporation of Walsol* (1733) Kel. W. 245.

[75] *R v. Carter* (1774) 1 Cowp. 220.

[76] *R v. Corporation of Maidstone* (1739) (Lincoln's Inn, Hill 16, f. 108).

[77] *Derby Mercury*, 7 February 1777.

[78] *The History and Proceedings of the House of Lords, from the Restoration in 1660, to the Present Time, Vol. 8* (London: 1741–43), 502.

warranto information usually involved allegations of infringements of this customary election law. There were three broad categories of infringements: (i) that the officer was not eligible to be nominated; (ii) that the election was not by the proper electoral college; or (iii) that the manner of the holding of the election had infringed customary rules.

Mayors could be prosecuted by quo warranto information on the ground that they had not satisfied some condition of eligibility. In 1748, the title of the mayor of Wareham was challenged on the ground that the mayor had not, in accordance with the customary requirement, first been lawfully elected as a capital burgess.[79] Prior service as sheriff was alleged to be a condition of mayoral eligibility in Poole; the title of John Masters was challenged on the ground that he had not served as sheriff.[80] A number of prosecutions were based on an infringement of a requirement that the candidate for mayor had been a burgess.[81] A dispute in Westbury in 1742 arose from an allegation that there had been an infringement of the convention that the nominees for mayor should be two councillors selected by the current mayor.[82]

Most charters would authorise the corporation to elect 'one or more of the discreet men of the borough, to be a burgess or burgesses', but without specifying the conditions for being recognised as a 'discreet man'.[83] Eligibility to be elected to the office of burgess or freeman was usually claimed through two customary routes: servitude (having served for seven years as an apprentice to a freeman) or patrimony (being born the eldest son of a current freeman). Attorneys employed to contest freemen claiming title through servitude would consult the entries of apprenticeship in corporation books or would obtain testimony from neighbours prepared to vouch that the freeman had not served for the full seven years.[84] Church registers and freemen admissions rolls were checked in order to disprove title by patrimony by showing that the defendant's father had been admitted on a date later than, rather than before, the birth of his son.[85] The titles of a series of Portsmouth

---

[79] Daniel Dugdale, 6 May 1748 (PRO, KB 1/9/5); *R v. Lewis* (1758) 2 Keny. 497 (New Radnor).

[80] Benjamin Skutt, 17 October 1748 (PRO, KB 1/9/6).

[81] *R v. Mayor of Weymouth* (1740) 7 Mod. 373.

[82] *R v. Hillier* (27 November 1742) (PRO, KB 1/7/5).

[83] *R v. Carter* (1774) 1 Cowp. 220, 226.

[84] *R v. Fenn* (1768) (PRO, KB 28/266); *R v. Lilly* (1768) (PRO, KB 28/266); *R v. Rowe* (1769) 4 Burr. 2287.

[85] Re Borough of Colchester, Affidavit of John Casketter (10 May 1768) (PRO, KB 1/17/4).

burgesses were challenged on the ground that they had been children when they were first admitted.[86] The claim of the Corporation of Exeter to elect non-residents as freemen was the subject of a prosecution in 1730[87]; similar challenges were taken against the Corporation of Durham in 1767[88] and the Corporation of Portsmouth in the mid-1770s.[89]

A second category of dispute involved more far-ranging constitutional questions about which borough constituency could exercise electoral rights. Freemen were becoming increasingly assertive in claiming political rights. The legality of a Maidstone by-law which excluded the 900 male inhabitants who made up the 'commonalty', was the basis of a series of quo warranto challenges in the 1760s.[90] A Helston by-law which removed the voting rights of the freemen was the subject of a prosecution in 1772.[91] A dispute in Yarmouth involved the issue of whether the power of election of capital burgesses belonged to the manorial court or to the common burgesses meeting in the guildhall.[92]

A third category involved disputes about the administration of the election meeting. An appointment in Appleby was challenged in 1723 on the ground that the meeting had not been held in the 'Moot-Hall but at a tavern and it was a plain surprise'.[93] Failure to provide proper notice of the election was a common ground of challenge.[94] An election of capital burgesses in Bury St Edmunds was challenged on the ground that the custom that the hall keeper, or the serjeants at mace, gave one or two days' notice of a pending meeting ('in order to prevent surprise') had been infringed.[95] In Wigan, in 1773, it was alleged that the normal custom of ringing the bell loudly for seven minutes before an assembly for the admission of burgesses had been disregarded.[96] In Grampound, in

[86] R v. Bladen (1774) (PRO, KB 28/290, no. 6); R v. Carter (1774) Lofft. 516 & 1 Cowp. 58.
[87] R v. Heath (1730) 1 Barn. KB 416.
[88] R v. Vane (1767) (PRO, KB 28/261).
[89] R v. Monday (1777) 2 Cowp. 530.
[90] R v. Spencer (1766) 3 Burr. 1827; R v. Cutbush (1768) 4 Burr. 2204; A Short Treatise on the Institution of the Corporation ... of Maidstone from the year 1 757 to the Present Time (Maidstone, 1786), 17–20.
[91] R v. Head (1770) 4 Burr. 2515; Hoblyn v. The King (1772) 2 Bro. PC 329.
[92] R v. Leigh (1767) (PRO, KB 28/260, no. 2).
[93] Musgrave v. Nevinson (1723) 1 Str. 584.
[94] R v. Tucker (1727) 1 Barn. KB 26 (Lyme Regis).
[95] Re Bury St Edmonds, Affidavit of Orbell Ray and John Challis (25 April 1744) (PRO, KB 1/8/2).
[96] Re Borough of Wigan, Affidavit of John Jackson and others (29 April 1776) (PRO, KB 1/20/4). R v. May (1770) 5 Burr. 2681 (Saltash) is another instance.

1741, it was reported that the mayor had sworn freemen 'at a private meeting between him and some of his friends ... with an interest to multiply votes at the [general] election'.[97] The legality of the election of burgesses at Wigan was disputed on the ground that the bailiff was not present at the election meeting.[98] An election by less than the prescribed quorum provided clear grounds for quo warranto. Borough elections at Evesham in 1728, and at Yarmouth in 1760, were challenged on the ground that a majority of the aldermen and capital burgesses were absent.[99] The election of the mayor of Westbury, and the election of burgesses at meetings at which that mayor presided, were disputed by a quo warranto on the grounds of 'the major part of the legal common or capital burgesses not being present at such nomination or election'.[100]

The majority of prosecutions resulted in the targeted officers either disclaiming or being ousted. In the year preceding the 1761 general election, over 95 per cent of those prosecuted either disclaimed or were ousted.[101] In the year preceding the 1768 general election, the figure was over 80 per cent[102]; for the 1774 election, the figure was 60 per cent.[103] A large number of defendants simply disclaimed office rather than fight the quo warranto challenge. All of the twenty-four Ipswich freemen prosecuted in 1773 conceded rather than fight the quo warranto.[104] Defendants were deterred by the expense: the cost of their own legal representation as well as the risk of having to pay the other side's costs (which could vary between £50 and £200).[105] A borough member from

---

[97] Re Borough of Grampound, Affidavit of William Carkeet (4 November 1741) (PRO, KB 1/7/3).
[98] R v. Latham (1764) 3 Burr. 1485.
[99] Re Borough of Evesham, Robert Cook (21 November 1732) (PRO, KB 1/3/4); Francis Halford, 2 January 1733 (PRO, KB 1/3/4); R v. Grimes (1770) 5 Burr. 2598.
[100] Re Borough of Westbury, John Withers, 4 February 1749 (PRO, KB 1/10/1).
[101] This figure is based on the quo warranto prosecutions recorded in PRO, KB 28/233 (Easter 1760) to PRO, KB 28/237 (Easter 1761).
[102] The figure is based on the quo warranto prosecutions recorded in PRO, KB 28/261 (Easter 1767) to PRO, KB 28/265 (Easter 1768).
[103] The figure is based on the prosecutions recorded in PRO, KB 28/287 (Michaelmas 1773) to PRO, KB 28/291 (Michaelmas 1774).
[104] R v. Brown and others (PRO, KB 28/286 (Trin. 1773) & PRO, KB 28/287 (Mich. 1773)).
[105] Re Borough of Orford, costs £55 (1734) (PRO, KB 28/128); Re Borough of Grampound, costs £180 (1741) (PRO, KB 28/156); Re Borough of Droitwich, costs £50 (1750) (PRO, KB 1/10/2); Re Borough of Taunton, costs £55 (1746) (PRO, KB 28/178, no. 3); R v. Pickerill, costs £180 (1792) 4 Term Reports 809.

Yarmouth pleaded with the Court of King's Bench not to allow an information against him on the ground that the cost of defending his office even if it were to succeed 'would greatly tend to the impoverishment of himself and [his] family'.[106] A group of over sixty burgesses from Lyme Regis, who had been targeted by quo warranto, accused the prosecutor, the MP Henry Fane, of using the King's Bench to intimidate them from 'from supporting and defending their rights on account of the great and enormous expense'.[07] In a case from Portsmouth, Mansfield CJ accused the prosecutors of employing a litigation strategy which involved 'loading the parties with expense'.[108] The 1711 Act gave the court discretion to impose a fine in addition to the judgment of ouster and costs. Blackstone wrote that fines in quo warranto informations were 'nominal only',[109] and the Court of King's Bench also described the 'fine to the King in such as case' as 'merely nominal'.[110] In practice, the amount of the fine in the mid-eighteenth century was usually between £80 and £200[111] – a figure which was certainly more than nominal.

Quo Warranto and Historical or Systemic Invalidity

Two types of defect could infect whole swathes of titles. One category involved cases where the illegality had been long-standing and repeated. In 1740, John Olmius, a candidate for the constituency of Weymouth, received a letter from his election agent relating how he had been 'in [his] study reading a book entitled *The Student's Companion or Reason of Laws* by Giles Jacob' when he had hit upon a legal argument which would enable Olmius to accomplish the elimination of hundreds of hostile voters.[112] Since 1616, the mayor and all previous mayors had been,

---

[106] Re Borough of Yarmouth, Robert White (5 January 1760) (PRO, KB 1/14/3).
[107] Re Corporation of Lyme Regis (Zachariah Drower and others, 1 June 1779) (PRO, KB 1/21/6).
[108] R v. Monday (1777) 2 Cowp. 530.
[109] W. Blackstone, Commentaries on the Laws of England: Book the Third (Oxford, 1768), 263.
[110] R v. Pickerill (1792) 4 Term Rep. 809.
[111] R v. Seward, fine £99 (1734) (PRO, KB 28/128, no. 9); R v. Cribb, fine £166 (1734) (PRO, KB 28/128, no. 13); R v. Thomas, fine £85 (1747) (PRO, KB 28/181, no. 11); R v. Walker, fine £144 (1767) (PRO, KB 28/260, no. 4).
[112] J. Joyeaux to J. Olmius, 12 April 1740 (Wiltshire Record Office, Chafyn Grove papers, MS 865/478).

contrary to the terms of the charter, nominated by the aldermen, and not by the common burgesses. The logical effect was that 125 mayors had been illegally appointed and all of the officers (freemen, aldermen and burgesses) sworn in by those mayors had been illegally appointed. The House of Lords upheld the information and ousted the mayor.[113] Earlier, in a 1738 case from Maidstone, it was found that, in continuous breach of the 1619 charter of James I – which required the election of jurats by the mayor, jurats and the inhabitants – voting rights had been limited to the mayor and jurats alone.[114] The invalidity had been practised for over 100 years.

A second form of defect involved a long sequence of titles derived from a superior office holder whose own appointment was invalid. The office of freeman derived from the swearing into office by the current mayor. 'It had always been understood that when a bad mayor presides, all elections under him are bad.'[115] Accordingly, the titles of freemen sworn in by a mayor could be voided if the mayor's own title was defective. The election of the mayor of Westbury in 1743 – and the election of burgesses at meetings at which that mayor presided – was challenged by a quo warranto on the grounds of 'the major part of the legal common or capital burgesses not being present at such nomination or election'.[116] In 1774, over sixty burgesses were ousted from Portsmouth when the title of the mayor, Sir John Carter, was successfully challenged on quo warranto.[117] Such mass impeachments could be contrived. An earlier mayor might collusively agree not to contest a quo warranto challenge to his title, thereby enabling the destruction of the titles of those who derived their title from that collusive mayor. Such collusive strategies were suspected to have been employed by former mayors at Winchelsea in the 1760s[118] and Cambridge in the late 1780s.[119]

A number of doctrinal strategies were attempted in order to limit the destructive impact of an appointment by an officer with a bad title. One was the de facto officer doctrine: the principle that the acts of a

[113] *R v. Mayor of Weymouth* (1740) 7 Mod. 373; *R v. Tucker* (1742) 2 Bro. PC 304.
[114] *R v. Blunt* (1738) Andr. 293; W. R. James, *The Charters and Other Documents Relating to ... Maidstone* (London, 1825), 171–179.
[115] *R v. Corporation of Bridgewater* (1784) 3 Doug. KB 379.
[116] Re Borough of Westbury, John Withers, 4 February 1749 (PRO, KB 1/10/1).
[117] Robert East, *Extracts from the Records in the Possession of the Municipal Corporation of Portsmouth* (Portsmouth, 1891), 237, 238.
[118] *R v. Dawes* (1769) 4 Burr. 2277.
[119] Re Cambridge, John Mortlock (22 May 1789) (PRO, KB 1/26/2).

defectively appointed officer might be regarded as valid for the purpose
of protecting the title of officers who had innocently relied upon their
validity. However, the Court of King's Bench was reluctant, for policy
reasons, to apply the doctrine.[120] The concern was that a general understanding in the boroughs, that acts carried out by an improperly
appointed mayor would be saved, would reduce the incentive to lawfully
administer the appointment process: 'the constitutions of corporations
would be overturned as officers will be hereby encouraged not to adhere
to the terms of the charter'.[121] Another strategy was the void/voidable
theory of invalidity. Lord Hardwicke recollected that the void[122]/voidable
distinction was deployed in opposition to the argument that the failure of
the mayor of Portsmouth[123] to take the oath prescribed by the
Corporation Act 1661 invalidated all subsequent appointments of freeman made by the mayor. Since, it was argued, the non-compliance with
the 1661 Act merely made the appointment voidable (valid until voided
by quo warranto) rather than void (unlawful from the point of the entry
into office), the subsequent appointments were valid. Lord Hardwicke
noted that, in the end, the point had not been determined.[124]

The regulation by time limit of the period allowed for taking quo
warranto informations became the preferred technique for limiting the
opportunities for upsetting long-established titles. The Court of King's
Bench began to insert time limits early in the history of the process.
A quo warranto from Buckingham in 1711 (involving an alderman who
had been unlawfully appointed in an alehouse) was barred on the ground
that the defendant had 'continued in the office for several years'.[125]
In 1722, Harcourt told the House of Commons that, 'after eight or nine
years, the Court of King's Bench would never suffer an information [by
quo warranto] to be filed'.[126] In the 1720s, the court refused to grant a
quo warranto to set aside the appointment of burgesses in Malmsbury

---

[120] *R v. Lisle* (1738) Andr. 163.
[121] Ibid., 167 (serjeant Eyre).
[122] 13 Car. II, c. 1.
[123] Lord Hardwicke was probably referring to the prosecution which was the subject of *R v. Whitehorn* (1711) 10 Mod. 64. The void/voidable point is not referred to in the law report.
[124] *R v. Miller* (1736) (Middle Temple, Misc. 19, f. 43).
[125] *R v. Borough of Truro* (1727) 1 Barn. KB 19.
[126] 13 December 1722, 20 *Commons Journals* 78.

and Helstone after eight years; and Truro after six years.[127] During this decade, the Court of King's Bench began to develop a distinction between 'minute matters'[128] and 'small slips'[129] (where the prosecution must be initiated within a short period) from 'objections going to the whole of the election'.[130] Defects in the first category were to be prosecuted promptly. However, the public interest in enforcing legality in the boroughs required that claims involving more serious defects should not be impeded by strict time limits. In one case the defendant was prosecuted twenty-six years after his election.[131]

In the 1740 case from Weymouth, the challenge was targeted at the mayor who had been elected under a legal understanding of 125 years' standing, that an alderman was eligible for appointment as mayor.[132] Covertly, the Weymouth litigation was being managed on behalf of the Prime Minister, Robert Walpole. Walpole's use of quo warranto to disturb innocent borough officers, who had assumed for years that their titles were lawful, lay behind an opposition demand for legislative intervention. In 1743, a Bill for Quieting Corporations,[133] which proposed a time limit on questioning the acts of an illegally appointed officer by quo warranto, was introduced by the politically independent Lord Romney. The Bill, introduced three months after the conclusion of the Weymouth litigation, proposed that 'reasonable periods of time be limited' after which a quo warranto prosecution could not be initiated.[134] The Bill did not specify a limitation period: this was to be settled by the House of Lords. However, the House of Lords was unable to agree on a time period. It struggled to reconcile the principle that unlawful appointments

---

[127] *R v. Bowen Hart the Mayor and Burgesses of Malmsbury* (1722) 8 Mod. 55; *R v. Pyke* (1724) 8 Mod. 286 (burgesses holding office for fourteen years; quo warranto refused); *R v. Major de Helstone* (1725) 2 Str. 677 (eight years); *R v. Borough of Truro* (1727) 1 Barn. KB 19.

[128] *R v. Corporation of Truro* (1727) as explained in *R v. Corporation of Maidstone* (1739) (Lincoln's Inn, Hill 16, f. 112).

[129] *R v. Woodman* (1728) 1 Barn. KB 101.

[130] *R v. Corporation of Truro* (1727) as explained in *R v. Corporation of Maidstone* (1739) Lincoln's Inn, Hill 16, f. 112.

[131] *R v. Powell* (1722) 8 Mod. 165; *R v. Woodman* (1728) 1 Barn. KB 101. Twenty-nine years was regarded as excessive: *R v. Stephens* (1757) 1 Burr. 433.

[132] *R v. Mayor of Weymouth* (1740) 7 Mod. 373; *Tucker v. The King* (1742) 2 Br. 309. See n. 113 above.

[133] 'A Bill for Quieting Corporations' (7 March 1743) (Parliamentary Archives, HL/PO/JO/10/6/508).

[134] W. Cobbett, *The Parliamentary History of England Vol. 13* (London, 1812) 98 (17 March 1743).

should be amenable to correction on judicial review (a policy which favoured a longer time limit) with the principle that the settled expect-ations of officers who assumed that they had been validly elected should not be disturbed (a policy which favoured a shorter time limit). Lord Chesterfield thought that, in the case of an annual officer, the limit should be a couple of weeks. From the other side, Lord Cholmondeley (Walpole's son-in-law and a 'faithful friend to court power')[135] argued that the effect of a rigid prescription period was equivalent to providing that 'stolen goods not reclaimed in a certain time should remain forever the property of the thief'.[136] Lord Chancellor Hardwicke thought that it was impossible to establish a limitation period: a time of 'any long duration' would merely perpetuate the existing time limits set by the Court of King's Bench so that the Bill would 'have no effect', while a very short time would allow improper elections escape correction and encour-age 'injustice and violence by a law'.[137] Unable to agree on a time limit, Romney's Bill was heavily defeated.[138]

Parliament and Quo Warranto, 1767–1792

The question of the quo warranto time limit question arose once again in 1767. Sir Fletcher Norton had been retained as counsel for Nathaniel Dawes, a former town clerk of Winchelsea, who had been admitted as a burgess for thirteen years without any objection.[139] When, during argu-ment, the question of the appropriate time limit arose, the Court of King's Bench drew the line at twenty years: an application made after twenty years could never be admitted (though a delayed application within twenty years might be refused in the court's discretion). The twenty-year maximum – more than doubling the eight-year period employed at the beginning of the century – was justified on the ground that it was 'in analogy of the rules on bonds and highways'[140] and

---

[135] J. Burgh, *Political Disquisitions, Or, An Inquiry into Public Errors, Vol. 1* (London, 1774), 467.

[136] *The History and Proceedings of the House of Lords during the Second Session of the Third Parliament of King George II*, 11 March 1743, 510.

[137] Ibid., 512–513.

[138] Ibid., 17 March 1743, , 538; Edward Harley's Journal, 11 February 1743, 64.

[139] *R v. Dawes* (1767) 4 Burr. 2120.

[140] While there was no fixed limitation period in the case of bonds, the court had a discretion to dismiss on grounds of delay which it would exercise after a 'silence of eighteen years'; *Case of the Borough of St Ives* (1757) 2 Keny. 171.

equivalent to the period prescribed for many personal actions by the Statute of Limitations 1623.[141] The pro-prosecutor twenty-year time limit would not have been enough to protect Dawes (who had been in office for nineteen years) against prosecution.[142] In laying down the twenty-year limit, Mansfield made it clear that he was happy for Parliament to reduce the court's twenty-year limit[143] and while the case was adjourned, the issue was raised in the House of Commons in the spring of 1767. Fletcher Norton, who was acting for the Winchelsea defendants affected by Mansfield's new rule,[144] was one of those MPs who sponsored a 'Bill for Quieting Corporations and for Rendering More Speedy and Effectual Writs of Quo Warranto'.[145] As in 1742, the House could not agree on the length of the limitation period. It was reported that a 'number of hard names' had 'alarmed the gentlemen of the House'[146] against restricting the court's capacity to exercise judicial review by imposing too short a time limit. When, in November, the Winchelsea cases resumed, without any change in the law, Mansfield confirmed the principle that he had earlier suggested: that officers would be secure after the elapse of twenty years.[147] Mansfield CJ's generous time limit preferred the interests of the Crown over the interests of borough officers. Although the twenty-year maximum was said to be 'the ne plus ultra',[148] it was not binding on the Crown and a prosecution could be initiated, even after the twenty years, by 'the King himself . . . [acting] by his Attorney General'.[149]

Political opposition to Mansfield's pro-prosecutor rule was renewed in the House of Commons in 1770.[150] However, Mansfield's successor as Chief Justice, Lloyd Kenyon, continued, at first, to endorse Mansfield CJ's

---

[141] 21 Jac. 1, c. 16; *Winchelsea Causes* (1766) 4 Burr. 1962; *R v. Stacey* (1785) 1 Term Rep. 1.
[142] On the resumed hearing in the summer of 1767, the Court of King's Bench used its discretion to block the prosecution against Dawes (which had been taken within twenty years): *R v. Dawes* (1767) 4 Burr. 2120.
[143] *R v. Dawes* (1767) 4 Burr. 2022, 2023.
[144] *R v. Wardroper* (1766) 4 Burr. 1963.
[145] 31 *Commons Journals* 359, 14 May 1767.
[146] (1768) 30 *Scots Magazine* 82, 1 February 1768.
[147] *Winchelsea Causes* (1767) 4 Burr. 1962.
[148] *R v. Rogers, Burgess of Helston* (1770) 4 Burr. 2523.
[149] *R v. Dawes* (1767) 4 Burr. 2120, 2121; *R v. Wardroper* (1766) 4 Burr. 1963.
[150] 32 *Commons' Journals* 846, 30 March 1770; 'A Bill [With the Amendments] for the Further Quieting and Establishing Corporations; and for Rendering More Speedy and Effectual Proceedings in Writs of Quo Warranto, and Informations in Nature of a Quo Warranto', *House of Commons Papers*, 22 (1770).

twenty-year time limit: five months after he succeeded Mansfield, Kenyon applied the rule in the case of a Cambridge burgess who had been in office for twelve years.[151] However, in 1791, just three years later, Kenyon CJ dramatically changed policy.[152] He now acknowledged that the twenty-year period was oppressive to borough officers, and he prohibited the prosecution of a Newcastle freeman who had been illegally admitted nineteen years earlier.[153] The following day, the court laid down a general rule contracting Mansfield CJ's twenty-year period to six years. Not merely was the time limit stricter; Kenyon's rule in the Newcastle case did not, like Mansfield's rule, create an express exemption so as to enable the Crown to prosecute after six years.[154]

The Informations in the Nature of Quo Warranto Act 1792

Three months after the Newcastle freemen case,[155] Charles James Fox introduced, along with his famous Bill on the law of libel, a Bill on the 'Law of Informations in the Nature of Quo Warranto'.[156] Ultimately, what would become the Informations in the Nature of Quo Warranto Act 1792[157] did little more than place the six-year limit laid down by Kenyon CJ on a statutory basis – but with one important addition: the theoretical immunity of the Crown from the time limit was removed. Overriding the common law immunity of the Crown, the six-year time limit was also to apply when the application was taken 'by his Majesty's Attorney General, or other officer of the Crown, on behalf of his Majesty'. By contrast with the parliamentary concerns of the 1740s and 1760s, Fox's concerns were not especially with the protection of innocent borough officers from being expelled for historical defects. In fact, Fox seems to have considered Kenyon's six-year limit as slightly overrestrictive on prosecutors. Given that parliaments lasted seven years, he proposed that the period of limitations should be extended to seven or

---

[151] *R v. Bond* (1788) 2 Term Rep. 767.
[152] *R v. Dicken* (1791) 4 TR 282.
[153] Ibid.
[154] Ibid.; R. Gude, *The Practice of the Crown Side of the Court of King's Bench* (London, 1828), 377.
[155] The Newcastle ruling was announced on 10 February 1791, *The Times*, 11 February 1791.
[156] 20 May 1791, 46 *CJ* 624; (1790–92) 79 House of Commons Sessional Papers, Bills 1790–91 & 1792.
[157] 32 Geo. III, c. 58.

eight years (so that members of Parliament, towards the end of the parliamentary cycle could employ quo warranto to remove borough officers elected at the beginning of the cycle).[158] However, an amendment to Fox's Bill moved in the House of Lords by Chief Justice Kenyon himself reduced the period to six years; the result was Kenyon managed to give statutory effect to his own rule.[159]

Fox and his supporters justified the Bill by reference to deeper constitutional concerns. William Pitt the Younger made perhaps the more persuasive of the arguments in the Commons, objecting to the claim of the Court of King's Bench to regulate access to justice by extra-statutory rules of court. It was 'the province of Parliament to fix the time'; it was 'unconstitutional and unsafe' for the Court of King's Bench to legislate by rules of practice.[160] Fox, on the other hand, targeted the exemption of the Crown from the 1791 time limit. Fox's case for reform of quo warranto was probably not as compelling as his case for his more celebrated companion Bill for restoring the role of juries in libel prosecutions (which he was piloting through the Commons at the same time).[161] By Kenyon CJ's rule, Fox argued, the Attorney General, on behalf of the government, might move at any time.[162] The effect was that the government might disfranchise electors who were opponents of the government and who had been elected more than six years ago.[163] Boroughs, Fox argued in a speech which at points seemed overstated, were not 'safe' against the King.[164] He linked this 'danger to the liberty of the people' to the Chief Justice, Lord Kenyon; it was 'by the last rule of the Court of King's Bench [Kenyon's rule]' that the Attorney General 'on the part of the king, might move at any time'. But the exemption of the Crown from time limits – the principle of *nullum tempus occurrit regi*[165] – was a common law rule which, unless it was overridden by statute, was binding on Kenyon. Kenyon was hardly to blame for this orthodox legal

---

[158] 20 May 1791, *The Speeches of the Right Honourable Charles James Fox, Vol. IV* (London, 1815), 263.

[159] 5 June 1792, 33 *Parliamentary Register or History of the Proceedings and Debates of the House of Commons* (London, 1792), 227.

[160] *Bath Chronicle*, 26 May 1791.

[161] Libel Act 1792 (32 Geo. III, c. 60).

[162] 20 May 1791, W. Cobbett, *The Parliamentary History of England, Vol. 29* (London, 1817), cols. 573–574.

[163] *Derby Chronicle*, 26 May 1791.

[164] Ibid.

[165] *R v. Berkley* (1754) 1 Keny. 80 (the principle exempted the Crown from the time limits regulating certiorari).

principle. Kenyon's version of the rule was also slightly less prerogative-orientated than Mansfield's. Mansfield's rule had expressly exempted the Crown; Kenyon's had not. Fox's concerns about the government's liberty to evade quo warranto time limits were probably more theoretical than practical. There had been a time bar in operation since Mansfield's rule of 1767. Yet Fox did not name an actual instance in which the government had been able to evade the 1767 time limit. A search of the identity of quo warranto informants in the early 1770s shows no cases in which an application was made at the direction of an agent of the Crown.[166] Instead, when the government did use quo warranto, it hid behind private informants (like the attorney, Leonard Martin, who prosecuted on behalf of Walpole in the 1740s).[167] But since those relators concealed the fact that they were acting on behalf of the Crown, they would not have been able to rely on the prerogative exemption, and would have had to prosecute within the six-year limit.

The Quo Warranto Information in 1792

The statutory form of judicial review quo warranto established by the Municipal Corporations Act 1711[168] blended elements of criminal prosecution and civil proceedings.[169] This system of judicial review, in turn, resulted in the displacement of hundreds of borough electors. At the same time, the 1711 Act process was tainted by its association with dishonourable electoral strategy. The process was, as Lord Chalmondley put it in 1743, exploited by 'agents of faction' who acted 'under the pretence of public justice' to advance the 'particular interests of wicked men'.[170] The identity of the actual prosecutor was hidden behind a common informer; borough place holders were intimidated into disclaiming their office by fear of unsupportable costs and fines; litigation was sometimes funded by the government; collusive legal strategies were used to impeach the titles of political rivals; and officers, who for years had assumed in good faith that their title was secure, were ejected for concealed historic defects. Underlying the parliamentary

---

[166] PRO, KB 28/286 (Trinity 1773) to PRO, KB 28/292 (Hilary 1775).
[167] See the text at n. 62 above.
[168] 9 Anne c. 20.
[169] *Re Maidstone Corporation* (1739) Lincoln's Inn, Hil. 16, ff. 108, 112; *R v. Francis* (1788) 2 Term Reports 484.
[170] *The History and Proceedings of the House of Lords during the second session of the Third Parliament of King George II*, 11 March 1743, 510 (Lord Chalmondley).

efforts in 1743, 1767, 1770, and in the early 1790s, to rebalance the process was a concern to protect borough political life from those 'agents of faction'. Yet, despite its misuse, the 1711 Act did expand the presence of the rule of law in borough politics and provide an independent alternative – the Court of King's Bench – to the partisan House of Commons. The 1711 Act was the beginning of the broader constitutional tendency which gradually saw the investigation of electoral malpractice removed from Parliament to the courts, a process which would be completed when the Committee on Elections was shut down and the Parliamentary Elections Act 1868[171] transferred all election petitions to the Court of Queen's Bench.

---

[171] 31 & 32 Vict. c. 125.

8

Land, Credit and the Constitution

Debtor Protections and Catholic Rights in Eighteenth-Century Ireland

JULIA RUDOLPH

Several mortgage bills – aimed to allow so-called papists to lend money to Protestants on mortgages of land – were proposed, but failed to secure passage in the Irish parliament in the 1760s and early 1770s. Examples include a bill from 1764 "To ascertain what securities may be taken by persons professing the Popish religion for monies lent," and a bill from 1771 "To secure the repayment of money really lent and advanced by Papists ... to Protestants, on mortgages of lands, tenements and hered-itaments within the kingdom of Ireland."[1] Opponents of these bills trotted out familiar anti-Catholic attacks. MP Thomas LeHunt, for example, objected to the 1764 proposed bill as "dangerous to the Protestant interest," because it would undermine what were known as the "Popery laws" or the "penal code." Those laws were essential, he thought, not only because they kept Catholics from acquiring property and power but also because they worked to "reclaim [Catholics] from idolatry and heathenism."[2] James Caldwell, "an improving and enlight-ened landlord" who published on a range of political and economic topics, used even more pointed language and inflammatory analogies.[3] In his pamphlet against that same 1764 mortgage bill, Caldwell insisted

---

[1] 1763/64, "To ascertain what securities may be taken by persons professing the Popish religion for money lent, or to be lent by them, and also what remedies they may have recourse to for recovery thereof": www.qub.ac.uk/ild/?func=display_bill&id=1353; and 1771A. "To secure the repayment of money really lent and advanced by Papists, or persons professing the Popish religion, to Protestants, on mortgages of lands, tenements and hereditaments within the kingdom of Ireland": www.qub.ac.uk/ild/?func=display_bill&id=1772, Irish Legislation Database, Queens University Belfast.

[2] J. Kelly, 'Repealing the Penal Laws, 1760–75', in K. Costello and N. Howlin (eds.), *Law and Religion in Ireland 1700–1970* (Basingstoke 2021), 88.

[3] H. Andrews, 'Caldwell, Sir James (c. 1720–1784)', *Dictionary of Irish Biography*, www.dib.ie/biography/caldwell-sir-james-a1389.

that Catholics posed a threat to state and society. The state must treat them with firmness and even severity, he said, in the same way that the state would properly treat other religious groups that, for example, engaged in child sacrifice or worshipped trees.[4] While Caldwell endorsed the familiar assertion that men's consciences could not be forced, he resisted the conclusion that men could not be punished for their beliefs. Such state action was required in order to defend the religious and constitutional settlement achieved in 1689, he explained, since "popery necessarily includes notions contrary to the safety and well-being of a Protestant state, under a Prince who owes his succession to the abdication and exclusion of a popish king."[5] Caldwell defended his arguments as political prudence and denied that he was motivated by a desire to persecute Catholics.

Only a few years after the creation of that Protestant state in 1689, the Irish parliament had passed repressive legislation intended to punish Catholic beliefs and actions. This penal code prohibited Catholic religious practice and education, proscribed Catholic political and professional activity, and significantly inhibited Catholic property holding.[6] Mortgage legislation proposed six decades later clearly raised questions about continued enforcement of these penal laws, as opponents expressed concern that the legislation would undermine this foundation of the Protestant constitution. At a time of widespread debate about constitutional change in many parts of Britain's Atlantic empire, commentators like Caldwell firmly rejected any relaxation of those laws that prohibited Catholic landownership in Ireland. When he repeated familiar arguments about an association between "popery" and "tyranny," and invoked long-lived Whig defenses of the revolution as a triumph of "liberty" over "slavery," Caldwell took part in a contentious imperial

---

[4] J. Caldwell, A Brief Examination of the Question, Whether It Is Expedient Either in a Religious or Political View to Pass an Act to Enable Papists to Take Real Securities for Money Which They May Lend (Dublin, 1764), 5–7.

[5] Ibid., 7.

[6] J. Bergin, E. Magennis, L. Ni Mhunghaile and P. Walsh (eds.), New Perspectives on the Penal Laws, Eighteenth-Century Ireland, Special Issue No. 1 (Dublin, 2011); I. McBride, Eighteenth-Century Ireland: The Isle of Slaves (Dublin, 2009), ch. 5; W. N. Osborough, 'Catholics, Land and the Popery Acts of Anne', in T. P. Power and K. Whelan (eds.), Endurance and Emergence; Catholics in Ireland in the Eighteenth Century (Dublin, 1990), 21–56; J. G. Sims, 'The Making of a Penal Law (2 Anne c. 6) 1703–4' (1960) 12 Irish Historical Studies 46, 105–118; J. Rudolph, 'A Broker's Advice: Credit Networks and Mortgage Risk in the Eighteenth-Century Empire', in M. Lobban and I. Williams (eds.), Networks and Connections in Legal History (Cambridge, 2020), 199–205.

discourse about economy, jurisdiction and rights. Yet when he warned that the proposed mortgage bill was "a project which tends to make Protestants slaves to Papists," and would empower Catholics "to subvert the very being of the Constitution," he was not contributing to critiques of colonial slavery or imperial governance.[7] Rather, Caldwell drew upon an Irish patriot language, contrasting English liberties with continental tyranny, in order to amplify particular religious fears about the political, economic and social changes that might follow from the proposed legislation.[8]

Scholars generally interpret these mortgage bills, and the negative reactions to them, within the context of a broader controversy over Catholic relief that occurred in the 1760s and 1770s. James Kelly, for example, analyzes this "sequence of initiatives ... to secure legislative protection for [Catholic] lenders" as part of what he calls the "first attempts" to repeal the penal laws.[9] Kelly and other scholars also emphasize the significance of economic improvement in Ireland after 1750, and highlight growing constitutional challenges to Irish legislative dependence, in order to explain the Catholic relief efforts of these years.[10] Such histories of the penal laws and of Catholic emancipation are essential to a longer narrative about politics and religion, and are certainly important contexts for these legislative proposals and failures. But critics of the proposed mortgage legislation, like James Caldwell, didn't just talk about politics or religion. They also talked about debt law and property law.

---

[7] Caldwell, *Brief Examination*, 12, 21. For the longer history of discourse, and examples of similar language used in 1771 and 1774, see J. Marshall, 'Whig Thought and the Revolution of 1689–91', in T. Harris and S. Taylor (eds.), *The Final Crisis of the Stuart Monarchy: the Revolutions of 1689–91 in Their British, Atlantic and European Contexts* (Woodbridge, 2013), 71–86; C. L. Brown, *Moral Capital: Foundations of British Abolitionism* (Chapel Hill, NC, 2006), 46–48, 209–213; Kelly, 'Repealing Penal Laws', 89–91; M. J. Powell, 'Credit, Debt and Patriot Politics in Dublin, 1763–1784' (2010) 25 *Eighteenth-Century Ireland* 140.

[8] McBride, *Eighteenth-Century Ireland*, 17; C. Kidd, 'North Britishness and the Nature of Eighteenth-Century British Patriotisms', *Historical Journal* (1996) 39(2) 380–381.

[9] Kelly, 'Repealing Penal Laws', 86.

[10] Ibid., 78–79; J. Kelly quoted in P. Higgins, 'Matthew Carey, Catholic Identity and the Penal Laws' (2014) 49 *Eire-Ireland* 176–177; T. O'Connor, 'The Catholic Church and Catholics in an Era of Sanctions and Restraint, 1690-1790', in J. Kelly (ed.), *The Cambridge History of Ireland. Volume III. 1730–1880* (Cambridge, 2018), 278–279; D. Dickson, 'Society and Economy in the Long Eighteenth Century', in J. Kelly (ed.), *Cambridge History of Ireland. Volume III. 1730–1880* (Cambridge, 2018), 167; S. J. Connolly, *Divided Kingdom: Ireland 1630–1800* (Oxford, 2008), 384–420.

They referred to specific legal dangers Catholic mortgagees posed, some-times citing elements of writ and judgment process. In order to under-stand their fears, and to interpret these legislative failures, we also need to understand the history of mortgage law in Ireland and in the empire. How did these Irish bills look in the context of evolving mortgage practice? How did they look compared to other examples of mortgage legislation proposed, and sometimes passed, in eighteenth-century Ireland, England and other parts of the British Empire?

Since the end of the seventeenth century, when modern mortgage principles were distinctly articulated in English law, strong debtor pro-tections had been enshrined in the doctrine of the equity of redemp-tion.[11] According to this doctrine, a mortgagor retained a right to redeem his property, even after default on the loan, and this right could only be extinguished through a lengthy and difficult foreclosure process. While at common law a mortgage had long been understood as a form of property transfer, in equity mortgage was now defined as redeemable debt secur-ity. This equitable doctrine aimed to protect the mortgagor from avoid-able loss of property while also preserving the creditor's right to repayment of the loan, with interest and costs. This debtor-friendly doctrine was a critical feature of eighteenth-century mortgage agree-ments, litigation and legislation in England, Ireland, the Caribbean and North America, as mortgage lending spread across the British Empire.[12] Yet while mortgage doctrine promised key protections for debtors, pro-moting stability in landed property and stimulating new kinds of invest-ment, the nature and extent of debtor protections were frequently contested. Religious and political concerns shaped mortgage law and policy in Ireland, and so too did imperial and economic factors. As mortgage lending spanned imperial networks, and periodic credit crises emerged, mortgagees often pushed for increased creditor protections.

---

[11] R. W. Turner, *The Equity of Redemption: Its Nature, History and Connection with Equitable Estates Generally* (Cambridge, 1931); A. W. B. Simpson, *A History of the Land Law* (Oxford, 1986), ch. 10; D. P. Waddilove, 'Why the Equity of Redemption?', in C. Briggs and J. Zuijderduijn (eds.), *Land and Credit: Mortgages in the Medieval and Early Modern Countryside* (London, 2018), 117–148; W. Cornish et al., *Law and Society in England 1750–1950* (Oxford, 2019), 128–132.

[12] J. Rudolph, 'The Last Will and Testament of John Gardner Kemeys: Jamaican Mortgages and English Inheritance Disputes', in C. Griffiths and L. Korporowicz (eds.), *English Law, the Legal Profession and Colonialism: Histories, Parallels, and Influences* (Abingdon, 2024), 219–234.

The failure of numerous proposed mortgage bills in late-eighteenth-century Ireland must, then, be understood as contemporaries saw it, not only as a part of the history of the penal laws and Catholic emancipation, but also as part of the history of mortgage law and the testing of the equity of redemption. Concerns about deceit and mismanagement in mortgage were widespread at this time and, like other concerns about the growing credit economy, this disquiet was frequently expressed through statute. Indeed the "Dublin parliament passed more than 2300 acts between 1660 and 1800," Julian Hoppit calculates, "of which a half concerned economic matters."[13] Irish and British mortgage legislation often focused on restraining fraudulent debtors, but some legislators elsewhere in the empire also targeted predatory lenders. Thus, in drafting and debating their bills, Irish legislators likely considered the wider potential impacts of their proposals to enable Catholics to become creditors: Would passage of these laws necessitate new kinds of legal protections for debtors? How might these laws affect other creditors; would they undermine the security that other lenders, in other places, had fought for and won?

* * *

In the late seventeenth and early eighteenth centuries, as debtor-friendly mortgage doctrine took hold, Irish and English parliaments enacted several creditor-friendly mortgage laws. These laws promoted transparency and penalized the deceitful mortgagor who tried, surreptitiously, to solicit multiple loans. For example, a 1692 English Act Against Clandestine Mortgages denied "the benefit of equitable rules" to such debtors who mortgaged property without "notice of prior encumbrance."[14] It was understood that these mortgagors should not enjoy protections afforded by the equity of redemption. The Irish parliament passed a similar Act to Prevent Frauds by Clandestine Mortgages in 1697.[15] As part of these efforts to prevent harms caused by secretive sellers and mortgagors, legislators also considered bills to establish land registries in both England and Ireland. Proposals for a national land registry had been discussed in England for decades, but the idea gained new prominence among advocates of a national land bank during the

---

[13] J. Hoppit, *Britain's Political Economies: Parliament and Economic Life, 1660–1800* (Cambridge, 2017), 130.

[14] 4 & 5 William & Mary c. 16 (Eng.)

[15] 9 William 3 c. 11 (Ire.).

1690s' public policy debate known as the "battle for the banks."[16] The most successful land bank scheme, promoted by the lawyer and economic writer John Asgill, included detailed plans for a public register of deeds. Asgill articulated his arguments about the stability and elasticity of credit founded upon land in his 1695 *The Settlement of the Land Bank*, and published a second stand-alone proposal, entitled *An Essay on a Registry, for Titles on Land*, in 1698. As Asgill explained, a registry would not only confirm land values underpinning his proposed bank, but would also guarantee transparency and avoid secret liens, which were known threats to creditors' interests.[17] Similar arguments about the importance of registration as a vital tool in the fight against fraud were made by other advocates, and although attempts to introduce a national registry ultimately failed, local deed registries were established in England soon after the turn of the century. Legislation created a registry in the West Riding of Yorkshire in 1704, and subsequent acts established local registries in the East Riding and in Middlesex in 1707–1708.[18]

The Irish parliament successfully launched its own comprehensive registry of deeds at this time with the 1707 Act for Irish Registration of Deeds, which created a national, rather than simply local, system of registration.[19] While this Irish act shared some of the goals of English legislation, it is important to emphasize that its passage was not simply an indication of direction or control from Westminster. By the early eighteenth century, Irish lawmakers were practiced at skirting restrictions on legislative independence imposed by Poyning's Law. Members of the Irish parliament initiated legislation in the form of "heads of bills" and

[16] Between 1691 and 1695 several economic projectors, including Hugh Chamberlen, John Briscoe, Nicholas Barbon and John Asgill, produced land bank designs and polemics. D. Rubini, 'Politics and the Battle for the Banks, 1688-1697' (1970) 85 *English Historical Review* 693; R. Kleer, 'Fictitious Cash: English Paper Finance and Public Money 1689-97', in C. I. McGrath and C. Fauske (eds.), *Money Power and Print: Interdisciplinary Studies on the Financial Revolution in the British Isles* (Newark, DE, 2008), 82; C. Wennerlind, *Casualties of Credit: The English Financial Revolution, 1620-1720* (Cambridge, 2011), 114–121.

[17] J. Asgill, *Settlement of the Land Bank* (London, 1695), 3–4.

[18] 2 & 3 Anne c. 4 (Eng.), 6 Anne c. 62, 7 Anne c. 20, 8 George 2 c. 6 (GB). F. Sheppard and V. Belcher, 'The Deeds Registries of Yorkshire and Middlesex' (1980) 6 *Journal of the Society of Archivists* 274.

[19] 6 Anne c. 2, amended in 8 Anne c. 10 (Ire.). This "Act for the public registry of all deeds, conveyances and wills [that shall be made of any honours, manors, lands tenements and hereditaments]" was approved after two unsuccessful bills to establish Irish registries failed before the English Privy Council in 1697 and 1705: www.qub.ac.uk/ild/?func=display_bill&id=728; www.qub.ac.uk/ild/?func=display_bill&id=860.

while these bills would still be scrutinized, and possibly rejected, by the British Privy Council, Irish MPs played a major role in framing laws.[20] It is possible that the framers of the Act for Irish Registration of Deeds were influenced by contemporary arguments for land registration, like those circulated by John Asgill, whose "Essay on a Registry, for Titles on Land" appeared, with extended debate, in a Dublin edition in 1701.[21] Also significant is the fact that these Irish legislators were operating during the lengthy period of Catholic dispossession imposed in Ireland after 1689. Like earlier English legislation, the Irish Act was framed as a necessary response to the general dangers of deception and fraud, but it further singled out the particular threat of fraud practiced "especially by papists, to the great prejudice of the protestant interest."[22] This statutory language has led some scholars to describe the Irish registry as an adjunct of the penal laws.[23]

At a time of property seizure and land transfer, when accusations of manipulation, deceit and violence were lodged against Protestants as well as Catholics, the Irish Acts for the registering of deeds and against clandestine mortgages were intended to ensure property title, and prevent deception in mortgage, leasing and sales. These Acts were shaped by Protestant determination to prevent Catholic evasion of the penal laws, but they were also informed by other areas of concern in contemporary property and debt law. The widespread use of mortgages in estate management in Ireland as well as England meant that mortgage doctrine was of particular interest and that new questions arose. With regard to formerly Catholic-owned property, for example, it was unclear what remedies would be available for creditors of a mortgaged estate that

---

[20] J. Kelly, 'The Making of Law in Eighteenth-Century Ireland', in N. M. Dawson (ed.), *Reflections on Law and History: Irish Legal History Society Discourses and Other Papers, 2000–2005* (Dublin, 2006), 270. J. Kelly, *Poyning's Law and the Making of Law in Ireland, 1660–1800* (Dublin, 2007), 11 and ch. 3; Connolly, *Divided Kingdom*, 202, 235.

[21] P. A. Walsh, 'Asgill, John 1659–1738', *Dictionary of Irish Biography*, https://doi.org/10.3318/dib.000238.v1; B. Twomey, *Personal Financial Management in Early Eighteenth-Century Ireland: Practices, Participants and Outcomes* (unpublished PhD dissertation, Trinity College Dublin, 2018), 84–85.

[22] "For securing purchasers, preventing forgeries and fraudulent gifts and conveyances of lands, tenements and hereditaments, which have been frequently practiced in this kingdom, especially by papists, to the great prejudice of the protestant interest thereof." 6 Anne c. 2, *The Statutes at Large, Passed in the Parliaments held in Ireland* (Dublin, 1786), vol. 4, 112.

[23] P. Roebuck, 'The Irish Registry of Deeds: A Comparative Study' (1972) 18(69) *Irish Historical Studies* 64–65; J. Howell, 'Deed Registration in England: A Complete Failure?' (1999) 58(2) *Cambridge Law Journal* 377.

had been forfeited, and where title remained in dispute.[24] Further, when
Catholic landowners managed to hold on to their estates, despite seizures
and the growing number of repressive laws, the interpretation of debtor
protections was changeable and contested. Family settlements and entails
created before 1703 had helped some Catholic families to safeguard
property, and even "to circumvent inheritance restrictions," like the
gavelling clause mandating subdivision of estates of inheritance, that
were part of the 1704 penal legislation targeting Catholic landownership.[25] Although Catholics could not legally hold mortgages on the lands
they retained, some Catholics did manage to mortgage their property to
sustain these family settlements, sometimes as part of collusive actions
with Protestant discoverers.[26] Other Catholic landowners were able to
secure mortgages after agreeing to convert to Protestantism, and this
added to already widespread concern about debtor deceit. Creditors took
note of the possibility of false conversion, leading mortgage lenders in
Ireland, and in other parts of the British Empire, to try to check property
deeds now validated at the registry in Dublin, and to seek assurances
from local informants about the religious convictions of potential
borrowers.[27]

Creditor suspicion about mortgage fraud and deception was, however,
not only directed at Irish Catholics. Heavily indebted Protestant landowners in Ireland also relied on mortgages in order to maintain and

[24] Rudolph, 'Broker's Advice', 200–201. The general issue of repayment to Protestant
creditors was a question posed early in the Williamite settlement: see the discussion of
the debt of Colonel John Browne and the articles of Limerick in E. Kinsella, 'In Pursuit of
a Positive Construction: Irish Catholics and the Williamite Articles of Surrender,
1690–1701' (2009) 24 *Eighteenth-Century Ireland* 25–29.

[25] R. Fitzpatrick, 'Catholic Inheritance under the Penal Laws in Ireland' (2020) 44(166) *Irish
Historical Studies* 224, 227–229; see also K. J. Harvey, 'The Family Experience: The
Bellews of Mount Bellew', in T. P. Power and K. Whelan (eds.), *Endurance and
Emergence; Catholics in Ireland in the Eighteenth Century* (Dublin, 1990), 177–178.

[26] Harvey, 'Family Experience,' 172; T. P. O'Neill, 'Discoverers and Discoveries: The Penal
Laws and Dublin Property' (1983) 37(1) *Dublin Historical Record* 2, 6–7. For an example
of the contest over discovery and the equity of redemption see *Foot v. Nagle* in G. E.
Howard, *Several Special Cases on the Laws against the Further Growth of Popery in
Ireland* (Dublin, 1775), 84–88.

[27] 8 Anne c. 3 s. 27–30 (Ire.) An Act for Explaining and Amending an Act Intituled, An Act
to Prevent the Further Growth of Popery; Rudolph, 'Broker's Advice', 205–207; C. Bailey,
Irish London: Middle-Class Migration in the Global Eighteenth Century (Liverpool, 2013),
95–96. On the significance of Catholic Irish merchant networks see also J. Bergin, 'Irish
Catholics and Their Networks in Eighteenth-Century London' (2015) 39(1) *Eighteenth-
Century Life* 75–85, 89–92.

expand family wealth. Taking on mortgage debt was an accepted way to charge an entailed estate so as to raise marriage portions for daughters, produce maintenance for younger sons, and provide for wives' trusts and jointures.[28] The earls of Donegall, aristocratic proprietors of Belfast, afford a good example of how this wide recourse to mortgage could stimulate creditor concern. The fourth earl, who suffered from chronic physical and mental illness, succeeded to his title in 1706. Soon after, the family moved from Belfast to England and estate finances were then taken over – and mismanaged – by trustees. Creditors challenged this estate administration and many of the Donegall debts, including several large mortgage loans, were "entangled in a web of lawsuits and legal settlements" for decades.[29] The fifth earl, more capable and more ambitious, inherited and increased these debts after he succeeded to the title in 1757. In addition to the mortgages, unpaid portions, annuities, and legacies he inherited, the fifth earl acquired new mortgage loans worth tens of thousands of pounds. He borrowed this money from individual lenders, and from Hoare's Bank in London, in order to finance the purchase and improvement of Fisherwick Park. This was an estate in Staffordshire, England that he had recently purchased from another heavily indebted Irish landowner, the fifth Viscount Massereene.[30] The fifth Earl of Donegall further embarked on "a major programme of urban improvement" in Belfast which established some of its features that still endure today.[31] Donegall not only took out major loans to finance these projects but he also raised rents and levied new fines on some of his properties in Belfast and elsewhere in Ulster. These actions contributed to the outbreak of agrarian protests – what were known as the "Hearts of Steel" risings – in County Antrim between 1770 and 1772.[32]

Irish Protestant property owners, both lesser gentry and great peers like the earls of Donegall looked to debtor protections in mortgage

[28] D. Wilson, *Women, Marriage and Property in Wealthy Landed Families in Ireland, 1750–1850* (Manchester, 2009) 20; P. Roebuck, 'Landlord Indebtedness in Ulster in the Seventeenth and Eighteenth Centuries', in J. M. Goldstrom and L. A. Clarkson (eds.), *Irish Population, Economy and Society* (Oxford, 1981), 153–154.

[29] S. J. Connolly, 'The Origins of Public Space', in D. Bryan, S. J. Connolly and J. Nagle (eds.), *Civic Identity and Public Space: Belfast since 1780* (Manchester, 2019), 19; Roebuck, 'Landlord Indebtedness', 139–140.

[30] W. A. Maguire, 'Absentees, Architects and Agitators: The Fifth Earl of Donegall and the Building of Fisherwick Park' (1977/78–1981/82) 10 *Proceedings of the Belfast Natural History and Philosophical Society* ser. 2, 6.

[31] Connolly, 'Origins Public Space', 20.

[32] Maguire, 'Absentees', 8–12; Roebuck, 'Landlord Indebtedness', 137–138.

doctrine as a way to ensure that they would be able to hold on to their estates. Many mortgage deeds enrolled at the Irish Registry made clear reference to that doctrine by using the term "equity of redemption" or including a "proviso or condition of redemption."[33] Mortgagees to these Protestant landowners also sought protections: pro-creditor legislation against clandestine mortgages and for establishing deed registers could help them make sure that borrowers weren't lying about prior liens, or about the extent and current value of their properties. Further pro-creditor legislation was developed to help mortgagees bring difficult debtors more swiftly to account since, as we can see from the Donegall example, redemption claims could be prolonged and litigation could drag on.[34] Given the expense and complexity of mortgage litigation in particular, some remedies had to be devised so as to preserve and promote credit. As the Irish legal writer G. E. Howard explained in his *Treatise on the Rules and Practice of the Equity Side of the Exchequer in Ireland*, men bringing bills of foreclosure often encountered "infinite delay" and this kind of obstruction and frustration might lead some of them to become suspicious of the entire legal system. "If something be not speedily done, to remedy this every Day growing Evil," Howard warned, "it will at length come to that Pass, that not any Man in his Senses will lend his Money on any Security in the Kingdom."[35]

Mortgage laws that addressed creditor concerns about procedural delay included an Irish Act for the Relief of Mortgagees, passed in 1733, when "the first serious banking crisis in Ireland" was connected to a general downturn in credit.[36] At a time when it was seen as important to open up credit, this Irish Act offered increased protection,

---

[33] Brendan Twomey avers that "the explicit citing of an equity of redemption term" was a "regular feature" in the first 200 "satisfied and discharged" mortgage deeds he surveyed. Twomey, *Personal Financial Management*, 119. These terms appear throughout the Irish registry, in later as well as earlier volumes considered by Twomey. See, for example, Registry of Deeds (ROD) 1 166 99, 5 363 2074, 72 57 4907, 108 24 74434, 247 6 15787.

[34] See, for example, continued negotiations over mortgage lending and repayment between Donegall and representatives at Hoare's Bank: letter to Earl of Donegall 1784, Private Letter Book 1778–1784, Hoare's Bank, London, HB/8/T/3 fol. 76; Earl of Donegall, n.d., and Earl of Talbot to Messrs Hoare, Bankers, 15 April 1795, Hoare's Bank, London.

[35] G. E. Howard, *A Treatise on the Rules and Practice of the Equity Side of the Exchequer in Ireland* (Dublin, 1760), vol. 1, xxv.

[36] L. M. Cullen, 'Problems in and Sources for the Study of Irish Economic Fluctuations 1660-1800' (2014) 41 *Irish Economic and Social History* 3–4; Dickson, 'Society and Economy', 155. A total of eight Dublin banks failed between 1727 and 1760 Powell, 'Credit, Debt and Patriot Politics in Dublin', 124.

and thus encouragement, to lenders The Act specifically addressed the problem of mortgagors who "absconded or [have] gone out of the kingdom" to avoid their creditors' suits. It detailed the legal responsibilities of resident estate agents, and clarified the steps by which a bill of foreclosure would move toward a final decree in the Irish Chancery.[37] This law would not only have impacted mortgagors who had only temporarily fled at a time of crisis, but also Irish absentees, and great debtors, like the earls of Donegall who had been living in England for decades. This legislative relief for creditors was part of the development of mortgage law that informed later debates about whether legislation should openly recognize and extend protection to Catholic mortgagees too. In these earlier decades there were some who already defended Catholic lending, arguing that since Catholics had "engrossed to themselves a great share of the trade and commerce," this expansive Irish Catholic merchant wealth was a reservoir of credit that ought to be acknowledged and accessed.[38]

More broadly, 1733 was a moment of economic and political upheaval in Britain and other parts of the empire, when complaints about deceits, speculation and "shameful frauds" were fueled by any number of controversies, including the excise crisis, increased risks in colonial credit markets and a stock market plunge.[39] The Westminster parliament addressed credit and investment concerns in legislation like the Colonial Debts Act 1732, which aimed to protect British merchant creditors, Barnard's Act 1734, intended to suppress the more speculative methods of securities trading or "stockjobbing," and the Act for the More Easy Redemption and Foreclosure of Mortgages passed in 1734.[40] Like the Irish Act of 1733, this British mortgage legislation outlined methods for promoting creditor rights. Both British and Irish legislators sought to protect mortgagees by establishing specific steps by which a cooperative mortgagor participated either in redemption or foreclosure processes. At the same time, both bills maintained the principle of debtor

---

[37] 7 George 2 c. 14 (Ire.). J. Gabbett, *A Digested Abridgement and Comparative View of the Statute Law in England and Ireland* (Dublin, 1812), vol. 2, bk. 3, 339–340.

[38] *Some Considerations on the Laws Which Incapacitate the Roman Catholicks of Ireland from Purchasing Lands, from Taking Long or Beneficial Leases, and from Lending Money on Real Securities* (Dublin, 1740), 19–20.

[39] M. J. Daunton, *Progress and Poverty: An Economic and Social History of Britain, 1700–1850* (Oxford, 1995), 310; S. Banner, *Anglo-American Securities Regulation: Cultural and Political Roots, 1590–1860* (Cambridge, 1998), ch. 3.

[40] 5 George 2 c. 7, 7 George 2 c. 8, 7 George 2 c. 20 (GB).

redemption rights enshrined in mortgage doctrine. Indeed, the Irish Act for the Relief of Mortgagees included several sections setting out extended times for mortgagors to respond to decrees of foreclosure as a way to preserve absentees' ability to redeem their mortgages.[41] A subsequent amendment, passed in 1739, offered some clarification of this decree process in yet another attempt to protect mortgagees against mortgagors who failed to participate.[42] The goal common to Irish and British legislation for "relief" and "easy redemption and foreclosure" was to allow for a mortgagor's redemption of property, but at the same time to expedite the decree process for the benefit of the mortgagee.

It was only much later that methods for mandating debtor cooperation, and ensuring payment, were enacted in Ireland. In 1772 an Irish Act for Rendering Securities More Effectual provided for the appointment of a "Receiver" in those cases where a lender had received no mortgage interest payments for over a year. The Receiver was empowered to gather "such part of the rents of the mortgaged premises" necessary to meet the mortgagor's obligations "to pay such arrear of interest, and also the accruing interest . . . until the whole of such interest due on the said mortgage be discharged."[43] This Irish Act was another example of extending protection for creditors at a time when money was tight. In 1770, a credit crisis had affected certain Irish banks and merchants, and by 1772 there was a widespread financial crisis throughout Britain and the empire.[44] Protections for creditors were broadly defended as necessary steps in order to promote national, commercial and imperial success.

The Irish Act for Rendering Securities More Effectual established enhanced supervision of debtors by creating an additional salaried administrator, the Receiver, who was to be involved in a landowner's affairs. Many, if not most, Irish landowners, residents as well as absentees, already employed agents, attorneys, surveyors and accountants to assist in running their estates. But those men were supposed to work for their landowner's benefit, and even before the 1772 Act lawmakers had raised questions about collusion between deceptive agents and indebted

---

[41] 7 George 2 c. 14, sects. 3–8 (Ire.); Gabbett, *Digested Abridgment*, 340.

[42] 13 George 2 c. 9, sects. 1–3 (Ire.).

[43] 11 & 12 George 3 c. 10 (Ire.).

[44] Cullen, 'Problems and Sources Irish Economic Fluctuations', 4, 7; J. Hoppit, 'Financial Crises in Eighteenth-Century England' (1986) 39(1) *Economic History Review* (new series) 51–54.

landowners. Two bills aimed to 'better regulat[e] agents, receivers and attorneys" had been proposed, but failed, in the 1740s and 1750s. These mid-century regulatory proposals generally focused attention on willful corruption and undue influence, but there was also disquiet "about the ease with which Catholics had moved into this work" as agents.[45] The court-appointed Receiver mandated by the 1772 Act was meant to be a check on a corrupt agent's power, and also a limit on a landowner's options. The Receiver's function was to advance the creditor's interests; the point of the 1772 legislation was to root out debtor frauds and evasions, and to compel a recalcitrant mortgagor to stay up to date on mortgage payments.

Similar questions about agency, and problems regarding absentee-ism, were also prevalent in Jamaica at this time. But in that part of the British Empire remedies for fraud were not solely aimed at debtors and agents. They were also sometimes aimed at creditors. Warnings about "malicious and crafty creditors" who threatened planter power had been aired in angry response to the Colonial Debts Act of 1732.[46] In subsequent years the Jamaican Assembly passed legislation against creditor deceits, seeking to exercise some control over creditor power. They enacted laws in 1740 and 1751 requiring regular and transparent accounting by mortgagees in possession, as well as by attorneys, trustees and executors, so as to ensure that any profits coming out of mortgaged plantations would be accurately recorded. While legislation in the early 1780s did bring the Jamaican foreclosure process into line with the creditor-friendly procedures outlined in earlier British and Irish legislation, Jamaican legislators took care to retain the require-ment for mortgagee honesty in accounting in order to protect planter interests.[47] If British and Irish mortgage legislation mainly focused on fraudulent debtors, these colonial legislators also targeted predatory lenders.

---

[45] T. Barnard, *A New Anatomy of Ireland: The Irish Protestants, 1649–1770* (New Haven, CT, 2003), 211–212, 225. As Barnard notes, proposed legislation to ban Catholic agents failed in 1749: www.qub.ac.uk/ild/?func=display_bill&id=1999, and 1755: www.qub.ac .uk/ild/?func=display_bill&id=2103.

[46] S. D. Smith, *Slavery, Family, and Gentry Capitalism in the British Atlantic* (Cambridge, 2006), 166–167.

[47] 13 Geo. II c. 9, 24 Geo. II c. 19, 25 Geo III c. 10, 33 Geo. III c. 21 (Jamaica). J. H. Howard, *Laws of the British Colonies, in the West Indies and Other Parts of America, Concerning Real and Personal Property and Manumission of Slaves* (London, 1827), 50–52, 54–56, 70–73.

It is likely that worries about powerful and predatory lenders also motivated some Irish lawmakers to reject the so-called popish mortgage bills of the 1760s and 1770s. They did so in the context of this persistent pro-creditor trend in eighteenth-century mortgage legislation. Participants in debate were aware of developments in credit and debt law. They referenced leading cases, citing English and Irish precedents that called into question the practice of Catholic mortgage lending. And they used the language of the law to argue their points. James Caldwell, for example, elaborated on the specific legal dangers that Catholic mortgagees posed. In his publication against the 1764 bill, Caldwell warned that if Catholics were allowed to lend on mortgage, they might actually come into possession of Protestant lands as tenants in *elegit*. In the event of an unpaid mortgage debt, he explained, the Catholic creditor who obtained judgment could choose a writ of execution called *elegit*; this writ directed the sheriff to deliver half of the debtor's lands to the creditor, who then utilized these lands to extract wealth in order to discharge the debt owed.[48] The "right of Papists levying their debts by elegit" was a point of contention in Irish parliamentary debate in part because any claim to *elegit* would be in conflict with early eighteenth-century British legislation and English case law, as well as with a recent decision in the Irish courts.[49] James Caldwell joined that debate, arguing that even if it were permissible for Catholics to hold only half of the estates of Protestant mortgagors through *elegit*, it would mean that "their power and influence [would] be encreased to a dangerous degree."[50] Caldwell did acknowledge that mortgage law should protect the Protestant borrower's right to redeem his debt since, according to the doctrine of the equity of redemption, even if a mortgagor defaulted on the loan, he had an equitable right which could only be ended by a court's decree of foreclosure. But in practice, Caldwell said, the Protestant debtor would

---

[48] As Caldwell's contemporary, the English legal scholar William Blackstone explained, the creditor then "held, occupied and enjoyed [these lands] until his debt and damages [were] fully paid." This kind of possession was another kind of "conditional estate, created by operation of law, for security and satisfaction of debts." W. Blackstone, *Commentaries on the Laws of England, Book II*, ed. Simon Stern (Oxford, 2016), 108–109. For a discussion of the longer history of *elegit* and the common-law mortgage, see D. P. Waddilove, 'The Mendacious Common Law Mortgage' (2018) 107(3) *Kentucky Law Journal* 435–438.

[49] J. P. Day, 'The Catholic Question in the Irish Parliament, 1760–82' (MA thesis, National University Ireland, 1973), 63; Kelly, 'Repealing Penal Laws', 85–86. The relevant statutes and case law were summarized in G. E. Howard, *Several Special Cases on the Laws against the Further Growth of Popery in Ireland: 1720–1773* (Dublin, 1775).

[50] Caldwell, *Brief Examination*, 14.

not be so well protected: "it is also well known," he noted, "that the agreement between the debtor and creditor may be so managed, as that neither the debtor nor his heir can redeem without such loss as will make the redemption a moral, though not a physical impossibility."[51]

The 1772 Act for Rendering Securities More Effectual, the only mortgage bill to be enacted in Ireland in this period of failed bills, outlined another way for a mortgagor to meet his interest payments and so, perhaps, avoid foreclosure. The Act gave the mortgagee an alternative process to *elegit*, a way to get a return on his investment without taking possession of a mortgaged property and so, if "papist" lending were permitted, could preclude a Catholic mortgagee from seizing Protestant lands. Further, passage of the 1772 Act occurred at the same time as the Irish legislature notably provided for some Catholic landholding, by ratifying an Act that allowed "every papist or person professing the popish religion, who shall be desirous to employ his industry and money for the improvement of the kingdom," to take long leases on bog land.[52] These two Acts were ratified at the same time as the legislature again took up the question of whether such wealthy Catholics could employ their "industry and money" as mortgagees.

Questions about debt process remained at issue in the debate. A legal commentator such as G. E. Howard, who published his collection of *Several Special Cases on the Laws Against the Further Growth of Popery in Ireland* in 1775, reassured contemporaries that debtor protections in mortgage law remained strong. Howard demonstrated that Catholic possession of Protestant property through mortgage was not a particular threat by citing Irish and English precedents against a Catholic right to claim *elegit* or pursue foreclosure.[53] Further, Howard actively defended the proposed bills to allow Catholics to lend on mortgage. Indeed, like other proponents of change, he argued that such mortgage loans would bind Catholics more closely to state and society, serving as what he called "a further pledge for their peaceful conduct," since Catholic money would be tied up in Protestant lands and out of reach for many years. "[S]urely the most prejudiced . . . must admit," Howard concluded, "that a rich papist could be a far more formidable enemy with money in his chest, than if it were out upon a mortgage, when twenty battles might be

---

[51] Ibid., 16.
[52] 11 & 12 George 3 c. 21 (Ire.); Kelly, 'Repealing Penal Laws', 91.
[53] Howard, *Special Cases*, 201–202, 294–295, 314–315.

fought before he could command a single shilling of it."[54] Here Howard referred to existing impediments to foreclosure and highlighted the mortgagor's equity of redemption – his persistent right to redeem. Howard viewed this aspect of mortgage doctrine as a powerful protection against any creditor, Catholic or other, who might threaten to foreclose.

Although another bill to "secure the repayment of money really lent and advanced by Papists" failed to secure passage in 1773/74, these ongoing arguments about mortgage doctrine were significant. They contributed to the change that was achieved in the "breakthrough" Catholic Relief Act a few years later.[55] Questions about creditor power clearly informed fears of Catholic power, and the testing of the equity of redemption was central to the debate over constitutional change.

---

[54] Ibid., vii–viii.
[55] Kelly, 'Repealing Penal Laws', 91–95.

9

Constitutional Change, Law and Grattan's Parliament

MAIKE SCHWIDDESSEN

The years 1782 and 1783 remain striking moments in the constitutional memory of Ireland. If, as Henry Grattan declared in the Irish House of Commons, 'the Sixth of George the First took away your Constitution',[1] the amendment of Poynings' Law, and the repeal of the Declaratory Act in 1782, returned fundamental constitutional rights to the Irish Parliament. Both Acts had been symbols of English supremacy over Ireland, and the legislative changes were celebrated as a step towards greater Irish independence. But the changes are viewed in two ways. While they were celebrated at that time and super-elevated later by Irish nationalists, less significance is nowadays attributed to the so-called Constitution of 1782, which is often seen as a mere 'change on paper'. Long before 1782, the Irish Parliament could influence legislation to be introduced to Ireland by proposing 'Heads of Bills', and the amendment of Poynings' Law largely affirmed an established legislative procedure. The degree of legislative independence achieved in 1782 fell short of full independence, for the British executive still had significant control over the Irish Parliament and determined Irish politics. The constitutional changes of 1782–83 were symbolically significant, but (apart from the return to the Irish House of Lords of its appellate jurisdiction, a solid constitutional gain) their practical impact was limited. Neither the Irish Parliament as a legislature nor the laws it subsequently enacted were much affected. For these reasons, it remains doubtful whether the 'Constitution of 1782', although an important symbol in the constitutional history of Ireland, was in fact a *constitution* that brought about

---

[1] As Henry Grattan referred to the Declaratory Act, 6 Geo. I, c. 5 [GB] (1719); 'Henry Grattan's Speech to the Irish House of Commons', 19 April 1780, in H. T. Dickinson (ed.), *Ireland in the Age of Revolution, 1760–1805*, Part I, Vol. 2 (1779–1782) (Abingdon, 2016), 59.

significant constitutional change – terms, defined by the House of Lords' Select Committee on the Constitution, that are examined below.

This chapter seeks to offer a new look at the constitutional implications of the changes of 1782–83, first, by studying the concept of constitutional change and, secondly, by analysing the legislation passed by the Irish Parliament before and after the point at which it achieved its legislative independence. The focus is on the economic legislation enacted. Analysis of the changes of 1782–83, and of the legislation of the Irish Parliament, allows for a better understanding of the extent of the constitutional change and of its impact on lawmaking. Constitutional change and the law are always interacting with each other. Acts of Parliament have been the usual devices that brought about constitutional change in the United Kingdom and Ireland: and constitutional change in turn has influenced future legislation. The question in the present case is whether constitutional change influenced the subsequent legislation of Grattan's Parliament.

Comparison of the legislation of the Irish Parliament before and after 1782–83 shows, for example, that there was a marked continuity in the field of economic policy. Long before 1782, the Irish Parliament, by using the 'Heads of Bills' procedure, could shape its economic and social legislation, and continued to do so after 1782–83. In looking at the economic legislation, the focus in this chapter is on the linen industry, on the big infrastructure projects represented by roads and canals, and on the Dublin Paving Board, which was one of several municipal institutions in Dublin that was improving living conditions in the city. A large part of the legislation passed by the Irish Parliament in the eighteenth century was on economic and social issues, and a case study of these three areas shows the impact the legislation made.

The 'Constitution of 1782'

Three Acts, passed in the summer of 1782 and the spring of 1783, two by the United Kingdom Parliament and one by the Irish Parliament, are credited as securing the legislative independence of the Irish Parliament. Poynings' Law of 1495 and the Declaratory Act of 1719 had undermined the sovereignty of the Irish legislature, the one for centuries, and the other for the previous six decades. Legislative independence meant greater independence for the Irish legislature from the authority of the United Kingdom Parliament and executive than it had enjoyed before.

Poynings' Law declared the dependence of the Irish Parliament first on the English and eventually the United Kingdom executive.[2] The Irish Parliament was to be summoned by the British monarch and his Councils. It provided that the right to initiate laws in the Irish Parliament lay with the United Kingdom and Irish Privy Councils. The Irish Parliament had no right to initiate its own legislation. It could only approve or reject Bills introduced by the United Kingdom executive.

The Declaratory Act was passed by the United Kingdom Parliament in 1719 following the case of *Annesley v. Sherlock*.[3] The 1719 Act deprived the Irish House of Lords of its judicial functions. The United Kingdom House of Lords, and not the Irish House, would henceforth be the final Court of Appeal for cases originating in the Irish courts. Further, the Act stated that the United Kingdom Parliament could legislate for Ireland. The subordination of Ireland to the British Crown was thus prescribed in law.

At the end of the seventeenth century, the Irish Parliament started to circumvent the prohibition on initiating legislation by introducing what were called 'Heads of Bills'.[4] Heads of Bills were sent from the Irish House of Commons or Irish House of Lords to the Irish and the United Kingdom Privy Councils which then had to approve them. Either Privy Council could reject or amend the Heads of Bills. After their approval – be it with or without amendment – the legislative proposals were sent back to the Irish Parliament, now in the form of accustomed Bills. The Houses of Parliament in Ireland then had the option of approving or rejecting the Bill. If the Bill was approved by both Irish Houses, it received royal assent. The procedure of the Heads of Bills was recognised by the United Kingdom executive and firmly established well before 1782.[5] Through this 'detour' of the Heads of Bills, the Irish Parliament could take part in initiating its own legislation. In fact, the majority of the Irish statutes enacted in the eighteenth century passed through this

---

[2] 10 Hen. VII, c. 4 [IR] (1495).

[3] 6 Geo. I, c. 5 [GB] (1719). For the details of the case see A. Lyall, *The Irish House of Lords, A Court of Law in the Eighteenth Century* (Dublin, 2013), 45–7.

[4] The only difference between Bills emanating from the Privy Councils and Heads of Bills from the Irish Parliament lay in the initial wording: J. Kelly, *Poynings' Law* (Dublin, 2007), 46.

[5] For detail on the Heads of Bills see, for example, Kelly, *Poynings' Law*; C. I. McGrath, 'Government, Parliament and the Constitution: The Reinterpretation of Poynings' Law, 1692–1714' (2006) 35 *Irish Historical Studies* 160.

procedure,[6] but the restrictions on the legislative powers of the Irish Parliament were the subject of a constant constitutional debate.

After the achievement of 'Free Trade' in 1780,[7] the call for 'legislative independence' became louder. It had been discussed politically for some time when, early in 1782, the Volunteers took the lead. At their Dungannon Convention, held in the County Tyrone town, on 15 February 1782, the Volunteers demanded constitutional reforms. Among the Resolutions of the assembled Volunteers was one that declared that the powers of the Privy Councils under Poynings' Law were unconstitutional and that only the King, Lords and Commons of Ireland had the power to make laws for Ireland.[8] Two months later, on 16 April 1782, Henry Grattan made his famous speech in the College Green Parliament, when he insisted 'that the kingdom of Ireland is a distinct kingdom, with a parliament of her own, the sole legislature thereof'.[9] The demand for legislative independence was conceded shortly afterwards. On 21 June 1782, the United Kingdom Parliament repealed the Declaratory Act of 1719.[10] This meant that the United Kingdom Parliament could no longer legislate for Ireland, and that the Irish House of Lords regained its appellate jurisdiction, becoming again the ultimate Court of Appeal for Ireland. Four weeks later, on 27 July, Poynings' Law was amended by the Irish Parliament through what became known as 'Yelverton's Act', an Act that consisted of four sections.[11] The first and the second of these declared the new legislative procedure: the Irish Privy Council and the United Kingdom Privy Council were merely to certify, 'without addition, diminution, or alteration' of the same, Bills that were

---

[6] Kelly, *Poynings' Law*, 115, 162, 204, 244, 312.

[7] The 'Free Trade' agitation (1778–80) was a political campaign of the Volunteers and Irish Patriots demanding the removal of British trade restrictions imposed on Irish commerce. The British ministry removed most trade restrictions from Ireland in 1779–80. N. Garnham, *The Militia in Eighteenth-Century Ireland, In Defence of the Protestant Interest* (Woodbridge, 2012), 102.

[8] C. H. Wilson, 'A Complete Collection of the Resolutions of the Volunteers, Grand Juries, &c. of Ireland, which Followed the Celebrated Resolves of the First Dungannon Diet', in H. T. Dickinson (ed.), *Ireland in the Age of Revolution, 1760-1805*, Part I, Vol. 2 (1779–1782) (Abingdon, 2016), 143.

[9] 'The Parliamentary Register: or History of the Proceedings and Debates of the House of Commons of Ireland of 1781-2', Tuesday, 16 April 1782, in H. T. Dickinson (ed.), *Ireland in the Age of Revolution, 1760-1805*, Part I, Vol. 2 (1779–1782) (Abingdon, 2016), 167, 188.

[10] 22 Geo. III, c. 53 [GB] (1782).

[11] 21 & 22 Geo. III, c. 47 [IR] (1782).

initiated by either the House of Commons or House of Lords of Ireland.[12] The Privy Councils of both countries could neither change Bills of the Irish Parliament nor introduce Bills of their own, but the United Kingdom Privy Council still retained a right of veto. The third section provided that no Bill could be certified before a meeting of the Irish Parliament had taken place. The final section affirmed that the Irish Parliament was summoned by the British monarch.

The third statute that became part of the scheme of legislative independence was the United Kingdom Renunciation Act of 1783. Henry Flood was the leader of those who had argued that the repeal of the Declaratory Act was not enough, in that the United Kingdom had not 'renounced' the right to legislate for Ireland. On 17 April 1783, following this constitutional debate, the Renunciation Act[13] was passed by the Westminster Parliament. This Act was also succinct. By its two sections any right to legislate for Ireland was renounced, and it was also declared that no writ of error, appeal, or any proceeding from any court in Ireland could be heard by any court in Great Britain.[14]

One consequence of the 'Constitution of 1782' was that in the eighteen years between 1782 and the Union, the years which became known as those of 'Grattan's Parliament', the Parliament in Dublin enjoyed greater freedom than it had ever had before 'Yelverton's Act' had abolished the need for the Irish Parliament to use the Heads of Bills procedure to initiate its own legislation, and the sole right to initiate legislation henceforth lay with the Irish Parliament. Still, that did not imply that the Irish Parliament had gained full sovereignty, for the United Kingdom executive could still veto Irish legislation. Irish nationalists, from the time of O'Connell to the beginning of the twentieth century, had a rosy view of the successes of 'Grattan's Parliament', and were accustomed to point to the arrangements of 1782–83 as a model for a restored Irish Parliament.[15] But was their veneration of these constitutional changes exaggerated; and did the changes even rank as constitutional changes?

---

[12] 21 & 22 Geo. III, c. 47, s. 1, 2 [IR] (1782).
[13] 23 Geo. III, c. 28 [GB] (1783)
[14] Regarding the wording of the Act see A. Lyall, 'The Irish House of Lords as a Judicial Body, 1783–1800' (1993–95) 28–30 Irish Jurist 314, 324–5.
[15] O. Coquelin, 'Grattan's Parliament (1782–1800), Myth and Reality', in O. Coquelin, P. Galliou and T. Robin (eds.), Political Ideology in Ireland, from the Enlightenment to the Present (Newcastle upon Tyne, 2009), 42, 45–6; G. O'Brien, 'The Grattan Mystique' (1986) 1 Eighteenth-Century Ireland 177.

What Constitutes 'Significant Constitutional Change'?

To establish whether a constitutional change took place in 1782, it is necessary to determine the meaning of the term. Finding definitions of 'constitution' and 'constitutional change' is not the least challenging task in constitutional law. For most of us nowadays a 'constitution' is a single codified document that prescribes the organisation of a state, although the notion of a single document is a relatively new concept. Historically, a constitution meant the fundamental laws of a country, written and unwritten. A few countries, such as the United Kingdom and San Marino, still have uncodified constitutions. The understanding of what a 'constitution' is differs from place to place, depending on whether or not it is codified, and also varies over time, for a constitution is always an evolving process. In the same way the meaning of 'constitutional change' is not static, but a developing concept.[16]

Definitions in the Reports of the House of Lords Constitution Committee

Much benefit has been derived from the definitions of these terms found in the Reports of 2001 (and later years) of the House of Lords Select Committee on the Constitution.[17] They provide very valuable guidance, for their basis is the concept of an uncodified constitution, such as still exists in the United Kingdom, and was the 'Constitution of 1782'.

In their First Report of 2001, the Constitution Committee defined 'Constitution' as 'the set of laws, rules and practices that create the basic institutions of the state, and its component and related parts, and stipulate the powers of those institutions and the relationship between the different institutions and between those institutions and the individual'.[18] With respect to 'constitutional change', the Constitution Committee

---

[16] On 'constitutional change' see for example X. Contiades and A. Fotiadou, 'Introduction, Comparative Constitutional Change: A New Academic Field', in X. Contiades and A. Fotiadou (eds.), *Routledge Handbook of Comparative Constitutional Change* (Abingdon, 2021), 1–2, 7–8; on the development of the term 'constitution' see D. Gosewinkel, 'The Constitutional State', in H. Pihlajamäki, M. D. Dubber and M. Godfrey (eds.), *The Oxford Handbook of European Legal History* (Oxford, 2018), 946.

[17] The 'Constitution Committee' advises the House of Lords on the constitutional implications of public bills and enquires into wider constitutional issues.

[18] Select Committee on the Constitution, *First Report* (2001–2), *Reviewing the Constitution, Terms of Reference and Method of Working* (HL Paper 11, London, 2001), para. 20.

acknowledged that any definition was challenging to find.[19] Examples can be given, but there cannot be an exhaustive list or a final definition. In its Fifteenth Report of 2011 the Committee offered this non-exhaustive list of what a 'constitutional change' could embrace[20]:

- any alteration to the structure and composition of Parliament;
- any alteration to the powers of Parliament, or any transfer of power, as by devolution or international treaty, which would in practice be difficult to reverse;
- any alteration to the succession to the Crown or the functions of the monarch;
- any substantial alteration to the balance of power between Parliament and government, including the conferment of unduly broad or ill-defined powers to legislate by order;
- any substantial alteration to the balance of power between central government and local authorities;
- any substantial alteration to the establishment and jurisdiction of the courts of law, including any measure that would place the exercise of power beyond the purview of the courts, or which would affect the independence of the judiciary.

Following this enumeration of possible examples of constitutional change, the Constitution Committee recognised that some constitutional changes are of higher significance than others. For this reason, any constitutional change needs to be examined in two steps: first, as to whether it is to be deemed 'constitutional', and second, 'whether it is so significant that it really ought to merit further delay and discussion'.[21] In their First Report in 2001, the Constitution Committee had already emphasised the importance of 'significance', stating that the Committee aimed to focus on 'significant constitutional issues'.[22] The consequence is that the importance of a constitutional change is less the change itself than its significance. This inevitably means that an element of subjectivity affects the definition[23]: if it did not, the term 'constitutional change', extended to a wide range of issues which only slightly touch the 'heart' of a constitution, would be apt to become boundless.

Restricting the interpretation to 'significant constitutional changes' allows us to focus on the major changes that bring about a notable

---

[19] Select Committee on the Constitution, *Fifteenth Report* (2010–12), *The Process of Constitutional Change* (HL Paper 177, London, 2011), para. 11 ff.

[20] Ibid., para. 11.

[21] Ibid., para. 13.

[22] Constitution Committee, *First Report* (2001–2), para. 22, emphasis in the original.

[23] Constitution Committee, *Fifteenth Report* (2010–12), para. 14.

alteration in a constitutional structure. In its First Report of 2001, the Constitution Committee suggested a neat test for significance that involves a pair of homonyms beginning with 'p'. The 'two p's' are the frequently misspelled words 'principal' and 'principle'. The test is this: 'In order to be significant, a constitutional issue needs to be one that is a *principal* part of a constitutional framework and one that raises an important question of *principle*.'[24]

It is a definition that still includes an element of subjectivity, especially with regard to the latter word, but it does permit a better understanding and narrowing down of what 'significant' constitutional changes are. By way of example, changes in the electoral system would be 'constitutional', but significant only in the case of major changes. Such major changes could be modifications to the voting system or to the political franchise whereas minor changes like alterations to regulations prescribing how officials count the votes would not likely be deemed a 'significant' constitutional change.[25]

In applying these definitions to the events of 1782–83, what must be factually determined is whether there were 'significant constitutional changes' – that is, changes to a *principal* part of the constitutional framework of Ireland, and if an important question of *principle* was raised.

Applying the Test of the 'Two P's'

Changes Touching the Irish House of Lords

The return to the Irish House of Lords of its judicial functions is clearly a 'significant constitutional change' within the Constitution Committee's definition. As seen above, a constitutional change can consist of a 'transfer of powers'. The repeal of the Declaratory Act transferred powers from the United Kingdom House of Lords to the Irish House of Lords. It further effected another aspect of the above definition: a 'substantial alteration to the establishment and jurisdiction of the courts of law'.[26] Recognition of the determinations of its highest court has to be a pillar of the constitution of any country, so a *principal* part of the Irish constitutional framework was concerned. A question of *principle* was also

---

[24] Constitution Committee, *First Report* (2001–2), para. 22, emphasis added.
[25] Constitution Committee, *Fifteenth Report* (2010–12), para. 14.
[26] Ibid., para. 11.

raised: the issue of the relationship between the Irish and the United Kingdom judiciary. The Irish House of Lords, having recovered powers that it did not possess between 1719 and 1782, was again a judicial body.[27]

Changes Affecting the Parliament as a Legislative Body

Changes in the legislature are clearly 'constitutional changes' within the contemplation of the Constitution Committee, for gaining the sole right to initiate laws was a 'transfer of powers' from Great Britain to Ireland. The previous right of the two Privy Councils to initiate Bills and to amend Heads of Bills interfered with the right of the Irish Parliament to legislate. This power was now greatly diminished, and the influence of the United Kingdom executive and legislature over Irish legislation was curbed. The Renunciation Act went further in confirming the powers of the two Houses of Parliament. The changes modified the constitutional relationship between Ireland and Great Britain, especially the relationship between the Irish legislature and the United Kingdom executive. A *principal* part of the constitutional framework of Ireland was thereby affected. The first 'p', 'principal', is thus easily satisfied.

The second 'p', 'an important question of principle', is much more difficult to establish. The question might be answered differently at different times, and any answer is subjective; but one can argue that a question of principle is always raised if visible and tangible changes come about which are likely to have a significant influence upon the course of future politics. With regard to the legislation of 1782–83, visible and tangible changes could be brought about *internally* within Ireland because the country now had the sole right to initiate legislation. There could be similar changes *externally* that would affect the relationship between Ireland and the United Kingdom because the Irish Parliament had gained more powers. But even if no changes were to be clearly visible to us, the question of *principle* would still be apt to arise when considering the perspective of contemporaries. Whether a constitution should be interpreted with strict adherence to the text or in accordance with the original perception is a continuing debate;[28] but what contemporaries

---

[27] In the three volumes of 'Ridgway's Parliamentary Cases', sixty-eight appeals are noted between 1784 and 1796: see Lyall, 'The Irish House of Lords as a Judicial Body', 329.

[28] On the interpretation of 'constitution', see for example L. B. Solum 'What Is Originalism? The Evolution of Contemporary Originalist Theory' in G. Huscroft and B. W. Miller (eds.),

understood, in particular the public opinion of the time, has to be taken into account in determining the meaning of a constitutional change at any given time, for this has a bearing on assessing the impact and importance of a constitutional change – that is, on its 'significance'.

Analysis of the Laws Passed Subsequent to the Constitutional Changes

The Irish Parliament made use of its newly acquired right to initiate legislation and passed more Acts in the seventeen years prior to the Union than ever before. Between 1783 and 1800 the total number of public and private Acts passed was 1,057 (an average of 62.2 per year). By comparison, in the preceding seventy-nine years, between 1703 and 1782, the total number of public and private Acts passed was 1,131, only 74 Acts more (an average of 14.3 per year).[29]

Yet, on closer scrutiny, the legislation passed between 1783 and 1800 was characterised more by quantity than quality. Grattan's Parliament was often praised for bringing about an economic upswing; but the reality is that only a few Acts changed Irish society and the economy with tangible effect. The economic upswing under Grattan's Parliament was mainly due to advantageous economic conditions after the end of the American War of Independence and to private investment.[30] It was not attributable to the legislation of the Irish Parliament, and an analysis of the social and the economic initiatives of the Irish Parliament before and after 1782–83 reveals a strong element of continuity.

Foster's Corn Law is an example of an Act passed after 1783 that had a visible beneficial impact on the Irish economy, although favourable economic conditions were also significant. This statute, passed in the first parliamentary session after legislative independence, granted

The Challenge of Originalism, Theories of Constitutional Interpretations (Cambridge, 2011), 12, in particular 22–4; B. H. Bix, 'Constitutions, Originalism, and Meaning' in G. Huscroft and B. W. Miller (eds.), *The Challenge of Originalism, Theories of Constitutional Interpretations* (Cambridge, 2011), 285; F. Gárdos-Oroz and Z. Szente, 'The Art of Constitutional Interpretation' in F. Gárdos-Oroz and Z. Szente (eds.), *Populist Challenges to Constitutional Interpretation in Europe and Beyond* (Abingdon, 2021), 29.
29 Kelly, *Poynings' Law*, 162, 244, 312, 357.
30 Coquelin, 'Grattan's Parliament (1782–1800)', 46–7; J. Innes, 'Legislating for Three Kingdoms, How the Westminster Parliament Legislated for England, Scotland and Ireland, 1707–1830', in J. Hoppit (ed.), *Parliaments, Nations and Identities in Britain and Ireland, 1660–1850* (Manchester, 2003), 15, 30–1; O'Brien, 'The Grattan Mystique', 177.

subsidies on the export of grain, and restricted the import of grain except in times of scarcity.[31] The Act undoubtedly had a positive impact, and encouraged tillage farming and flour milling; but it also came into force at an opportune time. Foster's Corn Law may have supported the upturn in the Irish corn trade, but it did not initiate it. An increase in English imports of corn from Ireland (that was very profitable to Ireland) was already discernible in the early 1770s. That Ireland had become the principal supplier of corn to England was the main reason for the success of Foster's Corn Law.[32]

As with Foster's Corn Law, the majority of the Acts passed by the Irish Parliament after 1783 that dealt with the economy and society tended more to maintain long-established trends than to effect major change in their own right. This can be seen when analysing legislation affecting the linen trade, infrastructure projects to do with canals and roads, and the Dublin 'Paving Board'. The first two examples belong to the most important areas of the economic legislation of the Irish Parliament. The linen industry was at the time the most important industry in Ireland, and infrastructure was the backbone of a thriving trade on the island. The Dublin Paving Board is a representative example of the municipal legislation of the Irish Parliament, which had similar effects in most Irish towns.

Linen Laws

Several Acts, by different means, supported the Irish linen industry. These included Acts on export bounties, grants, premiums for applying new techniques, the establishment of spinning schools, and above all the establishment of the Linen Board in 1710.[33] The linen industry is the only industry that received continuous subsidies from the Irish state from the seventeenth century until the nineteenth century.[34] After legislative

---

[31] 23 & 24 Geo. III, c. 19 [IR] (1783).

[32] A. P. W. Malcomson, *John Foster (1740–1828), The Politics of Improvement and Prosperity* (Dublin, 2011), 69–70; L. M. Cullen, *Anglo-Irish Trade, 1660–1800* (Manchester, 1968), 49.

[33] The Board of Trustees of the Linen and Hempen Manufactures of Ireland promoted and controlled the Irish linen industry as a regulatory authority. It was established by the Act 9 Anne, c. 3 [IR] (1710).

[34] D. Dickson, *Old World Colony, Cork and South Munster 1630–1830* (Cork, 2005), 203–4. Even the infamous English Woollen Act (10 Wil. III, c. 16, [GB] (1698)) indirectly supported the Irish linen industry. It prohibited the export of Irish woollen products to

independence, about twenty-five linen laws were passed by the Irish Parliament between 1783 and 1800. Most of these Acts related to duties, bounties and grants, and most of them usually extended expiring earlier Acts.[35] The last Act of Parliament which introduced a new element into the linen legislation was an Act passed by the Irish Parliament in the same parliamentary session as 'Yelverton's Act' in 1782, namely 21–22 George III, chapter 35. This Act of 57 sections provided for various measures. Among others, it prohibited the use of lime in bleaching, amended the regulations regarding linen seals, and introduced linen inspectors. The provisions on linen seals and the prohibition of lime in bleaching were not new, both measures being a continuation of existing laws.[36] The introduction of linen inspectors was a new element. The Act of 1782 provided for nine 'inspectors for the counties' and two 'inspectors general', one for the province of Ulster and one for the three other provinces.[37] The inspectors undertook a supervisory role in the linen industry. 'County inspectors' were supposed to travel through their allocated areas to resolve disputes in the linen markets and to report to the Linen Board in Dublin about the current state of linen manufactures. The 'inspectors general' also travelled through their provinces and informed the Linen Board about the state of the linen markets.[38] Although the Linen Board had already appointed inspectors who travelled through the country to report on the state of linen manufacture before the Act of 1782, it was the first time that such an institution was created by an Act of Parliament. This measure was the last entirely new element introduced in the linen laws. The statutes passed after legislative independence dealt mainly with export and import bounties regarding flax seeds and also provided for grants, essentially representing a continuation of previous policy. The later Acts did not introduce new

England but instead England supported the Irish linen industry through favourable duties. Ireland could develop the linen industry as it was not competing with English interests.

[35] For example, 25 Geo. III, c. 11 [IR] (1785); 28 Geo. III, c. 8 [IR] (1788); 32 Geo. III c. 4 [IR] (1792).

[36] For example, 7 Geo. II, c. 10 [IR] (1733); 19 Geo. II, c. 6, s. 18 [IR] (1746); 3 Geo. III c. 34 [IR] (1763).

[37] 21 & 22 Geo. III, c. 35, s. 12, 27 [IR] (1782). One 'county inspector' was appointed for Co. Antrim, Armagh, Derry, Donegal, Down and Tyrone; one for Co. Cavan, Fermanagh and Monaghan; one for Co. Louth, Meath and the town of Drogheda; one for Co. Sligo, Mayo and Galway.

[38] Whereas the 'county inspectors' had certain rights to enforce the laws, the 'inspectors general' could only advise and report back to the Linen Board.

measures to reform the linen industry, such as those passed in the first half of the eighteenth century, when the Linen Board was established.

Infrastructure: Turnpike Roads and Inland Navigation

A continuation after legislative independence of the policy of the first half of the eighteenth century can also be seen when analysing the Irish Acts on infrastructure, in particular Acts on turnpike roads and inland navigation. The main legal incentives for improving roads were provided by the Irish Parliament in the first half of the eighteenth century. Acts of Parliament transferred the management of certain roads to turnpike trusts which could charge tolls in compensation for the maintenance of the roads. Those Acts were copies of English Acts,[39] but all originated as Heads of Bill in the Irish Parliament. Between 1729 and 1837 about 2,040 miles of turnpike roads were created by Acts of the Irish Parliament.[40] However, by 1782 it had been acknowledged that the system of turnpike roads was defective. The tolls on the roads that were intended to finance their maintenance were never sufficient, with the result that the turnpike trusts became heavily indebted and were forced to take on continuing loans. Some Acts tried to diminish the debts by restricting the interest payable, expanding the duration of the time allocated to the turnpike trusts, or increasing the amount of the toll. The extension of the Turnpike Acts continued after legislative independence, but, although the financial problems of the trusts were known, no legislative attempt was made to relieve the trusts or to change the system. The turnpike road system existed unmodified from 1729 until its abolition in the 1850s. From beginning to end, it was shaped by the Acts of the Irish Parliament.

Similarly, Acts dealing with inland navigation were a continuous policy of the Irish Parliament before and after 1782. Throughout the eighteenth century the Irish legislature had promoted inland navigation, first through the founding of statutory corporations, later through encouraging private investment in canals. There was no shift in the policy after legislative independence. A first Act encouraging inland navigation was passed in 1715.[41] In 1729, in the same session in which the first statute for a turnpike road was passed, four commissions, one for

---

[39] D. Broderick, *The First Toll-Roads, Ireland's Turnpike Roads 1729–1858* (Cork, 2002), 44.
[40] Ibid., 232.
[41] 2 Geo. I, c. 12 [IR] (1715).

each province, were set up to promote further inland navigation.[42] This led to the building of the Newry Canal and the Coalisland (Tyrone) Canal in Ulster. In 1751 the Corporation for Promoting and Carrying on an Inland Navigation in Ireland was established by another Act of Parliament.[43] This corporation took charge of the inland navigation throughout the whole island of Ireland. Constructions at the Grand Canal towards Sallins and along the Shannon commenced in the mid-1750s. Further works were undertaken along the Boyne, the Barrow and the Lagan Canal.[44]

The major legislation regarding inland navigation after legislative independence was passed in 1787, 1789 and 1790. The Corporation for Promoting and Carrying on an Inland Navigation of 1751 had been found to be inefficient. This body was heavily in debt, for which reason it was dissolved by an Act of 1787.[45] Instead, local corporations for each of the rivers were set up, although in the long term these proved to be equally inefficient. In 1789, a scheme was set up to encourage individuals to invest in inland navigation through debentures. The Royal Canal, as seen in an Act of 1790, was mainly financed through this scheme.[46]

The legislation regarding canals passed after 1782 placed inland navigation in private hands, the better to finance its construction. This was a major shift in the financing of inland navigation, yet it did not take place because the Irish Parliament had gained more powers after legislative independence but because of the failed policy of the same parliament before 1782.

The Dublin Paving Board

The municipal legislation shaped by the Irish Parliament in the eighteenth century was likewise relatively unaffected by the constitutional legislative changes of 1782–83. Various institutions existed in the city of Dublin and other Irish towns that aimed at improving living conditions and promoting trade. Each institution was founded for a specific purpose by an Act of Parliament. Best known is the 'Wide Street

---

[42] 3 Geo. II, c. 3 [IR] (1729).
[43] 25 Geo. II, c. 10 [IR] (1751).
[44] P. Clarke, 'The Royal Canal 1789–1993' (1993) 46 *Dublin Historical Record* 46.
[45] 27 Geo. III, c. 30 [IR] (1787).
[46] 30 Geo. III, c. 20 [IR] (1790). Works on the Royal Canal began in Dublin at the Cross Guns Bridge, Phibsborough and lead towards Kilcock; on the development of the Royal Canal see Clarke, 'The Royal Canal 1789–1993', 46–9.

Commission', founded in 1757, which built and expanded some of Dublin's narrow streets and bridges to their modern size.[47]

The Paving Board in Dublin, which was founded in 1774, was one of the last such institutions established in the Irish capital.[48] Between its foundation and the Act of Union three further Acts were passed, two that preceded and one that followed legislative independence.[49] These Acts extended the competences of the Board, which was responsible for a variety of tasks that influenced both the street surfaces of Dublin and everyday life.[50] As its name suggests, the Board was responsible for paving the streets properly. In addition, it bore responsibility for cleaning the streets, and for lighting them at night. It initiated street signs and house numbers and was responsible for erecting fountains that provided drinking water for the poor. It regulated the markets and played an important role in the design of buildings, influencing the ornamentation of the façades of houses. The most controversial of the three Acts was that of 1784, which changed the structure of the Board and provided for the transfer of its supervision from the Corporation of Dublin to the House of Commons.[51] There were debates about the Board, its structure, members, tasks and finances, but there was no major shift in the policy of the Paving Board after 1782, which throughout its history was an institution that was entirely shaped by the legislation of the Irish Parliament.

The conclusion from studying these examples of the Irish Parliament's enactments is that no major changes occurred after legislative independence, and that no visible and tangible changes internally within Ireland were attributable to the acquisition of the right to initiate legislation. Reform of the legislative process did not affect the laws

---

[47] 31 Geo. II, c. 19 [IR] (1757). Among others, the Wide Street Commission was responsible for the building and expanding of the Essex-bridge, Sackville Street, Parliament Street and Westmoreland Street. Another example of such a municipal institution is the Ballast Board which aimed to expand the Dublin harbour and was founded in 1707 by an Act of the Irish Parliament (6 Anne c. 20). Similar Ballast Boards were founded in Cork, Galway, Sligo, Drogheda and Belfast in 1729 by another Act of the Irish Parliament (3 Geo. II, c. 21).

[48] 13 & 14 Geo. III, c. 22 [IR] (1774).

[49] 15 & 16 Geo. III, c. 20 [IR] (1775–76); 21 & 22 Geo. III, c. 60 [IR] (1781–82); 23 & 24 Geo. III, c. 57 [IR] (1783–84).

[50] For detail on the Paving Board, see F. O'Cionnaith, *Exercise of Authority, Surveyor Thomas Owen and the Paving, Cleansing and Lighting of Georgian Dublin* (Dublin, 2015).

[51] Ibid., 83–9.

themselves, which remained the same; and continuity was the hallmark of Irish economic and social policy.

A Constitutional Change 'On Paper' that Contemporaries Regarded as a Great Issue of Principle

English Influence on the Irish Parliament after 1782–1783

Looking at English influence on the Irish legislature after 1782–83, there is no more sign of constitutional change externally than there was internally. Despite the constitutional changes, Great Britain retained its substantial influence on the Irish legislature. While the United Kingdom Privy Council could no longer change the wording of an Irish Bill, it still retained a right of veto, which meant that the government of the United Kingdom retained a vital tool of control over Irish legislation. No Bill of which it did not approve would pass the Privy Council.[52]

The United Kingdom Privy Council used its veto only rarely, but the British executive still asserted influence.[53] The best example of continuing British influence on the Irish legislature is found in the passing of the Catholic Relief Acts of 1792 and 1793, which were not home-grown initiatives of the Irish Parliament but passed because of pressure from Britain even against concerns of Dublin Castle.[54] A 'recommendation' from London was like an order; and the Irish Parliament deferred to the United Kingdom's wishes.[55] The Lord Lieutenant of the day, John Fane, tenth Earl of Westmorland, pointed this out incisively:[56] 'The object of England must be to govern Ireland. She has in the present constitution a parliament formed of such materials that England always has and probably always will be able to manage; and she has a sect deficient in numbers but possessing the property, magistracy, and influence in the country pledged to maintain that establishment.' Grattan's Parliament was not at all independent of the influence of the United Kingdom executive.

---

[52] J. Kelly, *Prelude to Union, Anglo-Irish Politics in the 1780s* (Cork, 1992), 235–6, 241, 247.

[53] Between 1783 and 1800, only four bills were rejected. Thirty bills were sent back to Ireland with 'objections'. Kelly, *Poynings' Law*, 344–50, 357.

[54] T. Bartlett, *The Fall and Rise of the Irish Nation: The Catholic Question 1660–1830* (Dublin, 1992), 131–4, 155–62; G. O'Brien, 'Revolution, Rebellion and the Viceroyalty 1789–99', in P. Gray and O. Purdue (eds.), *The Irish Lord Lieutenancy, c. 1541–1922* (Dublin, 2012), 114, 117–18.

[55] Bartlett, The Fall and Rise of the Irish Nation, 138.

[56] Quoted in ibid., 132.

Absence of Evidence that the Constitutional Changes Influenced Subsequent Legislation

The conclusion to which we come is that the constitutional changes of 1782–83 that might have had an effect on the legislative process in fact had little direct impact either internally in Ireland or externally in the relationship with Great Britain. This is not surprising given that the Irish Parliament, with the Heads of Bills procedure, had invented an effective method of making its own laws before 1782, and that after that year the United Kingdom Privy Council still retained its right of veto. Both before and after 1782, only Acts that did not threaten British interests became law. Things effectively remained the same, and the changes of 1782–83 were changes 'on paper', changes *de jure* but not *de facto*. The Irish Parliament gained no more real power; and recognition of the right to initiate legislation was largely symbolic.

The Symbolic Importance of 1782–1783

If the changes of 1782–83 are viewed with scepticism from today's perspective, it is clear that they were very significant for the people who articulated public opinion in 1782. As pointed out above, in determining the significance of a constitutional change, the point of view of contemporaries, those proximately concerned, should be taken into account. In the eighteenth century, the restrictions imposed on the Irish Parliament by Poynings' Law and the Declaratory Act were continually being discussed as a grievance. Indeed, Henry Grattan pithily asked the rhetorical question: 'What is Poynings' law, and the unconstitutional power of the Irish or English Privy Council, but a grievance?'[57] From the perspective of contemporaries, 'legislative independence' was a 'flexing of muscles' in the direction of Great Britain, and the result a victory in a cause for which they had long contended. It was an important symbolic step for Ireland in the constitutional relationship with the United Kingdom. On this basis, from contemporaries' point of view, a 'principal question' was raised, and a significant constitutional change did indeed take place in 1782–83.

Reflecting that the constitutional changes of 1782–83 were introduced by three Acts of Parliament that did not of themselves much affect later

---

[57] 'The Parliamentary Register: or History of the Proceedings and Debates of the House of Commons of Ireland of 1781–2', Tuesday, 16 April 1782, at 185.

laws, it falls to consider what else might have been needed for a constitutional change to have had a significant impact on subsequent lawmaking. Going back to the Constitution Committee's 2001 Report, we find that an essential element in the definition of 'constitution' involves arrangements for the regulation of the relationship between the institutions of state and the individual.[58] A constitution has the aim of maintaining peaceful coexistence in a society. Any constitutional change that affects the relationship of the state's institutions to the individual may automatically have a significant impact, notwithstanding that the terms of the change itself deal only with the institution and not with individuals directly.

Parliamentary reforms of a type that would have affected the people were not sought in 1782–83, and at the time they would have stood little prospect of enactment. After legislative independence, when reforms were called for, which would have included Catholic enfranchisement, they foundered for a decade on the rock of the Catholic Question.[59] When that question was partially tackled, in the Catholic Relief Act of 1793, which extended the franchise to Catholic forty-shilling freeholders, this was a statute that had a greater potential to have a long-term effect on the constitution than the legislative independence of 1782 itself, for it might ultimately have effected a great change in the composition of the Irish Parliament. In 1793, that Parliament had only seven more years of existence, and the sole election that took place before the Union was that of 1797, which produced no significant change in the representative composition of the House of Commons; but the effect that laws such as the Relief Act which impact individuals directly might ultimately have had on the Irish Parliament is a proper subject for conjecture.

However, even though the importance that Irish public opinion placed on the constitutional changes in 1782–83 was much exaggerated, we yet may retain a lingering sense that the Irish Parliament, had it survived and been able to reform itself, might justly have looked back to 1782 as a significant step in an evolutionary constitutional legislative process.

---

[58] '[A]nd stipulate the powers of those institutions and the relationship between the different institutions and between those institutions and the individual.' Constitution Committee, *First Report* (2001–2), para. 20.

[59] J. Kelly, 'The Parliamentary Reform Movement of the 1780s and the Catholic Question' (1988) 43 *Archivium Hibernicum* 95.

10

Sir John Ross Bt

The Last Lord Chancellor of Ireland, 1921–1922

RICHARD MCBRIDE

Introduction

John Ross holds his place in history as the last Lord Chancellor of Ireland. He was also the only Presbyterian ever to hold that office.[1] Although his period as Lord Chancellor was comparatively short, the reported cases heard by him are of note. Ross's path to the metaphorical Irish Woolsack, while seemingly conventional, did differ from that of many of his predecessors and his consciousness of being a Presbyterian, his path to office and his retirement away from the limelight will all be examined.[2]

The events in Ireland during Ross's lifetime formed the backdrop to his career – the Land War from 1879 to 1882, the Home Rule debates between 1886 and 1914, the Easter Rising in 1916, and the ensuing Anglo-Irish War. The Government of Ireland Act 1920, although principally creating home rule parliaments for Southern Ireland and Northern Ireland also recast the role of Lord Chancellor of Ireland. The subsequent Anglo-Irish Treaty of 1921 and the creation of the Irish Free State in 1922 led to the complete abolition of the role, and the enforced, and not entirely happy, retirement of Ross.

Early Years

John Ross was born in Londonderry on 11 December 1853 where his father was the redoubtable Reverend Robert Ross, Minister of Fourth Derry

---

[1] N. Wells, Ross, Sir John, first baronet (1853–1935), Lord Chancellor of Ireland, in *Oxford Dictionary of National Biography* (Oxford, 2004).

[2] The Lord Chancellor of Ireland ceased to sit on the actual Irish Woolsack after the Act of Union 1800. The Irish Woolsack may still be seen in the former Irish House of Lords in Dublin.

Presbyterian Church on Artillery Street within the city walls. During John's youth in Derry and later, Reverend Ross so expanded his congregation that in 1879 it moved outside the city walls to a new purpose-built church (designed by noted Belfast architects Young & Mackenzie) in Carlisle Road.[3] Reverend Ross became Moderator of the Presbyterian Church in Ireland in 1886.[4] John Ross published two volumes of memoirs in 1924 and 1927, and these provide us with a view of how he saw his world.[5] He describes his father as, variously, 'the most gentle of men', 'a man quite incapable of any lengthened belief in human wickedness', but one who 'strictly enforced' family worship and who was a Liberal in his politics.

Against this family backdrop, John Ross was educated at Foyle College, where he was a friend of Percy French, the poet and songwriter, composer of 'The Mountains of Mourne'. During his time at Foyle, Ross notes in his memoirs his encounter with Christopher Palles, the future Chief Baron of the Exchequer, and how this influenced him to enter the legal profession – of which more below. Ross entered Trinity College, Dublin in 1873 to read Classics, where he obtained a Foundation Scholarship in 1876. In his memoirs he notes that he was one of the first Presbyterians to do so, the religious tests having only recently been abolished by the University of Dublin Tests Act 1873. He graduated BA in 1877 and LLB in 1879.

Ross's interest in the law as a career was sparked while still a schoolboy in 1868 when he saw Christopher Palles QC in action in an election petition hearing.[6] The Conservative candidate, a son of the Duke of Abercorn, had lodged a petition against the victorious Liberal, Richard Dowse QC. However, acting for Dowse was Palles, who won the case. This was much to the admiration of the young Ross, who wrote that he was 'blown away' to such an extent that 'henceforth [he] lived for only one thing – to achieve success at the Bar of Ireland'. He developed and maintained a lifelong admiration for and friendship with Palles, whom he regarded as 'the greatest of the Irish judges', despite differences of religion and denomination.[7]

---

[3] P. Harron, *Architects of Ulster: Young & Mackenzie, a Transformational Provincial Practice 1850–1960* (Belfast, 2016), 148–149.
[4] 'Former Moderators' (*Presbyterian Church in Ireland*), www.presbyterianireland.org/Utility/About-Us/Historical-Information/Former-Moderators.aspx, accessed 10 June 2022.
[5] Sir John Ross, *The Years of My Pilgrimage* (London, 1924); and Sir John Ross, *Pilgrim Scrip: More Random Reminiscences* (London, 1927).
[6] Ross, 1924 (n. 5), 14.
[7] Ross, 1927 (n. 5), 15; and V. T. H. Delany, *Christopher Palles, Lord Chief Baron of Her Majesty's Court of Exchequer in Ireland 1874–1916, His Life and Times* (Dublin, 1960), ix, 153–154.

On the other side of the political spectrum, Ross also enjoyed a close friendship with another lawyer, Edward Carson, forged during their time at Trinity College.[8] Initially, they followed similar paths: Ross followed Carson in being called to the Irish Bar in 1879 and they both became MPs – Carson for Dublin University and Ross for Londonderry City – in the 1892 general election.

Ross's parliamentary career only lasted three years (1892–1895) and after that it was his judicial career that became more important, with his appointment in 1896 as a land judge in the Chancery Division of the High Court of Justice in Ireland.[9] Again, a trailblazer, he was the first Presbyterian to be appointed as a High Court judge in Ireland. Lawrence McBride has suggested that this appointment was solely because of lobbying on his behalf by the Duke of Abercorn (the older brother of the defeated election candidate in 1868).[10] Whether this is true or not, he was clearly a highly regarded lawyer by this time and described by F. E. Ball as 'able, courageous and consistent'.[11]

Northern Ambitions

While Ross made much in his memoirs of having been Lord Chancellor of Ireland, particularly the last person to hold that office, he omits any mention of his earlier efforts to secure another senior legal position – Lord Chief Justice of Northern Ireland (LCJNI).[12]

Despite being Dublin-based since his appointment to the bench in 1896, Ross maintained his connections with Ulster. Despite his tendency to anti-partitionism, he continued to identify with the Ulster Unionists. So, with the passing of the Government of Ireland Act 1920, Ross's first ambition was not to be Lord Chancellor of Ireland. This role was still held by Sir James Campbell. Instead, Ross, in a series of letters in summer 1920, lobbied Walter Long to become Lord Chief Justice of Northern Ireland.[13] Long had been leader of the Ulster

---

[8] H. Montgomery Hyde, *Carson, The Life of Sir Edward Carson, Lord Carson of Duncairn* (London, 1953).

[9] Ross, 1924 (n. 5), chapter XIV.

[10] L. McBride, *The Greening of Dublin Castle: The Transformation of Bureaucratic and Judicial Personnel in Ireland,1892–1992* (Washington, DC, 1991), 74.

[11] F. Elrington Ball, *The Judges in Ireland, 1221–1921*, vol. 2 (London, 1926), 324.

[12] Ross, 1924 (n. 5), 297.

[13] Two letters, dated May–June 1920, from Sir John Ross to Walter Long found in Wiltshire & Swindon Archives Ref. 947/336.

Unionists from 1906 to 1910 and at the time of Ross's lobbying he was not only First Lord of the Admiralty but also chair of the so-called *Long Committee* of the British cabinet which had overseen the drafting and enactment of the 1920 Act.[14] In his letters to Long, Ross stated his desire to be the new Lord Chief Justice of Northern Ireland on the passing of the 1920 Act. He also displayed antipathy towards the then-incumbent Lord Chancellor, Campbell, by expressing to Long his refusal to acknowledge the consent of Campbell, as a precondition of such an appointment.

Sir James Craig, the holder of the new office of Prime Minister of Northern Ireland, appointed Denis Henry as Lord Chief Justice of Northern Ireland.[15] Whatever Ross's feelings about this, he was not to remain without a senior post and was even to conduct the swearing in of Henry as Lord Chief Justice of Northern Ireland while on holiday.

The Lord Chancellorship

The departure in June 1921 of Sir James Campbell as Lord Chancellor was reported as being 'startling'.[16] Ross wrote in his memoirs that he was 'astonished' at his own appointment and even believed that Campbell had not received any letter of removal.[17] Colum Kenny has provided a different outlook on some of Ross's machinations in 1919.[18] Given the sentiments expressed in Ross's letters to Walter Long, this astonishment may indeed be a little hard to believe. Nevertheless, the appointment of Ross was lauded, it being observed in *The Irish Law Times* that he was 'one of the most popular members of the Judiciary, and his appointment has been exceedingly well received by the profession'.[19] In fact, the reporter further enthuses:

---

[14] C. Moore, *Birth of the Border: The Impact of Partition in Ireland* (Dublin, 2019).

[15] É. Phoenix, 'The Life and Career of Denis Henry (1864–1925): Barrister, Ulster Unionist Politician and First Lord Chief Justice of Northern Ireland' in B. Dickson and C. McCormick (eds.), *The Judicial Mind: A Festschrift for Lord Kerr of Tonaghmore* (Oxford, 2021).

[16] Editorial, 'Week to Week', *The Irish Law Times* (Dublin, 2 July 1921), 162.

[17] Ross, 1924 (n. 5), 293.

[18] C. Kenny, '"Degradation of the Irish Bench" – Colum Kenny on Sir John Ross and a Private Plea in 1919', *The Irish Times* (Dublin, 9 August 2021), An Irishman's Diary, www.irishtimes.com/opinion/degradation-of-the-irish-bench-colum-kenny-on-sir-john-ross-and-a-private-plea-in-1919-1.4643048, accessed 21 February 2022.

[19] ILT (n. 16).

His genial manner, his unvarying courtesy to the Bar and to solicitors, his manly independence, his fairness to litigants, and his patience in listening to the arguments addressed to him while they are to the point, have all contributed to make him a very popular judge. His strong common sense is perhaps his outstanding quality on the Bench; but this does not obscure his firm grasp of legal principles and his knowledge of case law and practice. He is also a man of affairs. We anticipate for him great success in his new office.[20]

Having lost out to Sir Denis Henry, Ross contented himself with the role of permanent Lord Chancellor for life, and President of the new High Court of Appeal for Ireland. One of his first functions as the new Lord Chancellor was, however, not a judicial one.

Speaker of the Senate of Southern Ireland

In an echo of the role of earlier Irish Lord Chancellors as Speaker of the Irish House of Lords until the Act of Union 120 years before, Sir John Ross became Speaker of the short-lived Senate of Southern Ireland. The Senate had been envisioned as the upper house of the legislature of Southern Ireland under the Government of Ireland Act 1920. *The Irish Times* provides an interesting account of the two meetings held by the Senate before it rose for the final time, labelling the totality of proceedings a 'hollow mockery'.[21] It is interesting to note that the 1920 Act, while appointing the Lord Chancellor an *ex officio* senator, made no specific mention of the Lord Chancellor becoming Speaker. However, at the opening meeting of the Senate it was taken as read that the Lord Chancellor should have that role. At that meeting, the Marquess of Sligo noted 'that unfortunately our Speaker, the Lord Chancellor, is, through illness, unable to attend'. Accordingly, the Senate elected another senator, Sir Nugent Everard, as Deputy Speaker. The account in *The Irish Times* of the second meeting on 13 July 1921 (the only one attended by Ross) was scathing: 'Except among casual passers-by, a police inspector, and a few constables the arrival of members went almost unnoticed. The cinematograph operators might as well have stayed at home . . . the entire proceedings being over in fifteen minutes.'[22]

---

[20] Ibid., 163.

[21] Duty reporter, 'The Southern Irish Parliament. Formal Opening Ceremony', *The Irish Times* (Dublin, 29 June 1921), 5.

[22] Duty reporter, 'Meeting of Southern Parliament. Senate thanks the King. Another Adjournment', *The Irish Times* (Dublin, 14 July 1921), 4.

The Irish Times reported that Ross arrived at the offices of the Department of Agriculture and Technical Instruction preceded by two tipstaffs, as befitted the Lord Chancellor. No mention is made of whether one of the tipstaffs carried the Lord Chancellor's Mace. However, the Mace was to become an object of dispute in the following year. During the fifteen-minute sitting, Ross presided over the passing of two motions, one of which was for adjournment *sine die*.

What do we learn from this brief episode? Ross, according to his memoirs, was upset that his absence from the first sitting because of 'a slight return of a haemorrhage' stoked rumours of a deeper problem, even that he had 'had a stroke of apoplexy, and was in a dying condition'.[23] He does not mention the second meeting at all.

The High Court of Appeal for Ireland

Ross's judicial experience is demonstrated in the reported cases heard by the High Court of Appeal for Ireland, which, after 1920, was the only court in Ireland where the Lord Chancellor had a role. Ross himself contended that the High Court of Appeal 'got through a great deal of important work while it lasted'.[24] An analysis of these cases will show clear trends in the legal and jurisprudential direction Ross wished to pursue.

The role of Lord Chancellor assumed by Ross in 1921 was much changed from that of his predecessors. The Government of Ireland Act 1920 had redefined the role in terms much more equivalent to that of other senior judges than had been the case under the Supreme Court of Judicature (Ireland) Act 1877. The two most significant changes were that the Lord Chancellor now had tenure for life (in theory) and his judicial role was no longer in the Chancery Division but as president, *ex officio*, of the new High Court of Appeal. The reason for this change in tenure was that the Lord Chancellor was now no longer a member of the government (which he had been since the Act of Union 1800) and, as such, could retain his office despite political changes. The High Court of Appeal was established by section 42 of the Government of Ireland Act 1920 and was to sit above the Courts of Appeal for Southern Ireland and Northern Ireland. Its jurisdiction and composition were set out in section 43 of the Government of Ireland Act 1920. In addition to the Lord

---

[23] Ross, 1924 (n. 5), 294.
[24] Ibid., 295.

Chancellor, the other (*ex officio*) judges of the court were Sir Denis Henry (LCJNI) and Sir Thomas Molony, technically the Lord Chief Justice of Southern Ireland but styled as the Lord Chief Justice of Ireland (CJ).[25] The Chief Justices could nominate another judge from their jurisdiction to sit in their stead.[26] There were provisions for additional judges to sit and for situations where the Lord Chancellor was unable to sit.[27] However, in the majority of the ten reported cases only three judges ever sat, although the reasons for this are not noted by the case reporters.

The High Court of Appeal was reported to have met for the first time on 15 December 1921.[28] However, in the House of Commons it was noted to have been active only from February 1922.[29] The ten reported cases in the *Irish Reports* contain varying amounts of detail, while *The Irish Law Times* provides a more journalistic record of the High Court of Appeal's proceedings. From an analysis of *The Irish Law Times* for the same period, at least fifteen cases were heard by the High Court of Appeal during its existence, Ross having heard the vast majority. Since 1866, the Law Reporting Council of Ireland had been the near sole provider of 'authorised' law reports, a system which had come in for criticism from various quarters.[30] Taking these sources together provides a more rounded insight into how Ross acted as Lord Chancellor. Of the ten reported cases, only eight contain reports of substantive judgments.[31] Of these, four concern insurance or compensation claims directly or indirectly related to the security situation in Ireland at the time.[32] The remainder concern matters of constitutional law/jurisdiction, court procedure, banking law and land law.

Before looking at the insurance and compensation cases, the most common case type in the reported judgments, an examination of *Leyburn v. Armagh CC (No. 1)* illustrates the stance that Ross took overall.[33] As mentioned, the civil unrest in Ireland at the time was to

---

[25] Government of Ireland Act 1920 (GIA 1920) s. 42(1).

[26] Ibid., s. 42(2).

[27] Ibid., s. 42(2)(a) & (b).

[28] *The Irish Law Times* (Dublin, 17 December 1921), 313.

[29] HC Deb, 16 February 1922, vol. 150 cc. 1139–90.

[30] E. G. Hall, *The Superior Courts of Law – 'Official' Law Reporting in Ireland 1866–2006* (Dublin, 2007), 74–155.

[31] The two cases with no substantive judgment reported are *Loughnan v. O'Sullivan* [1922] 1 IR 160 and *Re Keane* [1922] 2 IR 221.

[32] F. S. L. Lyons, 'The War of Independence, 1919–21' in W. E. Vaughan (ed.), *A New History of Ireland: Ireland under the Union, II 1870–1921*, vol. VI (Oxford, 1989).

[33] [1922] 2 IR 15.

come into play in most of the reported cases heard by Ross and this is
one on point. It dealt with an appeal by Armagh County Council from
an order for criminal injuries compensation under the Local
Government (Ireland) Act 1898. The original order was made on
28 June 1921 by the Armagh County Court Judge and then appealed
to the Court of Appeal in Ireland sitting in Dublin. This appeal was
made before the commencement, on 1 October 1921, of the relevant
provisions of the Government of Ireland Act 1920.[34] After that date,
the Court of Appeal in Ireland was deemed to be the Court of Appeal
for Southern Ireland: the judgment of the Court of Appeal in Ireland
(by then the Court of Appeal for Southern Ireland) was delivered on
9 November 1921. As a result, a further appeal was then possible to the
new High Court of Appeal for Ireland. Ross sat on this case with Chief
Justice Molony and Lord Justice Andrews, their decision being unanimous. Initially, Ross dealt with an issue touching on the jurisdiction of
the High Court of Appeal for Ireland, it being argued that the former
Court of Appeal in Ireland had final jurisdiction. Interestingly, Ross
began his judgment by looking to Lord Selborne's judgment in an
English case containing the dictum that 'where there are general words
in a later statute ... you are not to hold that earlier ... legislation ...
[is] altered ... merely by force of such general words'.[35] Following on
from this, Ross entered into a discussion of the constitutional framework, as interpreted by him, engendered by the Government of
Ireland Act 1920. His conclusion was that the court was, in effect, a
constitutional court 'for the determination of the mutual rights and
obligations of the component parts of [Ireland] '.[36] He went on to
clarify that the jurisdiction of the (former) Court of Appeal in Ireland
has been transferred to the Courts of Appeal in Southern Ireland and
Northern Ireland. The jurisdiction of the High Court of Appeal for
Ireland was entirely novel, being a creation of the Government of
Ireland Act ('a Court separate and distinct').[37] For a political unionist,
Ross concluded his judgment with an altogether rather unusual statement: 'In view of the ultimate unity of the country ... uniformity of
the law is of the first importance ... and that could only be secured by

---

[34] Order in Council fixing Appointed Days for certain purposes under the Government of
Ireland Act 1920 (Statutory Rules &Orders 1921/1527).
[35] *Leyburn v. Armagh CC* [1922] 2 IR 15, 17.
[36] Ibid., 18.
[37] Ibid., 19.

the action of the High Court of Appeal exercising jurisdiction over all Ireland.'[38]

However, it is not really that unusual a statement for Ross to have made. It was well known that he opposed the creation of two differing jurisdictions and the resulting splits.[39] Ross, by his words, appears to be, if not anti-partition entirely, certainly averse to its implications for the legal world. This places him, despite being an Ulsterman, more in the Southern Unionist mindset than that of the Ulster Unionists. This is perhaps a reason why Sir James Craig did not appoint him to be Lord Chief Justice of Northern Ireland.

Leyburn No. 1 was the prelude to the much lengthier *Leyburn v. Armagh CC (No. 2)*, the first of the insurance/compensation cases that will be examined.[40] *Leyburn No. 2* covers not only compensation issues but also further matters of jurisdiction and constitutional law and, as such, shows how these issues were being considered by Ross against the backdrop of the political and security situation in 1921–22. In this case, the High Court of Appeal for Ireland heard the substantive claim concerning the theft of weapons and ammunition and the destruction of two hats during a raid on the home of a special constable in Tynan, County Armagh. The Court of Appeal in Southern Ireland (previously the Court of Appeal in Ireland) had earlier decided that compensation (totalling £19) for both the stolen weapons and the damaged hats should be paid under the Malicious Injuries Code. Ross, in a unanimous judgment for the High Court of Appeal, held that as the weapons were only stolen and not destroyed compensation was not payable in respect of them; compensation was only payable in respect of the damaged hats (£1). The judgment of the Court of Appeal in Southern Ireland was reversed. This judgment goes to show Ross's conservatism when dealing with issues connected with what he stated to be public money. As to the jurisdiction of the High Court of Appeal for Ireland, Ross again underlined that the:

> High Court of Appeal has a more extensive jurisdiction than any appellate tribunal that has hitherto existed in Ireland. It is not a substitution for any former appellate Court. It is the High Central Court which is necessary for the determination of the mutual rights and obligations of the component parts of the federal system contemplated by the [Government of Ireland

---

[38] Ibid.
[39] Kenny (n. 18).
[40] [1922] 2 IR 58.

Act 1920]. It is the supreme guardian of the Constitution and the pivot
upon which all the Constitutional machinery was intended to turn.[41]

Ross went further in his analysis and compared the transfer of jurisdiction under the Government of Ireland Act 1920 to the Courts of Appeal
in Southern Ireland and Northern Ireland from the Court of Appeal in
Ireland to the transfer of jurisdiction under section 23 of the Judicature
Act 1877 from the Court of Appeal in Chancery (and the other previous
appellate courts) to the Court of Appeal in Ireland. He reasoned that
since the High Court of Appeal was 'separate and distinct' it was not
'bound by [the] decisions' of the previous Court of Appeal.[42] However,
he acknowledged that the Court 'is bound to consider with the utmost
reverence and respect the decisions' of the previous Court of Appeal.
In this case, Ross noted that the Malicious Injuries Code only provided
for compensation where property had been destroyed, not stolen.
He cited *McDowell v. Dublin Corporation* for the proposition that public
authorities cannot be made responsible for compensation for theft.[43]
Other cases were considered, particularly *Kirby v. Kerry CC*, where
Ross overruled the decision of the (former) Court of Appeal,[44] and
agreed with the view of Molony CJ at Assizes that 'compensation should
not be given for ... goods stolen'.[45] Molony CJ was one of the assenting
judges in the High Court of Appeal in *Leyburn (No. 2)* – it is possible that
Ross was influenced by this. *The Irish Law Times* remarked that in their
view Ross's judgment 'settles authoritatively the question whether compensation can be claimed in cases of pure larceny, though it leaves the
question whether compensation can be claimed in cases of malicious
injury combined with larceny, one of some doubt'.[46] This contemporary
commentary also illustrates Ross's caution in making judgments beyond
the law familiar to him.

The question of compensation occasioned by the ongoing civil dis-
turbance in Ireland and paid by a local government authority was again
considered in *McKnight v. Armagh CC*.[47] In this case, a police barracks in
Camlough, County Armagh was attacked and, in the course of relieving

[41] Ibid., 62.
[42] Ibid.
[43] [1903] 2 IR 541.
[44] [1921] 2 IR 388.
[45] *Leyburn No. 2* (n. 34), 64.
[46] *The Irish Law Times* (Dublin, 18 March 1922), 65.
[47] [1922] 2 137.

the barracks, certain other premises were destroyed by the army and police. The question before the High Court of Appeal was whether compensation was not due because the damage was caused by the military acting under lawful orders or was due because it was the result of the original malicious attack. Ross noted that the law was unequivocally 'that the damage must be the direct consequence of the wrongful act'.[48] He considered *Noblett v. Leitrim CC* and in particular the judgment of Campbell, Lord Chancellor of Ireland (LCI) who interpreted previous judgments of Chief Baron (CB) Palles.[49] Ross was very clear that he disagreed with Campbell LCI (a contemporary of his at university and during his legal and political career) and, in particular, with Campbell's analysis of Palles CB's judgment in *Ballymagauran Dairy Society v. Cavan CC*.[50] Ross distinguished *Noblett* because it was grounded upon 'legal ideas and conditions of society which have passed away'.[51] Ross bemoaned the state of Ireland in a lengthy peroration:

> Armed bands in large numbers were contending all over the country; they were inflicting reprisals by destroying the property of persons supposed to be in sympathy with one side or other; they frequently came long distances in motor cars; the ordinary criminal courts had ceased to be operative; the inhabitants were powerless to suppress the crimes or to attempt to bring the offenders to justice.[52]

He went on to state that while he had sympathy with the 'innocent sufferers' in this case it would be 'unjust and unreasonable' to place the burden of compensation on the ratepayers. This is another example of Ross's conservatism when dealing with the spending of public money.

Linked to these cases are those concerning insurance claims for vehicle theft directly or indirectly as a consequence of the security situation. These received much attention by W. N. Osborough as test cases concerning such claims.[53] The first is *Cooper v. General Accident Assurance Corporation*, where the insurance company defendant wished to rely on an exception to the insurance policy which excepted liability 'for loss or

---

[48] Ibid., 146.
[49] [1920] 2 IR 143.
[50] [1915] 2 IR 85.
[51] *McKnight* (n. 47), 148.
[52] Ibid.
[53] W. N. Osborough, 'Forcibly Commandeered and Owners' Insurance: The Deciding of Two Test Cases in the 1920s', in W. N. Osborough, *Studies in Irish Legal History* (Dublin, 1999), 296–314.

damage occasioned through riot or civil commotion within the land limits of Ireland'.[54] At first instance the trial judge had held for the plaintiff, stating that the area concerned was not subject to 'riot or civil commotion'. The King's Bench Division dismissed an appeal by the defendants; the defendants then appealed unsuccessfully to the Court of Appeal in Southern Ireland. In a lengthy judgment, Ross allowed the appeal 'deeply conscious of our responsibility in overriding seven Judges of distinction'. However, in overturning the decision of those judges, Ross showed that he was not averse to taking potentially controversial decisions. His fellow judges hearing this case, Sir Charles O'Connor, Master of the Rolls and Andrews LJ concurred. The final case in this group was *Boggan v. Motor Union Insurance Co.*[55] This case, concerning the insurance of a car stolen by armed men, was the last reported judgment of the High Court of Appeal for Ireland. Ross sat with Sir Charles O'Connor MR and Henry LCJNI, the report merely stating that 'after argument the Court affirmed the order of the Court below'.[56] This, 27 November 1922, was the last time Ross sat as Lord Chancellor and just over a week later the statute abolishing his office and his court received the Royal Assent.[57]

Of course, not everything was dominated by the political and security situation – normal life continued and disputes arose. In *Coneys v. Morris*, we see Ross having to consider quite detailed points of banking law.[58] The brief facts were that Morris was the principal on a promissory note to the National Bank on which Coneys, a customer of the bank, was surety. Some years after the death of Morris, the bank set off the amount of the note (which was payable but unpaid) against monies due to Coneys from the bank. Coneys claimed, as a creditor of Morris, the ability to administer Morris's estate in respect of the indebtedness due under the note. The bank's counsel argued that the bank had a lien over the assets of its customer (Coneys) and, consequently, was able to recover from the estate of the principal (Morris). The Court of Appeal in Southern Ireland upheld the judgment of the High Court that Coneys was not a creditor in respect of the monies which the bank had applied discharging the note.

---

[54] [1922] 2 IR 38, 39.
[55] [1922] 2 IR 222.
[56] Ibid.
[57] HC Deb, 5 December 1922, vol. 159 c. 1609.
[58] [1922] 1 IR 136.

Ross, hearing the appeal on this case with Sir Charles O'Connor MR and Henry LCJNI, dismissed the appeal.[59] Ross expressed 'a difficulty in understanding how there can be a lien by bankers on customers' money'.[60] He cited an authority referenced in *Harte's Law of Banking* as having provided him with guidance.[61] Having concluded that no lien could exist in this case because there were no assets to which a lien could attach, he went on to consider specifically whether the banker's right of set-off (rather than other classes of set-off) could apply. He held that it could not, stating that 'the banker's ... right of set-off ... can only be exercised where there are in existence legal enforceable debts'.[62] In Ross's view, there were no such debts and, as such, the banker's right of set-off did not arise. His judgment shows knowledge of a complex area and his readiness to consult one of the leading texts of the time as well as case law. The case is unaffected by the civil unrest underlying life in Ireland, unlike some of the subsequent cases heard by Ross.

Ross had spent much of his judicial career (1896–1921) as a land judge in the Chancery Division of the High Court of Ireland, so with *Wycherly v. Flynn* he returned to familiar territory.[63] This case concerned the provisions of a lease, particularly as to the reduction in rent where the tenant could pay a lower amount if he paid all taxes, rates, charges, and impositions affecting the land. Ross, sitting with Andrews LJ and Dodd J, held that the provision in the lease was not a covenant but merely an option. As such, the tenant could not pick and choose which provisions suited him and he had to comply with all of the specified provisions, including payment of all rates and taxes, and performance of certain other acts, in order to obtain a reduction in rent in accordance with the terms of the lease.[64]

As seen from the analysis of the above cases, Ross had a penchant for detail and the final reported case of his which will be considered, *James Crean & Son Ltd v. McMillan*, played to that strength.[65] This case concerned an appeal relating to the taxation of costs on a commercial

---

[59] Charles O'Connor (31 December 1854–18 October 1928), last Master of the Rolls in Ireland and Sir Denis Henry Bt (7 March 1864–1 October 1925), first Lord Chief Justice of Northern Ireland.

[60] *Coneys v. Morris* (n. 57), 137.

[61] *Roxburghe v. Cox* (1881) 17 Ch. D 520 (CA).

[62] *Coneys v. Morris* (n. 57), 137.

[63] [1922] 2 IR 169.

[64] Ibid., 170.

[65] [1922] 2 IR 105.

case in respect of the sale of goods. The claim and counterclaim were both dismissed with costs, yet the plaintiff objected to the method of taxing the defendant's costs. The High Court of Appeal in Ireland heard the appeal in relation to the taxation of costs from the Court of Appeal in Southern Ireland. Ross observed that at 'first sight this would appear to be a very simple matter', and that it 'is the duty of this Court to settle matters of principle to be applied in the taxation of costs'.[66] However, he was reluctant to declare general principles for wider application and restricted himself to deciding in respect of the facts alone. Despite this, he stated that 'in strict justice it would appear that each party should pay the costs of the matter in which he fails'.[67] He stated that rules for taxation must be not only 'rough rules' but also 'definite rules', so giving the impression of simultaneously wanting a general and specific approach. He cited an English case of 1879, *Saner v. Bilton*, which set out the 'clear and simple' rule which had been followed in Ireland as well.[68] His subsequent discussion of the English and Irish cases led him to conclude that where a counterclaim is not a true, independent claim but merely a form of defence to the claim, 'the Taxing Master should not apportion [costs], but simply allow such extra costs as have been incurred by reason of [the] counterclaim'.[69] This provides evidence of Ross's desire to follow established precedent in England as well as his inclination to avoid using one case to change rules of general application. It also illustrates his conservative and cautious legal outlook even in a time of great political and constitutional change.

From the analysis of these reported cases, it can be seen that Ross applied himself to a variety of legal problems. In his judgments he reveals himself at first as being forceful in his defence of his role and the place of the new High Court of Appeal for Ireland. However, his judgments on other matters display a degree of caution and conservatism. As a consequence of events, the existence of Southern Ireland as an entity (if only as an inchoate one) was short-lived.[70] With only Northern Ireland emerging from the Government of Ireland Act, there was no need for the High Court of Appeal for Ireland so that, going forward, appeals from the Court of Appeal in Northern Ireland went to the Judicial

---

[66] Ibid., 128.
[67] Ibid., 129.
[68] (1879) 11 Ch. D 416.
[69] *Crean v. McMillan* (n. 63), 130.
[70] A. S. Quekett, *The Constitution of Northern Ireland* (Belfast, 1928).

Committee of the House of Lords. The Irish Free State (Consequential Provisions) Act 1922 abolished both the High Court of Appeal for Ireland and the office of Lord Chancellor of Ireland on 5 December 1922.[71]

Ross's judgments often display a degree of caution and conservatism. The legacy of the High Court of Appeal for Ireland has been considered by others.[72] Ross's personal contribution still resonates, notably his conscious desire to position the High Court of Appeal firmly as the 'guardian of the constitution'.

The Lord Chancellor's Mace. Abolition and Final Years

One interesting note to Ross's time as Lord Chancellor comes from the rather testy correspondence he entered into in late 1922 with Hugh Kennedy, at the time chief legal adviser to the Provisional Government of the Irish Free State, with regard to the Lord Chancellor's mace.[73] Ross refers in his memoirs to be 'past understanding' Kennedy's justifications for the Lord Chancellor's mace being retained by the Provisional Government.[74] Kennedy wrote in his letter of 23 October 1922 that it was 'the view ... [of] the late [Michael] Collins ... [and] the view of the [Provisional] Government ... that the mace, which was properly the symbol of the Lord Chancellor's authority as Speaker of the House of Lords, was no longer appropriate to that office' as section 44 of the Government of Ireland Act 1920 had transformed the Lord Chancellor into 'a purely judicial personage'.[75] Indeed, Ross acknowledged this state of affairs in his judgment in *Leyburn v. Armagh CC*.[76] In his letter of 24 October 1922, Ross set out five numbered arguments as to why the Lord Chancellor's mace should be his property[77]:

1. Under no circumstances could the mace be the property of *one* of the two Governments existing in Ireland.

---

[71] *The Irish Law Times* (Dublin, 2 December 1921), 289.

[72] Osborough (n. 52), 296.

[73] R. Keane, 'Hugh Kennedy', *Dictionary of Irish Biography* (Dublin, 2012), www.dib.ie/biography/kennedy-hugh-a4483, accessed 16 February 2022.

[74] Ross, 1924 (n. 5), 297.

[75] Letter, dated 23 October 1922, from Hugh Kennedy to John Ross found in National Archives of Ireland (NAI), Department of the Taoiseach (TSCH)/3/S4257.

[76] Ibid.

[77] Letter, dated 24 October 1922, from John Ross to Hugh Kennedy found in NAI, TSCH/3/S4257.

2. There is no connection between the office of Speaker in the Irish House of Lords and the function of the Lord Chancellor as a member of the Executive.

3. Where there is no express regulation, custom and use are conclusive. The mace has always been exhibited in the court where the Lord Chancellor has jurisdiction as a judge.

4. After the Act of 1920, nobody ever thought of depriving the Lord Chancellor of his mace. The question would never have been raised had it not been for the events occurring at the destruction of the Four Courts.

5. In the Act of 1920 the great seal is expressly mentioned and there are no general words; therefore things should remain as before.

Despite stating that he had other arguments which he will not raise he added that '[t]he last holder of an office on the disappearance of his office would by custom – nobody having a better title – retain the symbol as an heirloom; as for instance, in the case of the great seal on the Sovereign's death, the mace of the Irish House of Parliament [sic]'.[78]

After the Act of Union 1800, the mace of the (defunct) Irish House of Commons had come into the ownership of the last Speaker of that chamber, John Foster.[79] However, none of Ross's arguments were specifically addressed by Kennedy. The matter concludes with Kennedy forwarding the correspondence with Ross to the Secretary to the Provisional Government, stating that the mace 'should not be handed over to the Lord Chancellor in the altered circumstances of his office'.[80] If this is what Ross described as 'past understanding', it is perhaps more evidence that he either did not understand or did not want to understand that what was taking place was a more full-scale legal and constitutional change than that effected by the Act of Union. This is illustrated by his views following the Treaty and the abolition of his office, which left him without a role. His memoirs allude to his hatred of the settlement under the Treaty. In the first volume of his memoirs, he quips: 'Then came the Treaty, which I do not discuss'.[81] He assails the merits and necessity of the Treaty in an entire chapter of the second volume of his memoirs.[82]

---

[78] Ibid.

[79] P. Thorne, *The Royal Mace in the House of Commons* (London, 1990).

[80] Memorandum, dated 26 October 1922, from Hugh Kennedy to the Secretary to the Provisional Government found in NAI, TSCH/3/S4257.

[81] Ross, 1924 (n. 5), 295.

[82] Ross, 1927 (n. 5), chapter XVI, 244–254.

Despite all of that, the Lord Chancellor's mace ended up with the National Museum of Ireland in 1925.[83] It can today be seen in a cabinet in a corner of the National Museum of Ireland at the Collins Barracks in Dublin.

After the events of 1922, Ross sold his Dublin residence and initially moved to London, where he was unable to find a judicial position. He therefore retreated to the new Northern Ireland and the estate he had inherited from his father-in-law in south Tyrone. He became increasingly frustrated with his isolation from his former Dublin life. For example, his invitations to Thomas Bodkin, Director of the National Gallery of Ireland to come to Sixmilecross (ostensibly to see Ross's art collection) were repeatedly rebuffed.[84] Nevertheless, according to the newspaper reports of his illness and death he kept busy in his local area. He passed away on 17 August 1935, and it is fitting to conclude with the evocative report of his funeral from *The Londonderry Sentinel*:

> Amid the heather-clad hills of Tyrone and surroundings in which he had lived for many years, honoured, loved, and respected by all, the remains of Sir John Ross . . . distinguished son of Londonderry, last Lord Chancellor of Ireland, brilliant advocate and judge were laid to rest in Dunmoyle churchyard.
>
> The funeral was of the simplest character and an expression of the personality of a great man who valued and loved the simple things of life. Apart from the members of the family . . . there were only a few distinguished friends, including His Grace the Governor of Northern Ireland, who had been associated with him either on the bench, at the bar, or in political life.[85]

Conclusion

In a different era, Sir John Ross may have gone on to become one of the most influential judges of his generation. That he was able, despite his background as an Ulster Presbyterian, to ascend through the ranks of the Dublin legal world to the position of Lord Chancellor of Ireland is testament to his drive and determination. Proof of his skill as a lawyer, and in particular as a judge, is evident in the few judgments he was able to deliver in Ireland's last all-island superior court.

---

[83] NAI, TSCH/3/S4257.
[84] Library of Trinity College Dublin (IE TCD MSS) 7007 945–974 Sir John Ross.
[85] 'Funeral of Sir John Ross', *The Londonderry Sentinel* (Londonderry, 22 August 1935), 4.

11

Lord Birkenhead, Ambiguity and the Irish Border

Lawyers and the Anglo-Irish Treaty

COLUM KENNY

Creative ambiguity can be a useful tool for negotiators in complex circumstances. An example of ambiguity found in the agreement for an Anglo-Irish Treaty signed in London on 6 December 1921 is enshrined in Articles 1 and 11–12. Irish nationalists took these to mean that the agreement constituted Ireland as an all-island Irish Free State, only giving Northern Ireland a right to exclude itself *subsequently* from that state and in the manner specified in that agreement, so that (as Article 12 put it), 'the powers of the Parliament and the Government of the Irish Free State shall *no longer* extend to Northern Ireland' (emphases added). The Sinn Féin negotiators had insisted all along that those partitioning the island should formally recognise in principle the intrinsic unity of Ireland.

United Kingdom unionists preferred to interpret the agreement as having from the outset excluded Northern Ireland from the new state, albeit providing for Northern Ireland to be included after one month unless it formally indicated in the meantime that it wished to remain outside the Irish Free State. Unionists pointed to words in Article 11: '*Until* the expiration of one month from the passing of the Act ... the powers of the Parliament and the Government of the Irish Free State shall not be exercisable as respects Northern Ireland' (emphasis added). In practice, Northern Ireland could remain outside the Irish Free State either way.

However, if creative ambiguity can help to get a complex treaty across the line of agreement, it may also have unforeseen or negative consequences. This has been very evident from recent disputes over the Northern Ireland Protocol of the 'Brexit' agreement. Further ambiguity in the Anglo-Irish Treaty of 1921 was likewise problematic. Under

A version of this chapter was published in *Irish Jurist*, 68 (2022), 1–24.

Article 12, should Northern Ireland resolve to be separate from the Irish
Free State,

> a Commission consisting of three persons, one to be appointed by the
> Government of the Irish Free State, one to be appointed by the
> Government of Northern Ireland, and one who shall be Chairman to be
> appointed by the British Government shall determine in accordance with
> the wishes of the inhabitants, so far as may be compatible with economic
> and geographic conditions, the boundaries between Northern Ireland and
> the rest of Ireland.

Each side construed the meaning of those words differently.

The Irish negotiators had convinced themselves that they had won a
major concession – that this mechanism would ensure large transfers of
territory from the six counties of Northern Ireland into the Irish Free
State. The British thought otherwise, and they were convinced that the
Privy Council would back their interpretation. Privately, the greatest
lawyer on either side, Lord Chancellor Birkenhead (F. E. Smith),
appeared to have something of a bad conscience about the matter.
Nearly three years after the agreement, he wrote bluntly to his fellow
negotiator with the Irish, Austen Chamberlain:

> The plain truth is that rightly or wrongly we offered to the Free State
> representatives a certain consideration for their signatures. The consid-
> eration was that a Commission should be created, three members of
> which should be nominated, one by us, one by the Free State and one by
> the Northern Government ... In my judgment it is futile to reply that
> certain extremists in the South of Ireland, and many organs of the Press
> are making excessive and even absurd claims for the possession of
> Ulster territory. Every one of us knew that such claims had been made
> in the past and would be made in the future. We decided that they
> should be pronounced upon by a Commission. We decided upon the
> appropriate formula for reference to this Commission. Having satisfied
> ourselves that the words employed were only capable, upon a fair and
> competent construction, of the meaning which we placed upon them
> we assented to the addition of other words at the earnest entreaty of the
> Irish negotiators. We should not have agreed to the insertion of these
> words if we had not believed that they were powerless to effect the
> meaning of the article taken as a whole. But holding this belief, and
> accepting the responsibility of it, we were not prepared in the desperate
> circumstances of our negotiation to run the risk of a breakdown by
> objecting to the inclusion of words which apparently made it easier for
> the other side, but which we were satisfied could not change the plain
> meaning of the article upon which the Commission had to pronounce.
> In other words we agreed upon a reference to the Commission which

many of us knew to be disputable but which we were certain could only
be decided in one way.[1]

In his first sentence, Birkenhead's reference to 'consideration' highlights
the fact that the Irish believed there was a deal done. The deal was that in
return for the nominal recognition of essential Irish unity that the Treaty
afforded Sinn Féin, the Irish allowed for Northern Ireland to opt out of
the Irish Free State – but only provided that the British facilitated
significant adjustments to the border created at Westminster more than
a year earlier.

Prime Minister Lloyd George himself was dismissive of the existing
borderline created by the Government of Ireland Act 1920.
On 10 November 1921 he wrote to James Craig, leader of the Ulster
unionists, warning that if Northern Ireland remained in the United
Kingdom,

> Customs barriers would have to be established between Northern and
> Southern Ireland over a jagged line of frontier. The inconvenience of this
> arrangement would be considerably enhanced by the fact that there must
> of necessity be large elements of the population on both sides whose
> sympathies will lie across the border. The natural channels of trade would
> be arbitrarily obstructed. The difficulty of working any such arrangement
> would be unceasing, the cost considerable, and the vexation to traders
> continuous.[2]

He soon added another warning:

> The existing state of central and southeastern Europe is a terrible example
> of the evils which spring from the creation of new frontiers, cutting the
> natural circuits of commercial activity, but when once such frontiers are
> established they harden into permanence. Your proposal would stereo-
> type a frontier based neither upon natural features nor broad geographical
> considerations by giving it the character of an international boundary.
> Partition on these lines the majority of the Irish people will never accept,
> nor could we conscientiously attempt to enforce it.[3]

These were clear and prescient indications that Lloyd George regarded
the Irish border as both unsettled and unsettling. The leader of the Irish
negotiators, Arthur Griffith, had pointed out that elections already
showed clear nationalist or republican majorities in the counties of

---

[1] Churchill Archives Centre, Churchill College, Cambridge [CHAR] 2/570: Birkenhead to
Chamberlain, 22 August 1924.
[2] *The Times* (London), 14 December 1921.
[3] Ibid.

Fermanagh and Tyrone, and he and Michael Collins expected these counties – along with portions of counties Down and Londonderry – to be allowed to be transferred into the Irish Free State. It never happened. Indeed, it was partly because of the deaths of Griffith and Collins in 1922 – and partly because of the civil war that raged that year and in 1923 – that the Boundary Commission ultimately came to nothing and the border remained where it was.

One might say, from Birkenhead's British perspective, that the lawyers got things precisely right. He was confident that the Boundary Commission – and ultimately the Privy Council – would follow precedent in such matters and construe the powers of the commission very narrowly. The Irish in 1921 virtually ignored the possibly significant role of the Privy Council. But as ambiguities gave rise to administrative and political problems, the referral of Article 12 to the Privy Council by the British government in 1924 led to what Cabinet Secretary Thomas Jones described in quotation marks as a 'beastly awkward' decision. In July that year, Jones observed in respect to the drafting of the Treaty that 'though there were half a dozen famous lawyers among the plenipotentiaries, it is notorious that a lawyer cannot draft his own will clearly'.[4]

It is not evident who Jones had in mind as 'famous lawyers'. Of the five Irish plenipotentiaries, one was a solicitor and one a barrister. Éamonn Duggan had become a solicitor in Ireland in middle age and had a modest practice – when the British were not interning him for his republican activities. He was a TD (member of Dáil Éireann, the revolutionary parliament set up by Sinn Féin after that party swept to victory in Ireland in the 1918 UK general election). George Gavan Duffy TD had passed all his law examinations in England *magna cum laude* and was admitted a solicitor there in 1907. Griffith had urged him to return to live in Ireland: '[b]oth your skill as a solicitor and your name would be of material assistance'. He did not return immediately but was on the non-resident executive of Sinn Féin in 1908–10.[5] He was a member of Roger Casement's legal team in the latter's trial for treason in London in 1916, when F. E. Smith, later Lord Birkenhead, prosecuted the case. According to George Gavan Duffy's son, George's partners in his solicitors' firm told

---

[4] T. Jones, *Whitehall Diary, Vol. 3: Ireland 1918–1925*, ed. K. Middlemas (London, 1971), 234 (31 July 1924).
[5] G. M. Golding, *George Gavan Duffy (1881–1951): A Legal Biography* (Dublin, 1982), 21; R. Davis, *Arthur Griffith and Non-Violent Sinn Féin* (Dublin, 1974), xvi, 28–9, 33, 47, 60, 66, 87, 174–5.

him that if he persisted in Casement's defence he would have to leave the practice. Subsequently, 'without notice, his name was removed from the firm'.[6] He then moved to Ireland and, obtaining exemptions as a qualified solicitor, was called to the Bar in Dublin in 1917. He was elected a Sinn Féin MP in 1918, and represented many republican clients.[7] After independence he was to pursue a legal career rather than a political one, and in 1946 was appointed president of the Irish Free State's high court. According to Hogan, he earned 'a remarkable reputation' as a judge.[8] But it is hard to see how in 1921 Jones might have thought either Duggan or Gavan Duffy to be of much professional value in matters of constitutional or Dominion law. Even Éamon de Valera, the Sinn Féin leader and president of Dáil Éireann in Dublin, privately described the two men as 'mere legal padding'.[9] De Valera himself, for reasons long debated and contested, did not participate in London in the treaty negotiations.

The two leading secretaries on the Irish team, Erskine Childers and John Smith Chartres, also had some legal education. It seems that the pair undertook most of the drafting of documents on the Irish side, with occasional assistance from professional advisers who visited the delegates' rented Irish headquarters in Hans Place. Theirs were remarkable appointments. By late 1921, the Anglo-Irish Childers was close to de Valera. The latter described Childers as 'an intellectual republican' and said privately that he was sent to London partly to give Robert Barton (the fifth delegate and a near cousin and close friend of Childers) 'added strength' as 'a retarding force'.[10] Childers had studied classics and law at Cambridge, but was never called following his admission to the Inner

---

[6] C. G. Duffy, 'George Gavan Duffy', *Dublin Historical Record*, 36 (1983), 90–106 at 90–2, noting that one of George Gavan Duffy's tutors was Edward Jenks, 'whose *Digest of English Civil Law* was a legal masterpiece'.

[7] D. Foxton, *Revolutionary Lawyers: Sinn Féin and the Crown Courts in Ireland and Britain 1916–1923* (Dublin, 2008), 414.

[8] 'Duffy, George Gavan (1882–1951), politician and judge', by G. Hogan, in *Dictionary of Irish Biography* (open access: hereafter *DIB*); Golding, *George Gavan Duffy, passim*; T. Mohr, 'George Gavan Duffy and the Legal Consequences of the Anglo Irish Treaty, 1921–1923', *Northern Ireland Legal Quarterly*, 74 (2023), 323–61.

[9] De Valera to McGarrity, 21 December 1921, quoted at length in S. Cronin, *The McGarrity Papers: Revelations of the Irish Revolutionary Movement in Ireland and America 1900–1940* (Tralee, 1972), 107–11. Duffy, 'George Gavan Duffy', 93, points out that his father had earlier that year 'had a dispute with de Valera'. This was upon de Valera arranging to be nominated on 26 August 1921 as 'president of the Irish Republic', when the position under the Dáil constitution adopted in April 1919 was just 'president of the ministry elected by Dáil Éireann'.

[10] De Valera to McGarrity, 21 December 1921, in Cronin, *The McGarrity Papers*, 107–11.

Temple in 1892. Instead, he worked in England as a civil servant and soldier. He had a 'cultivated English accent'.[11]

Childers had written a book, published in 1911, exploring models of home rule for Ireland. In it he stated that 'nobody of sense, in or out of Ireland' supposed that Ireland's best interest lay outside the Empire. Ironically, in 1921 nobody on the Treaty team was more sensitive than Childers to the possibility of imperial considerations overriding republican ambitions.[12] For his part, from his surviving diaries it is evident that Childers thought of himself as something of a constitutional or Dominion expert, drawing up policy documents for his side on matters such as 'Law and Fact in Canada', and was enraged at being sidelined during the Treaty negotiations.[13] That Childers was left outside the conference room door in Downing Street was partly due to the fact that he and Griffith did not agree and did not get along well with one another, and partly due to the fact that some of the British delegates intensely disliked him. This had a consequential effect because it also meant that corresponding British officials were excluded more often than otherwise, as Jones noted: '[t]he Treaty was not drafted as an Act of Parliament would be drafted. Officials were frequently excluded from the Treaty negotiations, chiefly because of Childers'.[14] Chamberlain certainly did not share Childers' assessment of his own skills, remarking to Birkenhead on one occasion that a certain document 'is not Collins or even Griffith. It is a second rate attorney's – in other words Erskine Childers' draft'.[15]

Chartres, born in England to Irish parents, was admitted to King's Inns in Dublin in 1884, but not called to the Bar until 1908, by Middle Temple in London. Before World War I, Chartres was employed by the London *Times* as its 'head of intelligence' (news research, indexing and

---

[11] F. Hackett, 'Great Haileyburians: II. Erskine Childers', in *The Haileyburian*, April 1935; Inner Temple admission records (online) F. Hackett, *The World* (New York, 30 October 1922): see newspaper cutting from *The World* at National Library of Ireland [NLI] MS 41,780/1-19/20 (1), Letters from Moya Llewelyn Davies.

[12] E. Childers, *The Framework of Home Rule* (London, 1911); F. Cruise O'Brien, 'Home Rule: and After', *Irish Review*, 1 (1912), 573–8 at 576; T. Mohr, 'Irish Home Rule and Constitutional Reform in the British Empire, 1885–1914', *Revue Française de Civilisation Britannique*, XXIV:2 (2019), 1–17 at 3.

[13] Childers Diaries: Trinity College Dublin MS 7,814, f. 78 (entry for 1 December 1921); 'Childers, (Robert) Erskine (1870–1922), British civil servant, author and Sinn Féin propagandist', by M. A. Hopkinson, *DIB*.

[14] Jones, *Diary*, 234 (31 July 1924).

[15] University of Birmingham, Chamberlain Papers, AC 31/2/46/84: Chamberlain to Birkenhead, 30 October 1921.

reference), at a time when Edward Grigg (who later became Lloyd George's private secretary and who in 1921 helped his fellow official Lionel Curtis to draft the boundary commission proposal) worked for *The Times* as head of its colonial department. Chartres had a practice at the Bar and wrote books on the judicial interpretation of statutes.[16] Both he and Childers were employed gathering intelligence for British government departments immediately before their respective conversions to Irish republicanism. Each helped to run guns to the Irish Volunteers (the emerging 'IRA'). From 1917 Chartres also contributed articles to Arthur Griffith's latest weekly paper, *Nationality*, under the pen name *Haud Immemor* ('not forgotten').[17] By late 1921, Chartres had moved to Berlin as a Sinn Féin representative, but was then requested to go to London for the Treaty talks. According to Nancy Power, who assisted him in Berlin, Frank Pakenham was 'misled' about Chartres' claim to expertise: 'John Chartres did not pose as a constitutional lawyer. In a conversation with a friend at the time he emphasised that he had explained to Arthur Griffith that, while willing to do his best, he was not a constitutional lawyer but a common lawyer.'[18]

And who on the other side, among the seven British plenipotentiaries, was a 'famous lawyer'? Neither Chamberlain, nor Winston Churchill fitted Tom Jones' description. Prime Minister Lloyd George himself had been a solicitor, but he owed his fame to politics rather than to law. Laming Worthington-Evans MP was the head of a firm of solicitors with personal expertise in company law, but his fame outside that circle was not great. Gordon Hewart was respected as legal counsel and in 1919 had become attorney general for England and Wales. To that extent, he was by 1921 'famous' as a lawyer, although – according to an unflattering profile by Professor Robert Stevens of the University of

---

[16] C. Bewley, *Memoirs of a Wild Goose* (Dublin, 1989), 77–8 (published in 1989 but written at least twenty years earlier); *Student Admission Papers and Call Book*, 1884 (Honourable Society of King's Inns MSS); *Registers to the Admissions to the Honourable Society of the Middle Temple* (London, 1949), vol. 2, 648 (7 January 1885).

[17] B. P. Murphy, *John Chartres: Mystery Man of the Treaty* (Dublin, 1995); 'Childers, (Robert) Erskine', by M. A. Hopkinson, *DIB*; N. Power, 'Chartres meets Collins', *Irish Independent*, 4 November 1935. *Nationality* first appeared in June 1915; publication ceased immediately after the Easter Rising in 1916 but resumed in February 1917.

[18] Power, 'Chartres meets Collins'; F. Pakenham, *Peace by Ordeal* (London, 1935), 141–2, 240. This book by Frank Pakenham, later Lord Longford, has been the single most influential work on the treaty negotiations. I have warned elsewhere of relying on it unduly: C. Kenny, 'Redeeming Dev, Damning Griffith: Pakenham's *Peace by Ordeal*', *History Ireland*, 30:4 (2022), 14–15.

Oxford – his subsequent career as lord chief justice of England was 'not distinguished'.[19] Hamar Greenwood, who was chief secretary for Ireland during the War of Independence, was a king's counsel and bencher of Gray's Inn. He was infamous in Ireland for his association with the undisciplined Crown forces known as Black and Tans and 'Auxiliaries', but not particularly famous in Britain as a lawyer.[20]

In reality, of the seven British and Irish plenipotentiaries who were qualified to practise law, there was just one who was undoubtedly a 'famous lawyer'. This was F. E. Smith, Lord Birkenhead, who would be 'remembered as a great lord chancellor' of England and Wales. He was an accomplished practitioner, and also for years an 'apparently extreme' supporter of Ulster's unionists. He had attended some militant unionist rallies in Ulster against Home Rule and he earned the nickname 'Carson's galloper'.[21]

The Legal Advisory Committee

There was at least one Irish lawyer who foresaw that the ambiguities in the Treaty might not all work out well for the Irish side. This was John O'Byrne. He was among the members of a small 'Constitutional and International Law Committee' that the Dáil ministry set up in early October 1921, under the auspices of the Minister for Home Affairs, Austin Stack. The committee's membership was drawn from a small band of lawyers who were prepared to run new courts set up by the Dáil. The junior barrister James Nolan-Whelan was employed as its secretary. The committee was intended to advise on all legal matters relating to the Treaty negotiations.[22]

---

[19] 'Hewart, Gordon, first Viscount Hewart (1870–1943), judge', by R. Stevens, *Oxford Dictionary of National Biography (online* (hereafter *ODNB*); R. F. V. Heuston, *Lives of the Lord Chancellors, 1885–1940* (Oxford, 1964), 625. Personal tributes to him in the House of Lords, following his death, included Lord Chancellor John Simon describing him as having 'filled the position of Lord Chief Justice with unfailing dignity and courtesy and authority': *HL Debates*, vol. 127, cols. 427–31 (6 May 1943).

[20] R. MacLaren, *Empire and Ireland: The Transatlantic Career of the Canadian Imperialist Hamar Greenwood, 1870–1948* (Montreal, 2015), 29, 33, 36, 47, 289.

[21] 'Smith, Frederick Edwin, first earl of Birkenhead (1872–1930), lawyer and politician', by J. Campbell (*ODNB*). Edward Carson was a leader of the Ulster unionists.

[22] Letters of Austin Stack to J. Nolan Whelan, concerning a constitutional and international law committee set up by the Ministry of Home Affairs: with a few associated documents, 1921 (NLI MSS 15,052).

Nolan-Whelan soon sent Stack a list of lawyers who had agreed to attend the committee's first meeting. There were just three names on it, all junior counsel: Charles Bewley (who later claimed to have been the first barrister to appear in the Dáil courts), James A. Murnaghan and John O'Byrne. He also pointed out 'the objections to a large committee'.[23] Bewley would later write in a memoir that he lunched every day at Hans Place during a visit to London in November 1921, but it was Nolan-Whelan, Murnaghan and O'Byrne whom in December 1921 Griffith in Dáil Éireann described as 'the constitutional lawyers associated with the plenipotentiaries'. It is not obvious in what particular way any of these merited being described specifically as a *constitutional* lawyer. However, as well as being a practitioner, Murnaghan was part-time professor of jurisprudence, Roman law and international law at University College Dublin. O'Byrne and Murnaghan would subsequently be appointed members of the committee tasked in 1922 with drafting the Free State Constitution.[24]

John O'Byrne's Role

John O'Byrne (1884–1954) was then a junior counsel. He was to be appointed to the Irish Supreme Court in 1940 by a Fianna Fáil government, and his career has been favourably sketched by a current judge of that chamber.[25] O'Byrne wrote, as will be seen later, that in 1921 he warned Griffith about ambiguities in the draft article relating to the proposed boundary commission. Before being called to the Bar, he had been a respected official of the Irish Land Commission. When he was called in 1911, a regional paper commented that his academic distinctions were 'convincing evidence that he is a lawyer of unquestioned ability, who will bring to the practice of the law a mind deeply versed in the knowledge of legal lore'. Because of his academic distinctions, he was first amongst others to be called in January

---

[23] Ibid.

[24] *Irish Independent*, 21 November 1921; *Evening Herald*, 8 December 1921; *Dáil Debates*, 16 December 1921; Bewley, *Wild Goose*, 67–70, 78; B. Farrell, 'The Drafting of the Irish Free State Constitution: I', *Irish Jurist*, 5 (1970), 115–40. F. Callinan, *T. M. Healy* (Cork, 1996), 567–82, has suggested that Tim Healy KC was also substantially involved in advising the Irish delegates in London.

[25] 'O'Byrne, John (1884–1954), lawyer and judge', by G. Hogan, *DIB*; *Irish Times*, 15 January 1954, for a glowing 'appreciation' of O'Byrne on his death.

1911.[26] On O'Byrne's death in 1954, Chief Justice Conor A. Maguire stated that 'his success at the Bar had been immediate; among a group of very brilliant juniors he quickly had climbed into, and won, his place in the front ranks of lawyers, and he had acquired one of the biggest practices at the junior Bar'.[27]

O'Byrne had appeared before Maguire in 1920, when the latter sat in the Dáil Courts as a land settlement commissioner.[28] This aspect of O'Byrne's life has received little attention. As a young man he had joined the Irish Republican Brotherhood and was, in the words of Denis Gwynn, 'one of the early Sinn Féiners'.[29] During the Great War, when it was said to be difficult to find senior lawyers who were not reluctant to represent members of the nationalist Volunteers in Ireland, O'Byrne became known as one of a number of junior counsel who acted willingly for them. He was active not only in the revolutionary courts set up by Dáil Éireann, seemingly both as counsel and as a judge, but also continued to act as a barrister in the Crown courts, where his clients included Irish county councils that were defying the British by refusing to submit their accounts for audit.[30] In 1924, he was to be appointed attorney general of the new state, being permitted to become a king's counsel immediately beforehand in an otherwise 'unprecedented appointment of a junior counsel' to that office.[31]

Michael Collins, one of the five Irish negotiators in London, was also friendly with Crompton Llewelyn Davies and his Irish wife Moya O'Connor, the latter a daughter of an Irish nationalist MP. Davies was a wealthy partner in a leading City firm of solicitors in London, had once been an adviser to Lloyd George and had worked as solicitor to the Post

---

[26] *Nationalist and Leinster Times*, 11 February 1911; *Freeman's Journal*, 19 January 1911; *King's Inns Barristers 1868–2004*, ed. Kenneth Ferguson (Dublin, 2005), 320.

[27] Obituary and Tribute, *Irish Law Times & Solicitors' Journal*, 88 (1954), 26; *Irish Press*, 14 January 1954, includes a photograph of O'Byrne.

[28] C. A. Maguire, 'The Republican Courts', *Capuchin Annual 1969*, 384.

[29] Bureau of Military History, Witness Statements Nos. 168 (Melinn), 766 (Patrick McCartan), 868 (Kearney) and 1,765 (O'Kelly), all at www.militaryarchives.ie/collec tions/online-collections/bureau-of-military-history-1913-1921/witnesses/ (accessed 20 February 2024).

[30] *Irish Examiner*, 19 January 1954, for Gwynn; Bureau of Military History, Witness Statements 418/Úna C. Stack, 420/Wyse-Power, 619/Seán O'Duffy, 708/Conor A. Maguire, and 1,769/Little.

[31] R. Keane, 'The Voice of the Gael: Chief Justice Kennedy and the Emergence of the New Irish Court System 1921–1936', *Irish Jurist*, 31 (1966), 205–25.

Office. The couple appear to have been radicalised by the events of 1916 in Ireland, and Davies was subsequently dismissed for his sympathies with Irish republicans.[32] Moya wrote that they were introduced to Collins in 1918 by Art O'Brien, president of the Sinn Féin organisation in England and Wales, and thereafter 'from 1918 until his death we saw Mick very often, both in London and Dublin'.[33]

Nolan-Whelan attempted to furnish relevant documentation to the Irish delegates in accordance with Dáil Éireann's wishes. On 21 October, he wrote that he was advised from London (by whom is unclear) that 'authorities as to ratification [are] listed in Halsbury's *Laws of England* sub title Constitutional Law', and that he intended to provide promptly the judgments in the best cases listed there as well as any more recent authorities.[34] However, the delegates' principal source of information on Dominion constitutions and on the slowly increasing autonomy of countries such as Canada, Australia, New Zealand and South Africa may have been Hessel Duncan Hall's recent book on the Commonwealth, with each member of the Irish delegation being equipped with a copy if it.[35]

Constitutional Considerations

On 18 November 1921, more than a month into negotiations, Thomas Jones sent the Irish delegates a draft treaty, or 'tentative suggestions for a treaty', as Griffith described the document. On 21 November, Birkenhead, in the presence of Chamberlain, asked Jones to impress on Griffith the need for as few changes to the draft as possible:

> I [Jones] asked what were the kind of points on which A. Griffith was likely to make difficulties. He replied that it was only at their last interview that the P.M. had ventured to broach the question of the appeal to the Judicial Committee of the Privy Council. This had been wrapped up in

---

[32] *The Times* (London), 25 November 1935; 'Davies, Moya Llewelyn (1881–1943), political activist', by Patrick Maume, *DIB*; NLI, MS 38,207/3/10 (2), Letters to Alice Stopford Green, copy of letter from Crompton Llewelyn Davies to Lloyd George, 24 July 1916.

[33] NLI, MS 41,780/13, Correspondence from Moya Llewelyn Davies to P. S. O'Hegarty (early 1940s); M. Forester, *Michael Collins: The Lost Leader* (Dublin, 1971), 104, 201, 225, 228, 292.

[34] *Halsbury's Laws of England*, 31 vols. (London, 1907–17), vol. 6, 'Constitutional Law', particularly at 439–42; Stack to Nolan-Whelan.

[35] H. D. Hall, *The British Commonwealth of Nations – A Study of Its Past and Future Development* (London, 1920); T. Mohr, 'George Gavan Duffy and the Irish Free State on the International Stage, 1921–1923', *Irish Studies in International Affairs*, 32 (2021), 261–78, at 263–4.

Clause II – 'The position of Ireland in relation to the Imperial Parliament and Government and otherwise shall subject as aforesaid be assimilated as nearly as may be to that existing in the case of Canada.' This appeal to the Privy Council was, in F.E. [Smith]'s view, a vital matter, and Chamberlain agreed with him, and said that if there were a breach of the pact alleged there would have to be an appeal and it would be very undesirable to bring it forward in Parliament.[36]

The manner in which favourable references to the Irish Free State enjoying the same Dominion status as Canada might implicitly 'wrap up' the new state in the jurisdiction of the Privy Council, and thus determine how Article 12 on the Boundary Commission might be construed, were of considerable significance but had been expressed somewhat coyly. Jones seems to have been concerned that the Irish might be disadvantaged in that respect. He noted in his diary: 'I mentioned the point of the Sinn Féin leaders having some technical adviser to help them and the Lord Chancellor suggested Frank Russell, the son of Lord Russell of Killowen [1832–1900], and "a much better lawyer than his father". He was a Home Ruler and could give them first rate technical advice.'[37]

The Irishman Charles Russell had been the first Roman Catholic to be appointed Lord Chief Justice of England and Wales.[38] His son Francis Xavier obtained a first in jurisprudence at Oxford, where in 1887 'his brilliant speech in favour of home rule caused A. V. Dicey, notwithstanding his disapproval of the proposed reform, to write a letter of congratulation to Russell's father'. Birkenhead had been so impressed by Frank as a barrister that in 1919 he caused him to be appointed a high court judge in chancery in England.[39] It would have been remarkable had Frank actually given advice to the Irish delegates as Birkenhead suggested. He might well have guided them wisely on the tricky Treaty articles concerning the Boundary Commission and the oath. But there appears to be no evidence that he was consulted. If Pakenham is correct, at the outset of the peace talks Minister Austin Stack – who declined to attend them as a delegate and who was hostile to the very idea of an agreement that did not give Sinn Féin pretty much all that it demanded – had himself pressed the Irish negotiators to consult 'some authority of

[36] Jones, *Diary*, 169 (21 November 1921).
[37] Ibid., n. 59.
[38] 'Russell, Charles (1832–1900), Baron Russell of Killowen, lord chief justice of England and Wales 1894–1900', by R. Keane, *DIB*.
[39] 'Russell, Francis Xavier Joseph [Frank] [1867–1946), Baron Russell of Killowen', by P. Gibson, *ODNB*.

recognized standing, a foreigner if need be, even an Englishman if a man like Lord Bryce could be obtained'.[40] The octogenarian Bryce, formerly chief secretary for Ireland (1905–1907), was actually not an Englishman but a liberal Ulster-Scots Presbyterian. He was also a barrister and academic whose study of the US constitution, *The American Commonwealth*, had become a classic. His essay, 'Flexible and Rigid Constitutions', has been praised in modern times by Judge David Edward of the European Court of Justice as 'a precedent for the consti-tution of the European Union, in both its federal and regional aspects'.[41] In the event, Bryce also does not appear to have been consulted in 1921.

On 23 November 1921, at a sub-conference in Downing Street attended by Griffith, Collins and Barton for the Irish and Lloyd George, Chamberlain and Birkenhead for the British, it was agreed that Birkenhead should meet Griffith and Collins again the following day at the House of Lords and – according to what Childers wrote that Barton told him – Collins 'suggested bringing a constitutional lawyer, naming Chartres'. In a letter to de Valera later that day, Griffith stated that it was Birkenhead who suggested the Irish bring such a lawyer. The British Cabinet Secretary Thomas Jones noted '[a] further conference arranged for Thursday morning'.[42] Childers was fuming about his exclusion from this.[43] Jones made a contemporary note of the Thursday conference, at which Ireland's relationship to the Crown was discussed. In the room were Lord Chancellor Birkenhead, Attorney General Hewart, Griffith, Collins, Gavan Duffy and John Chartres: 'the last two as constitutional lawyers', wrote Jones. He added that 'Chartres started some historical disquisition and was shut up brusquely by F.E.' This image of Birkenhead 'brusquely' silencing one of the Irish 'constitutional lawyers' surely speaks of the relative status of the advisers on each side. Jones told his

[40] Pakenham, *Peace by Ordeal*, 142–3.
[41] 'Bryce, James, Viscount Bryce (1838–1922), jurist, historian and politician', by C. Harvie, *ODNB*; D. Edward, 'The Community's Constitution – Rigid or Flexible? The Contemporary Relevance of the Constitutional Thinking of James Bryce', in D. Curtin and T. Heukels (eds.), *Institutional Dynamics of European Integration: Essays in Honour of Henry G. Schermers* (Dordrecht, 1994), 57–78.
[42] Childers Diaries, Trinity College Dublin MS 7,814, f. 64v (23 November 1921); Jones, *Diary*, 173 (23 November 1921); Griffith to de Valera, 23 November 1921 (NAI, DE 2/304/1) states that it was Birkenhead who suggested the Irish bring a constitutional lawyer to the meeting.
[43] Childers Diaries, TCD MS 7,814, ff. 64v-5 (Thursday 24 November 1921), adding that, afterwards, 'AG apologised to GD in car'.

diary: 'it was hard to see how any formula can reconcile our position and theirs'.[44]

Meanwhile, Childers had had to wait outside in the private secretary's room where Lionel Curtis, second secretary to the British team, engaged him in conversation. Curtis and Childers had attended the same private school, Haileybury College near Hertford, and both fought for the British in the Boer War and wrote much about South Africa. Curtis was an influential public servant who had been called to the Bar and who had developed special expertise in respect of the constitutional and Dominion structure of the British Empire.[45]

The junior counsel John O'Byrne was also asked by Griffith that week to draft objections to certain points that Griffith had written out on matters concerning defence, but Griffith 'asked me nothing', complained Childers.[46] Remarkably. Chartres departed for a mission to Berlin that weekend and was absent for the final sessions of the peace conference.

O'Byrne's Warning

On an urgent return journey to Dublin for a crucial Cabinet meeting, just three days before the Anglo-Irish Treaty agreement was signed on 6 December 1921, Griffith had a signal discussion with John O'Byrne about the Boundary Commission provision. Some time before his death in January 1954, O'Byrne recalled their conversation that day:

> A.G. had with him the draft of the proposed Treaty. On the journey from Euston to Holyhead, he and I went through it clause by clause. When we came to the clause dealing with the boundary, A.G. tapped it with his finger and said, 'I believe that this will make the position of the North quite untenable'. I asked him how much territory he considered he would get. His answer was: 'The greater part of Tyrone and Fermanagh and portions of south Co. Down and south Armagh.' I pointed out to him that I considered that the clause was too vague and that it left too much power to the Boundary Commission. I suggested that some unit (such as a Barony or Electoral Division) should be specified, that a vote should be taken in such a unit and that the unit should automatically come to us or stay in the North according to the majority of the votes. He immediately

[44] Jones, *Diary*, 174 (24 November 1921).
[45] Ibid.; Pakenham, *Peace by Ordeal*, 137–40. Curtis had been called to the Bar but did not practise: 'Curtis, Lionel George', by A. May, *ODNB*.
[46] Childers Diaries, TCD, MS 7,814, ff. 67, 75v.

saw the point, but said that he did not know whether it would be possible
at that stage to have the clause altered. In fact it was not altered.[47]

The die was cast. The stress on Griffith and his colleagues was terrible
and the meeting in Dublin, after a long journey by rail and boat, was
fractious and unhelpful. It was a hybrid event, at times a formal Cabinet
session but at times also including Childers and others. Childers claimed
at it that the status of the new state as envisaged in the draft Treaty at that
point would be lower than that of a Dominion and said that the word
'exclusively' in one clause was particularly significant: 'A.G. said that we
should have a constitutional lawyer to interpret "exclusively". I said two
such lawyers had been brought by him to London and had been there for
some time and could have been consulted.'[48]

Faced with an ultimatum to sign within hours the draft as it then stood
or have the British immediately resume war in Ireland, the Irish delegates
signed articles of agreement on 6 December 1921. The agreement for a
treaty was still subject to approval by the UK parliament and by Dáil
Éireann.[49] John O'Byrne sailed back into Dun Laoghaire on 8 December
with the delegates. Also on board was James Nolan-Whelan.[50]

Birkenhead's Bulgarian Precedent

British ministers spun the 1921 agreement as a victory,[51] not least to beat
down their more intransigent die-hard imperialist and unionist opponents
in England. Chamberlain and others were soon representing Article 12 on
the Boundary Commission as far less significant than its unionist critics

---

[47] P. Colum, *Arthur Griffith* (Dublin, 1959), 295–6.
[48] Childers Diaries, TCD, MS 7,814, f. 83 (3 December 1921). This was presumably a
reference to the word 'exclusively' as found in Art. 4 of '"Tentative Suggestions" for a
Treaty presented by Thomas Jones to Arthur Griffith, London, 16 November 1921': NAI,
DE 2/304/1, or in Art. 1 of the 'Memorandum by the Irish delegates on their proposal for
the association of Ireland with the British Commonwealth, London, 28 November 1921':
NAI, DE 2/304/1.
[49] C. Kenny, *Midnight in London: The Anglo-Irish Treaty Agreement 1921* (Dublin, 2021).
[50] *Evening Herald*, 8 December 1921. For an obituary, see *Irish Law Times & Solicitors'
Journal*, 88 (1954), 26. Both O'Byrne and Murnaghan were to work closely on the
committee that drafted the constitution of the Irish Free State: *Irish Independent*,
21 November 1921; Farrell, 'Drafting of the Irish Free State Constitution: I', 115–40.
Also see Stack to Nolan Whelan; *Evening Herald*, 8 December 1921.
[51] E.g. TNA, CAB-23-27-17, 'Conclusions of a meeting of the Cabinet held on Tuesday,
6 December 1921, at 12.30 p.m.'

feared.[52] Birkenhead soon wrote a brilliant, if from an Irish nationalist perspective outrageous, legal opinion on the import of the Article. He did so during 1922, for a former Conservative prime minister Arthur Balfour. At the time Balfour seemed poised to withdraw his support from Lloyd George's Liberal–Tory coalition government and to rally Tory critics of the Anglo-Irish Treaty. By summoning up his great professional expertise in order to deny plausibly that the agreement could mean Northern Ireland losing any of its counties, Birkenhead's political intervention kept Balfour on side for the government. This legal opinion proved useful again in 1924, when published strategically to further British political interests.[53]

Perhaps only a brilliant lawyer could have made the arguments for Balfour that Birkenhead did, in terms more exquisite than John O'Byrne might have imagined when he warned Griffith of the article's weakness. Birkenhead's letter to Balfour was a masterpiece of special pleading and political advocacy.[54] Indeed, on 24 October 1921 at the seventh session of the peace talks, Birkenhead had made some reference to his interest in international law and Griffith had deferred to him as follows: 'On a point of international law I cannot say. You are an authority.'[55]

How well matched were Griffith's advisers to Birkenhead? Did Professor James A. Murnaghan's expertise as a part-time professor in international law extend to familiarity with the Treaty of Berlin that established the principality of Bulgaria, for example? This was a most germane 'precedent' according to Birkenhead. In his opinion, as expressed in his letter to Balfour, 'the *main* purpose [emphasis added]' of Article 12 of the Anglo-Irish Treaty was to preserve Northern Ireland as an entity if its parliament desired. He claimed that Northern Ireland under the Treaty was 'regarded as a creature already constituted' and thus not brought into existence by the Treaty (a contestable argument). He added that it was 'by way of proviso that a modification of boundaries is contemplated' and wrote: '[t]his seems to me to differ in no way from the ordinary precedents set in innumerable Treaties between European States during the 19th century'. He argued that the only difference between the Bulgarian and Northern Ireland circumstances was that in the case of Bulgaria there was just one document (the Treaty of Berlin), whilst in the case of Ireland there were

---

[52] E.g. Chamberlain: see *HC Debs*, vol. 149 cols. 357–8 (16 December 1921).
[53] K. Matthews, *Fatal Influence: The Impact of Ireland on British Politics, 1920–1925* (Dublin, 2004), 75–7.
[54] Full text at ibid., 288–90.
[55] Jones, *Diary*, 143.

two (the Government of Ireland Act 1920 and the Treaty). The lord
chancellor then delivered his *coup de grâce*:

> It appears to me inconceivable that any competent and honest arbitrator
> could take the opposite view. If the article had meant what Craig now
> apprehends that it does [a substantial repositioning of the border], quite
> obviously the Agreement would have been drafted in very different words.
> I might remark incidentally that I can hardly suppose that in that case the
> duty would have been committed to a Commission. The natural course
> would have been that the Governments concerned should retain every-
> thing but details in their own hands, in accordance with the precedents of
> Treaties. But assuming that it was intended that a Commission should
> operate which might conceivably wholly change the character of Northern
> Ireland by enormous reductions of its territory, I think it would have been
> necessary to say.

Birkenhead proceeded in the same letter to articulate for Balfour what he
felt would have had to have been stated in Article 12 if substantial
changes in the Irish border had been intended. He concluded: 'I have
no doubt that the Tribunal, not being presided over by a lunatic [under
Article 12 the British appointed the Boundary Commission's chairman],
will take a rational view of the limits of its own jurisdiction and will reach
a rational conclusion.' This was an ingenious, not to say disingenuous,
argument from no less a legal expert than the lord chancellor. Even if one
cannot say for certain that he was simply using his professional position
for political ends, it is difficult to conclude that he acted honourably by
signing the agreement for a Treaty. For he was well aware that the Irish
took an entirely different view of Article 12, a view that he categorised as
'honest if hotheaded', a phrase ostensibly doctored out of his opinion for
Balfour when the Tories published it in 1924.[56] It is clear from
Birkenhead's correspondence cited above, and from a letter sent to
Churchill by Lionel Curtis,[57] that the terms of the provision for the
appointment of the Boundary Commission in Article 12 of the Treaty
were such that the British were confident that any outcome of the
Boundary Commission's deliberations would not involve extensive
reductions in the area of Northern Ireland.

That confidence was evidently supported by what they regarded as a
silent term of the Treaty itself, one that meant implicitly that the Privy

[56] Matthews, *Fatal Influence*, 169–70, 290.
[57] Bodleian Library, Special Collections, Lionel Curtis MS 89, ff. 76–83, Lionel Curtis to
Winston Churchill, 19 August 1924.

Council in London would be the arbiter of any dispute but one that would be 'difficult to explain to public' if made more explicit.[58] The British thought that Privy Council judges could be depended upon to take the same view as Birkenhead if it came to interpreting Article 12 and that this would render the Boundary Commission of marginal significance. Just as Chamberlain later alleged to a receptive Pakenham that Griffith had done a 'secret' deal with Lloyd George on the Boundary Commission, the British soon claimed that the Irish had accepted the Privy Council's jurisdiction during the 1921 negotiations, but had specifically requested that no reference be made to it in the text of the Treaty. Their claim, like Chamberlain's to Pakenham, 'was only raised at a time when leading members of the Irish delegation – Collins and Griffith – were no longer in a position to contradict [or even to qualify] this version of events', both men having died in August 1922.[59]

There was certainly a lack of clarity in respect of aspects of the Anglo-Irish Treaty, but these fudges were at least partly deliberate and political. That such fudges may also return to haunt the parties that made them is a fact of which we have been forcefully reminded in respect to the post-Brexit Northern Ireland Protocol that was agreed between the European Union and Britain in October 2019.[60]

---

[58] Jones, *Diary*, 164–5, 178 (14, 15 and 29 November 1921).
[59] Thomas Mohr, *Guardian of the Treaty: The Privy Council Appeal and Irish Sovereignty* (Dublin, 2016), 30.
[60] See e.g. 'Dominic Cummings: Ireland and UK fudged Protocol problems to "figure out later"', *Irish News*, 22 July 2021, reporting a BBC interview of Cummings by Laura Kuenssberg.

12

The British–Irish Negotiations on the Drafting of the 1922 Constitution of the Irish Free State

THOMAS MOHR

Introduction

The negotiations concerning the text of the future Constitution of the Irish Free State that took place in the summer of 1922 do not receive the level of historical attention devoted to the Treaty negotiations of late 1921. This is unfortunate as the British–Irish negotiations on the 1922 Constitution could be seen as a sequel or even a continuation of the Treaty negotiations. Many Irish nationalists viewed the negotiations on the constitution in these terms in 1922. This ensured that the future constitution was the subject of passionate debate before a single word of it was drafted. The future Constitution of the Irish Free State was raised repeatedly in the Dáil debates of late 1921 and early 1922 on the acceptance of the 'Articles of Agreement for a Treaty signed between Great Britain and Ireland', popularly known as 'the Treaty', signed in London on 6 December 1921. Supporters of the Treaty declared that the future constitution would reflect the full scope of Irish nationalist aspirations.[1] Opponents of the Treaty warned that the constitution would be a crushing disappointment. They argued that the future constitution would have to recognise Dominion institutions including the King, the Governor General and the appeal from the Irish courts to a court in London called the Judicial Committee of the Privy Council.[2]

This chapter will explain the context behind the creation of the draft Irish constitution in 1922 and why the British government insisted that it

---

[1] For example, *Dáil Debates*, vol. T, no. 3, col. 160, 15 December 1921; no. 4, col. 210, 16 December 1921; no. 5 cols. 257–60, 17 December 1921; no. 7, cols. 60–3 and 71, 20 December 1921; no. 8, cols. 86 and 97, 21 December 1921; no. 9, cols. 130 and 150, 22 December 1921; and no. 10, cols. 194, 199 and 204, 3 January 1922.

[2] For example, *Dáil Debates*, vol. T, no. 3, cols. 163–5, 15 December 1921; no. 6, cols. 24, 27–8 and 38–42, 19 December 1921; no. 8, cols. 116–17 and 126, 21 December 1921; no. 9, col. 154, 22 December 1921; and no. 10, cols. 174 and 181–3, 3 January 1922.

be substantially revised. It will avoid a blow-by-blow account of the negotiations and the evolution of draft constitutional provisions. Accounts that follow this approach are already available.[3] Instead, this chapter will focus on the negotiating strategies developed in Dublin and London to secure key objectives. It will attempt to explain why the pro-Treaty Irish provisional government produced a draft constitution that largely ignored the Dominion settlement at the heart of the Treaty signed in December 1921 and why there was never any real possibility of the British government accepting such a constitution. British rejection of the draft Irish constitution was followed by a short period in which London and Dublin had to face the terrible prospect of a collapse of the Treaty settlement. Contingency plans proved unnecessary when the Irish provisional government agreed to a radical revision of the draft constitution. This chapter will conclude with an assessment of Irish and British priorities in negotiating the draft constitution.

Creating a Draft Constitution

On 24 January 1922 a 'constitution committee' was formally appointed by the Irish provisional government and held its first meeting in Dublin's Mansion House.[4] It was appointed to create a preliminary draft that the provisional government might adapt into a final text. The committee would eventually present the provisional government with three options – Drafts A, B and C – as the basis of the future constitution. In March 1922 the provisional government would select Draft B, which was adapted over the following three months to produce a new Draft D.

Although some scholars have referred to the 1922 Constitution as 'Michael Collins' Constitution', he only attended two meetings of the drafting committee.[5] Nevertheless, he was officially the chairman and he

---

[3] One of the best and most detailed accounts is Joseph M. Curran, *The Birth of the Irish Free State, 1921–1923* (Tuscaloosa, AL, 1980), 200–18. For analysis of British–Irish negotiations on the non-contentious aspects of the draft constitution, see Thomas Mohr, 'British Involvement in the Creation of the Constitution of the Irish Free State' (2008) 30 *Dublin University Law Journal* 166.

[4] National Archives of Ireland (NAI), S8952, Constitution Committee, report of first meeting, 24 January 1922.

[5] D. H. Akenson and J. F. Fallin, 'The Irish Civil War and the Drafting of the Free State Constitution' (1970) 5(1) *Éire-Ireland* 10, 13; 5(4), 28, 64 and speech of Taoiseach Micheál Martin at https://merrionstreet.ie/taoiseach_michel_martin_td_address_at_academic_conference_on_the_centenary_of_the_establishment_of_the_irish_free_state.html (accessed 16 November 2023).

bore primary responsibility within the provisional government for creating a constitution. Collins, accompanied by Arthur Griffith, gave important instructions at the first meeting of the constitution committee. He told the committee to ignore institutions common to the constitutions of the existing Dominions. Collins specifically asked that the provisions of the Treaty dealing with the King's representative (Governor General), the parliamentary oath and naval defence be omitted from the constitution.[6] He told the committee: 'I would, however, like strongly to emphasise that we must not allow considerations as to whether or not the British pass our Constitution to influence us unduly. The thing is to get the Constitution, then let us fight for it if necessary.'[7]

Members of the constitution committee, acting on their own initiative, decided to insert provisions that made very limited references to the Treaty and the King's representative in Articles 74 and 75 dealing with external relations. Even these token gestures failed to follow Dominion precedent.

One of the most important features that had distinguished Draft B from Drafts A and C was an innovation concerning 'extern ministers' inspired by the Constitution of Switzerland. These extern ministers would be members of the government but need not be members of the Oireachtas. They would not have to signify their acceptance of the Treaty or take the controversial parliamentary oath demanded by that settlement and would not bear responsibility for the conduct of external affairs. It is likely that Collins was attracted to this scheme by the possibility of allowing Éamon de Valera and his supporters into government and thereby healing the divide over the Treaty. The possibility of a coalition government that included opponents of the Treaty was strengthened by an electoral agreement known as the 'Collins–de Valera pact', concluded in advance of the election of June 1922.

The conclusion of the 'Collins–de Valera pact' together with the activities of opponents of the Treaty, including an IRA incursion into the Belleek and Pettigo districts of Northern Ireland, would later be blamed for raising British suspicions as to the good faith of the Irish provisional government during the negotiations on the 1922

---

[6] Articles 3, 4 and 6 of the Articles of Agreement for a Treaty between Great Britain and Ireland, 1921. NAI, S8952, Constitution Committee, report of first meeting, 24 January 1922.

[7] NAI, constitution committee, S3, first meeting, 24 January 1922.

Constitution.[8] The drafting process had already been complicated by two earlier commitments made by the provisional government in the spring of 1922. The first agreement was made with Irish opponents of the Treaty and included a commitment to publish the draft constitution in advance of an anticipated general election that eventually took place on 16 June 1922.[9] The second complication arose when the provisional government agreed to give the British government a confidential preview of the draft constitution before it was published.[10] These dual commitments reflect the unfortunate reality in which the provisional government found itself in 1922, stuck between the irreconcilable forces of Irish opponents of the Treaty and the British government. As Tom Garvin notes, satisfying both was clearly 'an impossible task'.[11]

As events transpired, the British government rejected the draft constitution when it was presented on 27 May 1922. Prime Minister David Lloyd George described it as 'a complete evasion of the Treaty and a setting up of a Republic with a thin veneer'.[12] Austen Chamberlain, leader of the Conservative party, called it the constitution of 'a republic scarcely covered by the thinnest monarchical varnish'.[13] He concluded that the draft was a negation, rather than an evasion, of the Treaty.[14] The British cabinet soon realised that the Irish provisional government must have instructed the drafters of the constitution to ignore aspects of the Treaty.[15] The entire Treaty settlement now hung in the balance.

---

[8] NAI, provisional government minutes, 1/1/2, 2 June 1922. Collins blamed the activities of opponents of the Treaty. See León Ó Broin (ed.), *In Great Haste – The Letters of Michael Collins and Kitty Kiernan* (Dublin, 1996), 175 and 183; and *Dáil Debates*, vol. 1, cols. 498–9, 20 September 1922. For Griffith's views see The National Archives [TNA], CAB 43/3 SFC 40, letter from Mr Arthur Griffith to the prime minister, 2 June 1922. Those of Kevin O'Higgins can be found at *Dáil Debates*, vol. 1, cols. 1008–9, 29 September 1922. See also Leo Kohn, *The Constitution of the Irish Free State* (London, 1932), 79; Curran, *Birth of the Irish Free State*, 204; and Alan J. Ward, *The Irish Constitutional Tradition* (Washington, DC, 1994), 175.

[9] *Irish Independent*, 23 February 1922, 5.

[10] TNA, CAB 43/6. 22/N/60(6), approval of draft constitution, 26 February 1922.

[11] Tom Garvin, *1922: The Birth of Irish Democracy* (New York, 1996), 174–5. See also F. S. L. Lyons, *Ireland since the Famine* (London, 1985), 459; and Oonagh Walsh, *Ireland's Independence* (London, 2002), 95.

[12] TNA, CAB 43/1 22/N/148(3), meeting of British signatories, 27 May 1922.

[13] Robert C. Self (ed.), *The Austen Chamberlain Diary Letters, 1916–1937* (Cambridge, 1995), 190.

[14] TNA, CAB 43/1 22/N/148(3), meeting of British signatories, 27 May 1922.

[15] TNA, CAB 23/30, CAB 31(22), the situation in Ireland, 1 June 1922.

The Drafting Instructions of the Irish Provisional Government

How had matters reached this impasse? What were the Irish provisional government's strategic priorities in creating and presenting the draft constitution brought to London in May 1922? The provisional government, having agreed to give London a confidential preview, now needed a strategy to justify its draft constitution and ensure that it would emerge largely intact from the negotiations that would follow.

The first and most obvious strategy followed by the provisional government was to interpret the provisions of the Treaty to provide as much autonomy as possible. George Gavan Duffy, minister for foreign affairs and a signatory of the Treaty, used a close reading of the text of the Treaty to argue that there was nothing in the text that suggested the controversial parliamentary oath was mandatory for all members of the Oireachtas.[16] However, as seen earlier, the constitution committee, following their instructions, pushed matters further and substantially excluded references to the King, the Governor General and the Privy Council appeal from the text.

The second strategic departure was based on Article 2 of the Treaty, which linked the constitutional status of the Irish Free State to that of the Dominion of Canada in terms of 'law, practice and constitutional usage'. This important provision was one of the most ambiguous in the entire text of the 1921 Treaty. The term 'constitutional usage' was particularly unclear and was often interpreted as meaning much the same as 'practice'.[17] Nevertheless, it could not be denied that a considerable gap had opened since the mid-nineteenth century between 'law' and 'practice' in the relationship between the United Kingdom and Canada. The provisional government decided that the provisions of the draft constitution would be a synthesis of 'law' and 'practice'. It hoped that the use of a 'synthesis approach' would allow the 1922 Constitution to reflect constitutional realities in the existing Dominions and so avoid inclusion of allegedly obsolete legal provisions.[18]

The final strategic priority was to create constitutional provisions that left the door open to coalition government with opponents of the Treaty.

---

[16] Gavan Duffy would later resurrect these arguments in the Dáil. See Thomas Mohr, 'George Gavan Duffy and the Legal Consequences of the Anglo-Irish Treaty, 1921–1923' (2023) 73 *Northern Ireland Legal Quarterly* 55, 75–6.

[17] For example, see *Dáil Debates*, vol. T, no. 3, cols. 167–8, 15 December 1921.

[18] Michael Collins had embraced this approach before signing the Treaty in 1921. See Ward, *The Irish Constitutional Tradition*, 172.

As mentioned earlier, this was probably the main consideration behind the choice of Draft B with its provision for extern ministers. This consideration is also likely to have influenced the exclusion of the divisive parliamentary oath from all drafts overseen by the provisional government.

How confident was the provisional government in its ability to persuade London to accept this draft Irish constitution? In late 1922, when the negotiations were long over, two members of the provisional government, Kevin O'Higgins and Ernest Blythe, claimed that they had regarded the draft constitution brought to London as an ambitious opening gambit in a bargaining process with the British government. They referred to it as a 'try on', an overly ambitious opening bid in a bout of high-stakes bargaining. O'Higgins claimed that the Irish delegation had aimed high and so 'we brought over something which we felt ourselves we could not get and which if the position were reversed – if we were in the English position and the English were in ours – we certainly would not concede'.[19] Ernest Blythe also argued that the draft constitution was an unrealistic opening gambit when he told the Dáil: 'I never had any belief whatever that the British would agree to all that was in the draft that was taken over to London, and, for my part, I believe the draft went outside the terms of the Treaty, and was such as we had no right to expect would be agreed to.'[20]

How accurate were assertions that the draft constitution brought to London was merely a 'try on'? Although Collins understood in the spring and summer of 1922 that difficulties might lie ahead with the British government, it is hard to identify his negotiating tactics on the constitution. No document appears to have survived indicating the provisions that Collins was prepared to trade and those on which he was determined to take a stand. In fact, it is clear from the minutes of the provisional government that the final text of the draft constitution was only approved on 25 May, the day before it was brought to London.[21] There was little time for strategy and Collins' attention appears to have been firmly fixed on mollifying opponents of the Treaty and on averting the approaching Civil War.

George Gavan Duffy remained convinced in May 1922 that the Irish delegation that travelled to London with the draft constitution were

[19] *Dáil Debates*, vol. 1, col. 1008, 29 September 1922.
[20] Ibid., col. 382, 18 September 1922.
[21] NAI, provisional government minutes, 1/1/2, 25 May 1922.

seriously under-estimating the task before them. He was convinced that the only member of the delegation that fully appreciated the challenge was Hugh Kennedy, law officer to the provisional government and future Chief Justice of the Irish Supreme Court. In fact, even Kennedy seemed to under-estimate the obstacles facing the Irish negotiators. He had not anticipated that the British government would reject the synthesis approach to drafting the constitution and so insist that the formal law that applied to the Dominions be replicated in the draft Irish constitution. Kennedy, writing six years after the conclusion of the negotiations, still could not bring himself to believe that in signing the Treaty that the Irish negotiators had agreed 'to dance a constitutional *danse macabre* with the bones of an obsolete colonial skeleton'.[22]

British Strategy and the Draft Irish Constitution

The British government was not ignorant of the nature of the draft constitution that was being prepared by the Irish provisional government in early 1922.[23] Despite this information, it remained difficult for the British government to formulate a strategy when they were dealing with a document whose details they only knew from scattered fragments of revelations and leaks. Nevertheless, several priorities were settled in advance of the anticipated preview of the draft constitution.

The first priority was to ensure that the prime minister, David Lloyd George, be personally present when the draft constitution was delivered to London. Thomas (Tom) Jones, a leading British civil servant who held the post of deputy secretary to the cabinet, later wrote that this was necessary to prevent the rest of the British government from rejecting the draft at first glance.[24] The sense of pessimism of British officials concerning the draft Irish constitution long preceded their first view of the text.

The most important British negotiating priority was ensuring that the future Irish Free State and its constitution adhere to precedents maintained by the existing Dominions. British insistence on sticking closely to Dominion models had been maintained consistently from the beginning of the Treaty negotiations and were reflected in Articles 1 and 2 of that

---

[22] H. Kennedy, 'The Association of Canada with the Constitution of the Irish Free State' (1928) 6 *The Canadian Bar Review* 747, 754.

[23] TNA, CAB 23/30, CAB 27(22), Constitution of the Free State, 16 May 1922.

[24] T. Jones, *Whitehall Diary* (Oxford, 1971), 199. See also TNA, CAB 23/30 CAB 27(22), the Constitution of the Irish Free State, 16 May 1922.

agreement. The British government was eager to ensure that the future Irish constitution be recognisable as the constitution of a Dominion.[25] Lord Hewart, a signatory of the Treaty who now held the post of Lord Chief Justice of England, concluded that 'very drastic' changes would be required when the draft Irish constitution was discovered not to adhere to this model.[26] Austen Chamberlain even suggested that 'a constitution in harmony with the Empire could be framed *de novo*'.[27]

The British government was aware of the Irish argument that 'law, practice and constitutional usage' in the Dominions should be treated as a synthesis in drafting the 1922 Constitution. This synthesis approach to drafting the Irish Constitution had been anticipated long before the signing of the Treaty. British negotiators were determined to reject this argument and demand that 'law' and 'practice' be treated separately. This meant enshrining core constitutional provisions in the Irish Constitution that mirrored those of the existing Dominions while following Dominion practice in the interpretation and application of these provisions.[28] Practice was, after all, constantly evolving and was often too messy and inconsistent to be translated into legal provisions. Lloyd George would later tell Irish negotiators that safeguards as to practice could not be embodied in a constitution. He made clear, with brutal frankness, that Irish negotiators should have raised such objections before signing the Treaty.[29]

The British government also followed a strategy of linking the fates of the Treaty and the 1922 Constitution. Lloyd George, speaking in the House of Commons on 14 December 1921, made clear the consequences

---

[25] For example, see TNA, CAB 43/1, SFB 4th, memorandum of Dominion status, 15 October 1921; CAB 23/30, CAB 27(22), the Constitution of the Irish Free State, 16 May 1922; CAB 43/2, SFB 3 memorandum on Dominion status by Lionel Curtis, 17 October 1921; CAB 43/2, SFB 40, memorandum by Lionel Curtis, 10 December 1921; CAB 43/2, SFB 55, note on the draft Irish constitution, 27 May 1922; CAB 43/3, SFC 35, memorandum on the draft Irish constitution, 29 May 1922; CAB 43/2, SFB 59, memorandum on the draft constitution for the Irish Free State, 29 May 1922, and CAB 23/30, CAB 31(22), the situation in Ireland, 1 June 1922.
[26] TNA, CAB 43/1 22/N/148(3), meeting of 27 May 1922.
[27] Ibid.
[28] For example, TNA, CAB 43/1, SFB 4th, memorandum of Dominion status, 15 October 1921, and CAB 43/3, SFC 35, memorandum on the draft constitution of the Irish Free State, 29 May 1922.
[29] TNA, CAB 43/7 22/N/163, interview between the Prime Minister and Mr Griffith and Mr Collins, 1 June 1922.

that would follow if the future constitution were not in accord with the terms of the document signed just over a week earlier. He declared that '[a]ny proposal in contravention of this Agreement [the Treaty] will be ultra vires'.[30] The British prime minister also made clear what would happen if attempts were made to revise the Treaty settlement itself. He had 'no doubt at all' that amendments would be moved in Ireland 'to leave out certain restrictions and limitations and qualifications'. 'Once they are inserted', he warned, 'the Treaty goes'.[31] When the British government rejected the draft constitution in May 1922 it soon became obvious that the entire settlement was in jeopardy. It is difficult to detect any element of bluff or insincerity in this approach. Lloyd George privately predicted a breakdown in negotiations soon after seeing the text of the draft constitution.[32]

British suspicions as to future Irish adherence to the Treaty settlement was a significant feature of preparations for negotiations on the future constitution. The British government became convinced in early 1922 that a device had to be placed in the constitution to ensure that the future Irish Free State would be bound to adhere to the Treaty. This would result in the insertion of the provision in the final text of the 1922 Irish Constitution that would become known as the 'Repugnancy Clause'.[33] This would provide that any Irish law, including the constitution and amendments to it, found inconsistent with the Treaty would be rendered null and void. It should be noted that determination to insert such a device, and the suspicion that underpinned it, long preceded the finalisation of the Collins–de Valera agreement and other events in mid-1922 that might have led to doubts as to Irish good faith with respect to the Treaty settlement.[34] It had also been decided before the signature of the Treaty in December 1921 that the Privy Council appeal should be used to ensure adherence to the settlement.[35]

[30] *Hansard*, House of Commons, vol. 149, col. 42, 14 December 1922.
[31] Ibid., col. 43.
[32] Jones, *Whitehall Diary*, 203.
[33] Section 2 of the Constitution of the Irish Free State (Saorstát Éireann) Act 1922 [Irl] and preamble to the Irish Free State Constitution Act 1922 (Session 2) [UK]. The term 'repugnancy clause' was created by Leo Kohn to refer to these provisions. See Kohn, *Constitution*, 98.
[34] For example, see TNA, CAB 43/2, SFB 40, memorandum by Lionel Curtis, 10 December 1922, and CAB 27/153, CP 3653, report of the attorney-general's committee, 24 January 1922.
[35] Thomas Mohr, *Guardian of the Treaty* (Dublin, 2016), 28–9.

The Confidential Preview of the Draft Constitution

On 27 May 1922, an Irish delegation led by Collins and Griffith brought their draft constitution to London. They were immediately placed on the defensive when they met British signatories of the Treaty. The British response to the draft constitution was overwhelmingly negative. Lloyd George asserted that it was the constitution of a republic in disguise with no concessions made to the Canadian yardstick. He highlighted the diminution of the position of the King, the absence of any reference to the parliamentary oath, the absence of an appeal to the Judicial Committee of the Privy Council and provisions allowing the Irish Free State to make its own treaties independently of the common foreign policy of the Commonwealth. These were all matters that struck at the very heart of imperial unity. Collins remained ominously silent on receipt of this news. Griffith protested that the draft constitution had been drawn up in a hurry. Nevertheless, he made it clear that the Irish provisional government had intended that the text conform to the Treaty. He was willing to consider any arguments to the contrary but insisted on being presented with specific instances of purported breaches. Lloyd George promised a detailed legal analysis that would illustrate just how far the draft constitution departed from the Treaty.[36] Austen Chamberlain made it clear that the British government desired substantive changes to the draft constitution and not merely the amendment of a line here and there. Lloyd George hinted at a resumption of hostilities if the draft constitution represented the provisional government's final word.[37] In private, Lloyd George reflected that Griffith was 'straight' but he had serious doubts concerning Collins, who he described as 'just a wild animal – a mustang'.[38] Collins wrote to his fiancée, Kitty Kiernan: 'Things are serious – far far more serious than anyone at home thinks. In fact it is not too much to say that they are as serious as they were at the worst stage of the negotiations last year.'[39]

On 29 May, British officials completed a written analysis of the draft Irish constitution that decisively rejected the synthesis approach.

---

[36] TNA, CAB 43/7, 22/N/162, draft Irish constitution, 27 May 1922.

[37] TNA, CAB 43/6 22/N/60(8), conference on Ireland with Irish ministers, 27 May 1922, and CAB 43/7 22/N/162, meeting between the British and Irish signatories, draft Irish constitution, 27 May 1922.

[38] TNA, CAB 43/1 22/N/148(3), meeting of British signatories, 27 May 1922, and Jones, *Whitehall Diary*, 206.

[39] Ó Broin, *In Great Haste*, 175.

It claimed that strong objections had been made at the most recent imperial conference, a meeting of the governments of the United Kingdom and the Dominions, against any attempt to crystallise the custom and practice of the Dominions in a written document. The analysis concluded that any variation from the accepted constitutional forms could not be sanctioned by the British government without reference to and consent from the imperial conference.[40] The British officials who wrote this analysis knew that imperial conferences required years of advance planning and that it was impossible to convene a new one in the summer of 1922.

Hugh Kennedy drafted a response to the British legal analysis that was intended to defend the synthesis approach to drafting the constitution. Kennedy's memorandum included a lengthy assault on the 'English Common Law' which caused some confusion. It also rejected comparisons between Ireland and the Dominions, which British officials interpreted as an attack on Articles 1 and 2 of the Treaty.[41] The British government was aghast when presented with this memorandum, and negotiations with Kennedy came to an abrupt halt.[42]

The failure of the talks to secure revision of the draft Irish constitution combined with the hostile reaction to Kennedy's memorandum led to a significant rise in political tensions. The British cabinet seemed convinced that the Irish negotiators appeared to have reverted to their pre-Treaty position. It decided that Lloyd George should write directly to Arthur Griffith making clear that the draft constitution was 'wholly inconsistent' with the Treaty and was also incompatible with Dominion status. The letter, sent on 1 June 1922, asked a series of direct questions on whether the Irish Free State would adhere to Dominion positions on citizenship, the position of the Crown, the power to make treaties, the Privy Council appeal and the parliamentary oath. The sixth and final question asked if all members of the Irish provisional government were prepared to sign a declaration accepting the Treaty as required by Article

---

[40] TNA, CAB 43/3, SFC 35, memorandum on the draft Irish constitution, 29 May 1922, and CAB 43/2, SFB 59, memorandum on the draft constitution for the Irish Free State, 29 May 1922.

[41] TNA, CAB 43/2, SFB 60, observations on the criticism of the British government on the draft Irish constitution, 31 May 1922, and CAB 43/7 22/N/163, interview between the Prime Minister and Mr. Griffith and Mr. Collins, 1 June 1922.

[42] UCDA, P4/1252, Kennedy to Conor Maguire, 10 June 1936 and TNA, CAB 23/30, CAB 31(22), Appendix, draft constitution of Irish provisional government, note on progress of negotiations.

17 of that document.[43] Lloyd George demanded clear answers to all six questions to avoid a breakdown of negotiations.[44] The British government was fully aware that the Irish provisional government was being asked to choose between a break with London or a break with de Valera and other Irish opponents of the Treaty.[45] Lloyd George told his cabinet that the Irish negotiators seemed slow to grasp this reality. He believed that Griffith might have come to this realisation while Collins appeared to remain in denial.[46]

Irish opponents of the Treaty had already presented the provisional government with the same choice in demanding full independence even if it meant a break with London. Harry Boland, a leading Irish opponent of the Treaty, declared in the Dáil 'let us see if in this Constitution the independence of the country can be gained by Parliamentary methods'.[47] Boland also made clear the alternative when he added: 'if the Constitution be such that England cannot accept it, I hold that with the forces of the Republic in the field, when the break comes, we can force England to accept a Constitution satisfactory to all'.[48]

The entire Treaty settlement appeared to be hanging over a precipice by the beginning of June 1922. The provisional government could no longer delude itself over whether it could produce a constitution that would satisfy both the British government and Irish opponents of the Treaty.

British Proposals in the Event of Breakdown of Negotiations

The British government had long anticipated the possibility of a breakdown of the Treaty settlement and possible courses of action had been under review since at least February 1922.[49] All contingency plans focused on the twenty-six counties of 'Southern Ireland'. They demanded a complete severance of communications between Northern Ireland and the rest of the island imposed by the British military. The proposed

---

[43] TNA, CAB 43/2, SFB 62, letter from the prime minister to Mr A. Griffith, 1 June 1922.
[44] Ibid.; and TNA, CAB 23/30, CAB 32(22), cabinet meeting of 2 June 1922.
[45] TNA, CAB 23/30, CAB 32(22), cabinet meeting of 2 June 1922.
[46] Ibid.
[47] *Dáil Debates*, vol. S2, no. 13, col. 473, 19 May 1922.
[48] Ibid.
[49] TNA, CAB 27/161, PGI (A) 1.

military frontier might not necessarily have followed the existing border on the island of Ireland.[50]

The earliest plans demanded the complete cessation of all trade and communications between the twenty-six counties and Great Britain, Northern Ireland and other parts of the British Empire. This plan was abandoned as inadequate to compel the Irish provisional government to fall into line.[51] A more radical plan of total naval blockade was later developed with a variation that involved the complete occupation of Dublin.[52] Once again, this would have involved a forcible closure of the border with Northern Ireland. Legal analyses concluded that there was little to prevent such action under the Covenant of the League of Nations. Nevertheless, the authors of this radical scheme recognised that it would expose the British government to serious domestic and international pressure.[53]

By June 1922, the dominant scheme was a compromise between these two plans. This involved the occupation of key Irish ports and the seizure and control of Irish revenue. Once again, there was to be a military closure of communications with Northern Ireland. It was estimated that a small fraction of existing Irish revenue would be left to the provisional government.[54] The objective was to compel the provisional government to concede to British demands without resorting to outright war. Exploratory discussions on this plan within the British cabinet revealed doubts, including a risk of descent into renewed conflict. Hamar Greenwood, chief secretary for Ireland, was convinced that attempts to occupy Dublin would see the city 'burnt in twenty-four hours'.[55] Winston Churchill repeatedly drew analogies between an Irish attempt at secession from the British Empire with that of the Confederate States from the United States of America in the 1860s.[56] Lloyd George feared that British forces occupying the ports would inevitably be drawn into the interior to protect southern unionists.[57]

---

[50] Jones, *Whitehall Diary*, 208–9.
[51] TNA, CAB 27/161, PGI (A) 5.
[52] Ibid., 5 and 8.
[53] Ibid., 5 and 7.
[54] Ibid., 9; and TNA, CAB 23/30, CAB 31(22), the situation in Ireland, 1 June 1922.
[55] Jones, *Whitehall Diary*, 208.
[56] For example, TNA, CAB 43/7 22/N/162, examination of the draft Irish constitution, 27 May 1922, CAB 43/1, 22/N/148(3), meeting of 27 May 1922 and *Hansard*, House of Commons, vol. 154, col. 2144, 31 May 1922.
[57] Jones, *Whitehall Diary*, 208.

The Irish Provisional Government and Crisis in the Treaty Settlement

Irish ministers considered the prospect of a breakdown of the Treaty settlement in a series of meetings in early June 1922. Arthur Griffith told a cabinet meeting that 'the position was very serious and the British will not hesitate to go back to war if they are not satisfied on the Constitution'.[58] Michael Collins appeared genuinely shocked by the British rejection of the draft constitution and also contemplated the real prospect of a breakdown of the Treaty settlement.[59] He was in a state of some emotional agitation throughout the negotiations and his own correspondence described the talks as 'bad beyond words', 'really awful' and 'ghastly'. By 1 June, Collins wrote 'I feel I can do no more good here' and returned to Dublin.[60]

Brian Murphy argues that Collins' return to Dublin after the early stages of negotiation 'was tantamount to an admission that he had lost the battle for his own views on the Constitution'.[61] However, his return to Dublin was accompanied by the formation of a new plan that restored his optimism in reaching a settlement. Collins now proposed the radical solution of abandoning the draft constitution whose creation he had supervised. He proposed publishing 'a skeleton Constitution and leaving to the Treaty the points upon which it can speak for itself'.[62] Under this scheme, the detailed document whose creation he had sponsored would be thrown to the winds. Instead, the Irish Free State would develop a constitution that was largely unwritten.

Collins tried to convince his cabinet colleagues that the British government would accept this solution and that the door to coalition with de Valera remained wide open. He argued that the British government would accept the proposal on extern ministers and the omission of the oath from the text. Collins also maintained that de Valera, in joining a coalition, would effectively accept the Treaty. He was confident 'that the English will meet us on an unwritten Constitution' and that 'They are

---

[58] UCDA, P4/205, cabinet meeting, 3 June 1922.
[59] Jones, *Whitehall Diary*, 203.
[60] Ó Broin, *In Great Haste*, 176 and 183.
[61] B. P. Murphy, 'Nationalism: The Framing of the Constitution of the Irish Free State, 1922 – The Defining Battle for the Irish Republic', in J. Augusteijn (ed.), *The Irish Revolution, 1913–1923* (London, 2002), 140.
[62] UCDA, P4/204, cabinet meeting, 2 June 1922.

willing to leave "law" plus "practice" unwritten'.[63] Hugh Kennedy poured cold water on the feasibility of the proposal for a skeleton constitution.[64] The British government had made clear that it required a constitution that was recognisable as that of a Dominion. Only George Gavan Duffy, an increasingly peripheral figure, offered vocal support for Collins' scheme and continued to support the proposal long after Collins had abandoned it.[65] Collins maintained his skeleton constitution proposal during cabinet meetings on 2, 3 and 5 June, but failed to convince his colleagues.[66] He did not participate in drafting a response to Lloyd George's six questions, which will be described at a later stage, and he did not join Arthur Griffith when he returned to London on 6 June to resume negotiations. Collins faded from the negotiations and from the drafting of the constitution from this point onwards.[67]

Brian Murphy writes: 'Why Collins did not go to London for the final constitutional talks is, in many ways, just as intriguing a question as why de Valera did not go to London for the Treaty negotiations.'[68] The comparison is not straightforward. De Valera did not attend the Treaty negotiations and rejected the final settlement produced by them. By contrast, Collins did engage with the negotiations in 1922, albeit at the peripheries, and did accept the revised draft constitution that finally emerged.

Nevertheless, it is difficult to deny that Collins seriously misjudged the drafting of the constitution. Akenson and Fallin note that 'The Constitution being proposed by Collins went beyond de Valera's and Childers' Document No. 2 in its statement of Irish independence and sovereignty'.[69] F. S. L. Lyons writes that the provisional government 'went as far as they dared in approximating their constitution to the concept of external association'.[70] Michael Laffan concludes: 'Despite heroic efforts Collins failed in his efforts to smuggle a disguised republic

---

[63] Ibid.
[64] UCDA, P4/206, cabinet meeting, 5 June 1922.
[65] UCDA, P4/207, Gavan Duffy to Collins, 3 June 1922 and P4/208, Gavan Duffy to Collins, 7 June 1922. See also Mohr, 'George Gavan Duffy', 67.
[66] UCDA, P4/204, 205–6.
[67] Collins did attend a meeting in London on 13 June but most of the redrafting had been completed by this time and the main topic for discussion concerned safeguards for southern Protestants.
[68] Murphy, 'Nationalism', 140.
[69] Akenson and Fallin, 'Irish Civil War', 36.
[70] Lyons, *Ireland Since the Famine*, 458.

into the constitution, he was unable to advance beyond the gains which had been secured during the treaty negotiations the previous December.'[71] Collins' fixation on placating opponents of the Treaty had led to a serious misreading of the British negotiating position, which had always sought an Irish constitution with provisions similar to the Dominions on matters such as the King, the Governor General and the Privy Council appeal. This had been made clear by the six questions presented by Lloyd George which required a response from Irish negotiators.

The Resumption of Negotiations

The period of tension and anxiety that accompanied the 1922 negotiations on the draft Irish constitution were described by some contemporaries as being worse than the negotiations that preceded the signing of the Treaty in late 1921.[72] The negotiations were also complicated by British misgivings as to the Collins/de Valera pact and Irish indignation at sectarian violence in Belfast which frequently intruded into discussions. Collins had declared that 'this gulf is unbridgeable' in the early stages of negotiation and contemplated the possibility of a resumption of armed conflict.[73] Lloyd George also seemed convinced of the likelihood of a break.[74]

The period of tension was finally relieved by the arrival of a taxicab at Downing Street on 2 June 1922 bearing Griffith's response to Lloyd George's six questions. This proved to be a watershed. *The Times* recorded that five minutes later British ministers dispersed with 'smiles of relief on their faces'.[75] Griffith had given satisfactory answers to the six questions subject to certain reservations on the Privy Council appeal that the British government believed could be overcome. He had effectively conceded that major amendments would have to be made to the draft constitution of the Irish Free State.[76] These amendments were negotiated in the days that followed by Hugh Kennedy and Lord Hewart, Lord Chief

---

[71] M. Laffan, *The Resurrection of Ireland – The Sinn Féin Party 1916–1923* (Cambridge, 1999), 398.

[72] Jones, *Whitehall Diary*, 203; and Ó Broin, *In Great Haste*, 175.

[73] Jones, *Whitehall Diary*.

[74] Ibid., 203 and 208.

[75] *The Times*, 3 June 1922, 8.

[76] TNA, CAB 43/3, SFC 40, letter from Mr. Arthur Griffith to the prime minister, 2 June 1922 and CAB 23/30, CAB 33(22), 2 June 1922.

Justice of England, under the supervision of their respective governments. The resulting text, published on 16 June 1922, was very different
to the original draft Irish constitution. Leaks in the drafting process from
before June 1922 ensured that the public were aware of this reality.

The King and the Governor General now appeared in multiple provisions of the draft constitution while the Privy Council appeal was recognised in Article 66. Amendments were also made to Articles 46 and 49 to
ensure compatibility with the defence provisions of the Treaty. The Irish
provisional government decided to adopt a policy where, in the event of
British representatives insisting on the insertion of the letter of Canadian
law in the constitution, Irish representatives should insist that the practice that applied in Canada should also be explicitly embodied in the
constitution.[77] This strategy ensured that three direct references to
Canada and one to Australia would appear in the text of the constitution.[78] These amendments would not prove to be particularly significant in practical terms. Far more significant additions included insertion
of the text of the Treaty in a schedule to the constitution together with an
entirely new 'Repugnancy Clause' which, as mentioned earlier, guaranteed the supremacy of the Treaty over all Irish law including the new
constitution. The controversial parliamentary oath was now included in
the provisions of the constitution and its obligatory nature for all Irish
parliamentarians and members of government was made clear.[79]

The detailed and complicated negotiations that accompanied the
redrafting of the provisions of the draft Irish constitution that took place
between 6 and 15 June 1922 have been stereotyped as acts of Irish
'surrender', 'capitulation', 'humiliating concession' and 'Turning Tail'.[80]
Akenson and Fallin decline to examine these negotiations on the basis
that they 'require little description, since they merely consisted of the
Irish surrendering to the British objections'.[81] Garvin asserts that on
2 June 1922, 'the Irish gave in completely'.[82] These conclusions as to
the latter stages in the British–Irish negotiations reflect unfortunate and
inaccurate stereotypes. The absence of realism in the creation of the draft
Irish constitution did ensure that many inevitable concessions had to be

[77] NAI, provisional government minutes, 1/1/2, 6 June 1922.
[78] Articles 41, 51 and 60 of the 1922 Constitution of the Irish Free State.
[79] Articles 17 and 55 and second schedule of the 1922 Constitution of the Irish Free State.
[80] Akenson and Fallin, 'Irish Civil War', 53, 55, 58–61.
[81] Ibid., 61.
[82] Garvin, 1922, 175.

made in a short period of time. Yet the Irish negotiators did not concede all British demands and did enjoy negotiating successes of their own. A comprehensive account is beyond the scope of this chapter. Nevertheless, examples include Irish refusal to accept strict adherence to the Canadian model in the method of constitutional amendment, a refusal to link the status of Irish citizenship to imperial legislation and securing cherished provisions emphasising Irish popular sovereignty without any symbolic reference to the King.[83]

On 15 June 1922, the British signatories approved the text of the revised draft constitution. The duration of the negotiations ensured that the provisional government just barely fulfilled its promise to publish the draft constitution in advance of the Irish election of 16 June. The text was published on the morning of the election. Opponents of the Treaty were swift to condemn the draft constitution.[84] Nevertheless, the ensuing election resulted in a decisive majority for parties that supported the Treaty. They won 92 seats while opponents won just 36 out of the 128 seats available. The Treaty and the draft constitution were, for the moment, secure.

Conclusions

Michael Collins remained convinced during the negotiations of May and June 1922 that the British government had rejected the draft Irish constitution based on suspicions raised by the activities of opponents of the Treaty.[85] Hugh Kennedy blamed the newly appointed law officers, Sir Ernest Pollock and Sir Leslie Scott, who faced Kennedy at various junctures during the course of the constitution negotiations. Kennedy believed that their report on the draft constitution had 'set the British Cabinet wild with the ideas they suggested, starting with the proposition that we should have taken one of the Dominion models and followed it somewhat slavishly'.[86] Other sources blame the Collins–de Valera pact

[83] NAI, S4285A, Hugh Kennedy to provisional government, 11 June 1922; provisional government minutes, 1/1/2, 12 June 1922; UCDA, P4/365, notes on draft constitution, 1922 and TNA, CAB 43/7 22/N/163, report on draft Irish constitution, June 1922.

[84] See T. Mohr, 'Opposition to the 1922 Irish Free State Constitution', https://papers.ssrn.com/sol3/papers.cfm?abstract_id=4487179 (accessed 25 November 2023).

[85] See references in n. 8 above.

[86] UCDA, P4/1252, Kennedy to Conor Maguire, 10 June 1936. Pollock and Scott were just two members of a group of legal experts who wrote the relevant report.

for raising British suspicions as to the good faith of the provisional government.[87]

British cabinet records do not support any of these theories. The British government had long assumed that the Irish Constitution should adhere to Dominion models, a position made clear in internal deliberations before and after the signing of the Treaty.[88] Lloyd George privately dismissed the significance of the Collins–de Valera pact in analysing the draft constitution soon after it was brought to London.[89] The fundamental objective of the British government in 1922 was to ensure that the future Irish Constitution could be presented as a Dominion constitution in order that the Irish Free State itself could be presented as a Dominion. Lloyd George summarised the dispute with the Irish provisional government over the draft constitution in the following terms: 'Are they prepared to accept the constitutional position of the other Dominions or not? That is the issue.'[90] Austen Chamberlain demanded a constitution 'in harmony with the Empire'.[91] Lloyd George made this position clear in his letter to Griffith sent on 1 June 1922, which concluded that 'as Ireland no less under the Treaty than before is a member of the Community of Nations known as the British Empire, the other member of that Community cannot permit her to adopt a Constitution that is out of harmony with that under which those members of the Commonwealth enjoy the fullest measure of freedom and security'.[92]

The failure of the Irish provisional government and its negotiators to fully appreciate the negotiating priorities of their opponents was a serious blunder. By contrast, the British government fully understood the Irish desire to obscure Dominion law with Dominion practice and, in so doing, attempt to mollify opponents of the Treaty. Unfortunately, these objectives were incompatible with wider British policy that demanded that the secession of the territory of the Irish Free State from the United Kingdom should not also be seen by the international community as secession from the British Empire and Commonwealth. The British government understood Irish negotiating priorities from the start,

---

[87] For example, Ward, *Irish Constitutional Tradition*, 175; and Kohn, *Constitution*, 79.

[88] See TNA, CAB 43/1, SFB 4th, memorandum of Dominion status, 15 October 1921, and CAB 43/3, SFC 35, memorandum on the draft constitution of the Irish Free State, 29 May 1922.

[89] TNA, CAB 43/7 22/N/163, examination of the draft Irish constitution, 27 May 1922.

[90] TNA, CAB 43/1 22/N/148(3), meeting of British signatories of the Treaty, 27 May 1922.

[91] Ibid.

[92] See TNA, CAB 43/2 SFB 62, letter from the prime minister to Mr A. Griffith, 1 June 1922.

whereas their Irish counterparts only grasped British priorities when the negotiations were well advanced.

One of the most striking features of the negotiations concerns the position of Michael Collins. As seen earlier, the draft 1922 Constitution is sometimes referred to as 'Michael Collins' Constitution' or 'Collins' draft'.[93] The constitution was his project and, although he had little direct involvement in the technical drafting, there can be little doubt that he had the final word in shaping the format of the draft Irish constitution. Yet Collins is striking for his relative absence from the British–Irish negotiations. He faded into the background after the initial exchanges and it was left to Arthur Griffith to take the lead in dealing with the British government. This ensured that Griffith would be blamed by some contemporaries and subsequent historians for the inevitable compromises that followed.[94]

Collins proved willing to ditch the draft constitution in the aftermath of its rejection by the British government and to replace it with a short 'skeleton constitution' published in conjunction with the Treaty. His conviction that the British would accept a largely unwritten constitution that excluded the parliamentary oath and other Dominion features was out of touch with reality. On 2 June, Collins told his cabinet colleagues that, 'on assurances from us they will give us a very liberal interpretation of the Constitution, for they are more concerned with our good faith than with our Constitution'.[95] On the very same day, the British cabinet was discussing possible military responses if the text of the constitution could not be made to conform with their interpretation of the 1921 Treaty.[96] On the other side of the coin, Collins' belief that coalition with de Valera would amount to de facto acceptance of the Treaty by all parties was also out of touch with reality. The draft constitution was not a 'try on', as described by O'Higgins and Blythe, but the product of wishful thinking that focussed almost entirely on satisfying the objectives of opponents of the Treaty while ignoring those of the British government.

George Gavan Duffy was correct in his assessment that the Irish negotiators who travelled to London with the draft Irish constitution had greatly under-estimated the task before them. The Irish negotiators

---

[93] See Akenson and Fallin, 'The Irish Civil War'; and speech of Taoiseach Martin.
[94] For example, see *The Plain People*, 25 June 1922, 1. See also Akenson and Fallin, 'Irish Civil War', at 58–61; and Murphy, 'Nationalism', 141.
[95] UCDA, P4/204, cabinet meeting of 2 June 1922.
[96] Jones, *Whitehall Diary*, 208–9.

seemed genuinely surprised at the strength of British rejection of the draft constitution. Austen Chamberlain wrote of their reaction in a letter to his sister: 'And they seem – nay, they are – genuinely surprised that we view it so gravely. . . . We are miles asunder & they talk as if we had only to cross the street.'[97]

Irish negotiators realised too late that wider British interests required that constitutional provisions shared by the Dominions be inserted into the draft Irish constitution. There is no evidence of bluff in the stance of the British government, which was fully prepared to take some form of military action if negotiations broke down. Once this became apparent, the Irish negotiators agreed to redraft the text that had been brought to London. They soon found themselves arguing on unfamiliar issues such as the Privy Council appeal, the reservation of Dominion legislation and imperial legislation. The approach taken by the provisional government in creating the draft Irish constitution had largely ignored these legal institutions which resulted in inadequate preparation when the time came to consider their insertion into the text. Consequently, Irish negotiators faced a serious knowledge gap while their opponents had far greater experience and resources at their disposal. In these circumstances, the best that Irish negotiators could do was to demand the insertion of references to practice followed in Canada and Australia in the text of the future Irish Constitution.[98] As mentioned earlier, this was an awkward device that produced few real benefits.

Irish ministers and officials did learn from the experience of the British–Irish negotiations of 1922. When the Irish Free State began to seek constitutional reforms at the imperial conferences of the late 1920s and early 1930s, its politicians and diplomats researched the finer points of constitutional law in the Dominions and made detailed preparations as to how undesirable features could be minimised or removed.[99] The narrowing of this knowledge gap ensured that Irish negotiators travelled to London with a sense of pragmatism as to what could be achieved and a clear understanding of the negotiating priorities of the British government. These features provided the foundations of success in negotiation at the imperial conferences of 1926, 1929 and 1930 that had proved elusive in 1922.

---

[97] Self, *Austen Chamberlain*, 190.
[98] See Articles 41, 51 and 60 of the 1922 Constitution of the Irish Free State.
[99] See D. W. Harkness, *The Restless Dominion* (Dublin, 1969).

13

No Way to Run a Railroad

The Decline of the Great Northern Railway of Ireland after Partition

C. R. G. MURRAY

Introduction

The partition of Ireland fell heavily upon the Great Northern Railway of Ireland (GNR(I)). Prior to partition, it had been the most profitable of Ireland's private railway companies as a result of its dominance of the Dublin/Belfast route. It became, overnight, an international private railway company, obliged to conform to regulations imposed by both Ireland and Northern Ireland and responsible for managing new and frequently changing customs and regulatory requirements on the goods it carried. Its track crossed the border seventeen times, six of them on a single stretch at the 'serpentine Monaghan–Fermanagh boundary'.[1] The railway became increasingly associated with cross-border smuggling, and was immortalised (as the 'Southern Railway of Northern Ireland') in the 1937 Ealing comedy *Oh, Mr Porter!* The difficulties of operating the railway in these circumstances, and in the face of increased competition from roads, frequently mirrored the chaotic scenes of the fictionalised Buggleskelly station. Following a steady decline in the railway's fortunes from the 1920s onwards, the company was jointly nationalised by Ireland and Northern Ireland in 1953. This operation of the railway line by intergovernmental agreement was a leap beyond the previous tentative cooperation in a commercial venture in the context of the Erne hydro-electric scheme.[2] This chapter explores how two governments which

---

[1] E. Patterson, *The Great Northern Railway of Ireland* (Oakwood, 1962), 66.
[2] M. Kennedy, *Division and Consensus: The Politics of Irish Cross-Border Relations, 1925–1969* (Dublin, 2000), 135.

ordinarily did everything they could not to engage with each other found themselves jointly operating a railway.

This rare moment of cooperation provoked intense discussions between Stormont and the UK government, with the UK Treasury using the opportunity to tutor Northern Ireland in public spending discipline. It demanded the closure of unprofitable branch lines, precipitating the shuttering of almost all railway infrastructure west of the Bann, and blocked the purchase of German locomotives in favour of more expensive alternatives manufactured in Great Britain. This intervention undermined efforts to modernise the railway, which was dissolved in 1958, its assets being split between the Ulster Transport Authority (UTA) and Córas Iompair Éireann (CIÉ). This unusual episode thus involves the impact of sudden establishment of borders, efforts to mitigate barriers to trade in goods, North–South cooperation, the looming influence of German industry, a crisis in public service provision in Northern Ireland and fraught relationships between London, Belfast and Dublin. As such, it foreshadows the current context of post-Brexit Northern Ireland and illustrates the challenge of mitigating the effects of partition when the main actors find themselves at loggerheads.

Partition and the Railway

Twentieth-century Irish history often particularises the experience of partition, but partition was just one part of the extensive process of 'borderisation' across Europe after the First World War.[3] After 1922, the border became a dividing line between two polities whose leaders not only avoided direct engagement with each other but actively sought to define their own governance order against the other. From 1 April 1923, barriers to trade became extensive and quickly curtailed the now cross-border economy. The Common Travel Area enabled cross-border travel, but it did little to facilitate cross-border trade.[4] Railways, however, provided an enduring link across this boundary. They sometimes punctured this narrative of border-as-barrier altogether. The 'condom train' of 1971 demonstrated the absurdities of the Irish government's ongoing

---

[3] P. Leary, *Unapproved Routes: Histories of the Irish Border 1922–1972* (Oxford, 2016), 11.

[4] See C. Murray and D. Wincott, 'Partition by Degrees: Routine Exceptions in Border and Immigration Practice between the UK and Ireland, 1921–1972' (2020) 47 *Journal of Legal Studies* S145, S154–S158.

efforts to restrict access to contraception,[5] whilst the 'peace train', which began in 1989, sought to generate pressure for the removal of Articles 2 and 3 of Ireland's Constitution on the basis that they were being used to justify 'a campaign of murder' in Northern Ireland.[6] But more often they became a rare point of interrelationship which both governments had to manage.

Not that this was welcome to the new administrations in Dublin and Belfast. From the earliest days of partition, Sir James Craig was preoccupied by the potential for his counterparts in Dublin to use the Government of Ireland Act's Council of Ireland arrangements, intended to facilitate cooperation on a range of cross-border issues, to influence Northern Ireland's internal affairs.[7] This concern was acute in the context of railways because Dublin had a particular interest in the rail connections into Donegal, which all traversed Northern Ireland's territory.[8] The operation of the Council of Ireland was, however, delayed in 1922 and then dissolved following the agreement to set aside the Boundary Commission's outcomes in 1925.[9] Liam Cosgrave's administration wanted to have nothing to do with Northern Ireland or to be seen to rely on any part of the Government of Ireland Act's arrangements.[10] The GNR(I) was also excluded from the statutory amalgamation of railway companies which operated entirely within the Free State.[11]

This is not to say that the GNR(I) was left to its own devices. Even as it recovered from attacks on railway infrastructure and rolling stock during the War of Independence and Civil War, its stations and practices needed to be adapted to handle customs checks from 1 April 1923 onwards. Goods trains were subject to complex arrangements, with dutiable goods having to be grouped together in separate wagons wherever possible[12]

[5] E. Cloatre and M. Enright, 'On the Perimeter of the Lawful: Enduring Illegality in the Irish Family Planning Movement, 1972–1985' (2017) 44 *Journal of Legal Studies* 471, 476.

[6] D. Norris, 'History Takes a New Track' (1989) 279 *Fortnight* 14, 14.

[7] Government of Ireland Act 1920 (UK), s.10(2).

[8] See Public Record Office of Northern Ireland (PRONI) CAB/9/F/11/1, Letter from Sir James Craig to Directors, GNR(I) (2 February 1923), p. 1.

[9] Irish Free State Constitution Act 1922 (UK), s. 3(2) and Ireland (Confirmation of Agreement) Act 1925 (UK), s. 5.

[10] See C. Murray, 'The Partition of Ireland and the 1922 Constitution' in L. Cahillane and D. Coffey (eds.), *The Centenary of the 1922 Constitution* (London, 2024).

[11] Railways Act 1924 (Ireland). See H. Casserley, *Outline of Irish Railway History* (Newton Abbot, 1974), 147.

[12] The National Archives, UK (TNA) CUST 49/647, GNR(I): Special Circular to Staff (22 March 1923), p. 2.

and some sealed wagons having to be excluded from customs processes if they were beginning and ending their journey in one jurisdiction but being trans-shipped through the other.[13] Passengers, however, were subject to unpredictable delays and schedules had to be adapted to accommodate customs checks on baggage at the first stop after trains crossed the border.[14] Apportionment of assets and profits for taxation purposes was also a work in progress in the inter-war decades. It took years for the railway to agree the necessary concessions with customs officials to exclude activity as banal as the sale of on-train refreshments from duty requirements,[15] and when it came to apportionment of company profits for taxation purposes, all that the Free State government could say was that ultimately this was 'really a case of expecting the Commissioner to be reasonable in his demands on the railway company'.[16] All of this dislocation took its toll. In the same month the customs border came into effect, the GNR(I) instituted the first closure of a cross-border line; people and livestock were no longer travelling cross-border to the cattle fairs which had been so important to the operation of the Castleblayney–Armagh line. These challenges deepened in the 1930s, as the Ireland–UK trade war involved regular changes in tariffs, which then gave way to wartime rationing, with both generating incentives for smuggling.[17]

The Post-War Challenges

The profitability of railways in the war years gave way to a sudden crisis for the three major railway companies operating in Northern Ireland. The tragedy of the Ballymacarrett crash in January 1945 undermined the financial stability of the Belfast & Co. Down Railway. The Unionist government planning for the UTA had involved the ambition of rolling

---

[13] Composite reporting forms to cover all the different classes of wagon and truck on a goods train would not be agreed between the customs authorities in Dublin and Belfast until 1950; TNA, CUST 49/3386, Customs and Excise, Belfast, to Traffic Manager, GNR (I) (24 October 1950), p. 1.

[14] TNA, CUST 49/647, Notes of Interview between the GNR(I) Goods Manager and W. Young (Customs and Excise, Belfast) (6 March 1923), para. 10.

[15] TNA, CUST 49/979, W. Bailie (Traffic Manager, GNR(I)) to J. Large (Customs and Excise, Belfast) (19 December 1927), p. 1.

[16] Dáil Debates, Ernest Blythe (Minister for Finance), vol. 40, no. 20, Speech 147 (3 December 1931). Railways (Valuation for Rating) Act 1931 (Ireland), section 6(c).

[17] See B. Evans, *Ireland during the Second World War: Farewell to Plato's Cave* (Manchester, 2014), 98–99.

together, in one step, all public transport services operating solely within Northern Ireland's boundaries under a single public body.[18] But with the Belfast & Co. Down Railway 'heading rapidly towards bankruptcy', the government was obliged to expedite this element of its plan and roll it into the newly created UTA in October 1948.[19] The other parts of the puzzle were even more complicated. The Northern Counties Committee had already become part of British Railways when its parent company, the London, Midland and Scottish Railway, had been nationalised in January 1948. Sir Basil Brooke's government, notwithstanding its aversion to collectivisations, could not countenance that such an important element of Northern Ireland's transport policy would be directed from London, and promptly bought out British Railways for the grossly inflated figure of £2.7 million. With the UTA immediately saddled with extensive liabilities, the Transport Tribunal began the task of pruning unprofitable lines. In the same period the GNR(I) launched the 'Enterprise Express' as a non-stop service on the Belfast–Dublin route, designed to reduce mid-journey delays by ensuring that customs formalities were dealt with at either end of the line. The initial use of ageing steam locomotives, in part because the upheavals since the 1920s had deterred investment, meant that the service was beset by unreliability. The 1948 purchase of new steam engines was a backward step, with the company buying twenty new diesel railcars just two years later. These investments did not immediately restore confidence in the service, but did increase expenditure, and by 1950 the company was warning the governments in Belfast and Dublin that its losses were unsustainable.

In this period the Northern Ireland government found itself caught in a rail policy trap. Even after the nationalisation of most public transport services in 1948, Northern Ireland's law continued to be designed to regulate private providers rather than to run a nationalised railway service. This was a visible manifestation of Unionist aversion to nationalisation; as late as 1943 the records of the Cabinet sub-committee show that Brooke 'found some difficulty in understanding the force of the arguments put forward .. in favour of fusion of the transport interests as opposed to co-ordination, as provided for in the act of 1935'.[20]

[18] The legislation imposed a duty on the UTA to provide for an integrated system of road and rail transport; Transport Act (NI) 1948, s. 5.
[19] PRONI, CAB/4/721, Position of the BCDR: Memorandum by the Minister of Finance (30 June 1947), p. 1.
[20] PRONI, DEV/10/50/C/42, 'Northern Ireland Transport' (26 August 1943), p. 1.

Northern Ireland's Transport Act did not, for example, grant ministers powers to uplift fares equivalent to the legislation covering British Rail.[21] Even if ministers had such powers, and they had in essence eschewed the opportunity to include them in the legislation, the Northern Ireland government ordinarily baulked at the prospect of passing on increases in costs of public services to the electorate.[22] Whereas the British Transport Corporation spent the 1950s borrowing from the UK Treasury to manage its deficit, this was not an option that was open to the UTA, which was formally required, but always struggled, to operate in an economically viable manner. Industrial relations in the period were also strongly influenced by events in Great Britain. The year 1955 saw Northern Ireland rail workers undertake a prolonged strike alongside their British Rail counterparts, notwithstanding the distinct public bodies operating in Northern Ireland, and secure comparable wage rises.[23] These challenges were exacerbated by the increasingly parlous state of Northern Ireland's public finances; Northern Ireland was being pulled in policy directions it could scarcely afford. All of these concerns saw loud voices, including Sir Anthony Babington (a former Attorney General, appellate judge and now Chairman of the Transport Tribunal), argue for the prioritisation of road over rail in the 1950s.[24] This invidious policy picture aligns with Patrick Buckland's conclusion, with regard to Northern Ireland's welfare policy, that the major beneficiary of devolution in the middle part of the twentieth century was London, 'being relieved of direct responsibility for Northern Ireland's social problems'.[25]

The GNR(I) crisis thus saw Brooke's administration wrongfooted by a policy issue where its instincts pulled in contrary directions. Ministers were concerned that Dublin would buy out the railway and use it as an (expensive) way to embarrass the Unionist government. William McCleery, perhaps the most conciliatory of Brooke's

---

[21] Road and Rail Transport Act (NI) 1935 and Transport Act (NI) 1948 lacked comparable provisions to the Transport Act 1947 (UK), s. 85.

[22] See P. Greer, *Road versus Rail: Documents on the History of Public Transport in Northern Ireland 1921–1948* (Belfast, 1982), 128–129.

[23] The Transport Act (NI) 1948 did allow for the UTA to make proposals for fare increases to the transport tribunal, in an effort to shield the government from criticism, but it was reluctant to become a lightning rod for public complaint and repeatedly deferred fare increases even as the wage increases increased the UTA's operating costs.

[24] See A. Babington, *Report of the Transport Tribunal* (Belfast, 1952), Cmd. 310.

[25] P. Buckland, *The Factory of Grievances: Devolved Government in Northern Ireland, 1921–39* (Dublin, 1979), 175.

ministers, was thus dispatched to Dublin to try to feel out the coalition government's position. In August 1950 the GNR(I) crisis thus precipitated the first ministerial meeting between Dublin and Belfast in a quarter of a century.[26] But even when these concerns were allayed, with McCleery building up a rapport with his Dublin counterparts, the costs associated with the railway made financially conservative Unionist politicians blanch.[27] The financial pressures generated by the inadequacies of the Government of Ireland Act's terms, moreover, had recently seen it make extraordinary pleadings to the UK Treasury to enable Northern Ireland to match the nationalisation of healthcare provision.[28] When McCleery first mooted the possibility of line closures west of the Bann in 1950 in response to the parlous state of the GNR(I), he faced an intense backlash from both Nationalists and Unionists in the Northern Ireland Parliament. Abandoning these lines invited considerable embarrassment, but the prospect of nationalising the GNR(I) could not be easily reconciled with Stormont's straitened circumstances. For its part, the Irish government was concerned that it would get stuck with the costs of subsidising loss-making railway lines as Belfast's public transport policy shifted from rail to road. Its favoured solution of an All-Ireland Transport Board, however, offended Unionist sensibilities.[29]

Against this complex policy backdrop, talks between Dublin and Belfast over the railway dragged on for months. Even as the collapse of the railway appeared imminent in January 1951, the shareholders added a further complicating factor, rejecting an emergency offer by the two governments to purchase the railway company for £3.9 million, and holding out for a valuation of over twice that amount.[30] The governments' initial purchase price offer, an average of the GNR(I)'s stock exchange value over the previous three years, substantially overvalued a company in decline. The Shareholders' Protection Association lobbied representatives in the Dáil and Stormont throughout 1951, only

---

[26] Kennedy, n. 2 above, 124–125.

[27] See, for comparable pressures regarding social security, Buckland, n. 25 above, 159.

[28] See G. Walker, *A History of the Ulster Unionist Party: Protest, Pragmatism and Pessimism* (Manchester, 2004), 148–150.

[29] Kennedy, n. 2 above, 127–128.

[30] The UTA prepared a detailed timeline of the two governments' negotiations with shareholders in 1951, from which this summary is drawn; PRONI, UTA/23/CD/30, 'Notes on the G.N.R.(I.) Position' (1952), pp. 1–4.

accepting an improved offer of £4.5 million that November.[31] Following
the shareholder agreement,[32] corresponding legislation was introduced in
the Dáil and Stormont to give effect to the new arrangements, but would
not be enacted until 1953, with the two governments subsidising over £2
million in losses in the interim whilst the complex negotiations on the
management of the jointly nationalised entity proceeded.[33] Although the
Great Northern Railway Board (GNRB) was established to manage the
railway, with the two governments each appointing five members to the
Board, which was tasked with the priority of balancing the railway's
revenues and outgoings,[34] there was a persistent gloom around the
legislative debates. As Seán Lemass informed the Dáil, 'one of the most
difficult problems which arose during the negotiations' was not over how
to run cross-border services, but was instead 'to devise a procedure for
the termination of such common services'.[35] Both ministers had to sign
off on any termination of cross-border services, and if they did not, the
matter was put to a Tribunal.[36] Even as the agreement was signed to
aplomb in Belfast in August 1953, McCleery sounded a cautionary note:
'It is well to realize that the difficulties which overtook the company will
not disappear overnight with the passing from the old to the new.'[37] For
Micheal Kennedy, the closer cooperation became to becoming a reality, the
more the project assumed the appearance of 'a long-term liquidation plan',
with tracts of the corresponding Great Northern Railway Acts providing
the arrangements for winding down aspects of the GNR(I)'s operations.[38]
But if both governments were taking some notice of the pressure that the
GNR(I) was under, and preparing for the worst, this cannot be read as

---

[31] Dáil Debates, Seán Lemass (Minister for Industry and Commerce), vol. 138, no. 1, Speech
      76 (15 April 1953). Great Northern Railway Act 1953 (Ireland), s. 46.
[32] Shareholders continued to loudly complain that they had been the subject of 'blackmail'
      and that 'the Roman Catholic South and Protestant North had combined to commit a
      wicked act' as the preparation of the complex legislative arrangements delayed payments;
      'Delay in payment of G.N.R. acquisition price', Belfast Newsletter (28 February 1953).
[33] Unionist detractors in Stormont, such as Frederick Lloyd Dodd, raised objections that
      there was no relief on duty as the railway moved materials for its own maintenance
      between the jurisdictions, meaning that 'there was little possibility of the railway being
      maintained at a properly equipped and highly efficient level'; 'Move to withdraw G.N.R.
      Bill at Stormont', Northern Whig (14 May 1953).
[34] Great Northern Railway Act 1953 (Ireland), s. 7.
[35] Dáil Debates, Seán Lemass (Minister for Industry and Commerce), vol. 138, no. 1, Speech
      78 (15 April 1953).
[36] Great Northern Railway Act 1953 (Ireland), s. 24.
[37] 'McCleery and Lemass Sign Agreement', Northern Whig (11 August 1953), p. 1.
[38] Kennedy, n. 2 above, 136.

meaning that the collapse of the joint ownership scheme was an inevit-ability. To do so would be to neglect the (admittedly fitful) efforts to make this experiment in intergovernmental cooperation work after 1953.

The Operation of Joint Ownership, 1953–1958

The Northern Ireland government had aspirations to run public trans-port in a manner comparable to Great Britain, thereby demonstrating that Northern Ireland was an integral part of the United Kingdom. Nationalising the GNR(I) was part of this ambition. McCleery appointed the former general manager of the GNR(I), George Howden, as Chairman of the UTA to help integrate and coordinate services.[39] The most pressing problem, however, remained how to pay for the inflated cost of its acquisition. The Unionist government had some reason to expect that London might be receptive to providing financial backing for the Railway Agreement. It had already established a track record of 'evading' the strictures of the 1920 Act's finance arrangements in order to sustain public service provision.[40] In 1939, the UK Treasury had made an extraordinary subvention to Northern Ireland, writing off a large element of the imperial contribution, in part to support public transport policy.[41] The Treasury had, at the start of the 1950s, written off £1.5 million of the debt related to the purchase of the Northern Counties Committee railway, amounting to more than half of the purchase price, when Belfast's Ministry of Finance belatedly realised it had overbid for the asset.[42] These interventions gave rise to an expectation that the UK Treasury would support 'relative parity' in public service provision.[43] Throughout the GNR(I) crisis, moreover, the UK government had been broadly supportive of Belfast and Dublin adopting a cooperative approach, and after the agreement was concluded the Home Secretary

---

[39] When the new UTA Chairman heralded the prospects for greater coordination, Sir Anthony Babington remained sceptical that this could make a meaningful difference in light of the rise of the car; 'Tribunal Chairman says during U.T.A. hearing: "A Revolution Is Taking Place in Transport"', *Northern Whig* (22 July 1953).

[40] M. Wallace, *Northern Ireland: 50 Years of Self-Government* (New York, 1971), 157.

[41] See P. Arthur, *Special Relationships: Britain, Ireland and the Northern Ireland Problem* (Belfast, 2000), 25–27.

[42] TNA, T 233/1752, B. Maginess (NI Finance Minister) to R. Butler (Chancellor of the Exchequer) (11 July 1955), p. 1.

[43] P. Robson, 'Aspects of Public Expenditure in Northern Ireland' (1952) 19 *Journal of the Statistical and Social Inquiry Society of Ireland* 38, 43.

highlighted it in the Commons as the pre-eminent example of developments which 'show a lessening of the tension, and that is very acceptable to everyone in this House'.[44] Behind this public veneer of Home Office support, however, the Treasury seethed, and its senior officials had long awaited an opportunity to make 'these parochial die-hards ... face up to a touch of reality'.[45] The events which unfolded have remained difficult to piece together because key archival holdings within Northern Ireland remain closed, and it is only by reviewing the records generated by the UK Treasury that an account emerges of the Unionist government's efforts to defend the new arrangements.[46]

The first year of the GNR(I)'s existence as a jointly owned public body allowed for a review of its operations by the new Board, which completed an extensive report on the challenges facing the railway in September 1954.[47] It made for unhappy reading; much of the GRN(I) network was loss-making – to the tune of £457,000 in the 1953/54 financial year – and had been subject to prolonged underinvestment. Much of the historiography of subsequent events – insofar as analysis has touched upon this largely forgotten episode at all – has combined the Northern Ireland government's immediate efforts to cut GRN(I) costs alongside the previous cuts to the UTA rail network, indicating that it had never been committed to making a success of the joint venture.[48] The Northern Ireland government's response to this bleak assessment, however, was to attempt to back the GNRB, and seek additional financial support from London. Finance Minister Brian Maginess was instructed to approach the UK's Conservative government in July 1955 on the basis that 'much of the railway system in Northern Ireland should be retained', including the two different mainlines between Belfast and Derry-Londonderry (the one running south of Lough Neagh being the GNR (I) line), 'and be equipped with new motive units using diesel traction,

---

[44] Sir David Maxwell Fyfe, HC Deb., vol. 512, col. 284 (3 March 1953). See also TNA, DO 35/3910 'Great Northern Railway' (1948–1952). Leading Unionist politicians recognised many within the 1950s Conservative governments as 'sympathetic'; B. Faulkner, *Memoirs of a Statesman* (London, 1978), 22.

[45] See D. McMahon, *Republicans and Imperialists: Anglo-Irish Relations in the 1930s* (New Haven, CT, 1984), 278–279.

[46] There is little that can continue to justify the closure to the public of a record like this, seventy years after the events in question; PRONI, CAB/9/F/140/31, Great Northern Railway Company (I): Future of the Company (1952–1958).

[47] TNA, T 233/1752, GNRB, *Report on General Investigation into the Working of the G.N.R.* (15 September 1954).

[48] Kennedy, n. 2 above, 141–145.

and other rolling stock', which would require 'a very substantial sum of money'.[49] The justification for this policy was threefold. First, it would protect the employment of 4,800 railway workers. Second, the removal of rail facilities would impact upon 'Northern Ireland's prospects of future economic development'. Third, extensive closures would 'isolate' western parts of Northern Ireland 'severing their links with the capital'.[50]

Maginess' overture was expected; indeed, it had already been undermined. Just over a week before his letter arrived at the Treasury, the Permanent Secretary of the Ministry of Finance, and Head of the Northern Ireland Civil Service, Douglas Harkness, had made one of his regular visits to London to liaise with his UK government counterparts. There he had informed the Third Secretary, Edmund Compton, of all the weaknesses he perceived in the GNR(I) plan, and in particular that much of the required outlay of £5 million 'will be invested South of the Border where the main workshops and facilities of the G.N.R. are'.[51] Any capital expenditure on the GNR(I) was thus dismissed as 'throwing good money after bad'.[52] These conclusions set the tone for the memorandum prepared for the Chancellor of the Exchequer the following month, which concluded that the rail system was a mess and that much of the existing capital expenditure would have to be written off: 'Strictly financial considerations would indicate that the railways ought to be closed altogether; but this does not really seem to be practical politics, and it is fairly clear that some sort of railway system will have to be kept in Northern Ireland.'[53]

The memorandum advocated the closure of almost all of the GNR(I) network other than the mainlines between Dublin and Belfast and potentially Portadown and Derry-Londonderry, on the basis that these lines 'serve sparsely populated country ... and they might well be replaced quite adequately by road transport'.[54] This, however, had implications regarding the joint ownership of the GNR(I): 'The lines in question are probably of greater importance to the Government of Ireland since ... they offer the only direct rail link between the Republic and Donegal; in that case let the Government of the Irish

[49] Maginess, n. 42 above, 2–3.
[50] Ibid., 3.
[51] TNA, T 233/1752, E. Compton, 'Northern Ireland Transport' (18 July 1955), p. 1.
[52] Ibid., 1.
[53] TNA, T 233/1752, Memorandum: Northern Ireland Transport (15 August 1955), para. 12.
[54] Ibid., para. 13.

Republic exercise its right to keep them open and meet the losses incurred in running them.'[55]

Treasury officials also took a dim view of the lack of control that the Northern Ireland government was exercising over public transport fares and charges.[56] Overburdened by the pressing issue of speculation over UK exchange rate policy, the Chancellor of the Exchequer, R. A. Butler, only weighed into the discussions in mid-August. He held out the potential for some 'fresh capital' and that some of the existing losses might be 'written off', but only on the implicit basis of Treasury officials taking a lead on these decisions.[57] At the resultant meeting, the Treasury officials delayed any conclusion on dieselisation until line closures had taken effect.[58]

Through all of these back and forward discussions between Belfast and London, the GNRB waited. In the middle of July 1955, after the Northern Ireland Cabinet had agreed to back modernisation, the Ministry of Commerce had sought to immediately give the green light to diesel purchases to help stem operating losses. They were promptly rebuffed by Harkness in the Ministry of Finance, on the basis that any decision rested with London:

> It is clear that public transport in Northern Ireland is bankrupt unless there is a very substantial injection of State assistance ... [I]n these circumstances and now that we have gone to the Treasury for advice and assistance, it would be to my mind quite wrong and improper to agree to any capital expenditure on the part of the undertakings until we know the outcome of my Minister's approach to the Chancellor.[59]

Harkness, of course, was well aware of the direction that the Treasury would take. The discussions between the UK Treasury and the Northern Ireland government, however, were taking place in a closed box, with neither the Irish government nor the GNRB having any impression of the true position. A month later the Chairman of the GNRB made it clear to

---

[55] Ibid., para. 13.
[56] Lord Glentoran was instructed to upbraid Sir Anthony Babington for the 'embarrassment' of the transport tribunal's refusal to allow increased charges in the face of the losses that public transport in Northern Ireland was facing; PRONI, COM/64/4/74, Memorandum to the Minister of Commerce (25 July 1955), para. 4.
[57] PRONI, COM/64/4/74, R. Butler to B. Maginess (17 August 1955), p. 1.
[58] PRONI, COM/64/4/74, 'Future of Transport in Northern Ireland: Notes on a Meeting at H.M. Treasury' (1 September 1955), p. 3.
[59] PRONI, COM/64/4/74, D. Harkness (Ministry of Finance) to J. McKeown (Ministry of Commerce) (22 July 1955), p. 1.

Lord Glentoran, in the most extraordinarily frank terms, that this was no way to run a railroad:

> Who or what is causing the delay in giving a decision on the proposals submitted by the Board? I am told that it is not the Government here [Dublin] and your officials say the bottle-neck is in the Department of Finance or alternatively in London. A member of a Cabinet is a person like any other individual, so is a Civil Servant. A person takes a day, a week, or it may be a month to consider a given proposition and comes to a conclusion. . . . Any ordinary Board of Directors would decide the issue at one meeting. . . . Is a railway needed or not?[60]

He would continue to wait.

Another year was lost as line closures were announced and put to the respective transport tribunals for consideration without any movement on questions of investment for modernisation. Compton concluded that the £3 million paid by the Northern Ireland government for its share of the GNR(I) was a 'dead loss' and 'more loses are in prospect unless branch lines are closed down and more capital is put up (mainly in the form of diesel engines) to make the surviving main line (Dublin to Belfast) pay'.[61] These losses would, he fumed, eventually fall on the UK Treasury because of Northern Ireland's now-negative imperial contribution. The solution was intense Treasury oversight of all decisions around the GNR(I). The UK government would agree no further investment, and would certainly not sign off on the diesel engines from Germany which the GNRB had sought to purchase, without the Northern Ireland government following through with swingeing cuts. As the Second Secretary to the Treasury, Sir Herbert Brittain, confirmed: import '[d]uty must be charged on the German locomotives' if they were to operate on GNR(I) lines, even if they were formally based in Dublin.[62] This particular public procurement saga would rumble on into 1957, when even under a fresh tender process the German-manufactured engines remained cheaper and would be available more promptly than their British-manufactured competitors. The Northern Ireland government cavilled that 'if we disagree and say "buy British" (in part!) the South are likely to ask us to foot the bill' and wondered whether 'the U.K. declared intention of association . . .

---

[60] PRONI, COM/64/4/74, A. Reynolds (Chairman, GNRB) to Lord Glentoran (Minister of Commerce, NI) (18 August 1955), p. 1.

[61] TNA, T 233/1752, E. Compton (Third Secretary, UK Treasury) to Mr Painter (UK Treasury) (6 November 1956), p. 1.

[62] TNA, T 233/1752, Sir Herbert Brittain, Handwritten Note (4 June 1956).

with the proposed European free market' had any impact on the
Treasury's position.[63] The Treasury remained implacable in its opposition, and until the 1970s the Enterprise service would largely be left to
run using a hodgepodge of diesel railcar sets, designed for commuter
rather than intercity services.

Having exerted such pressure on the Northern Ireland government
to cut costs, the UK Treasury were unsurprised when the North and
South transport tribunals, tasked with making decisions on the future of
GNR(I) lines under the 1953 Acts, split over whether branch lines west
of the Bann should be closed. Sir Douglas Harkness (newly knighted) is
described as having a 'wicked gleam in his eye' as he reported that the
Treasury's pressure was having its desired effect in terms of the
retrenchment of the GNR(I) network in 1956: 'The next stage is for
the N.I. Government to proceed with the closure, it being open to the
Eire Government, if they wish to prevent it, to provide the extra
finance.'[64] By 1958, as a result of the cuts required by the UK government, the Dublin–Belfast GNR(I) mainline was the only remaining
railway to cross the Ireland/Northern Ireland border. The
Portadown–Derry/Londonderry mainline was also slated for closure,
but would receive a series of short-term reprieves until the final axe fell
after the Benson report of 1963.[65] The final GNRB annual report
bemoaned the lack of response from the governments in Dublin and
London to its efforts to 'rehabilitate and modernise' the railway, but
these complaints do not reveal the role that the UK Treasury was
playing behind the scenes.[66]

The Treasury's careful choreography, calibrated to shift some of the
public blame for the closure of so much of the network onto Dublin,
nonetheless came unstuck in June 1957 when Lord Glentoran, Belfast's
Minister of Commerce, announced that the Northern Ireland government intended to terminate the railway agreement at the five-year review
point stipulated in the 1953 Agreement.[67] As a result, Seán Lemass could
inform the Dáil that 'even if the Government here were prepared to meet

[63] TNA, T 233/1752, J. Morrison (NI Ministry of Finance) to S. Lees (UK Treasury)
(12 March 1957), p. 1.
[64] TNA, T 233/1752, E. Compton, Northern Ireland Transport (6 November 1956), p. 1.
[65] H. Benson, Northern Ireland Railways: Report (Belfast, 1963), Cmd 458.
[66] GNRB, Fifth (and Final) Annual Report and Accounts (1958), p. 3.
[67] See Kennedy, n. 2 above, 145.

the heavy cost of subsidising rail transport within the Six-County area, the termination of the agreement made that course impossible'.[68] Even at this point, the files indicate that the Brookeborough government's direct dealings with Irish ministers were limited; the most prominent element of intergovernmental discussion related to realising Northern Ireland's share of the value of the GNRB's most significant fixed asset, the Dundalk engineering works.[69] On 1 October 1958, what was left of the GNRB was dissolved and, under an agreement between Dublin and Belfast, its assets were split between CIÉ and the UTA and liabilities divided between the two governments.[70] In a final indignity for efforts to modernise Northern Ireland's rail transport, the UTA was obliged to purchase some of the ageing, former-GNR(I), steam locomotives from CIÉ in 1963 to maintain its services.[71]

The Aftermath

It has become an easy answer to attribute the general failings of devolution in the aftermath of the Second World War in the main to the sectarianism of successive Unionist governments. This thesis was neatly summarised by Patrick Buckland: 'the power of the government was used in the interests of Unionists and Protestants, with scant regard for the interests of the region as a whole'.[72] John Whyte, however, was notably sympathetic to the Northern Ireland government when it came to transport policy:

> Railways in Northern Ireland were losing money, and, as in Britain and the Republic, the government was obliged to close lines in order to limit losses. Far from being condemned in the west for closing one line, it should have received credit for at least keeping open the other line to Derry, through Ballymena and Coleraine, for the Benson report had recommended the closure of both.[73]

---

[68] Dáil Debates, Seán Lemass (Minister for Industry and Commerce), vol. 169, no. 4, Speech 310 (24 June 1958).

[69] PRONI, Lord Glentoran, 'Memorandum: Great Northern Railway – Dundalk Works' (10 September 1957), pp. 1–2.

[70] Great Northern Railway Act 1958 (Ireland), s. 3.

[71] J. Rowledge, *Irish Steam Locomotive Register* (Batley, 1993), 56.

[72] P. Buckland, *A History of Northern Ireland* (Dublin, 1981), 72.

[73] J. Whyte, 'How Much Discrimination Was There under the Unionist Regime, 1921–68?' in T. Gallagher and J. O'Connell (eds.), *Contemporary Irish Studies* (Manchester, 1983), 1, 25–30.

When the line it chose to preserve went through Unionist heartlands and maintained the connectivity and employment benefits for these areas, it is easy to see why sympathy for the Unionist government's predicament was in short supply. What the archival holdings illustrate, however, is the efforts of the Unionist government to keep large parts of the GNR(I) network in place. These were doomed by the UK Treasury's determination to make an example of railway cuts to force them, in the words of (the soon to be knighted) Edmund Compton, to 'pursue the path of financial rectitude'.[74] The financial settlement for devolution had undermined Northern Ireland's governance since the 1920s, and the scarcity of public resources only served to bring sectarianism in their allocation into sharp relief. These financial challenges also precipitated the decline in relations between the Conservative Party and Northern Ireland's Unionists, with the ennobled Lord Brookeborough even threatening Harold Macmillan with more equivocal support from Unionist MPs at Westminster in 1960 in order to secure more funding.[75]

The dysfunctional cooperation through the GNRB had lasted a mere five years. Even had the two governments been more minded to cooperate effectively, they would still have found themselves caught between a profound financial squeeze and the UK government's heavy-handed imposition of a shift towards a more road-centred transport policy. Notwithstanding the setback of 1958, Seán Lemass, who had effectively fronted the Irish government's efforts during the joint ownership of the GNR(I), would become synonymous with the high-profile efforts to reset relations between Ireland and Northern Ireland in the 1960s. He built on the GNR(I) experience with the olive branch of selective reductions in tariffs for products from Northern Ireland after he became taoiseach.[76] Even these initiatives were viewed with suspicion by Brookeborough's Cabinet, as being intended to 'differentiate Northern Ireland goods from those made in Great Britain', which they refused to encourage 'for political and constitutional reasons'.[77] It was not until Brookeborough was replaced as Prime Minister of Northern

---

[74] TNA, T 233/1752, E. Compton, Handwritten Note: Northern Ireland Transport (6 November 1956).
[75] See J. Smith, '"Ever Reliable Friends?": The Conservative Party and Ulster Unionism in the Twentieth Century' (2006) 121 *English Historical Review* 70, 97.
[76] See M. Kennedy, 'Towards Co-Operation; Seán Lemass and North–South Economic Relations: 1956–65' (1997) 24 *Irish Economic and Social History* 42, 42.
[77] PRONI, CAB/4/1161, Conclusions of a Meeting of the Cabinet (1 June 1961), p. 4.

Ireland by Terence O'Neill that the Stormont administration became more receptive to these overtures. Lemass' January 1965 meeting with O'Neill rapidly acquired the reputation of having inadvertently stoked intercommunal tensions within Northern Ireland which spiralled into the conflict.[78] Although such accounts set rather too much store on the Lemass–O'Neill dialogue as a catalyst for the conflict, Lemass' track record of dealings with the Northern Ireland government is a significant part of why the administrations thought they could achieve something substantive in 1965.

The failure of the GNRB initiative has had impacts which have persisted to the present day. Its legacy is keenly felt in the deficiencies in the transport infrastructure in the north west of Ireland. The Enterprise service was maintained, under an operating arrangement negotiated between the CIÉ and UTA, but it would remain subject to sustained underinvestment, and from the start of the conflict, intense security disruption, until 1997.[79] This lack of joined-up policy continues to be reflected in the Enterprise sharing tracks with the Dublin–Malahide Dublin Area Rapid Transit (DART) service, limiting the number of Enterprise trains and slowing the intercity service to a crawl as it nears Dublin.[80] The whole GNR(I) experiment thus has the feel of an idea out of time; it would become easier to run a cross-border railway against the backdrop of EU law,[81] which negated the need for complex customs arrangements (and which, post-Brexit, persists in this regard under the auspices of the Northern Ireland Protocol). There was, moreover, no established basis for cross-border dealings. After the intense period of negotiations to rescue the GNR(I) through joint ownership, the two governments sought to stand off from each other and engage only through the GNRB. Lemass would not develop any meaningful relationship with Lord Glentoran, who succeeded McCleery as Northern

---

[78] See C. Cruise O'Brien, *States of Ireland* (New York, 1972), 146–147. See also I. Hamilton, 'From Liberalism to Extremism' (1971) 17 *Conflict Studies* 5.

[79] That year saw Northern Ireland Railways and Iarnród Éireann relaunch the Enterprise service with a new fleet of locomotive-hauled coaches, making it by far the most modern rail service operating on the island at the time; see Northern Ireland Affairs Committee, *Northern Ireland Railways: Financial Provision for New Rolling Stock* (2000) HC 512, para. 7.

[80] Department for Infrastructure (NI) and Department of Transport (Ireland), *All Island Strategic Rail Review Consultation Paper* (November 2021), p. 17.

[81] See J. Anderson, 'Problems of Inter-State Economic Integration: Northern Ireland and the Irish Republic in the European Community' (1994) 13 *Political Geography* 53.

Ireland's Minister for Commerce.[82] For much of the period of joint ownership the archives illustrate that direct communications between the two governments were vanishingly rare, and ministers were left to divine their counterparts' intention through polite requests for copies of public speeches and reports. This was in no way comparable to the development of North–South cooperation under Strand 2 of the 1998 Agreement. The post-1998 arrangements should have provided an institutional foundation for a reconsideration of railway policy.[83] Railways, however, were not high on either the Irish government's or the Northern Ireland executive's list of priorities. It took many decades to return to the development of a cross-border rail policy in cooperative terms, and even today the ambitions of an all-island transport strategy faced delays caused by the stop–start nature of devolution in Northern Ireland.[84]

Conclusion

In *Oh Mr Porter!* – that classic Englishman-out-of-place comedy – the titular character finds himself waving off trains from Buggleskelly station to 'Ballyhooley, Ballyhelly and all the other Bally places', which turned out to uncomfortably reflect the level of interest shown by the UK Treasury's civil servants in Northern Ireland's transport infrastructure in the 1950s. The continued existence of the Fintona horse tram[85] into the mid-1950s was not treated by Treasury officials as a marker of persistent underdevelopment which needed to be addressed, but as illustrative of a rail transport system in Northern Ireland that was beyond reform and could be 'replaced quite adequately by road transport'.[86] The inadequacies of the devolution funding settlement had, by this juncture, generated multiple extraordinary funding requests from the Northern

---

[82] McCleery had been in failing health and retired from government (but not from active and senior roles in the Orange Order) immediately after the new GNR(I) arrangements were in place.

[83] See J. Anderson, L. O'Dowd and T. Wilson, 'Cross-Border Co-operation in Ireland: A New Era?' (2001) 49 *Administration* 6; and C. McCall, 'From Barrier to Bridge: Reconfiguring the Irish Border after the Belfast Good Friday Agreement' (2002) 53 *Northern Ireland Law Quarterly* 479.

[84] 'The review cannot be formally published until a Stormont minister is in place to sign it off'; L. Cullen, 'All-Island Rail Review: Londonderry to Portadown Line Recommended', *BBC News NI* (25 July 2023).

[85] Consistently misspelled as 'Filtona' in the Treasury documents, demonstrating the insouciance with which the issue was treated; Memorandum, n. 53 above, para. 13.

[86] Ibid., para. 13.

Ireland government and increasingly 'fraught' relations between Belfast and London.[87] When it came to the GNRB, the UK Treasury had had its fill of these efforts, adopting a narrow and costs-focused response. Key actors in this decision making would return to haunt Northern Ireland as it slid into conflict; Sir Edmund Compton would again demonstrate his loyalty to the UK government's position in producing an uncritical report into abusive interrogation practices in 1971.[88]

Amid the recriminations, in 1958 Seán Lemass publicly deplored the termination of the Railway Agreement as 'a backward step in the development of co-operation on matters of common interest affecting both parts into which our country is divided', but he laid the blame firmly upon the 'change of outlook regarding transport matters which has taken place in Belfast'.[89] There is, nonetheless, something missing from accounts which suggest that the story of the agreement was one in which '[t]he transport policies of Northern Ireland and the Republic were quite different, and the GNRB was caught in the middle'.[90] The Unionist government was, in this instance, playing a forced game. Its prioritisation, alongside Dublin, of the shareholders of an essentially bankrupt concern meant that from the outset of joint ownership they were focused on finding savings and not on the needs of the railway. They were, moreover, hemmed in by inadequate funding arrangements and a UK Treasury which did not see itself as being under any obligation to facilitate cross-border cooperation. As a result of this intervention, the best avenue for building substantive cross-border policy cooperation prior to the Northern Ireland conflict was summarily dissolved.

---

[87] Buckland, n. 25 above, 279.
[88] Sir E. Compton, *Report of the Enquiry into Allegations against the Security Forces of Physical Brutality in Northern Ireland Arising out of Events on the 9th August 1971* (1971), Cmnd 4823. See A. Deb and C. Murray, 'Sealing the Past: *McQuillan* and the Future of Legacy Litigation' [2022] *European Human Rights Law Review* 393, 394–395.
[89] Lemass, n. 68 above, Speech 325.
[90] Kennedy, n. 2 above, 146.

14

Fortuna Fortes Adiuvat

The Importance of Individuals in Estonian Constitutional Change

MERIKE RISTIKIVI, KATRE LUHAMAA AND KARIN SEIN

Introduction

In 1991, Estonia began its journey away from five decades under Soviet rule and toward constitutional and legislative reform. The Constitution of Estonia[1] adopted in 1992 marked the start of a decade-long quest to establish the rule of law and return to Western democratic norms. Given Estonia's relatively small population[2] and the correspondingly limited cadre of legal professionals available for this undertaking, individual contributions gained pronounced importance.

This chapter examines the dynamics of Estonia's legislative reforms during its transitional decade, with a focus on the influence and contributions of two key groups. The first comprises young, enthusiastic *tabula rasa* lawyers entering the scene with a fresh perspective, while the second consists of seasoned but open-minded leaders from the Estonian Soviet Socialist Republic (ESSR) establishment with a proclivity for Western democratic norms, who were ready to empower, inspire, and protect them. Grounded in empirical data from interviews conducted in 2020–2021 with twenty-five key legal figures[3] and a thorough analysis

The research leading to this chapter was supported by the Estonian Academy of Sciences (SSVOI21349).

[1] The Constitution of the Republic of Estonia (*Põhiseadus*), *Riigi Teataja* [State Gazette], 1992, 26, 349.

[2] In 1990, the population of Estonia was 1.56 million, with 40 per cent having moved to Estonian territory during the Soviet occupation. See, for example, H. Kulu, 'Sõjajärgne sisseränne Eestisse võrdlevas perspektiivis', *Akadeemia*, 11 (2001), 2379–2395.

[3] On the oral history method and the methodology behind these interviews, see the discussion by K. Sein and M. Ristikivi, 'Rearranging Legal Culture in Estonia

of primary legal documents, this chapter sheds light on the critical role individuals played in state-building during Estonia's turbulent 1990s. The narratives that emerge illuminate these actors' pivotal role in the state-building project, particularly amid that decade's turbulence. Unexpected opportunities and individual influences proved significant, underscoring how essential fortitude would prove for decision-making.

The analysis begins with a contextual overview of Estonia's historical and societal landscape from 1992 to 2002. This is followed by discussion of the generational divisions evident in the legal sector within the same timeframe. It incorporates perspectives from young state officials, some in the early stages of their legal careers, juxtaposed with insight from senior officials and politicians rooted in the Soviet legal framework. Acknowledging the contributions of an external foreign academic adviser affords a comprehensive view of the forces shaping Estonia's legal transformation over the course of the period under review.

Estonia's Historical and Societal Landscape

Until 1990, the Estonian legal system was tightly intertwined with the legal system of the Union of Soviet Socialist Republics (USSR).[4] Formally, power within the ESSR legal system was vested in people; de facto, it was held by the Communist Party and its members.[5] The ESSR's legal system did not recognise administrative or civil law in the modern sense,[6] and both it and the institutions overall were highly politicised and, at times, engaged in clear violations of the rule of law. For example, they fabricated politically underpinned criminal offences in the service of the Communist system.[7] The independence movement, in turn, was led by

1992–2002: Political Context and Factors of Success', *Rechtskultur*, 11 (2022), 163–164, https://doi.org/10.36213/11-5.
[4] E.g., see K. Luhamaa and M. Ristikivi, 'Rebuilding the Court System of Estonia after the Communist Regime', *Juridica International*, 31 (2022), 81–89, https://doi.org/10.12697/JI.2022.31.05.
[5] E.-J. Truuväli (ed.), *Põhiseadus teel* (Tallinn, 2008); *Eesti Nõukogude Sotsialistliku Vabariigi Konstitutsioon (Põhiseadus): vastu võetud Eesti NSV Ülemnõukogu 9. koosseisu erakorralisel, 9. istungjärgul 13. aprillil, 1978. aastal* (Tallinn, 1988).
[6] Interview with former Minister of Justice Prof. Paul Varul, Tartu, on 3 July 2020, summarised by Sein and Ristikivi, 'Rearranging Legal Culture', 86.
[7] E.g., *Political Arrests in Estonia 1940–1988, Vol. 1*, compiled and edited by Leo Õispuu (Tallinn, 1996).

a set of activists consisting of, on the one hand, Soviet dissidents and, on the other, critical intellectuals (mostly historians).[8]

Estonia had to rebuild its whole legal and institutional system. The process had two aspects: dismantling the interconnected legal systems of the USSR and ESSR and building a new legal system coupled with institutions that would lead to the re-establishment of the independent Estonian state.[9] In the course of the legislative process, the continental European legal system, particularly the German legal tradition, was chosen as the model for the forthcoming Estonian legal frameworks.[10] Private law had to be reformed especially extensively, as this was vital for a radical turn from a Soviet-style planned economy to a modern market economy with private initiative and private property at its core. Another reason for this major reform was that Estonia in the early 1990s was in desperate need of foreign investment – and investors needed a clear, firm message about the state's guarantees for their investments. In addition to the reforms in private law, initiatives were undertaken to reform public law and criminal law. Simultaneously, comprehensive restructuring was deemed necessary for state administration, the court system, and the prosecutor's office.[11]

The Tabula Rasa

Estonia's move away from Soviet legal traditions was influenced by the proactive efforts of its youth, who were leading the independence movement, supported by seasoned freedom fighters. These individuals played a critical role in distancing the nascent legal system from the stagnation and dependencies characteristic of the previous regime. Young legal professionals and scholars, less burdened by a legacy of entrenched connections to the Soviet legal elite, were central in initiating progressive legal reforms. Meanwhile, the freedom fighters utilised their experience

---

[8] M. Kukk, 'Political Opposition in Soviet Estonia 1940–1987', *Journal of Baltic Studies*, 24(4) (1993), 369–384, https://doi.org/10.1080/01629779300000261.

[9] For more comprehensive accounts of the transition process of Estonia, see, for example, R. Taagepera, *Estonia: Return to Independence* (New York, 2018); G. Smith, *The Baltic States: The National Self-Determination of Estonia, Latvia, and Lithuania* (London, 1994); W. R. Iwaskiw (ed.), *Estonia, Latvia and Lithuania: Country Studies* (Washington, DC, 1996).

[10] On the background of this choice, see further details from Sein and Ristikivi, 'Rearranging Legal Culture', 174–178.

[11] K. Sein and M. Ristikivi (eds.), *Õigusriigi taastamine. Eesti seaduste ja institutsioonide reformid 1992–2002* (Tartu, 2022), 9.

of history to guide these reforms, ensuring that they reflected Estonia's renewed commitment to democratic governance and autonomy.

The interaction between these groups facilitated a break from the Soviet era's institutional inertia, allowing for transformation that was as much a product of individuals' initiative as it was of collective will. The extent of their influence in the shaping of Estonia's legal framework becomes clear as one delves more deeply into the importance of individuals' agency in the country's transition to democracy.

The Fresh Face of Leadership and Decisive Factors in Reform

The first post-independence government under the 1992 Constitution of Estonia was headed by thirty-two-year-old historian Mart Laar, whose government served until 1994.[12] While land and property reform, as well as reforms to the court system, had been initiated in 1990–1991, civil law continued to be governed by the Civil Code of the ESSR of 1965,[13] and punishments were still handed down in line with Soviet penal law, the Criminal Code of the ESSR of 1961.[14] The interim government's stabilisation of the economy and completion of monetary reform set the stage for Laar's administration to undertake comprehensive legal reforms, despite its limited legislative experience. These reforms went uncontested by subsequent governments, signalling a collective commitment to transformation.

Free from Soviet *nomenklatura* influences, the administration sought to alter the status quo rapidly and fundamentally. The coalition pursuing this aim consisted of newly founded parties – the national conservatives (Isamaa), the Estonian National Independence Party (ERSP),[15] and the Moderates.[16] Its main objective was implementing the reforms necessary

---

[12] Mart Laar (born in 1960) served as Prime Minister of Estonia in 1992–1994 and 1999–2002.

[13] Civil Code of the Estonian SSR (*Eesti NSV Tsiviilkoodeks*) (Tallinn, 1965).

[14] Criminal Code of the Estonian SSR (*Eesti NSV Kriminaalkoodeks*) (Tallinn, 1963); Sein and Ristikivi, *Õigusriigi taastamine* 16. For details of the former ESSR codes during the transition, see, for example, P. Varul, 'Legal Policy Decisions and Choices in the Creation of New Private Law in Estonia', *Juridica International*, 5 (2000), 104–118; J. Sootak, 'Development of Estonian Criminal Law', *Juridica International*, 1 (1996), 52–55.

[15] Founded in 1988, the ERSP was led largely by Soviet-era freedom fighters and dissidents. See A. Kasekamp, 'Extreme-Right Parties in Contemporary Estonia', *Patterns of Prejudice*, 37(4) (2003), 403–405, https://doi.org/10.1080/0031322032000144483.

[16] B. Grofman, E. Mikkel and R. Taagepera, 'Fission and Fusion of Parties in Estonia, 1987–1999', *Journal of Baltic Studies*, 31(4) (2000), 329–357, https://doi.org/10.1080/01629770000000141.

for transition to a market economy, in accordance with Milton Friedman's principles, and fostering Estonia's integration into the Western world.[17] Efficiency, coupled with receptiveness to external legal ideas and innovation, was central to the transition programme.

Isamaa member Kaido Kama served as the inaugural Minister of Justice, in the first government. His ascension to this role was rather unexpected, as he had initially aspired to be Minister of Defence, a position that ultimately went to a member of coalition partner ERSP. Kama's nomination for the Ministry of Justice position was influenced by his legislative experience; he had spent several years in Estonia's Soviet-era Parliament, where he contributed to the Legal Affairs Committee, led the Property and Land Reform Committee, and crafted legislation in collaboration with the Ministry of Justice and its staff. This tenure had familiarised him with the inner workings of that ministry and with its personnel. Consistent with the tapestry of unconventional backgrounds characteristic of the time, his academic training was in architecture, not law. This unique perspective was not a disadvantage; rather, it aligned with the ministry's need to rethink law and the legal system fundamentally. After all, Estonia had embarked on constructing an entirely new legal framework.[18]

Societal confidence in the youth was palpable during this era. Alongside the notably young Prime Minister, the cabinet featured a number of ministers in their twenties and thirties who were charged with overseeing critical sectors.[19] When it came to reconstructing the banking and financial system, a deliberate choice was made to entrust the leading roles to young individuals, unfettered by ties to the Soviet planned economy and equipped instead with Western-style economic training.[20]

The government's efforts were supported by freedom fighters in the Parliament (*Riigikogu*), who were intent on attenuating the influence of the former ESSR elite and lessening the dependency on Soviet legal

---

[17] A. Kasekamp, *A History of the Baltic States*, 2nd ed. (London, 2018); M. Laar, *Pööre* (Tallinn, 2015), 189–197, 297–309.

[18] Interview with former Minister of Justice Kaido Kama, Tartu, 2 July 2020.

[19] For instance, Jüri Luik and Indrek Kannik, serving, respectively, as Minister of Defence and Minister of Foreign Affairs, were just twenty-seven and twenty-nine years old. Heiki Arike took on the role of Interior Minister at the age of twenty-eight. The cabinet also included Finance Minister Heiki Kranich, age thirty-three; Economy Minister Toomas Sildmäe, thirty-four; and Justice Minister Kaido Kama, who was thirty-five.

[20] For example, the managers of Hansapank, which was founded in early 1992 and quickly grew into the largest financial institution in the Baltics, were in their twenties and thirties.

doctrine and practices. For example, they exerted a decisive influence on the Constitution's development, as the Constitutional Assembly set aside the draft from the ESSR Minister of Justice in favour of the version proposed by freedom fighter Jüri Adams.[21] Similarly, they blocked the appointment of several ESSR Supreme Court justices, the chief justice among them, to the newly created Supreme Court.[22] Strong ties with the Estonian diaspora further cemented their dedication to strict political oversight and upholding of core values: efficiency concerns could not justify compromises relating to democracy and the rule of law. Nevertheless, the government and freedom fighters had acknowledged the pragmatic necessity of reforming the legal system. This entailed enforcement of transitional justice measures, albeit limited, alongside strategic engagement with the ESSR elite to ensure thorough renewal without perpetuating outdated concepts and practices in the reformed legal framework. Estonia only used written oaths of conscience until 2000 to exclude persons who had taken part in the Soviet repression from higher civil service positions.[23]

In September 1994, the government led by Laar tendered its resignation. A new government was formed under the leadership of Prime Minister Andres Tarand, which came to be known informally as the 'Christmas-peace government'. In this reconfiguration, Adams, who had been a prominent figure in the dissident movement, was appointed Minister of Justice. Though these years saw it function at times as a minority government, his tenure, which endured until April 1995, was marked by a dedication to maintaining the momentum of reform. A key achievement of this time was the enactment of the Commercial Code, a significant legislative undertaking co-ordinated with the young chairman of the Legal Affairs Committee, Daimar Liiv. Together, the seasoned dissidents and the new generation of legal experts pursued a shared vision: the swift replacement of the Soviet legal system, effectively marginalising the vestiges of the Soviet establishment.[24]

---

[21] Information about the five drafts of the Constitution discussed by Parliament and their approaches to court reform is provided by K. Luhamaa and M. Ristikivi, 'Eesti kohtusüsteem ja kohtunikkond reformide keskel 1988–1993', *Riigiõiguse Aastaraamat*, 3 (2022), 35.

[22] Luhamaa and Ristikivi, 'Rebuilding the Court System of Estonia after the Communist Regime', 87–88.

[23] The Constitution of the Republic of Estonia Implementation Act, *Riigi Teataja* [State Gazette], 1992, 26, 350, §6.

[24] Interview with former Minister of Justice Jüri Adams, Tallinn, 6 March 2020.

The victors in the 1995 elections were predominantly those parties and electoral alliances that had been in the opposition in the previous Parliament. Thus, the 1995 parliamentary election results reflected a resurgence of attention to societal groups whose interests had been sidelined amid the initial reforming fervour. The Estonian Centre Party and the Estonian Coalition Party, representing the centre left and centre right, respectively, along with Maarahva Ühendus (the Rural People's Union), echoed the electorate's desire to acknowledge and integrate broader interests, not least those of rural communities. Subsequent governments, led by Tiit Vähi and later Mart Siimann with Paul Varul as Minister of Justice, exemplified a nuanced approach to governance. Both Vähi and Varul, reform-embracing technocrats with roots in the Soviet establishment, symbolised the era's spirit of reconciliation and pragmatic engagement with the former elite. This period underscored the necessity of balancing the zeal of the reform-minded youth and dissidents against the experience and restraining influence of the old guard, reflecting the ethos of limited lustration that characterised the transition era.[25]

Lawyers' Generational Divide

As Estonia underwent legal transition in the 1990s, a generation gap was evident in the legal profession. Seasoned lawyers directed their expertise towards institutional/pragmatic reforms, such as revision to citizenship regulations and the overhaul of the monetary system, while newly minted legal scholars, many of whom were recent university graduates, concentrated on the theoretical underpinnings of legal drafting. These young civil servants shouldered the critical task of re-envisioning laws to meet the demands of an evolving democratic society. They embodied the advantage of being able to assimilate diverse legal principles from various established democracies, an endeavour in which the former legal establishment, constrained by outdated paradigms and perspectives inculcated by a Soviet education, had little to offer. Accordingly, it was the young professionals who were given broad discretion in legislative drafting roles, operating with minimal political interference. Such a setting was necessary for reconstructing the legal system from the ground up to accord with international democratic standards.[26]

---

[25] Sein and Ristikivi, 'Rearranging Legal Culture', 165–167, 170.
[26] Ibid.

Under Soviet rule, the political landscape of the ESSR was such that membership in the Communist Party, or at least candidacy for it, was a de facto prerequisite for any significant professional role within state institutions. The University of Tartu's Faculty of Law, as Estonia's lone legal education institution, mirrored this exclusivity by limiting admission to a select few. In the 1980s, places were capped at 50–55 full-time students per year. The dawn of the 1990s witnessed significant expansion, with the number admitted doubling to 100–120. This surge represented not only growing interest in the legal profession but also a strategic move to cultivate a new generation of legal experts equipped with a democratic ethos and a broader vision for Estonia's legal system.[27]

The Role of Young Civil Servants within the Ministry of Justice

Examining the contributions of young civil servants in the Estonian Ministry of Justice sheds light on their decisive impact on the legal reforms. Interviews revealed strategic personnel selection to be a crucial element in facilitating swift and effective legislative reform. The reform initiatives were deliberately assigned not to the seasoned officials steeped in Soviet legal training but to a cohort of young legal practitioners, some newly graduated and others still pursuing their studies. This approach stemmed from recognition of a certain doctrinal inertia inherent in the legal profession; lawyers often become entrenched in the conceptual frameworks featuring in their education. Disengagement from established, implicit doctrines is typically arduous. Consequently, it was evident to the decision-makers within the Ministry of Justice that entrusting the reform process to experienced lawyers whose education had mired them in the Soviet system would likely result in stagnation, since they might not even perceive a need for adjusting or outright abandoning the doctrines they had assimilated.[28] Mihkel Oviir, then Secretary General of the Ministry of Justice, articulated the sentiment thus: 'The Ministry of Justice needed young people who were eager to learn and who did not have to go through the trouble of forgetting the old'.[29]

---

[27] P. Pruks, 'Academic Legal Education in Estonia: Current State and Perspectives (Faculty of Law of the University of Tartu)', *Juridica International*, 1 (1996), 139.

[28] Interview with former Head of the Penal Law Department of the Ministry of Justice Priit Pikamäe, Tartu, 3 July 2020.

[29] Interview with former Secretary General of the Ministry of Justice Mihkel Oviir, Tallinn, 28 February 2020.

Kama, appointed as Minister of Justice in autumn 1992, recognised the foundational nature of the reforms initiated by his predecessors, Jüri Raidla and Märt Rask. A significant development during their tenure was the establishment of the Department of Economic Law, which subsequently focused on the drafting of civil law. It was within this new department that, in the final days of the Soviet regime, pioneering legislative frameworks for private enterprise, notably co-operatives, were first formulated.[30] 'The mood and the people had already changed there, and I don't remember that in the autumn of 1992 I had to fight with any Soviet-era persons. Anyway, the people who were in that building at the time, this hundred people, went along with the reforms.'[31]

Innovative Recruitment Strategies in the Ministry of Justice

In the search for capable young talent to take on the challenges of legislative reform, the Ministry of Justice engaged closely with the faculty at the University of Tartu, Estonia's only university at the time to offer a law degree. Academics from the university were instrumental to identifying students with expansive vision and a distinct interest in the complexities of legislative drafting. The legal field's intense demand for professionals was evident in the fact that most law students matriculating in 1992 had found employment by the end of their second year of study. The acute shortage had prompted recruiters to seek out those who either were nearing the completion of their law degree or had recently graduated.[32] Crucially, the Ministry of Justice sought out young, ambitious individuals who, instead of being inclined to offer perfunctory affirmations such as 'yes, Chancellor' or 'yes, Minister', demonstrated independent thought and dared to challenge the status quo.[33] Also, in those years it was not uncommon for chance to play a significant part in the recruitment of personnel. A case in point is the career of Priidu Pärna, who would later ascend to the roles of Vice-Secretary General and Secretary General of the Ministry of Justice. He recalled learning about the opportunity to contribute to the draft Law of Property Act through an informal tip from a peer, who

---

[30] Interview with Kama.
[31] Ibid.
[32] Interview with Pikamäe.
[33] Interview with Oviir.

mentioned that the working group was on the lookout for graduates proficient in German.[34]

Given the factors mentioned above, the legislative drafting divisions within the Estonian Ministry of Justice were staffed predominantly by recent law graduates. Foremost among the sought-after qualifications was, indeed, proficiency in the German language, coupled with an understanding of German legal principles. This was a strategic necessity: the decision to apply the associated legal tradition as a template for crafting Estonian legislation rendered such expertise crucial.[35] Simultaneously, the Ministry of Justice capitalised on the opportunity to send young civil servants to Germany for one to two years to pursue further legal studies. In addition to German, skills in English were vital for personnel at the ministry, permitting comprehensive engagement with and understanding of legislative and regulatory developments within the European Union. Young civil servants often possessed a distinct advantage over their middle-aged colleagues in terms of language proficiency, given the inadequate emphasis on foreign-language training in schools during the Soviet era.[36]

The successful recruitment of young, enthusiastic officials was a critical component in the success of Estonia's legal reforms. Exploring the methods used to attract and retain such individuals in the Ministry of Justice merits attention particularly on account of the context of low public sector salaries juxtaposed with the high demand for legal professionals at the time. Despite the competitive draw from law firms, notarial firms, and the business sector generally, the ministry adopted various strategies to attract young, gifted individuals to the civil service. Many young recruits were swayed by questions framed as contemplation of their legacy for the future: 'In 30–40 years, what stories will you share with your grandchildren? Will you recount the purchase of a Žiguli car that succumbed to rust after five years, or will you be able to say that you played a role in the unique process of shaping a nation's legal framework?'[37]

---

[34] Interview with former Vice-Secretary General of the Ministry of Justice Priidu Pärna, Tallinn, 28 August 2020.

[35] See also M. Ristikivi et al., 'An Introduction to Estonian Legal Culture', in S. Koch and M. M. Kjølstad (eds.), Handbook on Legal Cultures (Cham, 2023), 389–418, https://doi.org/10.1007/978-3-031-27745-0_11.

[36] Interview with former official of the Ministry of Justice Priit Kama, Tallinn, 28 August 2020.

[37] Interview with Oviir; interview with former Head of the Public Law Department of the Ministry of Justice Heiki Loot, Tartu, 30 October 2020.

Efforts were made to secure financial incentives for young civil servants as well. One noteworthy initiative was the provision of flats in a residential building constructed by the Ministry of Justice.[38] Key contributors to legal reforms also received supplementary compensation from funds designated for legal drafting, payments that were, at times, quite substantial.[39] Such financial considerations formed a key element of the ministry's strategy to attract, and retain, promising young lawyers. Beyond monetary incentives, the prospect of contributing to the country's legal framework offered a compelling career path. These young professionals were presented with an opportunity to shape the legal landscape of Estonia significantly. The enduring relevance of the legislation they drafted, much of which remains in force today, speaks to the significance of their work.[40]

Balance between Political Oversight and Autonomous Drafting

Fully comprehending the legislative process in Estonia during the reform years requires one to understand the atypical nature of political guidance at the time. While democratic governance usually involves politicians outlining specific legislative directions, this tradition was eschewed in the case of 1990s Estonia. Politicians provided only broad legislative objectives, leaving substantive policy decision-making to the discretion of the working groups. These groups, composed of civil servants and legal scholars, steered the course of legal policy effectively in the absence of conventional political directives.

That said, exceptions to this general legislative approach of the 1990s were visible in critical areas such as property and land reform, which had been initiated before the regaining of independence and been subject to long-term political debate. In these sectors, the necessity of explicit political consensus was clear and ministers aimed to establish clear political accord prior to the drafting phase, to streamline the work of the legal teams.[41] Similarly, the formulation of local government regulation was preceded by extensive, meticulous discussion within the

---

[38] Interview with Pärna; interview with the first Chief Justice of the Estonian Supreme Court, Rait Maruste, Tallinn, 6 March 2020.
[39] Interview with Pärna.
[40] Interview with Kama; interview with Loot.
[41] Interview with Kama.

coalition. The outcomes of these debates provided the Ministry of Justice with definitive mandates for the specific type of legislation to develop.[42]

Again, political involvement with most of the other legislative reforms was scarce or highly selective.[43] The crafting of the Law of Obligations Act serves as a textbook example of selectiveness. While that Act's comprehensive framing was drafted largely without political interference, specific areas such as regulation of rental agreements emerged as focal points for political debate and decision-making. This selective political focus was a strategic response to the urgent societal challenges posed by demands for restitution and restoration of pre-World War II property rights. Thus, while political influence was restrained on the broader stage of legislative development, with initial draft concepts too being subject to minimal ministerial scrutiny[44] (instead, the recommendations of the legislative drafting groups, along with foundational texts of model legislation, directed the drafting), it became concentrated in areas of direct engagement with pressing transition-linked issues of the time.

In the domain of public law, especially with respect to organisational structures, the influence of political directives was more substantial. Notably, prior to the introduction of the updated Civil Service Act,[45] comprehensive discussions held during cabinet meetings developed the structural blueprint for the ministries. Such a concerted strategy guaranteed that the foundational legal framework of the ministries corresponded with the collective strategic plan articulated at government level.[46]

In the sphere of penal law, ministerial engagement was commonly set within the boundaries of examining particular proposals. Priit Pikamäe, the head of the department for penal law during that period, recalls the considerable independence afforded to his team, marked by the absence of intricate political guidelines.[47] When looking back at those years, key legal figures consistently point out the lack of political direction in the selection of legal paradigms. They emphasise the extensive latitude

[42] Ibid.
[43] Interview with Oviir.
[44] Interview with Pärna.
[45] *Riigi Teataja* [State Gazette] I 6 July 2012, 1.
[46] Interview with Varul.
[47] However, Minister of Justice Varul brought with him his own legislative agenda, which would form the basis for the ministry's work plans at the time. Per this agenda, the aim was to complete the legal reforms, particularly those related to legal institutions. This was addressed in the interview with Pikamäe.

granted to civil servants in shaping legal statutes and core legal policy decisions – in marked divergence from the prescriptive norms that characterise the current legal environment.[48]

The induction of Rask as Minister of Justice in 1999 marked a significant shift in the functioning of the Ministry of Justice, bringing greater consistency with broader policy statements and strategic directives decided upon by politicians at the governmental level. Transition to this state of affairs was indicative of the maturation and refinement of Estonia's political machinery, reflecting advancement towards a more intricate and systematic approach to governance and legal drafting. Previous years' relatively limited political steering of the ministry's civil servants can be ascribed largely to the initial post-independence resource issues and to ambiguity as to the legal avenues available, both of which naturally constrained the formulation of comprehensive political directives.[49]

Challenges in Drafting Comprehensive Legal Codes

In the 1990s, Estonia's legal drafting was focused on the development of comprehensive legal codes for thorough regulation of various fields of law. Although the goal initially was to establish complete codes, the reality of legal and political complexities often led to creation of separate statutes such as the Property Law Act and Law of Obligations Act. Awareness of the need for systematic drafting and meticulous oversight in the area of civil law led to convening the High Commission of Civil Law. This commission was formed to provide 'quality control'[50] and guide the process of legal drafting, rather than exercise political oversight.

Established in December 1992 and presided over by Professor Varul, this commission featured eminent legal professionals – lecturers from the University of Tartu, judges, and Bar Association representatives – who had received their education during Soviet times and brought experience of those times to the table. The commission operated for more than a decade, serving until the adoption of the Law of Obligations Act in

---

[48] Interview with former officials of the Ministry of Justice: Villu Kõve, Martin Käerdi, and Harri Mikk, Tallinn, 27 August 2020; interview with former Head of the Land Registry and Notary Department of the Ministry of Justice Rein Tiivel, Tallinn, 28 February 2020; interview with Pärna.

[49] Interview with Oviir.

[50] Ibid.

2001.[51] The ministry's working groups were responsible for drafting and submitting legislation to the commission, which reviewed their work, making amendments or suggesting revisions as needed. The role of the High Commission was limited in the main to language editing for the drafts, the removal of unnecessary repetition and irrelevant provisions, and legal editing.[52] This commission provided a quality-assurance mechanism, thereby also securing the legal community's endorsement of the legislation drafted by the ministry's young staff. Addressing the balance between expertise and experience, Minister Varul stated in 1998: 'The members of the working groups are mostly young individuals with little experience in the legal drafting. They grasp the substance well, yet they lack the practised skill of translating their understanding into written legislation.'[53]

In several instances, the efforts at thoroughly revising existing legislation were not entirely successful. For example, the Law of Obligations working group faced an impasse with trade union representatives when dealing with employment contracts. This stalemate, partially attributable to the working group's inexperience, manifested itself in sub-optimal communication and some reluctance to work towards compromise. It led to employment contract regulation being omitted entirely from the Law of Obligations Act.[54] The Labour Code, prepared by the Ministry of Social Affairs working group, likewise fell at the enactment hurdle, leaving the Employment Contracts Act of 1992 – amended on several occasions since its passage – as the prevailing statute until 2009. It was not until 2008 that Estonia adopted its first modern Employment Contracts Act, consistent with the overarching principles of civil law.[55] Villu Kõve, who led the Law of Obligations Act working group, has said that the Employment Contracts Act of 2008, which remains in force, is significantly less favourable for employees than the draft prepared by the Ministry of Justice in 2000–2001, which was intended for incorporation into the Law of Obligations Act – particularly with respect to the provisions governing termination of employment contracts.[56]

---

[51] Interview with Varul.
[52] Interview with Pärna.
[53] M. Prööm, 'Intervjuu justiitsminister Paul Varuliga', *Juridica*, 3 (1998), 110.
[54] Interview with Kõve, Käerdi, and Mikk.
[55] *Riigi Teataja* [State Gazette] I, 2009, 5, 35.
[56] Interview with former official of the Ministry of Justice Villu Kõve, Tallinn, 27 August 2020.

The Role of Ministers of Justice and Senior Civil Servants

From 1995, the Ministers of Justice consistently had been drawn from the former establishment, figures who had played central roles in the final years of the ESSR. These individuals were among the reformists of the previous regime. Despite having been educated within the ESSR and possessing considerable professional and administrative experience from the Soviet era,[57] they remained committed to the established goal of joining the European Union and the North Atlantic Treaty Organization (NATO), and they maintained the momentum of the legal reforms.

In Vähi's inaugural cabinet of 1995, several ministers were appointed for reason of their special expertise rather than their political background. Varul was one of them. A civil law professor at the University of Tartu, who held the office Minister of Justice across two administrations, from April 1995 to March 1999, he left his mark with a series of institutional reforms that commenced with the overhaul of the prosecutor's office and culminated in the planning stages for new correctional facilities. Concurrent with these developments, the drafting of comprehensive legislation addressing key areas of law persisted.

Rask, with the liberal Estonian Reform Party, served as the decade's final Minister of Justice, holding the office from 1999 to 2003. During his term, a series of legislative reforms reached completion, resulting in the enactment of several lynchpin legislative acts that had been under development for half a decade or more. Among the seminal works were the new Penal Code, the Law of Obligations Act, the General Part of the Civil Code Act, and the Private International Law Act,[58] along with their corresponding implementing regulations. Whereas Ministry of Justice officials had previously played a significant role in shaping legal policy, it was during Rask's term that the major legal reforms reached completion and the legislative activities took a more traditional form.[59]

Over the decade of legal reforms, Estonia was served by six ministers of justice, yet it was Oviir,[60] in his longstanding role as Secretary General of the Ministry of Justice, who guaranteed continuity and acted as a driving force for significant reforms. He was particularly influential in

---

[57] Vello Pettai and Rein Toomla, *Political Parties in Estonia* (Washington, DC, 2003), 5.
[58] *Riigi Teataja* [State Gazette] I, 2002, 35, 217.
[59] Interview with Oviir.
[60] Born in 1942, he became the first Secretary General of the Estonian Ministry of Justice in 1992 and worked there until 2002.

mentoring an entire generation of young, aspiring civil servants. Oviir's tenure with the ministry can be traced back to the Soviet era, when he assumed leadership of the economic law division of the ESSR's Ministry of Justice in 1972. His ascent to the position of Secretary General was a condition set by Kama, who agreed to accept a position as the first Minister of Justice in Laar's government only if Oviir were appointed as stipulated.[61]

Many officials and key legislators from that era remember Oviir for displaying remarkably strong leadership qualities. Despite his Soviet-era education and ten-plus years' experience in Soviet institutions, he had an innate ability to attract and trust young, promising individuals, backed up by the readiness to defend them when this became necessary.[62] His significant contribution as Secretary General of the Ministry of Justice, especially to its staffing with suitable individuals, has been recognised by many of Estonia's leading lawyers, both his contemporaries and those active today. Drafters of extensive private-law legislation have reflected thus: 'I think only today do we understand how challenging it must have been for him to effectively isolate us, to allow us to do our job, and to shield us so that we could do it. In such a bureaucratic structure, that is an extraordinary accomplishment that should not be underestimated.'[63]

Oviir was crucial in recruiting several young officials who would go on to play highly significant roles in the legislative reforms.[64] Key figures were attracted to the Ministry of Justice also through the encouragement of Varul, who, upon becoming Minister of Justice in 1995, initiated a structural reform that included transforming the Soviet-era economic law department into an entity focused on private law and introducing new departments for public law, penal law, and legislative methodology. His extensive network as a professor at the University of Tartu informed the associated recruitment. In one notable move, he brought in twenty-four-year-old Heiki Loot, a consultant with the Supreme Court, to head the public law department in the same year.[65] Furthermore, Varul persuaded Pärna, also aged twenty-four at the time, to forgo a position as a

---

[61] Interview with Oviir.
[62] Interview with Kõve; interview with former Vice-Secretary General of the Ministry of Justice Juhan Parts, Tallinn, 19 August 2020; interview with former officials of the Ministry of Justice Heiki Loot and Madis Ernits, Tartu, 1 July 2021.
[63] Interview with Kõve, Käerdi, and Mikk.
[64] Interview with Varul.
[65] Loot commenced work as the Head of the Public Law Department in September 1995. Interview with Pärna; interview with Varul.

notary and instead become Vice-Secretary General. Thus, Pärna took charge of co-ordinating the Ministry of Justice's legislative drafting in 1995.[66]

Finally, in retrospect, Oviir's keen interest in technology stands out. He not only prioritised the development of electronic registers within the Ministry of Justice but also secured the necessary funding from the state budget.[67] In the latter half of the 1990s, some countries had already begun working towards electronic registers. With Austria's efforts in this area serving as inspiration, the concept of creating electronic judicial registers took root within the Estonian Ministry of Justice in those years. This idea would later be hailed as the inception of the Estonian e-state.[68]

Foreign Experts' Part in Shaping the Estonian Legal System: The Impact of Professor Peter Schlechtriem

In assessing the legal reforms, the influence of international legal scholars deserves particular recognition. While the foregoing discussion has highlighted the efforts of young Estonian jurists in drafting new legal statutes, supported by experienced political leaders, it is important to bear in mind that these individuals often lacked extensive legal education and practical drafting experience. To bridge this gap, the Estonian Ministry of Justice forged a partnership with the German Foundation for International Legal Cooperation (Deutsche Stiftung für Internationale Rechtliche Zusammenarbeit), established in 1992. This initiative, spearheaded by Germany's Minister of Justice Klaus Kinkel, was underpinned by German interest in supporting the economic and legal development of post-Soviet states.[69] Through this collaboration, Estonia benefited from a broad spectrum of support, encompassing legal drafting expertise, consultation with high-level German experts, institutional study visits, and professional training programmes.[70] Most importantly, in the early years

---

[66] Pärna worked as the Vice-Secretary General for legislative drafting at the Ministry of Justice until 2002, when he became Secretary General of the Ministry. Interview with Pärna.

[67] Interview with Kõve, Käerdi, and Mikk; interview with Parts; interview with Kama; interview with Pikamäe; interview with former Head of the Business Registry Department of the Ministry of Justice Viljar Peep, Tallinn, 17 August 2020.

[68] Interview with Parts.

[69] Interview with Varul.

[70] Interview with Oviir; interview with Kõve.

of the co-operation, distinguished German legal experts offered their advice for drafting of Estonian legislative acts.[71]

Among these experts, we cite Professor Peter Schlechtriem of the University of Freiburg for his notable contributions. Highly regarded for his extensive contribution to the international harmonisation of private law,[72] Schlechtriem acted as the main expert behind the shaping of the Estonian law of obligations: he wrote several expert briefs for the Estonian Law of Obligations Act, including material on the law of non-contractual obligations.[73]

His influence is unique in that, unlike many others', it extended beyond providing expert advice on legal drafting. In his trademark unassuming and modest manner, he moulded the legal education and awareness of an entire generation of young Estonian lawyers. His two textbooks on the German law of obligations were translated into Estonian in 1999 and 2000,[74] making them the first law-of-obligations textbooks adopted by Estonian law faculties. Furthermore, numerous young Estonian researchers had the opportunity to study law and complete their doctoral and master's theses under his guidance at the Faculty of Law of the University of Freiburg.

These Estonian scholars, the 'Freiburger Schule', introduced European legal thinking to Estonian legal practitioners. Many of them later assumed roles as Supreme Court judges, notaries, or university professors, exerting significant influence on the evolution of Estonian legal culture for decades to come In addition, Schlechtriem served as a foreign member of the editorial board for the Estonia-based law journal *Juridica International* and facilitated Estonian legal scholars' active contribution to the academic endeavour of drafting the European Civil Code. For over a decade, he proved himself a cherished friend of Estonia, in recognition of which the University of Tartu awarded him an honorary doctorate in 2002.[75]

---

[71] Interview with Varul.

[72] M. Schmidt-Kessel, 'Peter Schlechtriem', in S. Grundmann and K. Riesenhuber (eds.), *Private Law Development in Context: German Private Law and Scholarship in the 20th Century* (Cambridge, 2018), 252–257.

[73] E.g., P. Schlechtriem, *Gutachten zum Entwurf der Vorschriften über die widerrechtliche Schädigung* (unpublished manuscript, 1999).

[74] P. Schlechtriem, *Võlaõigus. Üldosa* (Tallinn, 1999); P. Schlechtriem, *Võlaõigus. Eriosa* (Tallinn, 2000).

[75] 'Peter Schlechtriem (2 March 1933–23 April 2007)', *Juridica International*, 12 (2007), 190.

Conclusions

In a nutshell, Estonia's experience underscores the lasting importance of individuals while simultaneously highlighting the need to strike a balance between innovation and practicality when undertaking extensive legal transitions. Instead of relying on officials with a Soviet-era education, these reforms were led by a new generation of legal practitioners, often recent graduates, not burdened by the constraints of Soviet legal doctrine. Their Western European education, their strong work ethic, and ample opportunities for fulfilling ambitious visions were central to reshaping Estonia's legal landscape.

While young and ambitious lawyers played a crucial role at the outset, the landscape shifted over time. The later phases of the reforms witnessed transition toward a more collaborative approach, with the younger generation of legal practitioners working alongside their more experienced counterparts, many of whom held a wealth of practical expertise. This collaboration between generations allowed for synthesis of new ideas and established practices, and it guaranteed institutional support. Thus, adjustment for balance contributed to the success of Estonia's legal transformation.

The lasting impact of these reforms continues to affect Estonia's legal framework. Furthermore, it offers valuable lessons for nations contemplating constitutional change in the modern era: it draws attention to the importance of maintaining the delicate equilibrium between innovation and tradition. Also, it highlights the value of willingness to change while underlining the significance of backing this up by identifying, nurturing, and harnessing the potential of individuals willing and able to take on the task of legislative innovation.

Moreover, this case study underscores the centrality of international support and collaboration for transition-related decisions at national level. Estonia benefited from non-intrusive assistance, including education, training, and expertise, which allowed the domestic drafters to shape the legislative agenda independently and make specific decisions as required. This approach empowered Estonians to chart their own course in legal reform while benefiting from international insights, expertise, and a supportive network with which they could ensure the compliance of the ensuing reforms with international standards and best practice.

15

First Nations Constitutional Recognition in Australia

Addressing Foundational Failures of Rule of Law

GABRIELLE APPLEBY AND MEGAN DAVIS

This chapter explores the complexity of the relationship between Australia's rule of law claims and the treatment of First Nations. This has been described by scholars as a 'paradox at [the] heart' of the Australian state,[1] giving rise to a 'crisis of constitutional legitimacy' caused by 'disagreement ... about the authority of the constitutional order itself'.[2] We argue that this crisis has two historical roots. First is the basis for the assertion of English sovereignty over the lands that would become Australia in 1788, the 'original grievance'.[3] Second is the imposition of a legal system and the evolution of 'rule of law' machinery and principles that were designed to curtail the arbitrary exercise of government power in the Australian colonies, while simultaneously denying access to the rule of law for the Aboriginal population of those lands. In both of these cases the rule of law was not neutral, but rather weaponised: to assess the Aboriginal people and their political and legal structures as being 'unworthy'.[4]

We place these two strands of Australia's rule-of-law history in a broader context of rule-of-law debates and failures in the Australian

---

[1] M. Krygier, 'The Grammar of Colonial Legality: Subjects, Objects, and the Australian Rule of Law', in G. Brennan and F. G. Castles (eds.), *Australia Reshaped: 200 Years of Institutional Transformation* (Cambridge, 2002), 220–60.

[2] G. Appleby, R. Levy, and H. Whalan, 'Voice versus Rights: A First Nations Voice and the Australian Constitutional Crisis of Legitimacy', *University of New South Wales Law Journal*, 46 (2023), 761, 765.

[3] See M. Davis, 'Ships That Pass in the Night', in M. Davis and M. Langton (eds.), *It's Our Country: Indigenous Arguments for Meaningful Constitutional Recognition and Reform* (Melbourne, 2016), 86–96, 93.

[4] We develop this position from an argument initially made in a narrower context by D. Manderson, 'The Law of the Image and the Image of the Law: Colonial Representations of the Rule of Law', *New York Law School Law Review*, 57 (2012), 153.

state. Aboriginal and Torres Strait Islander people's experience of the law and the Australian state intersect in myriad and complex ways with these debates. Their experience, and the rule-of-law architecture that developed to deal with them as a separate group, an 'other' within the Australian legal system, persist in the Australian legal system. We develop an argument that it is the foundational incoherencies that have continued to plague the Australian state and its claim to the rule of law.

In the final part of this chapter, we explore this continued crisis in light of the failed referendum to 'recognise' the unique status of First Nations people in the constitutional system. We consider the extent to which different structural reform proposals for recognition of First Nations – in particular proposals for constitutional rights protection and a constitutionally enshrined Voice (a representative advisory body) – address these incoherencies and their consequences. The proposals speak varyingly to history. The only reform that speaks to First Nations rights to a self-determined political status and to political participation, and provides a unique structural governance response to rule-of-law grievances, is a constitutionally enshrined Voice. The Voice proposal sought a new understanding of the rule of law that incorporates the status, laws and experiences of First Nations.

The rule of law frames this discussion for two key reasons. The first is its now well-accepted use in the discourse on the constitutional state in Australia. It is the touchstone against which the evolution of the legal system from a penal colony to a modern state has been assessed.[5] In the landmark and much-celebrated High Court of Australia decision in *Australian Communist Party v. Commonwealth* (1950), Dixon J referred to the rule of law as forming an assumption on which the Australian constitutional text was based.[6] In subsequent celebrated decisions relating to the rule of law, it has been used to explain the basis of constitutional guarantees to access the courts,[7] and to prevent the development of 'islands of power', immune from judicial oversight.[8] Following the

---

[5] D. Neal, *The Rule of Law in a Penal Colony: Law and Power in Early New South Wales* (Cambridge, 1991); V. Windeyer, 'A Birthright and Inheritance – The Establishment of the Rule of Law in Australia', *Tasmanian University Law Review*, 1 (1962), 635.

[6] *Australian Community Party v. Commonwealth* (1950) 83 CLR 1.

[7] Through section 75(v) and the guarantee of original jurisdiction to seek writs against officers of the Commonwealth: *Plaintiff S157/2002 v. Commonwealth* (2003) 211 CLR 476.

[8] *Kirk v. Industrial Court of NSW* (2010) 239 CLR 531.

Mason–Brennan eras in the High Court,[9] in which a series of rulings established new foundational and constitutional doctrine (for instance, in relation to native title, the implied freedom of political communication and separation of powers-based limitations on executive power of detention), conservative High Court justices invoked 'the rule of law' to defend a return to a more formalist and legalistic approach to constitutional interpretation.[10] The 'rule of law' is thus deployed, defended and celebrated as foundational: an assumption and a defence of Australia's entire constitutional ethos and the legitimacy of Australia's highest court.

The second reason is that claims and appeals to, and contests over, 'rule of law' that might be perceived to be occurring entirely separate to, and dislocated from, the rule-of-law issues experienced by First Nations, do affect First Nations people and intersect with their experience of the Australian state in a myriad of complicated and pervasive ways. Equal application of the law is explicitly disregarded in our constitutional system with Aboriginal people, the only 'race' against which the Commonwealth's power to make laws with respect to 'the people of any race for whom it is deemed necessary to make special laws' has been used.[11] They are also the only race for which the operation – and protections – of the Racial Discrimination Act 1975 (Cth) have been suspended. When the High Court handed down its ground-breaking decision in *Mabo v. Queensland* (No. 2) (1992), finding the common law of Australia recognised pre-existing native title claims of Aboriginal and Torres Strait Islander people, the court and its interpretative approach was attacked as 'activist' and 'political'.[12] Much of the critique and the attempted swing against the High Court's progressive interpretative trends were made by conservative jurists under the guise of protecting the court's legitimacy and 'the rule of law'.[13] The formalist, legalistic approach for which these judges advocated left Aboriginal and

---

[9] See further discussion of these eras in R. Dixon and G. Williams (eds.), *The High Court, the Constitution and Australian Politics* (Cambridge, 2015).

[10] M. Gleeson, *The Rule of Law and the Constitution* (Australian Broadcasting Corporation, Boyer Lectures, Sydney, 2020); D. Heydon, 'Judicial Activism and the Death of the Rule of Law', *Quadrant*, 47 (2003), 9.

[11] Section 51(xxvi) of the *Australian Constitution*.

[12] *Mabo v. Queensland (No. 2)* [1992] HCA 23; 175 CLR 1. See further T. Josev, 'The Persistent Pejorative: Judicial Activism', in G. Appleby and A. Lynch (eds.), *The Judge, the Judiciary and the Court: Individual, Collegial and Institutional Judicial Dynamics in Australia* (Cambridge, 2021), 163–86.

[13] See Heydon, 'Judicial Activism'.

Torres Strait Islander people in a number of cases without the substantive protection of the law, and at the whim of political agendas.[14]

Initial Claims and Evolution of Rule of Law

This section sets out two dimensions of the claims to the rule of law that have dominated the Australian historical discourse. The first is the initial legal foundation for the assertion of sovereignty on which the colonial and then federal legal system and 'rule of law' would be built. The second is the development of that legal system and evolution of the rule of law in accordance with English legal thought. In both instances, these historiographies have intersected with the experience of Aboriginal and Torres Strait Islanders of the rule of law in deeply troubling ways.

Initial Claims to Sovereignty

There is a well-recited mantra in Australia that the British assertion of sovereignty for its first colony in New South Wales was made not as a conquest, not through cession: it was 'settled'. And with 'settlement' came the peaceful acquisition of British sovereignty over the colonies, and the importation of the British common law, or at least as much of that law as could be applicable to the circumstances of a penal settlement. This was all juridically explained on the basis of an asserted legal fact: the land over which they were laying claim to sovereignty belonged to no one, termed *terra nullius* in more contemporary scholarship and cases. The basis of the claim lay in statements of international law, as enunciated by Sir William Blackstone (1765)[15] and Emmerich de Vattel (1758).[16] As Blackstone explained:

> Plantations, or colonies, in distant countries, are either such where the lands are claimed by right of occupancy only, *by finding them desart and uncultivated*, and peopling them from the mother country; or where, already cultivated, they have been either gained by conquest, or ceded

---

[14] For instance, in *Kartinyeri v. Commonwealth* (1998) 195 CLR 337, in relation to the interpretation of section 51(xxvi), and *Maloney v. The Queen* (2013) 252 CLR 168, interpreting special measures under the Racial Discrimination Act 1975 (Cth).

[15] W. Blackstone, *Commentaries on the Laws of England* (Oxford, 1765–69): we have used the 17th edition of 1830 (hereafter, Bl.Comm.).

[16] E. de Vattel, *Law of Nations or the Principles of Natural Law: Applied to the Conduct and the Affairs of Nations and Sovereigns*, trans. C. G. Fenwick (Washington, DC, 1916), Book 1, Chapter CVIII.

to us by treaties. And both these rights are founded upon the law of nature, or at least upon that of nations.[17]

The claim that the land was 'desart and uncultivated' was evidenced and determined, ultimately, by the observations and conclusions of the British themselves. In Captain James Cook's language, the inhabitants had 'no fix'd habitation but move on from place to place like Wild Beasts in search of food' and live 'wholly by fishing and hunting, but mostly by the former for we never saw one Inch of Cultivated Land in the Whole Country'.[18] Sir Joseph Banks wrote in his journal that when he went ashore at Botany Bay, he had seen 'nothing like people',[19] and that '[t]his immense tract of Land [is] thinly inhabited even to admiration'.[20] He would later testify to the House of Commons select committee looking at the establishment of the colony for transportation of convicts that:

> he apprehended that there would be little probability of any opposition from the natives, as during his stay there, in the year 1770, he saw very few, and did not think there would be above fifty in all the neighbourhood, . . . and those he saw were naked, treacherous, and armed with lances, but extremely cowardly, and constantly retired from our people when they made the appearance of resistance.[21]

Terri Libesman describes these statements as reflecting 'presumptions with respect to Aboriginal societies rather than evidence'.[22] In the 1889 Privy Council decision of *Cooper v. Stuart*,[23] in determining the application of the English law of perpetuities to a New South Wales land dispute, Lord Watson provided his own interpretation of Blackstone, and the position of the New South Wales colony. Lord Watson was even

---

[17] 1 Bl.Comm. 4 (emphasis added).

[18] J. Cook, *Journal of HMS Endeavour (1768–1771)* (first published in 1773, now available at www.nma.gov.au/exhibitions/endeavour-voyage/cooks-journal/new-holland-description), 86. See also *Cooper v. Stuart* (1889) 14 App. Cas. 286, 291 (Lord Watson).

[19] J. Banks, *The Endeavour Journal of Sir Joseph Banks* (25 August 1768–12 July 1771, available at https://gutenberg.net.au/ebooks05/0501141h.html#apr1770), entry for 29 April 1770.

[20] Ibid.

[21] Bunbury Committee on Transportation Journal of the House of Commons, 10 April 1779, vol. 37, 311.

[22] T. Libesman, 'Dispossession and Colonisation', in L. Behrendt, C. Cuneen, T. Libesman and N. Watson (eds.), *Aboriginal and Torres Strait Islander Legal Relations*, 2nd ed. (Oxford, 2019), 3–19, 7.

[23] (1889) 14 App. Cas. 286.

more favourable to the British than the original text, and accorded closely with the observations of Cook and Banks:

> There is a great difference between the case of a Colony acquired by conquest or cession, which there is an established system of law, and that of a Colony which consisted of a tract of territory practically unoccupied, without settled inhabitants or settled law, at the time when it was peacefully annexed to the British dominions. The Colony of New South Wales belongs to the latter class.[24]

Watson's extension of Blackstone has been described by Eddie Synot and Roshan de Silva-Wijeyeratne:

> The problem . . . is that Lord Watson took liberties with the definitions of 'practically unoccupied' and 'settled', resulting in an expansion of the applicability of occupation and settlement to lands legitimately occupied and possessed by peoples that colonial authorities otherwise characterised as being incapable of occupation and possession.[25]

As Ann Curthoys, Ann Genovese and Alexander Reilly have written: '[a]fter *Cooper*, a territory was understood to be *terra nullius* not only if it were uninhabited, but also if it had inhabitants but those inhabitants were without a recognisable law'.[26] To be recognisable as a legal system would likely then require the minimum pillars of a legal system that were dictated by the minimum characteristics of the rule of law: a set of laws, centrally promulgated, and enforceable by an independent arbiter. As Kristen Rundle has written, the rule of law is theoretically and conceptually underdeveloped to identify and describe Indigenous political and legal orders. That is 'not because indigenous traditions contain no idea of law-governed political order', but that 'indigenous conceptions of law-governed political order are organised around patterns of thought that run in very different directions'.[27]

Through a 'rule of law' lens, then, the initial sovereignty claims are deeply troubling at a number of levels. The assertion that these norms described by Blackstone and de Vattel are the law of nations, or even natural law, is the assertion by imperial powers of a normative position that justifies and facilitates the desired colonial expansion. Even if one

---

[24] Ibid., 291.

[25] E. Synot and R. de Silva-Wijeyeratne, '*Cooper v. Stuart*', in N. Watson and H. Douglas, (eds.), *Indigenous Legal Judgments* (Abingdon, 2021), 36–53, 38.

[26] A. Curthoys, A. Genovese and A. Reilly, *Rights and Redemption: History, Law and Indigenous People* (Sydney, 2008), 55.

[27] K. Rundle, *The Rule of Law Revisited* (Cambridge, 2023), 66.

were to accept the legitimacy of the normative justification, how would Indigenous populations contest the assertions by an imperial power that land was uncultivated? This was a legal system that they did not understand or operate within; and one which provided no ready forum for contesting the assertions of one party: the colonising state. It was an assertion that was very much in the imperial interests of the British: the British penal system was in crisis, and Britain was in desperate need of a solution to accommodate the increasing numbers of prisoners produced by its justice system. A simple claim to land would provide a parking place for the growing convict population and would, eventually, in the words of Brennan J in *Mabo (No. 2)*, underwrite 'the development of the Australian nation'.[28] Thus, the claim of sovereignty was a self-interested, unaccountable assertion of British state power, the very antithesis of the rule of law.

The claim was directly incoherent with the facts, including those known to the British at the time. First, there is now a large body of work, including judicial findings, that has developed to argue the inappropriateness of the claim that the land that became Australia was uninhabited, or uninhabited by those with a recognisable system of social governance and dispute resolution.[29] The extent to which this was understood by the British is revealed by the second fact. Settlement was not peaceful but occurred through ongoing, fatal and organised violence, including killings and massacres of entire Aboriginal families, communities and society. These were the result of the expansion of the colonial enterprise, and Aboriginal inhabitants of those lands fighting to protect their country and societies from invasion by a foreign state.

The incoherency of this position was finally accepted by the High Court in *Mabo v. Queensland (No. 2)*, but not in the complete way that might be thought, given the celebration of the case. Indeed, Daniel Lavery

---

[28] *Mabo (No. 2)*, 69.
[29] See e.g. *Milirrpum v. Nabalco* (1971) 17 *Federal Law Reports* 141, 267–9 (Blackburn J) (*Gove Land Rights Case*); N. L. Wallace-Bruce, 'Two Hundred Years On: A Re-examination of the Acquisition of Australia', *Georgia Journal of International & Comparative Law*, 19 (1989), 87; G. Simpson, '*Mabo*, International Law, *Terra Nullius* and the Stories of Settlement: An Unresolved Jurisprudence', *Melbourne University Law Review*, 19 (1993), 195; D. Ritter, 'The 'Rejection of *Terra Nullius*" in *Mabo*: A Critical Analysis', *Sydney Law Review*, 18 (1996), 5; S. Hepburn, 'Disinterested Truth: Legitimation of the Doctrine of Tenure Post-*Mabo*', *Melbourne University Law Review*, 29 (2005), 1; A. Fitzmaurice, 'The Genealogy of *Terra Nullius*', *Australian Historical Studies*, 38 (2007), 1.

has described the decision, which condemned the notion of *terra nullius* as unjust, discriminatory and ahistorical, as nonetheless exposing 'a troubling doctrinal paradox'.[30] The decision, particularly the judgment of Brennan J, accepts the position that the Aboriginal and Torres Strait Islander inhabitants of the land lived in accordance with recognisable legal systems, but leaves the acquisition of sovereignty untouched. Indeed, quoting the statement by Gibbs CJ (a subsequent critic of the *Mabo* decision) in *Seas and Submerged Lands Case*,[31] Brennan J accepts that '[t]he acquisition of territory by a sovereign state for the first time is an act of state which cannot be challenged, controlled or interfered with by the courts of that state'.[32] The recognition of sovereignty, Brennan J explained, 'is accorded simply on the footing that such a prerogative act is an act of state the validity of which is not justiciable in the municipal courts'.[33] The *Mabo (No. 2)* decision was one that looked at the consequence of acquisition of territory, not that act itself. Brennan J's position, by necessity, left the foundations of the assertion of sovereignty as resting on a peaceful settlement, resting on *terra nullius*, which itself rested on the idea that Aboriginal people had no recognisable legal system.

The conclusion in *Mabo (No. 2)*, ultimately, is that the Australian common law legal system recognises that there were pre-existing – and ongoing – legal systems that governed and govern Aboriginal and Torres Strait Islander communities. The existence of these legal systems, however, has an extremely limited effect: they may, if the circumstances are right, give rise to a common law claim to native title. In 2020, the Australian High Court recognised that the common law's recognition of the rights and interests drawn from Aboriginal law and custom, and connection to the land that would become Australia, gave rise to a constitutional limitation on the application of the 'aliens power' to members of the Aboriginal and Torres Strait Islander community.[34] The High Court's now embrace of the recognition of the status of traditional laws and custom of Aboriginal people sits directly in contradiction to the legal basis for the claim of English sovereignty over the land in 1788. But this consequence of recognition is simply left as

---

[30] D. Lavery, 'No Decorous Veil: The Continuing Reliance on an Enlarged *Terra Nullius* Notion in Mabo (No. 2)', *Melbourne University Law Review*, 43 (2019), 233.
[31] (1975) 135 CLR 388.
[32] *Mabo (No. 2)*, 31.
[33] Ibid.
[34] *Love v. Commonwealth; Thoms v. Commonwealth* [2020] HCA 3.

unresolvable: a political fact, an artefact of the arbitrary exercise of force and violence by the British state against the Aboriginal nations.

This position is unsatisfactory. As we explore in the final section of this chapter, it is unsatisfactory because it leaves unresolved the status of claims to sovereignty by First Nations.[35] These claims span the legal, political and spiritual. While they have been consistently denied in their legal form by the High Court, since *Mabo (No. 2)* they been given legal footholds. This is because assertions of First Nations sovereignty rests on the idea that 'it was never validly taken or given away'.[36] The incoherency of the legal position in regard to the basis of British sovereignty, coupled with the strength of advocacy and argument for ongoing First Nations sovereignty, represents an ongoing crisis for the legitimacy of the rule of law in the Australian state. As we have shown here, it is one that has not been able to be resolved by the courts. In the final section of the chapter we return to how other avenues of reform might offer solutions to this issue.

Evolution of Rule of Law

The second claim we seek to interrogate in the Australian myth-making with respect to rule of law is the remarkable evolution of the legal system that was imposed by the British on colonisation, from a penal state in which there was largely unfettered executive and legislative power bestowed on the Governor, to one in which the institutions and principles associated with the rule of law were developed. This is a view of colonisation as creating a legacy of rule of law. The development of 'free institutions' of the rule of law and democratic ideals included the introduction of independent courts, a crown prosecutor, trial by jury, a representative legislature with an expanded franchise, and eventually an accountable executive.[37] This massive transformation of institutions was, however, only for the colony and for the men and women who had come

---

[35] See, for instance, M. Mansell, *Treaty and Statehood: Aboriginal Self-Determination* (Annandale, NSW, 2016), chapter 5.

[36] S. Brennan, L. Behrendt, L. Strelein and G. Williams, *Treaty* (Annandale, NSW, 2005), 72, and at 73, other political objectives and claims to sovereignty as the basis for political advocacy for rights and governance. See also L. Behrendt, *Achieving Social Justice: Indigenous Rights and Australia's Future* (Annandale, NSW, 2003), 99.

[37] See further, e.g., Windeyer, 'A Birthright and an Inheritance'; B. Kircher, *An Unruly Child: A History of Law in Australia* (Abingdon, 1995); Neal, *Rule of Law in a Penal Colony*.

to Australia or been born under the colonial government. The status of Aboriginal people within this developing system of rule of law was ambiguous, arbitrary and violent: the antithesis of the rule of law. The expectations of the colonists and convicts might have been that they had natural-born rights to the liberal institutions and expectations of the rule of law. As David Neal argues, '[a] cluster of ideas known as the rule of law provided the major institutions, arguments, vocabulary and symbols with which the convicts forged the transformation'.[38] But this was not the expectation, or experience, of the Aboriginal populations. So, as Martin Krygier has asked, how do you come to terms with 'what happened to Australia's Aborigines while these remarkable achievements were underway'?[39]

The experience of colonisation, and the evolution of the rule of law in the colonial system for Aboriginal populations across the Australian colonies were diverse. That diversity was marked, however, by a number of shared experiences that demonstrate not just a vacuum of rule of law but an active denial of it and, as we have argued above, the weaponisation of the rule of law against Aboriginal people. The starting point for those exploring this juxtaposition is usually the Royal Instructions issued to the early Governors, and, in some cases, their own public proclamations, as to the treatment of Aboriginal people. The most famous of these instruments were those issued to Governor Philip:

> You are to endeavour by every possible means to open an intercourse with the natives, and to conciliate their affections, enjoining our subjects to live in amity and kindness with them. And if any of our subjects shall wantonly destroy them, or give the unnecessary interruption in the exercise of their several occupations, it is our will and pleasure that you do cause such offenders to be brought into punishment according to the degree of the offence.[40]

The status of Aboriginal people in the newly imposed legal system was not clear. Governor Philip's Instructions imply that they were *distinct* from the subjects of the colony. Did this mean they were subject to the laws of the colony, or their own laws? If they were subject to the laws of the colony, were they competent to give evidence in a colonial court so as to actually make use of those laws? This was a matter of great public and

---

[38] Neal, *Rule of Law in a Penal Colony*, 62.
[39] Krygier, 'Grammar of Colonial Legality', 220.
[40] Governor Philip's Instructions, 25 April 1787.

legal debate.[41] Legally, it would remain unsettled for decades, only being resolved in the 1836 decision in *R. v. Murrell*.[42] There, Burton J of the New South Wales Supreme Court found that Aboriginal people were subject to colonial laws. Aboriginal people had, in his words, 'not attained at the first settlement of the English people amongst them to such a position in point of numbers *and civilisation, and to such a form of Government and laws*, as to be entitled to be recognised as so many sovereign states governed by law of their own'.[43] This was explained, then, using the same justification for 'settlement'. Here, though, we see the language of 'civilisation', language that was often used, to deny not just the status of Aboriginal society and laws but their spiritual and religious lives.

The official role of the state in the frontier violence of dispossession was complex and multifaceted. There were instances of Governors involved in the legally sanctioned, armed (violent) 'pacification' of Aboriginal people.[44] There were many instances of state officers engaged in extensive, arbitrary massacres of Aboriginal people, which, while they were not sanctioned by the Governor or law, were tolerated and these individuals were not brought before the justice system for their violations.[45] There were other examples of Governors giving legal permission to settlers and the military to use force against Aboriginal people,[46] and in particular to defend themselves against violence as they pushed further into Aboriginal lands. 'Defend' in this situation was often the result of proactive incursions into Aboriginal land, resulting in armed resistance.[47] In this respect, the position of the colonial government in relation to this violence was consistent with

---

[41] As evidenced in the letters to the editor of various provincial newspapers; see e.g. those extracted in H. Reynolds, *This Whispering in Our Hearts Revisited* (Sydney, 2018).

[42] [1836] NSWSupC 35; although see also *R. v. Ballard (or Barrett)* [1829] NSWSupC 26; and *R. v. Bonjon* [1841] NSWSupC 92.

[43] *R. v. Murrell* [1836] NSWSupC 35 (emphasis added).

[44] See Governor Hunter, letter to the Duke of Portland, 20 June 1797, *Historical Records of Australia*, vol. 2, 24 (hereafter *HRA*).

[45] For instance, Major James Nunn, considered responsible for the massacre of potentially hundreds of Gamilaraay People at Waterloo Creek in 1836. See further *HRA* (22 July 1839), vol. 20, depositions at an inquiry into this encounter.

[46] See e.g. the instructions of Governor Macquarie in 1816: M. Organ, 'Secret Service: Governor Macquarie's Aboriginal War of 1816', *Proceedings of the National Conference of the Royal Australian Historical Society* (Mittagong, 25–26 October 2014).

[47] See e.g. H. Reynolds, *The Question of Genocide in Australia's History: An Indelible Stain* (Ringwood, Victoria, 2001), 56.

the English colonising mindset: that they were laying claim to a land occupied not by people that they or their law could recognise, but by 'savages'. To the British, Aboriginal people had no legal system or systems under which they might have a legitimate claim to land, that they might legitimately defend through force. Rather, for the British, the 'law' (their law) was on the one side of this conflict: the side of the colonists (their side).

Desmond Manderson has argued that not only was the rule of law not *for* Aboriginal people, its standards were weaponised in this context *against* Aboriginal people to deny them its protections.[48] This is a slightly different thesis from another which is undoubtedly true: that *law* was used against Aboriginal people. Some of the violence against the Aboriginal people was sanctioned by law. Later, law would provide the foundation for many of the policies of the protection era, the restrictions on liberty, the removal of children without consent, forced slavery. In these cases, 'law', and the mechanisms of the rule of law to enforce that law, was used against Aboriginal people. Manderson, however, claims that the standards of the 'rule of law' were also actively used against Aboriginal people in this context. This resonates with our argument, above, that the rule of law created a standard against which the Aboriginal legal systems were assessed, found wanting, and subjected to claims of British sovereignty.

Manderson states that the denial of rule of law to Aboriginal people is not 'subsidiary to its glorification but brought about by it'. This was because Aboriginal people were assessed as not 'worthy' of the rule of law: 'their own "savage spirit" ... prevented their attaining it'. The British, in order to bring them to a point of civilisation that would mean they could benefit from the rule of law, had to suspend the rule of law in relation to them. Manderson goes on:

> The very belief in the rule of law highlighted the apparent inadequacy of the Tasmanian Aborigines to benefit from it, and this in turn justified any and all measures to impose legal and social order on them. The more beautiful the ideal, the more inadequate the present state of the natives seemed. The more sincere the British commitment to our universal sameness, the more Aboriginal difference and resistance seemed a 'wanton' 'fierceness' to be subjugated or a 'weakness' to be fixed.[49]

---

[48] Manderson, 'Law of the Image'.
[49] Ibid., 164.

The experience of Aboriginal people of the 'remarkable' transformation of the Australian penal colonies into bastions of the rule of law is not just a paradox: its existence actively undermines the claims of 'rule of law' achievement in the colony. Indeed, the exceptionalism of the status of Aboriginal people, the suspension of the principles of the rule of law in relation to them, the impunity with which violence could be dealt out to them to achieve rule-of-law objectives for the colony, has created a set of culturally acceptable practices and exceptions – or rule-of-law 'machinery' – within Australia's rule-of-law system that continue to be felt.

This history demonstrates that Australia's rule-of-law system was developed alongside an acceptance that there were groups of 'others' who were not worthy of the rule of law, for whom the protections of the rule of law could be suspended, for their benefit, or the benefit of the state, or some combination of the two. This rule-of-law machinery has never stopped being used against Aboriginal people in ways that continue to undermine claims of the Australian state's rule-of-law achievements. Since the period of colonisation that we have outlined in this chapter, these have included an array of policies: the legal targeting and authorisation of the removal of Aboriginal children from their families; the almost unlimited discretion of the Protector of the Aborigines to dictate the lives of Aboriginal people – where they may live, whether they may travel, access to their children, what jobs they may hold; the suspension of racial discrimination statutes for Aboriginal people so as to implement targeted restrictions on their welfare.

The rule-of-law exceptions that have been created for First Nations people have become accepted – and acceptable – within the Australian state. They were initially deployed against Aboriginal people, but they have become part of the discretions and exceptions in the White Australia Policy, and the government's contemporary policy framework for processing asylum seekers. They have been used against those seen as undeserving of the rule of law: vulnerable or publicly reviled minorities, from asylum seekers to members of organised criminal gangs. Legal frameworks established to govern these groups often fall short of rule-of-law expectations of the rest of the community. These frameworks contain, for instance, altered court procedures and rules of evidence, almost unlimited ministerial discretion, attempts to remove the ability of refugees to appeal the government's decisions to the courts, the detention of children, limited access to work and welfare. These incursions are justified to *uphold* the rule of law, on the basis that somehow these people represent a threat to the rule of law, and the targeted suspension of the rule of law against them is required. The Australian state thus recognises and accepts as necessary certain rule-of-law incursions that can be traced back to the first denials of rule of law to Aboriginal people.

The Contemporary Movement for Constitutional Recognition of Aboriginal and Torres Strait Islander People in Australia

In this section, we move to consider the contemporary movement for recognition of Aboriginal and Torres Strait Islander people in the Australian constitutional system,[50] and the extent to which proposed reforms address the rule-of-law crises that flow from original claims and development of the Australian state and its relationship to First Nations.

The objectives of 'recognition' and structural reform are numerous, interrelated, contested and, needless to say, complicated. They have included a desire – one held almost always by non-Indigenous Australians and rejected by First Nations[51] – to recognise the historical fact of pre-colonial occupation by Aboriginal and Torres Strait Islanders. This has become known as 'minimalist' recognition. Recognition includes recognising the cultural sovereignty of Aboriginal and Torres Strait Islanders within the monolithic legal sovereignty of the Australian constitutional system, which would extend to recognition through rights of self-determination and political empowerment. Recognition includes addressing the possibility of negatively racially discriminatory government action. Setting aside minimalist recognition, these objectives have manifested as three ideas for change:

1. A modern agreement-making process, or treaty, which might be constitutional or extra-constitutional, and would include settlement of matters such as land and water rights, reparations and future self-government;
2. A constitutionally entrenched protection against racially discriminatory laws that would bind the federal and state governments and legislatures; and

---

[50] This contemporary discussion is not in ignorance of the long history for reforms that can be seen as amounting to recognition: D. Lino, *Constitutional Recognition: First Peoples and the Australian Settler State* (Annandale, NSW, 2018), particularly chapter 2.
[51] See Kirribilli Statement (Sydney, 2015).

3. Some sort of constitutionally enshrined political empowerment, such as the creation of a representative body engaged in the policy-making and legislative process.

In the lead-up to the 2007 election, Prime Minister John Howard on the eve of likely election defeat, promised to pursue recognition if re-elected.[52] He was not. In 2010, when the federal election returned a hung parliament, Prime Minister Julia Gillard made an agreement with independent MPs to undertake an inquiry into constitutional recognition. In 2012, the Expert Panel on Constitutional Recognition of Indigenous Australians reported,[53] making a number of recommendations that combined removal of outdated and racist provisions in the Constitution, symbolic recognition of cultural heritage and connection to land, and a new clause that would constitutionally guarantee protection against racially discriminatory laws. It was this last proposal that formed the substantive reform idea of the report.

The 2012 Expert Panel proposal was addressed to what was seen as a deficiency in the constitutional position, demonstrated by the history of adversely discriminatory laws. It was addressed, in many senses, to the rule of law: to the potential in Australia's constitutional system through section 51(xxvi) for negatively racially discriminatory laws to be enacted against groups, including Aboriginal and Torres Strait Islander people, who, historically, had been the target of these laws. The proposal for a non-discrimination clause would apply equally to all state actors in the Australian system: state and federal governments and parliaments would be bound by it. It relied on an independent court system for its enforcement. But while it was addressed to a rule-of-law failure, the anti-discrimination proposal did not provide any answer to the initial rule-of-law grievance of Aboriginal people, on which the legal institutions are built. It retained the legal and political institutions, and, indeed, retained confidence in their legitimacy and the final authority of the courts over Aboriginal people.

The Expert Panel's recommendations proved politically controversial in Australia, with pushback from the Conservative Party on the basis that it shifted power from the legislature to the courts. This reflects a long

---

[52] S. Brennan and M. Davis, 'First Peoples', in C. Saunders and A. Stone (eds.), *The Oxford Handbook of the Australian Constitution* (Oxford, 2018), 27–55, 31.

[53] *Expert Panel on Constitutional Recognition of Indigenous Australians*, Final Report (Canberra, 2012).

history in Australia of political protection of rights rather than constitutionalised and juridified rights protection. The Australian Labour Party never engaged with or responded to the 2012 report; rather, the issue was left to languish politically. This led to a group of Aboriginal and Torres Strait Islander leaders lobbying the government and opposition and demanding a new approach to recognition. This became known as the Kirribilli Statement (2015), requiring that the question be resolved through a greater level of *engagement* or 'dialogue' with the Aboriginal and Torres Strait Islander communities, to determine what sort of *substantive* – not minimalist – change was desired. The demands made in the Kirribilli Statement led to the creation by the Prime Minister (with the agreement of the Opposition Leader) of the Referendum Council, that oversaw the process that delivered the Uluru Statement from the Heart.

The Uluru Statement from the Heart

Within the Referendum Council, an Indigenous Steering Committee was developed which was responsible for the first Indigenous-designed and Indigenous-led series of civics-informed dialogues with Aboriginal and Torres Strait Islander people across Australia. These dialogues were designed to be culturally legitimate, as well as culturally sensitive, and responsive to Aboriginal and Torres Strait Islander needs. The purpose of these dialogues was to try to understand what form of recognition would meet the expectations of First Nations. The process was a historic, never-before-attempted exercise in self-determined political reform work, that has been well-documented elsewhere.[54] It culminated in the First Nations National Constitutional Convention at Uluru, which synthesised the recognition priorities from the dialogues conducted across the country and delivered the Uluru Statement from the Heart to the Australian people on 26 May 2017.

The Regional Dialogues process that led to the Uluru Statement pioneered a model of genuine deliberative consultation with Aboriginal and Torres Strait Islander communities on technical, sophisticated and highly contested issues of public policy and law. Aboriginal and Torres Strait Islander people were involved in the development of law reform proposals in a way that recognised their right to self-determination and

---

[54] See e.g. M. Davis and G. Williams, *Everything You Need to Know about the Uluru Statement from the Heart* (Sydney, 2021), 128.

their right to be involved in a culturally specific process. The process achieved an unprecedented national consensus within the Aboriginal and Torres Strait Islander community on constitutional and structural reform. The substantive changes that the Uluru Statement called for were, first, the constitutional entrenchment of a 'First Nations Voice'. While there was little detail provided in the Statement as to what the structure of Voice might look like, the dialogues cumulatively explicitly indicated that a body ought to be culturally representative of Aboriginal and Torres Strait Islander peoples, and, importantly, would represent First Nations, in recognition of their status not as a homogenous social group, but as distinct nations with distinct laws, customs and experiences. This body would have input into legislation passed by Parliament. In this way, the dialogue process not only modelled inclusive and deliberative self-determination but also ongoing self-determination. The second call was for the creation of a Makarrata commission to oversee a process of agreement-making, that is, treaty-making, at a national level, and also to be responsible for overseeing a process of truth-telling.

The proposed reforms of the Uluru Statement are pragmatic and forward-thinking; they speak to structural reforms to the place of Aboriginal people in the constitutional institutions of the state. This is a place that has previously been denied to them as a group of 'others' who could be excluded at will. The new constitutional position proposed under the Uluru Statement would recognise Aboriginal and Torres Strait Islander people as having a unique claim, and so incapable of being excluded in the future. The establishment of a First Nations Voice would be an acceptance of the previous denial of the position of Aboriginal and Torres Strait Islander people, and denial to them of law, through its attempt at structural redress. The establishment of a First Nations Voice would be a political act of recognition of the assertions of sovereignty on which Aboriginal and Torres Strait Islander people base their claims. It would not change the High Court's legal position on sovereignty, but the document that lays the foundations for the constitutional state would recognise a group of people with a unique claim on the state. This unique claim speaks to the currently unresolved foundation of the legal system. The Voice might not be a complete or direct response to that incoherency, but it would operate as a recognition of its existence, and, more than that, an attempt to redress it through structural changes that are designed to address the particular rule-of-law failures that have become regularised for First Nations people.

The Voice was intended to be a vehicle through which there is an explicit constitutional recognition of the systems of laws and customs that govern First Nations communities – not simply as a historical matter, but as ongoing, vibrant, evolving societies. The Voice was intended to be comprised of representatives selected by First Nations in accordance with their own laws and customs. Further, the work of the Voice, and ultimately its advice to government, was predicated not just on the fact that First Nations have different life experiences, but also in recognition that there are different cultural norms and practices that should inform the development of policy. Implicitly recognised in the establishment of the Voice, then, was the recognition of the contemporary cultural, political and legal systems of First Nations, a constitutional acknowledgement of a plurality of legal systems.

A constitutionally guaranteed voice in the political process would allow First Nations to be at the table when decisions are made as to whether to suspend the law as it affects them. It would allow First Nations a voice at the table when decisions are made about what is in their 'best interests', and what 'special measures' might need to be enacted, directed at them, to address these. It would allow First Nations people a voice at the table in designing systems where government power is wielded over them: how much discretion is granted in these frameworks, and how will it be accountable? In this way, it would offer a way to break the cycle of rule-of-law machinery that was created at a time when the status of Aboriginal and Torres Strait Islander people in the state was ambiguous, arbitrary and violent. The Voice offered recognition of First Nations in the Constitution and a way forward from the initial grievance. It was intended to provide a new understanding of the relationship between Aboriginal and Torres Strait Islander people and the rule of law. Aboriginal people are not only subjects of the law, but they are constitutionally guaranteed voices in the future design – and remedying – of the institutions and processes of the rule of law. Up until this point, the ongoing evolution of the rule of law had been one in which the differentiated treatment of Aboriginal people was tolerated. It had always been thus. But it does not have to always be thus.

Conclusion

On 14 October 2023, the Australian people voted 'no' in a constitutional referendum to recognise First Nations people through the Voice. This means that any constitutional recognition of First Nations people is likely to be delayed for decades, much like the referendum for an Australian republic. It means that the racist elements of the Constitution are retained.

The reasons for the loss are complex, and will no doubt be the subject of ongoing analysis as Australians grapple with what this means for their constitutional future. The primary reason can be traced back to the lack of bipartisan support and the nature of the political campaign that was run by the Opposition.[55] The successful 'no' campaign was based on the argument that race does not belong in the Constitution and that Australia's Constitution and concomitant institutions are all imbued with formal equality. The failure of the Voice referendum maintains the status quo not only in policy but the crisis of constitutional legitimacy and the 'disagreement . . . about the authority of the constitutional order itself'.[56] The Voice was aimed at mitigating the impact of a legal system and 'rule of law' machinery and principles imbued with racism and the deliberate denial of access to the rule of law for the Aboriginal and Torres Strait Islander population. The failure of the Voice referendum and a twelve-year process of recognition means that the foundational incoherencies of Australia will continue. It is a bitter irony that it was these foundational incoherencies that were the drivers of the 'no' campaign.

[55] See S. Nakata, 'The Political Subjugation of First Nations Peoples Is No Longer Historical Legacy', *The Conversation*, 14 October 2023. See further exploration of the loss in G. Appleby and M. Davis (eds.), The Failure of the Voice Referendum and the Future of Australian Democracy (London, 2025).
[56] Appleby, Levy and Whalan, 'Voice versus Rights', 765.

16

The Rise and Fall of the UK Human Rights Act

BRENDA HALE

I read my law in Cambridge from 1963 to 1966 and in our first year we had an introduction to public international law. It was all about the law of war and the law of the sea. I do not remember a single reference to International Human Rights Law. It was solely concerned with the relationship between states, so I gave it up as soon as I could.

This is of course not at all surprising. The modern International Human Rights Law project was kicked off in the Charter of the United Nations in 1945. The Preamble declares that the people of the United Nations are determined 'to reaffirm faith in fundamental human rights, in the dignity and worth of the human person, and in the equal rights of men and women and of nations large and small'. Among the Purposes of the United Nations listed in article 1 are 'to achieve international co-operation in ... promoting and encouraging respect for human rights and for fundamental freedoms for all without distinction as to race, sex, language or religion'. Note the emphasis on international co-operation which chimes with the UN's emphasis on the sovereignty of the nation state. Then came the Universal Declaration of Human Rights in 1948, with its ringing declaration 'that all human beings are born free and equal in dignity and rights' and its ambitious list of rights, which has formed the basis of many later human rights instruments, whether from the United Nations itself, or from regional bodies, or indeed in national constitutions. But the UN's enthusiasm for binding human rights instruments quickly waned and did not revive until the 1960s.

In the meantime, the Council of Europe, then only the twelve democracies in western Europe and Turkey, decided to go it alone and produced the European Convention on Human Rights in 1950. The Preamble reaffirmed 'their profound belief in those fundamental freedoms which are the foundation of justice and peace in the world and are best maintained on the one hand by an effective political democracy and on the other by a common understanding and observance of the human rights on which they depend'. Whether the notions of 'political democracy' and 'fundamental human rights' can be reconciled with one another is open to debate. Conor Gearty, for example, has argued that there is an inherent tension between the human rights project and political democracy.[1] Democracy means that the will of the majority, as expressed through their democratically elected representatives, must prevail. The human rights project means that there are certain rights which are protected against violation even if the majority wills it.

The Convention came into force in 1953, but until 1998 member states could choose whether or not to accept the jurisdiction of the European Court of Human Rights. The United Kingdom did not do so until 1966. The Convention gives the Court jurisdiction, not only over complaints brought by one member state against another, but also over complaints brought by 'any person, non-governmental organisation or group of individuals claiming to be the victim of a violation' by a member state. There have been cases between member states – most notably, for us, the case brought by Ireland against the United Kingdom complaining that the 'five techniques' used by the British in interrogations in Northern Ireland violated the article 3 prohibition of 'torture' or 'inhuman or degrading treatment or punishment'. In 1978, the Court held that the techniques did amount to inhuman or degrading treatment but not to torture.[2] The British judge[3] dissented, save in respect of the specific violations which the United Kingdom did not dispute, and voiced his 'emphatic opinion that if a commendable zeal for the observance and implementation of the Convention is allowed to drive out common sense then the whole system will end by becoming discredited'. His particular concern was enlarging the terms of the Convention 'so as to include concepts and notions that lie outside their just and normal scope'. That is a complaint which is frequently heard today.

More numerous than complaints by states, however, have been complaints by individuals, and it is in these cases that the Court's doctrines have been most clearly established. Principal amongst these is the notion, established in *Tyrer v. United Kingdom*,[4] that the Convention is a 'living instrument' which must develop to keep pace with changing social

---

[1] C. Gearty, 'Spoils for Which Victor? Human Rights within the Democratic State' in C. Gearty and C. Douzinas (eds.), *The Cambridge Companion to Human Rights Law* (Cambridge, 2012), 214 at 215.

[2] *Ireland v. United Kingdom* (1979–80) 2 EHRR 25. The Irish asked the Court to revise its judgment after new evidence came to light in 2014, but the Court declined to do so.

[3] Sir Gerald Fitzmaurice.

[4] (1979–80) 2 EHRR 1.

attitudes and conditions. There is nothing new in this to UK eyes. In *Edwards v. Attorney General of Canada*,[5] the Judicial Committee of the Privy Council held that, while the word 'persons' in the British North America Act of 1867 might not have included women at the time, by 1929 it did include them: the British North America Act had 'planted in Canada a living tree capable of growth and expansion within its natural limits' and their Lordships did not wish 'to cut down its provisions by a narrow and technical construction but rather to give it a large and liberal interpretation'.

This approach was adopted in *Ministry of Home Affairs v. Fisher*,[6] where the Judicial Committee held that the word 'child' in the Constitution of Bermuda included a child born to unmarried parents, although at that time it would not have done so if contained in an ordinary Act of Parliament. But a Constitution was different:

> A Constitution is a legal instrument giving rise, amongst other things, to individual rights capable of enforcement in a court of law. Respect must be paid to the language which has been used and to the traditions and usages which have given rise to that language. It is quite consistent with this, and with the recognition that rules of interpretation may apply, to take as a point of departure for the process of interpretation a recognition of the character and origin of the instrument, and to be guided by the principle of giving full recognition and effect to those fundamental rights and freedoms with a statement of which the Constitution commences.

This was a firm rejection – by UK judges not noted for their radical ideas – of the American doctrine of originalism – that the text must read in accordance with the original intention of the drafters or as the original readers would have understood it. So we should not have been surprised or dismayed when the European Court of Human Rights adopted a similar approach.

The drafters of the European Convention were of course influenced by the content of the Universal Declaration. But they also had in mind the fundamental freedoms which the British had fondly assumed to be their birthright since at least the days of Sir Edward Coke in the seventeenth century and Sir William Blackstone in the eighteenth century. So it came as something of a shock when the United Kingdom began to lose cases in Strasbourg: early examples were *Golder*,[7] holding that it made no sense to

---

[5] [1930] AC 124, 136.
[6] [1980] AC 319, 329.
[7] (1979–80) 1 EHRR 524.

require a fair trial in the determination of civil and criminal cases if there was no right to go to court in the first place, so one was implied into article 6; *Tyrer*,[8] holding that judicially ordered corporal punishment of juveniles violated the prohibition of degrading punishment in article 3; *Sunday Times*,[9] holding that an injunction prohibiting publication of articles about the thalidomide scandal because of the risk of contempt of court violated the freedom of expression protected by article 10 (prompting another dissent for the British judge, who argued that the aim of protecting the authority and independence of the judiciary had been added at British insistence because of our law of contempt of court, unknown to the other members); *Dudgeon*,[10] holding that Northern Ireland's continued criminalisation of homosexual acts between adult men violated the right to respect for private life in article 8; *Young*,[11] holding that dismissal for refusing to join the British rail closed shop unions violated the freedom of association protected by article 11 (thus establishing that the right to do something might also imply the right not to do it – a feature which helped us to decide the so-called 'gay cake' case in Northern Ireland[12]); *Campbell and Cosans*,[13] holding that insisting on corporal punishment in school violated the parents' right to have their children educated in accordance with their religious or philosophical beliefs under article 2 of the First Protocol; *Silver*,[14] holding that censoring prisoners' letters to MPs and solicitors (but not to others) violated the right to respect for correspondence in article 8; and *Malone*,[15] holding that the unregulated common law allowing the police to tap private phones violated the respect for home and private life in article 8. I could go on – and note that by no means all of these were the result of primary legislation about which the UK courts could do nothing; some stemmed from the common law which might perhaps have been developed to meet the situation. Added to these shock defeats were several friendly settlements reached after the Commission had found a violation.

---

[3] (1979–80) 2 EHRR 1.
[9] (1979–80) 2 EHRR 245.
[10] (1980) 3 EHRR 40.
[11] (1981) 4 EHRR 38.
[12] *Lee v. Ashers Baking Co. Ltd* [2018] UKSC 49, [2020] AC 143.
[13] (1982) 4 EHRR 293.
[14] (1983) 5 EHRR.
[15] (1985) 7 EHRR 14.

Calls to incorporate the Convention into UK law began even before these shocks. Anthony Lester argued for this in a Fabian Tract, *Democracy and Individual Rights*, in 1968. Sir Leslie Scarman advocated it in his 1974 Hamlyn Lectures, *English Law – The New Dimension*. In 1978, a House of Lords Select Committee voted in favour of a Bill of Rights by six to five. Between 1969 and 1997, no fewer than eleven Bills were introduced in the House of Lords, mostly by Lord Wade and Lord Lester, six of which passed all their stages in the Lords and were sent to the House of Commons. In 1987, a Conservative MP, Sir Edward Gardner, introduced a private member's Bill to incorporate the Convention into the House of Commons. In 1996, the newly appointed Lord Chief Justice, Lord Bingham, used his maiden speech in the House of Lords to argue for incorporation.

It then became Labour Party policy. Jack Straw and Paul Boateng published a Consultation Paper in December 1996, *Bringing Rights Home: Labour's Plans to Incorporate the European Convention on Human Rights into United Kingdom Law*. The arguments were simple and some of them have resonances today. Because their rights were not protected in the UK courts, British people had to undergo the lengthy and costly process of applying to Strasbourg. British judges were denied the opportunity of building a body of case law which was properly sensitive to British legal and constitutional traditions. The European Court of Human Rights had not been able to benefit from experience of the UK legal system and was neither sufficiently familiar with, or sensitive to, British legal and constitutional traditions. Incorporation would reduce the degree of recourse to Strasbourg. It was implicit, if not spelt out, that it would reduce the proportion of cases which the United Kingdom lost there.

I well remember the excitement amongst the judges sitting on the woolsack to hear the Queen's Speech after Labour had won the General Election in May 1997. Her Majesty announced that 'A Bill will be introduced to incorporate in United Kingdom law the main provisions of the European Convention on Human Rights'. The Bill was introduced in December, along with a white paper, *Rights Brought Home: The Human Rights Bill.*[16] This pointed out that it had been thought when we ratified the Convention that the Convention rights and freedoms were already protected in British law. But it turned out that they were not. The

---

[16] 1997, Cm 3782.

rights originally developed with major help from the UK government were no longer actually seen as British rights. UK judges had a very high reputation internationally, 'but the fact that they do not deal in the same concepts as the European Court of Human Rights limits the extent to which their judgments can be drawn upon and followed'. With incorporation, we would be speaking the same language.

So the Human Rights Act 1998 was passed and came into force in 2000 after a massive training programme for all the judges. It did three basic things. First, it turned the rights contained in the Convention into rights in UK law: it became unlawful for a public authority to act incompatibly with a Convention right and any victim could bring proceedings for a remedy or rely upon the right in existing proceedings.[17] Second, the courts – and indeed everyone else – had a duty to read and give effect to all UK legislation in a way which was compatible with the Convention rights, so far as it was possible to do so.[18] Experience of a similar duty in EU law had taught us a number of techniques for doing this. Third, in deciding questions relating to the Convention rights, courts and tribunals had a duty to take into account the case law and decisions of the European Court of Human Rights and other Council of Europe institutions.[19] However, unlike EU law, if a provision in an Act of the UK Parliament could not be read and given effect compatibly, the courts had no power to ignore it or strike it down. The most they could do was to make a declaration of incompatibility,[20] a clear warning to Government and Parliament that the United Kingdom would lose if the matter went to Strasbourg, but leaving it to them to decide what, if anything, to do about it.

The Government White Paper did consider whether the courts should be given power to strike down incompatible provisions in Acts of the UK Parliament. After all, the European Communities Act had given them this power, so a Human Rights Act could also do so – unless and until it was repealed. Various compromise models were considered, in particular the one adopted in Canada when it decided to repatriate its Constitution and adopt a Charter of Fundamental Rights, which would allow the Supreme Court to strike down inconsistent laws. But the Canadian Parliament was allowed to pass laws 'notwithstanding' their

[17] HRA, ss. 6–9.
[18] HRA, s. 3.
[19] HRA, s. 2.
[20] HRA, s. 4.

incompatibility with the Charter rights, which the court could not strike down. In practice, very little use has been made of this power, but it is a safety valve which enables the will of the elected to prevail.

The government decided not to adopt either the EU or the Canadian solution, pointing out that the EU solution was a requirement of EU membership, whereas there was no such requirement in the European Convention. Parliamentary sovereignty should prevail. The authority of Parliament to make decisions about important matters of public policy was derived from the democratic mandate of its members, who were elected, accountable and representative. Allowing the courts to strike down Acts of Parliament would be likely on occasions to draw the judges into serious conflict with Parliament. The judges did not want this and the government had no mandate for such a change.

Quite right. The judges did not and do not want this. But that has not prevented their being drawn into conflict, if not with Parliament, then with more recent governments. By and large, the government's record of acting upon declarations of incompatibility has been impressive. There has always been intense frustration that the Convention does not allow foreign national criminals to be deported if there is a risk that they will suffer torture in the only country which will take them. Soon after the atrocities of 11 September 2001, there was legislation allowing the indefinite executive detention of suspected foreign national terrorists who could not be deported. In one of the earliest cases under the Act,[21] the House of Lords declared that this was incompatible, because it discriminated between foreign and home-grown suspected terrorists: how could detaining the foreigners be justified if it was not necessary to lock up the home-grown? To its credit, the then government allowed the legislation to lapse under its sunset clause and replaced it with something less draconian which applied to British and foreign nationals alike.

After 2010, the government became more openly critical of the Act. The only example of prolonged resistance to a declaration of incompatibility has been the blanket ban on sentenced prisoners voting, where the government held out for so long that the Council of Europe eventually gave in and accepted that some minor administrative changes would suffice. The Prime Minister declared that the idea of prisoners voting made him feel physically sick. On another occasion, when the Supreme Court declared that the inability ever to have one's name removed from

---

[21] *A (and Others) v. Secretary of State for the Home Department* [2004] UKHL 56, [2005] 2 AC 68.

the sex offenders' register was incompatible with the right to respect for private life,[22] the same Prime Minister introduced a remedial order to provide some machinery for doing so,[23] while questioning the sanity of our ruling and suggesting that we had forced him to do this. We had done no such thing. It was always up to Government and Parliament to decide what, if anything, to do about a declaration of incompatibility.

By then criticism of both the Strasbourg and the UK courts had been mounting. Certain sections of the media were, of course, upset that the courts were developing a tort of misuse of private information. The courts were public authorities. They had to act compatibly with the Convention rights, even in cases between private persons. So they had to balance a newspaper's right to freedom of expression against an individual's right to respect for their private life. *The Daily Mirror* was not entitled to publish photographs and details of supermodel Naomi Campbell's treatment for drug addiction.[24] But the newspapers had got used to being able to publish all sorts of private information, whether about celebrities or about ordinary people, and did not like their activities being restrained. They began to refer to the 'hated Human Rights Act'.

They were not alone. In a lecture in 2011,[25] Michael Howard, the former leader of the Conservative party, attacked the Strasbourg court for descending into the minutiae of the Convention rights and denying member states their proper margin of appreciation to interpret and apply the Convention in the light of local conditions. But he also attacked the UK courts for going beyond the Strasbourg case law in interpreting the Convention. In another lecture that same month, Jonathan Sumption QC,[26] soon to be a Justice of the Supreme Court of the United Kingdom, attacked the Strasbourg court for its detailed development of the general principles in the Convention, for deciding not only whether the member states had proper institutional safeguards for those rights but also whether it agreed with the findings of those institutions, and for attempting to apply the rights in a uniform manner throughout the

---

[22] *R (F (A Child)) v. Secretary of State for the Home Department* [2010] UKSC 17, [2011] 1 AC 331.

[23] Sexual Offences Act 2003 (Remedial) Order (SI 2012 No. 1883).

[24] *Campbell v. MGN Ltd* [2004] UKHL 22, [2004] 2 AC 457.

[25] Kingsland Memorial Lecture 2011, *The Human Rights Act: Bastion of Freedom or Bane of Good Government?*, https://policyexchange.org.uk/publication/the-human-rights-act-bastion-of-freedom-or-bane-of-good-government

[26] FA Mann Lecture 2011, *Judicial and Political Decision-Making: The Uncertain Boundary*, https://doi.org/10.5235/108546811799320844

forty-seven member states, despite the fact that 'the consensus necessary to support it at this level of detail does not exist'. After retiring from the Court, he expanded upon those views in his 2019 Reith Lectures.[27]

Fixing the Human Rights Act became a recurring theme of Conservative party manifestoes, although the proposals were subtly different each time. The 2010 Manifesto announced that 'to protect our freedoms from state encroachment and encourage greater social responsibility, we will replace the Human Rights Act with a UK Bill of Rights'. But from 2010 until 2015 the Conservatives were in coalition with the Liberal Democrats, so this didn't happen. In 2015, they promised to 'scrap the Human Rights Act and curtail the role of the European Court of Human Rights so that foreign criminals can be more easily deported from Britain' – a more radical proposal but for a more limited purpose. Somewhat to their surprise, they won the election. Active steps were taken within the Ministry of Justice, particularly while Dominic Raab was Minister for Human Rights from 2015 to 2016. By 2017, however, not only had little progress been made on the project, but it had been overtaken by the all-consuming demands of Brexit. Thus, Theresa May's manifesto declared that

> we will not repeal or replace the Human Rights Act while the process of Brexit is under way but we will consider our human rights legal framework when the process of leaving the European Union concludes. We will remain signatories to the European Convention on Human Rights for the duration of the next Parliament.

Understandably, most of the 2019 Manifesto was devoted to getting Brexit done, but the promise was to 'update the Human Rights Act and administrative law to ensure that there is a proper balance between the rights of individuals, our vital national security and effective government'. The plan was to 'set up a Constitution, Democracy and Rights Commission' in their first year.

In fact, that didn't happen. Instead, the government first set up the Independent Review of Administrative Law under Lord Faulks.[28] This found very little wrong with administrative law, but recommended some small changes. The government then consulted on some much more

---

[27] *Law and the Decline of Politics*, BBC, published as *Trials of the State: Law and the Decline of Politics* (London, 2019). For my riposte, see 'Dame Frances Patterson Memorial Lecture 2019: Law and Politics – A Reply to Reith', *Judicial Review*, 24(3) (2019), 205–216.
[28] *The Independent Review of Administrative Law*, 2021 CP 407.

radical changes but retreated when these were widely condemned. The resulting Bill contained the small changes.[29] Then the government set up the Independent Human Rights Act Review under Sir Peter Gross.[30] Its remit was not to look at the particular Convention rights but at the relationships, between the UK courts and the Strasbourg court and between the various branches of government in the United Kingdom. It too concluded that nothing much was wrong. Meanwhile the House of Commons and House of Lords Joint Committee on Human Rights produced its own report on the subject.[31] This noted that the Human Rights Act had had a wide impact outside the courtroom, Whitehall and Westminster. The duty of public authorities to act compatibly with the Convention right had embedded human rights amongst public authorities and reduced the need for litigation to enforce people's rights. Far from curtailing the scope of the Act, where rights did need enforcement in the courts, this should be accessible to all. So among other things the Equality and Human Rights Commission should be given the same powers to enforce human rights as it has to enforce equality rights.

Then the government produced its own Consultation Paper, ignoring most of the careful work of the Joint Committee and the Independent Review and proposing to replace with Human Rights Act with a 'modern Bill of Rights'.[32] On the plus side, the government was still committed to remaining a party to the Convention, to retaining all the substantive rights protected under the Human Rights Act, and to fulfilling its international obligations. Two of these are vital. One is the obligation in article 13 to provide an effective remedy before a national authority for everyone whose rights and freedoms set forth in the Convention are violated. The other is to retain the right of individuals to apply to the European Court of Human Rights and to abide by any final decision of that Court. Many of those who responded to the government's consultation judged its proposals against those obligations and found them wanting. But the government went ahead and introduced the Bill of Rights Bill.

The Bill had its first reading in the House of Commons on 22 June 2022 but there was no enthusiasm for it after Dominic Raab resigned as Lord Chancellor in April 2023 and it was withdrawn on

---

[29] It would become the Judicial Review and Courts Act 2022.
[30] *The Independent Human Rights Act Review*, 2021 CP 586.
[31] 2021 HC 89, HL Paper 31.
[32] *Human Rights Act Reform: A Modern Bill of Rights*, 2021 CP 588.

23 June. But it is worth remembering its main features to give us some idea of the threats it posed.

First, it began with some political sloganising – unnecessary statements of the blindingly obvious designed to appeal to the most vocal critics of the Human Rights Act. Thus, 'it is the Supreme Court (and not the European Court of Human Rights) that determines the meaning and effect of Convention rights for the purpose of domestic law'. But this has always been the case. The Supreme Court, and indeed any court which finally decides a case concerning the Convention rights, already determines their meaning and effect in domestic law. Taking the case to Strasbourg is not an appeal from the decision of the domestic court. That still stands. Even if Strasbourg finds that the United Kingdom has violated the Convention rights, the interpretation arrived at by the UK court is still binding on the lower courts unless and until the higher court decides to change it. Equally obvious are the statements that judgments, decisions and interim measures of the European Court of Human Rights are not part of UK domestic law and do not affect the right of Parliament to legislate.

After that came a series of provisions designed to uncouple the United Kingdom's interpretation and application of the Convention rights from Strasbourg. The duty to take into account Strasbourg and other Council of Europe jurisprudence was to be repealed. The duty to read and give effect to legislation compatibly with the Convention rights was to be repealed. The courts were to be told they should pay particular attention to the text of the Convention and could look at the *travaux preparatoires* – a nudge towards American style originalism which Strasbourg rejected long ago. (A nice little early example is *Campbell and Cosans*,[33] where the United Kingdom argued that the *travaux preparatoires* indicated that 'philosophical' had been added to the 'religious' opinions of the parents to cater for agnostics – the Commission countered that 'philosophical' clearly had a wider meaning.) The courts could only develop the Convention rights further than Strasbourg if they had no reasonable doubt that that was what Strasbourg would do with the case. The Supreme Court predicted correctly in *Rabone*,[34] but could we have had no reasonable doubt of this? And what good would the – again unnecessary – power to have regard to the development under the

[33] (1980) 3 EHRR 531.
[34] *Rabone v. Pennine Care NHS Trust* [2012] UKSC 2, [2012] 2 AC 72; see *Reynolds v. United Kingdom* (2012) 55 EHRR 35.

common law of any right which is similar to the Convention right do if the common law had developed the right further than Strasbourg had done? Tellingly, the one exception to no expansion was freedom of speech.

The one new right was a completely empty right to trial by jury. More striking was the cutting down of the existing Convention rights. There were to be no new positive obligations – that is, a duty on a public authority to do something. Worse still, the courts would be given a discretion whether or not to apply even those positive obligations already established – they would have to consider the burden it placed on the public authority concerned. So the victims of the police failure to catch John Worboys, the black cab rapist, much earlier might be left without a remedy.[35] And people alleging breaches of their fundamental rights would have to get permission to bring a claim when people alleging breaches of their ordinary everyday rights do not.

All in all, therefore, the Bill was likely to mean that more claimants would be denied an effective remedy here for the breach of their Convention rights, more would have to go to Strasbourg to vindicate their rights, and the United Kingdom would lose more cases in Strasbourg than it had been doing since the Human Rights Act came into force.

So should we breathe a sigh of relief that the Bill has been abandoned? I think not.

Once again there were dire mutterings about withdrawing from the Convention altogether, both before and after the UK Supreme Court ruled unlawful the government's plan to send some of the people entering the United Kingdom without permission to Rwanda.[36] But perhaps more realistically, and more troublingly, the government has shown itself willing to procure legislation in this context which restricts both the obligations of ministers to act compatibly with the Convention rights and the right of individuals to bring human rights claims before the UK courts. This began with the Illegal Migration Act 2023 and has continued with the Safety of Rwanda (Asylum and Immigration) Bill, which was given its second reading in the House of Commons on 12 December 2023. The Home Secretary, James Cleverly, stated on the

---

[35] *Commissioner of Police for the Metropolis v. DSD* [2018] UKSC 11, [2019] AC 196.
[36] *R (AAA (Syria)) and others v. Secretary of State for the Home Department* [2023] UKSC 42.

face of the Bill[37] that he was 'unable to make a statement that, in my view, the provisions of [the Bill] are compatible with the Convention rights'. This is scarcely surprising, as the Bill disapplies the operative provisions[38] of the Human Rights Act.

To return to Conor Gearty, in 2012, he posited two scenarios: in one, a radical socialist government is elected which 'legislates for the confiscation of much private property, the nationalisation of some profitable industry, and a vast increase in the power of the bureaucratic state in the fields of planning and environmental regulation'; in the other, a right-wing nationalist government is elected, which 'goes after immigrants and asylum seekers in a dramatically aggressive way'.[39] Under the British model, the law would be able to do next to nothing in reply. But Gearty believed that 'the culture of human rights, rooted in legal practice but also in society's common sense of basic standards, serves to support the ethical status quo against such plunges into extremism'.[40]

So whose view of common sense is to prevail?

---

[37] As required by the HRA, s. 19.
[38] Clause 3 disapplies ss. 2, 3 and 6 to 9 in defined circumstances.
[39] Gearty, 'Spoils for Which Victor?', 227–228.
[40] Ibid., 228.

17

Courting the Past

Reconstructing Ireland's Lost Legal Records, circa 1300–1922

PETER CROOKS, TIMOTHY MURTAGH AND
CIARÁN WALLACE, WITH JOEL HERMAN

Lex est defuncta, quia judicis est manus uncta.
Propter unguentum, jus est in carcere tentum.[1]

'The law is deceased, because the judge's hands are greased' ran a Latin maxim inscribed on page 30 of the small vellum codex known as the 'Red Book of the Exchequer'.[2] The scribe may have been poking fun at the contemporary reputation of the judiciary, whose venality was imagined to have cast 'right in chains'. If so, it was an in-joke – a reflexive piece of office

The Virtual Record Treasury of Ireland is hosted at Trinity College Dublin and Science Foundation Ireland's ADAPT Centre. The research is funded by the Government of Ireland under Project Ireland 2040 through the Department of Tourism, Culture, Arts, Gaeltacht, Sport and Media. The first phase of the research (2016–18) was funded by the Irish Research Council, New Horizons Scheme. The following abbreviations appear in this chapter after the first occurrence: BL: British Library; NAI: National Archives, Ireland; NLI: National Library of Ireland; PROI: Public Record Office of Ireland; PRONI: Public Record Office of Northern Ireland; *Rep. DKPRI: Reports of the Deputy Keeper of the Public Records of Ireland*; TNA: The National Archives, UK; VRTI: Virtual Record Treasury of Ireland; Herbert Wood, *A Guide to the Records Deposited in the Public Record Office of Ireland* (Dublin, 1919).

Throughout the chapter, we use a 'PROI-ID' in parentheses to identify archival collections destroyed in the PROI in 1922. The archival descriptions associated with these PROI-IDs are accessible through VRTI (www.virtualtreasury.ie).

[1] J. F. Ferguson, 'A Calendar of the Contents of the Red Book of the Irish Exchequer', *Proceedings and Papers of the Kilkenny and South-East of Ireland Archaeological Society*, 3 (1854), 35–52. A table of contents of the Red Book was prepared by the PROI: *Twenty-Fourth Rep. DKPRI* (1892), 96–7

[2] P. Crooks, 'The Charter Reforged: The Red Book, Materiality and Ireland's Magna Carta', in P. Crooks and T. Mohr (eds.), *Law and the Idea of Liberty in Ireland: From Magna Carta to the Present* (Dublin, 2023), 40–63.

satire by a scribe from inside the court.[3] The 'Red Book' was, in a sense, the foundation stone of English administration and record-keeping in Ireland. From the Middle Ages onwards, the king's law officers in Ireland would kiss the codex when taking their oaths, rubbing away the manuscript over centuries of use. At the core of the Red Book were the thirteenth-century statutes of England, laws 'given' to Ireland by that great legislator, Edward I (1272–1307). Prefaced to the Edwardian statutes was a version of Magna Carta itself, improved for Irish circumstances by the substitution of 'Dublin' and 'Liffey' for 'London' and 'Thames'. How appropriate, then, that the 'Red Book' eventually found its way to a repository on the north bank of the Liffey, within the Four Courts complex, in the Public Record Office of Ireland (PROI) established in 1867. There it was destroyed, together with hundreds of thousands of legal records dating from the mid-thirteenth to the late nineteenth centuries, in the Civil War that commenced at that very location in June 1922.[4]

The Virtual Record Treasury of Ireland (VRTI) aims to reconstruct digitally, in so far as is possible, the collections destroyed in the explosion and fire which occurred at the PROI on 30 June 1922.[5] The task is daunting when one considers the scale of the losses. Although the PROI had only been in operation for fifty-five years by the time it was destroyed, it could credibly be described as one of the most impressive archives in Europe for its continuous run of seven centuries' worth of legal records. Indeed, it was the PROI's success in gathering together the country's records that was to make its eventual destruction all the more devastating. As Herbert Wood (1860–1955), the deputy keeper (that is, chief archivist) of the PROI in 1922, was to lament: 'the very centralization of the documents has proved their undoing, and at one blow the records of centuries have passed into oblivion'.[6] Furthermore, legal records predominated within the PROI's collections: understanding the nature of the accumulated records, their archival arrangement and their intended

---

[3] For contemporary (official) concerns about corruption, see E. Biggs and P. Dryburgh, 'The State of the Irish Exchequer, c. 1284', in 'Special Issue – The Fire of 1922', *Analecta Hibernica*, 53 (2023), 59–95.

[4] P. Crooks, E. Johnston and T. Murtagh, '"For Fear of Oblivion": Archival Fragility and Persistence from the Middle Ages to 1922 – and Beyond', *Analecta Hibernica*, 53 (2023), 1–14. More generally, see P. Connolly, 'The Destruction of the Public Record Office of Ireland in 1922: Disaster and Recovery', *Archivum*, 42 (1996), 135–46.

[5] P. Crooks, C. Wallace, with D. Brown and G. Munnelly, 'How to Reconstruct a Lost Archive in the Digital Age: The Virtual Record Treasury of Ireland, The Fire of 1922, and the Archival Loss and Recovery Model (ALARM)', *Archives et Bibliothèques de Belgique* (in press).

[6] H. Wood, 'The Destruction of the Public Records: The Loss to Irish History', *Studies: An Irish Quarterly Review*, 11:43 (1922), 364.

purpose reveals a great deal about the development of the Irish legal establishment over the centuries and the nature of English rule in Ireland. The first section of this chapter describes the legal setting, character and functions of the PROI in the half-century after its foundation.

The Red Book of the Exchequer was only one part of the collection lost to the flames in 1922. Yet its loss, and the loss of the wider archive, were to cast a shadow over subsequent Irish historiography, restricting and shaping the efforts of those studying the country's past, and particularly complicating the efforts of legal historians. The Red Book is a useful entry-point into the twin themes of the later sections of the chapter, which concern the PROI's legal collections from the Anglo-Norman enrolments of the thirteenth century to the era of agrarian agitation in the late nineteenth century. First, loss and reconstruction. Although it was a single codex, and unusual for the attention that it garnered in its life as a physical artefact, the Red Book lives on through the many sources that can be aggregated to reconstruct its contents.

Law is lived, not merely enacted and enforced. This is our second concern. We look beyond the formalities of court documents to the lived experience of the law in Ireland. Surviving salvaged and substitute records reveal not only the institutional development of the courts and parliament in Ireland, but also – read against the grain – the character of Ireland as a colonial society. In a similar vein, a discussion of the Chief Secretary's Office analyses the growing executive oversight of law enforcement in the eighteenth and nineteenth centuries, illustrating the often-fractious interface between the law and the 'common people'. Finally, an account of the series of uniquely Irish legal institutions (the late nineteenth-century land courts) examines the role of law in transforming Irish rural society in the decades leading up to independence.

The General Law Record Repository

When the PROI opened at the Four Courts in 1867, it found itself nestled within a community of legal neighbours. Located inside Gandon's handsome Four Courts building were the Courts of Chancery, Exchequer, Common Pleas and King's Bench. On the streets and quays nearby, firms of solicitors and law searchers plied their trade. A short walk to the north lay the legal district around the King's Inns, the hub of the Irish legal profession and 'the single greatest influence' on the area.[7]

---

[7] T. Murtagh, *Spectral Mansions: The Making of a Dublin Tenement, 1800–1914* (Dublin, 2023), 42–7.

The PROI was the outcome of decades of campaigning by lawyers and scholars anxious to rescue Ireland's archival records from their perilous conditions. Legal cases produce paper and precedent, which in turn require efficient record-keeping. In an era before professional archives were established, Irish legal and other records had ended up in an alarming variety of unsuitable repositories. Attics and cellars in decayed government offices or private homes left centuries of legal records vulnerable to vermin, weather, fire and theft. A century earlier, in 1756, the Irish House of Commons had granted £5,000 to build a record repository on the north bank of the River Liffey.[8] But the plans for a record office evolved into an ambitious wholesale redevelopment to create a combined repository and law courts.[9] However, as discussions progressed, the record repository was dropped. Ultimately, when the foundation stone was laid in 1776, Dublin newspapers described 'a Suite of Buildings containing, the public Law Offices, the Hall and Law Library, for the Use of the Society of the King's Inns'.[10] There was no mention of a repository for the legal records. Archival decay and appeals for action continued, and indeed were heightened, after the Act of Union of 1800.

In 1810, Bartholomew Thomas Duhigg, barrister and author of two histories of King's Inns,[11] wrote to Lord Manners, lord chancellor of Ireland, advocating for the better preservation of the legal records. 'The general voice of this island demands an arrangement, illustration and preservation of legal records', he wrote, 'and the liberal spirit of Great Britain echoes that call.'[12] Duhigg's concern was prompted in part by the recent visitation in 1806 of members of the English Record Commission

---

[8] *Journals of the House of Commons of the Kingdom of Ireland*, 21 vols. (Dublin), v, 390; E. McParland, 'The Early History of James Gandon's Four Courts', *The Burlington Magazine*, 122:932 (1980), 727–33, 728.

[9] McParland, 'Early History of James Gandon's Four Courts'.

[10] E.g. *Dublin Journal*, 24–26 October 1776.

[11] P. M. Geoghegan, 'Sutton, Thomas Manners (1756–1842), 1st Baron Manners and Lord Chancellor of Ireland', in *Dictionary of Irish Biography* (online, open access: hereafter *DIB*).

[12] B. T. Duhigg, *A Letter to the Right Hon. Lord Manners [etc.] on the Expediency of an Immediate and Separate Record Commission, to Investigate, Illustrate and Arrange the Records of Ireland* (Dublin, 1810), 5. See C. Kenny, 'Duhigg, Bartholomew (c. 1751–1851), Political Activist, Antiquarian and Barrister', *DIB*. Duhigg was among the first four sub-commissioners of the Irish Record Commission (1810–30). The manuscripts of that Commission were preserved in the PROI, and many are now extant as NAI, RC. See M. C. Griffith, 'The Irish Record Commission 1810–30', *Irish Historical Studies*, 7 (1950), 17–38. The Commission's MSS are listed in P. Crooks, Z. Reid, J. Baldwin, C. Fahy and B. Gurrin, 'The Salved Records of 1922', *Analecta Hibernica*, 53 (2023), 35–9.

to survey Irish repositories. At this he 'sounded an alarm at the recorded wound, given to Ireland by having its legal muniments guided under a commission, in which this island is not named . . . and from which . . . all Irishmen were excluded'.[13] Duhigg's letter, which combined catastrophism and common sense, was to become a familiar refrain in the decades after the Union. Lawyers and historians repeatedly demanded parity of esteem for the centuries-old accumulation of Irish legal records, evidence, they thought, of the dignity of the kingdom of Ireland and its ancient association with the kingdom of England. This evidence sat in a 'ruinous state' and in imminent danger of destruction: '[s]uch an awful event would involve unoffending posterity in irredeemable barbarism, as if they were slaves crouching under an hereditary yoke'.[14] Such was the fear in 1810.

Westminster passed a public record act for England and Wales in 1838,[15] leading to the creation of a purpose-built repository at Chancery Lane, London, thirteen years later in 1851.[16] Ireland had to wait until 1867 for similar legislation. In Dublin, however, a suitable record repository was immediately available.[17] In the absence of an Irish record office, the courts had decided to build their own 'law record repository'. Construction took place between 1864 and 1867 on land especially acquired under the Four Courts (Dublin) Extension Act of 1858.[18] This extension of the courts transformed the local streetscape, clearing away many narrow alleyways with their taverns and stable yards, and reinforcing the dominance of the legal profession in the district (Figure 17.1).

As the building was nearing completion, the *Dublin Builder* described 'the general Law Record Depository', built at a cost of £40,000, as 'by far the most important in point of size and cost, of a public nature, that has been erected in Dublin for some years'.[19] A year later, however, when parliament passed the Act establishing a state archive for Ireland, it was decided that the premises would serve both the legal profession and the general public administration. The preamble to the Public Records (Ireland) Act 1867 noted the 'large and commodious building . . . erected in the neighbourhood of the Four Courts in Dublin for the purpose of

---

[13] Duhigg, *Letter to the Right Hon. Lord Manners*, 9.
[14] Ibid., 13.
[15] An Act for Keeping Safely the Public Records 1838, 1 & 2 Vict., c. 94.
[15] J. D. Cantwell, *The Public Record Office, 1838–1958* (London, 1991), 136–7.
[17] Public Records (Ireland) Act 1867, 30 & 31 Vict., c. 70, preamble.
[18] Four Courts (Dublin) Extension Act 1858, 21 & 22 Vict., c. 84.
[19] *Dublin Builder*, 1 July 1866, 166.

Figure 17.1   Robert French, photograph of the exterior of the Public Record Office of Ireland, taken c.1867, shortly before the archive's opening.
(National Library of Ireland, L_IMP_0008).

serving as a Public Record Office'.[20] Section 3 defined public records as: 'all Rolls, Records, Writs, Books, Proceedings, Decrees, Bills, Warrants, Accounts, Papers, and Documents whatsoever, of a public Nature, belonging to Her Majesty, or now deposited in any of the Offices or Places of Custody herein-after mentioned'.[21] Section 4 listed the courts whose records came under the Act, beginning with: 'All the Records of the Court of Chancery ... All the Records of the Courts of Queen's Bench, Common Pleas, and Exchequer, Probate and Admiralty Courts, and of the former Court of Prerogative', along with 'Records and Documents of any Courts ... which shall have ceased to exist'.[22] Thus, as most public records were actually court records, it was a simple matter to expand the new building's purpose from a 'Law Record Repository' into a more general 'Public Record Office' for Ireland.

The PROI was a modern, purpose-built archive. Occupying two buildings faced in cut granite, the sixty-metre-long archive sat at the west side of the Four Courts complex. Nearer the river was the three-storey Record

---

[20] Public Records (Ireland) Act, 1867, preamble.
[21] Ibid., s. 3.
[22] Ibid., s. 4.

House where the deputy keeper and his staff worked. At the heart of the Record House was the Search Room, a double-height space lit by an ornate glazed ceiling. From the Search Room, fireproof doors led across a three-metre firebreak to the record repository, which was always known as the 'Record Treasury'. The firebreak was designed to protect the vulnerable documents from the risk of fire in the administration block, with its open coal fires and gas lighting. The Record Treasury rose six storeys over a stone basement. Above the lofty atrium, a glass roof stretched the length of the building; matching arcades of tall arched windows ran along on either side. Ample natural light, and modern heating through hot-water pipes, reduced the risk of fire; to minimise the use of combustible timber fittings, cast iron walkways, stairs and shelving were used throughout. Standing in the centre of this impressive space, one was surrounded by centuries of Irish law; over 60 per cent of the Treasury's 200 storage areas held legal records.[23]

The court records were vast in scale, varied in format, confused in provenance and, not infrequently, rotten.[24] Yet the staff acted rapidly to establish order from chaos – or, rather, to establish the conditions whereby order might be incrementally imposed. The records of the Court of Common Pleas (PROI CCP), for instance, occupied 258 'presses' (that is, wall cupboards typically with doors) in the main Four Courts building, prior to their transfer to the Record Treasury. The bulk of these were in a fire-proofed 'Record Room', but others were laid on open shelves in the eastern wing of the Four Courts. A further 160 'sacks' were accumulated in the vaults of the basement, 'crowded together without any reference to their order' and in some cases rotting from 'contact with the damp stone'. In August 1870, transfer of these records began with the sacks, which were carried across the yard of the Four Courts and placed on the as-yet unshelved bays within the Record Treasury on the third floor. There the sacks were opened and 'cleansed', the bundles of records within inspected, and a rudimentary catalogue was created.[25] The records included deeds dating from the seventeenth century, judgment books from 1661 to 1760, and the court rolls, which were intact from 1663 but which also included an earlier court roll from the

---

[23] 'State of Bays' reports in successive annual reports culminating in *Twenty-Sixth Rep. DKPRI* (1894), 70–1.

[24] Wood, *Guide*, 62–3.

[25] *Third Rep. DKPRI*, 'Appendix No. 5. Extract from Report of James Mills, Esq., on the Records removed from the Court of Common Pleas, 1870'.

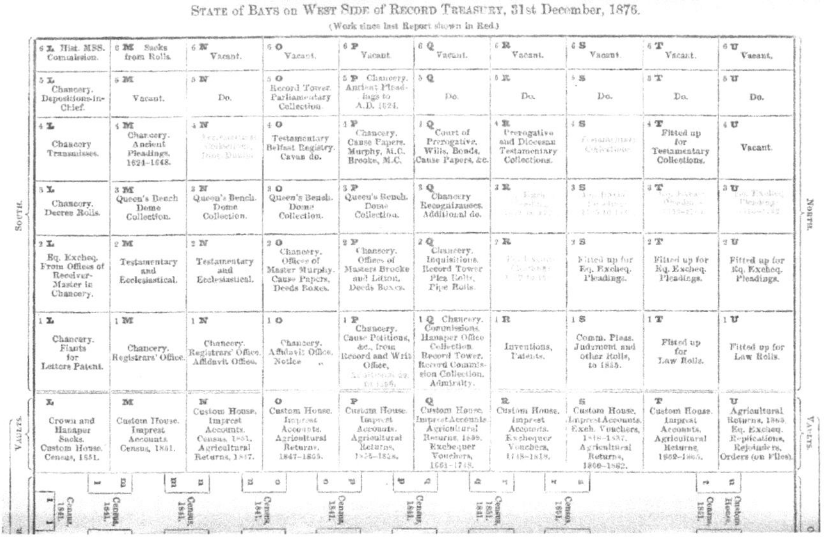

STATE of BAYS on WEST SIDE of RECORD TREASURY, 31st December, 1876.
(Work since last Report shown in Red.)

Figure 17.2 A schematic cross-section of the Record Treasury (East Side) from December 1876 showing sixty bays prepared for the receipt of court records. Approximately one-third of the bays are shown as 'Vacant'. The records of the Court of Common Pleas were, by 1876, sorted into six bays on the third floor (Bays 3-E to 3-K).

reign of Elizabeth I (specifically 1590–1591). During the first year of its existence, the staff of the PROI proved their worth, indexing 6,000 legal cases and cleaning, flattening and arranging a quarter of a million Chancery petitions[26] (Figure 17.2).

The new institution was placed under the overall authority of the master of the rolls, John Edward Walsh.[27] Walsh was, nominally, the keeper of the records, but a deputy keeper managed the daily operations of the archive. Among the names considered for the prestigious and lucrative post of deputy keeper were prominent scholars and antiquarians, but it was felt essential that the appointee should have a legal qualification. Samuel Ferguson QC (1810–1886) fitted the bill. A somewhat unspectacular barrister and a well-regarded poet,[28] he was

---

[26] *First Rep. DKRPI* (1869), 17.
[27] B. Hourican, 'Walsh, John Edward (1816–69), Judge and Writer', *DIB*.
[28] E. Patten, *Samuel Ferguson and the Culture of Nineteenth-Century Ireland* (Dublin, 2004).

also a renowned expert on ancient Irish texts.[29] Usefully, in the fraught atmosphere surrounding government appointments, Ferguson had no strong political affiliations. A surprising expertise in construction and metalwork proved a valuable asset. His knowledgeable response to structural issues which risked the Record Treasury's sixty-metre glass roof falling in, and his detailed designs for new shelving brackets, reflected Ferguson's lifelong interest in engineering, both large and small.[30]

Experience working with legal records was evidently viewed as a requirement for most senior staff appointments. The assistant deputy keeper was John James Digges La Touche (1838–1895), former chief clerk at the Rolls Office in the Four Courts, who would eventually succeed Ferguson in the top post This practice of maintaining legal expertise in the senior roles persisted. In 1899, the barrister Henry F. Berry (1847–1923) was appointed assistant deputy keeper.[31] The junior staff included clerks transferred from the Courts of Common Pleas and Chancery.[32] Expertise with legal records also made a difference for Richard Tucker, the first foreman of the PROI workmen. He insisted on, and received, higher wages to reflect his eighteen years working in the Rolls Office.[33]

The new Public Record Office had to find its place in the complex legal landscape of nineteenth-century Dublin. Operating under the authority of the master of the rolls helped to defend the archive against challenges from judges and the legal profession. In 1868, the master of the rolls saw off an attempt to make the PROI responsible for amending or updating entries in court records deposited with it, which would effectively mean creating new records. The master of the rolls insisted that each court appoint an officer to make such amendments, which would be recorded in a separate ledger.[34] This blurring of the distinction between the archival and record-creating roles arose again in 1870 when a Dublin solicitor insisted that Ferguson issue a certificate of vacate from the Court of Chancery for his client. The deputy keeper refused, and the master of the rolls referred the issue to the solicitor general and attorney general for

[29] G. Doyle, 'The Foundation and First Twenty Years of the Public Record Office of Ireland' (National University of Ireland, unpublished MA thesis, 1975), 209–11.
[30] Patten, *Samuel Ferguson*, 9; NAI, PRO/2/1/1, letters to Board of Works, 18 and 21 Jan. 1868.
[31] *Freeman's Journal*, 3 July 1899, 4.
[32] Doyle, 'Foundation and First Twenty Years', 245.
[33] NAI, PRO/2/2/1, 15.
[34] Doyle, 'Foundation and First Twenty Years', 292.

Ireland. To avoid litigation, they advised Ferguson to issue the vacate in this instance, but in future Chancery must appoint an officer to do so. This case was crucial in defining the PROI's purely archival role.[35] In 1871, Judge Robert R. Warren of the Court of Probate insisted on keeping all wills dated after 1821 indefinitely, for the convenience of the business of the court. However, a coordinated response by the master of the rolls and the crown law officers defused this threat to a core principle behind the whole archival enterprise.[36]

Because of their authenticated chain of provenance, records held in a state archive have evidentiary value. The 1867 Act required that: '[e]very copy of a record in the custody of the Master of the Rolls ... shall be received as evidence in any court'.[37] In consequence, much of the PROI's activity was producing certified transcripts of records for legal cases. The first fee for a certified copy was received on 26 February 1868, marking the start of the PROI's legal output. Fees were based on the age of the record, and consequently on the difficulty involved in deciphering and transcribing it. From February to December 1868, the clerks in the PROI transcribed almost 4,000 folios for legal clients.

A generation later, the passing of the Government of Ireland Act 1920 affected jurisdiction and raised a series of awkward questions about lines of responsibility. These were carefully itemised under the headings 'Difficulties' and 'Anomalies' by the then deputy keeper in a memorandum to the under-secretary for Ireland at Dublin Castle in February 1921.[38] Among the anomalies was the fact that the functions assigned to both the master of the rolls and the lord chancellor were stated in the Act to be assumed by the lord lieutenant. The lord lieutenant was previously the counter-signatory on orders for the removal (that is, the transfer to the PROI) of state papers from Dublin Castle. Would the lord lieutenant now both sign and countersign such orders? The new dispensation also meant the removal of the master of the rolls, an absence felt in

---

[35] Legal opinion of law officers of the Crown, Charles Robert Barry and Richard Dowse, 28 Oct. 1870, SPO Chief Crown Solicitor's Opinions, 1870/264, communicated by letter of the chief secretary to the master of the rolls. Doyle, 'Foundation and First Twenty Years', 295–6.

[36] Doyle, 'Foundation and First Twenty Years', 297–8.

[37] Public Records (Ireland) Act 1867, s. 10.

[38] NAI, PRO 2/1/83, M. J. McEnery to under-secretary, Dublin Castle, 28 Feb. 1921, printed with an introduction in C. Wallace, 'Queries, Difficulties, and Anomalies: A Memo on the Government of Ireland Act (1920) by Michael Joseph McEnery, Deputy Keeper of the Public Records', *Archivium Hibernicum*, 75 (2022), 143–61.

daily operations: the deputy keeper referred to his proximity, 'coming almost daily to the Four Courts', which made the master of the rolls 'very accessible for consultation ... on all matters connected with the records in which he took the deepest interest'.[39]

Ancient Rolls

While the bulk of the PRCI's legal archives dated from 1700 onwards, the staff of the PROI were, from the first, particularly attentive to their most ancient muniments. As Herbert Wood put it in 1912, when advertising the 'unexplored treasures' of the PROI: '[w]hat a mine of information is still lying buried in these old Rolls!'[40] Wood was specifically referring to the statute rolls which ran in a sequence of over 500 parchment rolls preserved with the records of the Court of Chancery from 1427 into the modern era (PROI C 1/111). The publication of these early statute rolls became one of the PROI's prestige projects. Henry F. Berry planned and edited the four massive volumes, totalling over 2,500 pages of text, translations and apparatus. The first instalment was not, in fact, based on an archival series in the PROI, where the surviving statute rolls only commenced in the fifteenth century.[41] Determined to begin at the beginning, Berry opened the first volume in the reign of King John (1199–1216), and for the rest of the period up to 1422, he created an archivally artificial, but historically invaluable, miscellany that drew on various repositories in Ireland and Britain, and in particular reproduced the statutes that had been transcribed into the Red Book of the Irish Exchequer. He titled this first volume *Statutes and Ordinances and Acts of the Parliament of Ireland, King John to Henry V*. It included what was to become the standard critical edition of the 'Statutes of Kilkenny, 1366' until the twenty-first century.[42]

Berry went on to prepare three more volumes of 'early statutes, Ireland', now taken directly from the PROI's own collection of original Irish statute rolls. Two, spanning the years 1427 to 1472, were published

---

[39] NAI, PRO 2/1/83, Letter Book (Out) 21 Feb. 1921–Mar. 1922, M. J. McEnery, deputy keeper, PROI to under-secretary, Dublin Castle, 28 Feb. 1921.

[40] 'Unexplored Irish Treasures', extant in RIA, 23 M 75 (Berry–Twiss Papers).

[41] Wood, *Guide*, 17.

[42] *Statutes and Ordinances and Acts of the Parliament of Ireland, King John to Henry V*, ed. H. F. Berry (Dublin, 1907).

before 1922.[43] The First World War delayed progress on the fourth volume, which was intended to cover the later reign of Edward IV from after the 'readeption' of Henry VI in 1470, and included statute rolls from 1473 to 1481.[44] This volume finally appeared just as the Second World War commenced in 1939. By this time, not only had the original editor, Berry, died (in 1923), but almost the entire sequence of statute rolls from the fifteenth century to the Act of Union had been consumed in the flames of 1922. The fourth volume consequently gained a new editor in James F. Morrissey (died 1952), assistant deputy keeper of the PROI. Morrissey had performed heroically after succeeding Herbert Wood to the role, though not initially to the rank, of deputy keeper of the PROI in 1923.[45] Among many other pressing duties, and with only a skeleton administrative staff, Morrissey rescued the 'early statutes' project by drawing together Berry's notes and translations made before 1922, as well as transcriptions of the statute rolls by the nineteenth-century Irish Record Commission.[46] The translations and indexing were carried out afresh under Morrissey's supervision by Dr Charles J. MacGarry, who died in January 1936 before the volume appeared in print. The project was struck by calamity for a fourth time when the printing works – Browne and Nolan's of Fenian Street, Dublin – was completely destroyed by fire on 16 August 1935.[47] The type of the text and MacGarry's translation were lost, but duplicate page proofs were intact in the PROI. These were photographed and reproduced by photo-lithography, but another five years passed before the volume appeared in print.[48]

---

[43] *Statute Rolls of the . . . reign of King Henry the Sixth* (Dublin, 1910); *Statute rolls of the . . . first to the twelfth years of the reign of King Edward the fourth* (Dublin, 1914).

[44] *Statute Rolls of the . . . twelfth and thirteenth to the twenty-first and twenty-second years of the reign of King Edward the fourth* (Dublin, 1939).

[45] D. Cregan, 'James F. Morrissey', *Analecta Hibernica*, 20 (1958), xv–xvi. Morrissey remained 'assistant deputy keeper', and the full role of 'deputy keeper' was left unfilled in 1938. See also G. O'Brien, *Irish Governments and the Guardianship of Historical Records, 1922–72* (Dublin, 2004), 22–40. Morrissey was also a member of the first Irish Manuscripts Commission (1928): M. Kennedy and D. McMahon, *Reconstructing Ireland's Past: A History of the Irish Manuscripts Commission* (Dublin, 2009), 15.

[46] An important recent addition to the analytical literature on the statute rolls is S. Booker, 'Widowhood and Attainder in Medieval Ireland', in T. Phipps and D. Youngs (eds.), *Litigating Women: Gender and Justice in Europe, c. 1300–c. 1800* (Abingdon, 2022), chapter 5, especially the discussion of parliamentary petitions at 83–5.

[47] '£180,000 fire damage: destruction of printing works', *Irish Times*, 17 August 1935.

[48] *Statute Rolls of the Parliament of Ireland, twelfth and thirteenth to the twenty-first and twenty-second years of the reign of King Edward the fourth*, ed. J. F. Morrissey (Dublin, 1939), lxxv–lxxvii. The progress of MacGarry's fresh translation work is reported by

Morrissey had been active after 1922 in organising the salvage operation at the Four Courts.[49] The sole survivor of 1922 among the statutes was the roll for the 'reformation parliament' of 29 Henry VIII (1536–1537), which happened to be in use in the public Search Room. Protected in the strong room adjacent to the public reading room of the PROI, the parchment roll survived the cataclysm.[50] The entire corpus of Chancery records from the patent and close rolls, as well as tens of thousands of 'rotulets' of medieval Exchequer rolls were destroyed.[51] The early plea rolls were luckier. Several were blasted out of the Treasury building during the conflagration. The parchment withstood the weather to be retrieved from the rubble in autumn 1922, and stored for posterity.[52] These plea rolls (PROI PR) were the survivors from a series highly prized by PROI staff as being among their earliest, and so greatest, historical treasures.

In their veneration for 'ancient rolls' – 'ancient' being a loose descriptor for 'medieval' – the PROI staff shared the spirit of their age.[53] The value of the early enrolments was well understood at the time, even though the academic study of history was a fledgling profession. In 1865, Thomas Duffus Hardy (1804–1878) and J. S. Brewer (1809–1879), who inspected Ireland's public records, wrote a long encomium to their inestimable value and importance in throwing light on

---

Morrissey in *Fifty-Seventh Rep. DKPRI* (1936), item 101, 55. We are grateful to Damian C. MacGarry, grandson of Charles J. MacGarry, for information on his grandfather's career.

[49] Z. Reid, J. Baldwin, P. Crooks and D. Brown, 'Retrieved from the Rubble: Reconstructing Ireland's lost Archive', in P. Murray, L. Humenuck, W. Bennett and L. Moon-Schott (eds.), *Mod Cons: Modern Conservation, Modern Conveniences, Modern Constraints [ICON Book & Paper Group Third Triennial Conference, 2021]* (London, 2022), 46–53.

[50] P. Connolly (ed.), *Statute Rolls of the Irish Parliament, Richard III–Henry VIII* (Dublin, 2002). The 'substitute material' underlying this volume is drawn from NAI, RC/13 (Irish Record Commission transcriptions of statute rolls), especially RC/13/8 and RC/13/9, as well as the salved statute roll (NAI, CH/1/1).

[51] P. Crooks, 'Reconstructing the Past: The Case of the Medieval Irish Chancery Rolls', in F. M. Larkin and N. M. Dawson (eds.), *Lawyers, the Law and History: Irish Legal History Society Discourses and Other Papers, 2006-2011* (Dublin, 2013), 281–309; R. Frame, 'Rediscovering Medieval Ireland: Irish Chancery Rolls and the Historian', in R. Frame (ed.), *Plantagenet Ireland* (Dublin, 2022), chapter 9.

[52] See 'Part 1 – Salved Records Listed before 2017', P. Crooks et al., 'The Salved Records of 1922', in 'Special Issue – The Fire of 1922', *Analecta Hibernica*, 53 (2023), 15–58, 33–4.

[53] For the phrase 'ancient rolls', see Wood, *Guide*, 59; 'The Irish Justiciary Rolls', *Irish Times*, 2 Nov. 1906. For a spirit of 'medievalism' among the new archivists of this period, see P. Crooks, 'Rescue the Records, Revisited', *Irish Archives: Journal of the Irish Society for Archives* (50th Anniversary Issue), 27 (2022), 26–36.

the social condition of Ireland from the earliest period since its conquest by England, the mode in which it was governed, and the various efforts made at successive intervals by its English rulers to awe or entice it into submission ... such documents cannot be regarded with indifference; without them the true history of Ireland never can be written; with the aid of them it has been reserved for such future historians to give the world a narrative of events surpassed by none in tragic interest or political significance ... Now, with the fresh aids afforded by the Government, and the access given by Calendars and Catalogues to the public muniments of the country, there is reason to hope that the future efforts of Irish scholars will be as much distinguished in the successful cultivation of this as it has been in other branches of their literature. On this point, as it seems to us, public opinion is unanimous.[54]

The earliest rolls emanating from the court of the justiciar – that is, the king's chief governor in Ireland – survived from the late thirteenth century.[55] By this time, the chief governor was already calling upon the experience and expertise of professional lawyers – those who would come to constitute a court or 'bench' of the justiciar, dispensing royal justice in Ireland on the king's behalf.[56] The plea rolls, typically rolls of parchment stitched at the head, recorded the cases heard before that court. These records were stored in Bermingham's Tower in Dublin Castle, where, in the early eighteenth century, they were kept in wooden presses. This did not protect them from the rain coming in through the ruined roof, or the risk from the fires in the kitchen located in the base of the tower. The Bermingham Tower was demolished in 1775, when the ancient records were placed in sacks and stored in Battleaxe Hall.[57] They came under the remit of the Irish Record Commission in 1810, and were transferred again into the Record Tower of Dublin Castle in 1815, which was the Commission's base of operations (Figure 17.3).

---

[54] NLI, MS 11219.

[55] The surviving evidence is listed in G. J. Hand, *English Law in Ireland, 1294–1324* (Cambridge, 1967), 219–50.

[56] See ibid., chapter 3; P. Brand, 'The Birth and Early Development of a Colonial Judiciary: The Judges of the Lordship of Ireland, 1210–1307', in W. N. Osborough (ed.), *Explorations in Law and History: Irish Legal History Society Discourses, 1988–1994* (Dublin, 1995), 1–48; P. Connolly, 'The Medieval Irish Plea Rolls – An Introduction', *Journal of the Irish Society for Archives*, 2:1 (1995), 3–12; P. Connolly, 'Pleas Held before the Chief Governors of Ireland, 1308–76', *Irish Jurist*, 18 (1983), 101–31.

[57] Wood, *Guide*, 59; C. Manning, '"But You Are the First to Build a Tower": The Bermingham Tower, Dublin Castle', *Ulster Journal of Archaeology*, 3rd series, 74 (2017–18), 145–54.

SOUTH VIEW OF THE RECORD TOWER,
IN THE
LOWER YARD OF THE CASTLE OF DUBLIN.

Figure 17.3 'South View of the Record Tower in the Lower Yard of Dublin Castle', *Reports from the Commissioners appointed by his Majesty to execute the measures recommended in an address of the House of Commons respecting the Public Records of Ireland,* Second Report (1819), 478.

The plea roll collection comprising more than 600 rolls was moved into the PROI in 1869.[58]

In the 1890s, PROI staff inspected their holdings and determined that earlier inventories of the plea rolls prepared by the Irish Record Commission in 1819 were confused and, at 'closer acquaintance', their calendars were adjudged to be 'unquestionably valuable for reference, yet very incomplete and unsuitable in form for publication'.[59] Led by James Mills (later deputy keeper of the PROI), a completely new catalogue and concordance was prepared and published in the mid-1890s.[60] From 1900, work began on a new calendar, to commence in the later reign of Edward I (1295–1307), which prioritised for publication the rolls of sessions held before the justiciar over common bench rolls. Two volumes of these 'justiciary rolls' appeared under Mills' editorship in 1905 and 1914.[61] Mills retired in May 1914 and died in September the same year, just as war was breaking out in Europe. Calendaring progressed slowly under Herbert Wood, author of the famous *Guide to the Records* in the PROI, who, together with his colleague, Albert Langham, had reached the year 1318 by the time of the fire. Their work remained unpublished in 1922, when the fire destroyed almost the entire corpus of plea rolls.

Fortunately, the handwritten calendar by Wood and Langham survived, presumably because it was in the Record House, where the administrative offices were located, rather than in the Record Treasury. A first portion of their work, covering 1307–1314, was revised for publication three decades later by Margaret C. Griffith (1911–2001), deputy keeper of the records, now acting under the authority of the Irish Minister for Justice. But seventy years on, the remaining manuscript calendar pages (1314–1318) have never been prepared for publication, and even more remarkably an intact plea roll (NAI, KB/1/1) remains unedited and little known. Given the intensity with which the published justiciary rolls have been worked over by generations of historians, the absence of accessible editions of the remaining plea roll material – whether salvaged, calendared, abstracted or stolen – is clearly an urgent priority.

---

[58] Wood, *Guide*, 59.

[59] *Thirty-Second Rep. DKPRI*, 25. The Irish Record Commission plan for abstracting the Plea Rolls appears in NAI, RC 7/1, accessible through VRTI (https://virtualtreasury.ie/item/NAI-RC-7-1-1).

[60] *Twenty-Sixth Rep. DKPRI*, appendix III, 'Early Rolls', 53–68; *Twenty-Eighth Rep. DKPRI*, appendix 1, 'Early Rolls of Judicial Proceedings', 39–56.

[61] *Calendar of the Justiciary Rolls of Ireland*, ed. James Mills et al., 3 vols. (Dublin, 1905–56).

What is the historical significance of this surviving evidence? The value lies not merely in the detail furnished on the legal and institutional transformation of Ireland a century after the conquest begun under Henry II (1154–1189). The plea rolls have proved to be sources for social history of the first importance, especially in the complex multi-ethnic society of conquered Ireland. In the view of Jocelyn Otway-Ruthven (died 1989), who was not an historian given to flights of fancy, 'they are more fascinating than any historical novel, giving us a most vivid picture of a society in which every man went armed, so that a pleasant evening in a tavern only too often ended in homicide'.[62] An example presents itself from one of the few intact, unpublished, plea rolls pulled from the rubble at the Four Courts (NAI, KB/1/1). The case, heard in County Kildare in 1313, arose from a quarrel over impounded livestock, which escalated into a brutal conflict between the family of Simon Clement and Robert Levetrot, the servant of William Donheved.[63] Following a dispute over a pledge for the beasts' release, Simon and his kin accosted Levetrot. William tried to mediate by inviting Simon for a drink. This was rebuffed, escalating tensions. The scuffle led to bloodshed and culminated in the killing of an unnamed Irishman associated with William, whose death required compensation:

> Simon gave him the lie and they began using abusive language to each other and came up close to each other so that their faces were almost touching and William pushed Simon away and hit him with his fist above the eyebrow; and one of those who had come with Simon hit William with an axe; and one of those who was with William hit Simon on the head, so that William and Simon both fell down; and in the fight an Irishman belonging to William, who had come to rescue his master, was killed, for whom William recovered compensation in the king's court. Adam de la Bere, being maimed, fled to William's house, pursued by Robert Clement with an axe and, when Adam tried to get in, a boy passed him out a lance; he turned back and struck Robert on the head, so that he fell to the ground. Robert at once got up and struck Adam and broke his arm.

Detail of this kind sheds light on the dynamics of a medieval community where ingrained cultures of honour and retribution – rancour and reconciliation – characterised interpersonal relations, albeit within the overarching structures of the common law.[64]

---

[62] A. J. Otway-Ruthven, 'Review of *Calendar of the Justiciary Rolls, Ireland, 1308–1314*', *Irish Historical Studies*, 11:41 (1958), 50–2.

[63] NAI, KB/1/1, m. 67d (pleas at Castledermot, Co. Kildare, 21 May 1313).

[64] Cf. P. R. Hyams, *Rancor and Reconciliation in Medieval England* (Ithaca, NY, 2003).

Another case from the same roll, heard at Cashel in October 1312, concerns a woman named Alice Prout.[65] Alice brought a possessory assize of *mort d'ancestor* (concerning her right to inheritance) before the chief governor, Edmund Butler, then hearing pleas at Cashel, County Tipperary. She claimed as heiress of her brother Adam that she should be permitted to inherit his lands. The weakness in her case was, however, that Adam was unavailable to present evidence in court, either in person or from beyond the grave. He was no longer on the island of Ireland. In his absence, his lands had been occupied by another man named Edmund Umfrey. In court, Edmund countered Alice's claim to the land by pointing to the fact that Alice could not prove that her brother was dead. Adam had left Ireland to go on pilgrimage. He intended to travel to Santiago de Compostela, and thence perhaps to Rome. He never returned alive, but nor was there proof that he was dead. Alice could not deny this. The court decided against Alice. Not only did she lose her case, she also suffered a financial penalty for making a false claim. Only her poverty exempted her from paying the fine.

The case of Alice Prout is important in its own right, and as a window into a lost world shaped by 'pragmatic literacy' and the growth of legal consciousness among wider segments of society.[66] It reveals an Ireland transformed across the previous century, since the English conquest introduced in its wake the common law.[67] Tipperary had become a shire, one of thirteen counties created in Ireland after the invasion as a means of exerting English royal government at local level.[68] We see an Ireland interconnected with Christendom and its well-trodden pilgrimage routes to Spain and Italy.[69] And we see a legal culture in which female inheritance is possible and access to the court system is permitted, albeit with constraints and within a decidedly patriarchal social context.[70] As Joanna

[65] NAI, KB/1/1, m. 4, pleas at Cashel, Co. Tipperary, 30 Sept. 1312.
[66] For these concepts, see R. Britnell (ed.), *Pragmatic Literacy, East and West, 1200–1330* (Woodbridge, 1997); A. Musson, *Medieval Law in Context: The Growth of Legal Consciousness from Magna Carta to the Peasants' Revolt* (Manchester, 2001).
[67] See, most recently, R. Frame, 'Ireland within the Plantagenet Orbit', in R. Frame (ed.), *Plantagenet Ireland* (Dublin, 2022), chapter 1.
[68] A. Empey, 'Conquest and Common Law', chapter 2 in P. Crooks and T. Mohr (eds.), *Law and the Idea of Liberty in Ireland: From Magna Carta to the Present* (Dublin, 2023); C. Veach, 'Conquest and Conquerors', in B. Smith (ed.), *Cambridge History of Ireland I: 600–1550* (Cambridge, 2018), especially 179–81.
[69] See B. Cunningham, *Medieval Irish Pilgrims to Santiago de Compostela* (Dublin, 2019).
[70] S. Booker, 'The Challenge of Writing Histories of "Women": The Case of Women and the Law in Late Medieval Ireland', *Irish Historical Studies*, 46 (2022), 224–43.

MacGugan's illuminating recent study of social memory and reputation has demonstrated, legal records are invaluable for reconstructing mentalities within elements of society normally beyond the scope of medieval evidence.[71]

The 'Nerve Centre' of Government

Writing in the aftermath of the fire, the Irish legal historian F. Elrington Ball (son of a lord chancellor of Ireland) wistfully recalled the great resources he had found in the PROI: 'of its contents use was especially made of, besides the plea rolls, the prerogative and consistorial wills and grants, the memoranda and summonister rolls, the exchequer inquisitions, the assize warrants'. However, he also highlighted the legal significance of records produced by the Chief Secretary's Office (CSO), listing 'the departmental, civil, and country correspondence' that stemmed from that office.[72] While the CSO records were comparatively recent in origin (the earliest dated from the late seventeenth century), they nonetheless represented a significant portion of the PROI's holdings. Wood's *Guide* lists 202 separate CSO archival series, several of impressive size and complexity, comprising many sub-series. In scale, this rivalled even some of the older categories of records held by the archive, such as courts with origins in the medieval period.[73] The scale should not be surprising. The CSO has been described as 'the nerve centre' of the Irish government, and as such it played a pivotal role in overseeing government operations, influencing legislation and shaping the country's legal framework until its dissolution in 1924.[74] Prior to this, the chief secretary acted as the head of the lord lieutenant's secretariat, but from the mid-eighteenth century the CSO emerged as a distinct entity charged with supervising the various departments of the executive government in Ireland.

The CSO was a non-judicial entity, yet it was one of crucial legal importance. The legal dimensions to its operational work ran along a number of lines. It played a significant role in the shaping of Irish legislation, with 'parliamentary management' forming a major part of

[71] J. MacGugan, *Social Memory, Reputation and the Politics of Death in the Medieval Irish Lordship* (Dublin, 2023).

[72] F. E. Ball, *The Judges in Ireland, 1221–1921* (London, 1926), xxi.

[73] Wood, *Guide*, 204–5.

[74] R. B. McDowell, 'The Irish Executive in the Nineteenth Century', *Irish Historical Studies*, 9 (1955), 265; T. Bartlett (ed.), *Macartney in Ireland, 1768–72* (Belfast, 1979), xiii–xiv.

the responsibilities of incumbent chief secretaries. During the eighteenth century, members of the executive in Dublin Castle (including the lord lieutenant and chief secretary) were not appointed by the Irish parliament, but instead reported to, and received their instructions from, the British Cabinet. Yet at the same time, the lord lieutenant was tasked with ensuring the passage of desired legislation through the Irish parliament in Dublin. This task became more hands-on during the tenure of Lord Lieutenant George Townshend, viceroy from 1767 to 1772 and the first viceroy to take up a permanent residence in Ireland.[75] Townshend's viceroyalty transformed the role of the chief secretary, becoming the primary manager of government business within the parliament, directing affairs from a seat within the Irish House of Commons.[76] Instead of relying on local powerbrokers to manage the business on behalf of the administration (an arrangement that had always had mixed results), the chief secretary now ensured that the government's legislative programme would be followed more closely.[77]

The fraught constitutional relationship between Ireland and Britain in the eighteenth century made this a complicated job, and the passage of legislation into law a confusing process. This resulted in the production of a wide array of legal documents alongside other local records such as parliamentary returns, appeals, precedents, law papers and proclamations.[78] After the Act of Union transformed this relationship by abolishing the Irish parliament, these and other records were carried by cart to a dilapidated private house on nearby Anglesea Street, before finding a dedicated space in the Dublin Castle complex. It was from this Parliamentary Record Office that they were moved to their final destination in the Four Courts (PROI PARL), where many of them would be destroyed in 1922.[79]

---

[75] M. J. Powell, 'Reassessing Townshend's Irish Viceroyalty, 1767–1772: The Caldwell–Shelburne Correspondence in the John Rylands Library, Manchester', *Bulletin of the John Rylands Library*, 89 (2013), 155–76.

[76] For the Irish parliament, see D. W. Hayton, *The Irish Parliament in the Eighteenth Century: The Long Apprenticeship* (Edinburgh, 2001); E. M. Johnston-Liik, *History of the Irish Parliament, 1692–1800*, 6 vols. (Belfast, 2002). For Townshend's reform project, see M. J. Powell, 'The Reform of the Undertaker System: Anglo-Irish Politics, 1750–67', *Irish Historical Studies*, 31 (1998), 19–36.

[77] Powell, 'Reassessing Townshend's Irish Viceroyalty', 157.

[78] J. Kelly, *Poynings' Law and the Making of Law in Ireland, 1660–1800* (Dublin, 2007).

[79] *Reports of the Commissioners Appointed by His Majesty to Execute the Measures Recommended in an Address of the House of Commons Respecting the Public Records of Ireland*, Second Annual Report, HC 1819 (545) xx, 551.

One of the most fruitful sources for reconstructing the legislative activity of the Irish parliament – namely, the bills that would ultimately become law – are the records of the English Privy Council.[80] Earlier legal precedent, including Poynings' Law and a later declaratory act, required that drafts of these bills be sent to the Privy Council in England for approval or amendment before being returned to be accepted or rejected by the Irish parliament.[81] As a result, these records reveal when bills arrived, if and how they were amended, and when they were approved by the English Privy Council before being returned to Ireland.[82] Some parliamentary returns were salvaged in 1922, but many more were lost, including most relating to the religious census of 1766.[83] The *Journal of the House of Commons*, which fortunately was printed, serves as a useful substitute for destroyed parliamentary materials, providing a formal account of the proceedings of parliament.[84] However, the *Journal* leaves out the debates through which laws were crafted and approved. Sources such as the 'Cavendish Transcripts' in the Library of Congress, the *Parliamentary Register* and reports carried by contemporary newspapers can be used to rebuild these debates.[85] The 'Cavendish Transcripts', which run through the years of the American War of Independence and to the outset of the French Revolution, are especially valuable in this regard. These transcriptions of shorthand notes, taken from the floor of the Irish House of Commons, represent the sole surviving 'record' of the speeches of 'Grattan's Parliament', giving us a window into the law-making process itself.[86]

---

[80]   For example, see the 'Irish Legislation Project' (www.qub.ac.uk/ild/), which reconstructed and digitised the legislation of the Irish parliament under the direction of David Hayton and James Kelly.

[81]   J. L. McCracken, *The Irish Parliament in the Eighteenth Century* (Dundalk, 1971), 13–23.

[82]   TNA, PC 2 (Privy Council: Register).

[83]   For a painstaking reconstruction of House of Lords returns for the religious census of 1766 (PROI PARL 88/30/5), see VRTI Gold Seam, '1766 Religious Census' (https://virtualtreasury.ie/gold-seams/1766-religious-census).

[84]   *Journals of the House of Commons of the Kingdom of Ireland*, 19 vols. (Dublin, 1796–1800). See also *Journals of the House of Lords*, 8 vols. (1779–1800).

[85]   Ireland: Parliament, House of Commons Debates, MSS 27292, Library of Congress; *Parliamentary Register, or History of the Proceedings and Debates of the House of Commons of Ireland*, 17 vols. (Dublin, 1784–1801). For an example of how this can be done, see J. Kelly (ed.), *Proceedings of the Irish House of Lords, 1771–1800*, 3 vols. (Dublin, 2008), accessible on VRTI (https://virtualtreasury.ie/item/IMC-2008-Lords).

[86]   J. Kelly, 'Review Article: Recording the Irish Parliament', *Eighteenth-Century Ireland*, 15 (2000), 164. Several volumes of the Cavendish debates are accessible on VRTI (https://virtualtreasury.ie/item/LOC-MS-27292)

While the archives of the Parliamentary Record Office were among the collections destroyed in 1922, it is clear that several of the larger CSO series also contained an abundance of material relating to parliamentary matters. For instance, 'Departmental Correspondence (British), 1683–1759' (PROI CSO 1/30), included letters received from lords lieutenant and their secretaries when in England, and from other departments in England, about civil and military business.[87] At the time of their transfer to the PROI, Sir John Bernard Burke (1814–1892), keeper of the state papers in Dublin Castle, made note of the significance of the CSO archives. Burke described how 'many of these letters, though written on public affairs, have the character of private correspondence, for they deal fully as much with the ordinary circumstances of the day as with public business'.[88] A later guide to the PROI would similarly describe how, 'in order to possess the clue to the government of the country', this series 'possesses high value', containing letters from all of the major British parliamentary figures of the day which, although they 'discuss public matters, still there are in them human touches'.[89]

After the Act of Union (1800), while all major decisions on Irish legislation were now taken in London, the administrative machine in Dublin Castle nonetheless remained in place. During the nineteenth century, the chief secretary, increasingly a cabinet-level appointment, spent the majority of his time in London, defending the government's Irish policies in Westminster. However, when parliament was not in session, the chief secretary was kept busy in Ireland, assembling information that would allow the drafting of new legislation, or answering queries from London. Once again, the records destroyed in 1922 included a crucial series that would have illuminated the mechanics of government between Dublin and London in the early nineteenth century. The vast series of *Official Papers, 1760–1830* (PROI CSO 1/31) included 'letters to the Irish Government from Public Departments or officials in England and Ireland, and papers connected therewith'.[90] This series was classified into sub-headings arranged by subject, including a number of sub-series

---

[87] Wood, *Guide*, 209.
[88] PROI, DKPRI 3/3, 'Appendix 1. To the Right Honorable the Master of the Rolls – The Third Report of Sir John Bernard Burke, C.B., Ulster, Keeper of the State Papers in the Record Tower, Dublin Castle, dated 1st February, 1871', accessed on VRTI.
[89] H. Murray, *A Short Guide to the Principal Classes of Documents Preserved in the Public Record Office, Dublin* (London, 1919), 29–30.
[90] Wood, *Guide*, 209.

with obvious interest to legal scholars, such as 'Courts of Law & Equity'[91] and 'Crown Solicitors'.[92] However, other series undoubtedly held material which shed light on the nature of Irish legal matters, such as the voluminous correspondence between the CSO and the Home Office.[93]

The lord lieutenant, and by extension the CSO, had the determining role in appointments to, and promotion within, the Irish bench. At the time of the Union in 1801, there were sixteen judges on the bench of the six superior courts in Ireland. With few exceptions, all were appointed by the crown and held office during good behaviour; they could only be removed by the crown or by an address of both houses of parliament.[94] As a result, judicial appointments and promotions were a subject of considerable discussion within Dublin Castle. While much of the internal correspondence of the CSO has been destroyed, the letters it sent to London, preserved in the archives of the Home Office, reveal a careful consideration of the make-up of the Irish judiciary.[95] Legal experience (particularly Irish legal experience) was obviously a criterion for appointment to the bench, but there was a clear link between political activity and legal promotion. In the years between 1801 and 1877, over half of those appointed to the bench in the Four Courts had sat in the British (or, before 1800, Irish) House of Commons. Even more remarkable is that nearly three-quarters of these appointees had been law officers of the crown.[96]

The lord lieutenant and chief secretary were regularly advised by – and, indeed, had a role in appointing – the crown law officers for Ireland. The Irish attorney general and solicitor general, just like their English counterparts, had the core function of advising the administration of the day on legal matters, making sure the lord lieutenant and the chief

---

[91] PROI, CSO 1/31/94, 'Official Papers, 1760–1831; Courts of Law & Equity; 1821–1831; Carton 302', accessed on VRTI.

[92] PROI, CSO 1/31/95, 'Official Papers, 1760–1831; Crown Solicitors; 1799–1831; Carton 307', accessed on VRTI.

[93] PROI, CSO 1/31/130–51.

[94] The exceptions were the judge of the prerogative court who was appointed by the Archbishop of Armagh, and the lord chancellor of Ireland who could be removed by different means. By the 1840s, the lord chancellor was usually selected by the Irish Bar. R. B. McDowell, 'The Irish Courts of Law, 1801–1914', *Irish Historical Studies*, 10:40 (1957), 366.

[95] Examples of Dublin Castle's recommendations concerning appointment of judges can be found in TNA, HO 100/37/79, 'Westmoreland to Dundas' (1792); TNA, HO 100/107/209, 'Hardwicke to Pelham' (1801), all accessed on VRTI.

[96] R. B. McDowell, *The Irish Administration, 1801–1914* (London, 1964), 107.

secretary acted legally. The CSO frequently received requests for legal advice from local magistrates, which they in turn referred to the solicitor or attorney general. The office of king's serjeant, almost always filled by members of the Irish Privy Council, was another key office in the extension and maintenance of royal authority in Ireland. By the beginning of the nineteenth century, there was a 'prime serjeant', as well as a second and third serjeant, although the importance of these roles had declined relative to those of attorney and solicitor general.[97] Together, these officials formed the cornerstone of Ireland's legal administration: their opinions on legislative matters were valued, and they often participated in discussions surrounding bills and committee work. The advice of the attorney and solicitor general can frequently be found in surviving private papers of chief secretaries, as well as in the regular exchanges between Dublin Castle and the government in London.[98] The Irish law officers were also critical to one of the key developments of the CSO in the nineteenth century: its growing supervision of the local administration of justice.

Given the significance of the CSO for Irish legal history, how might the devastating loss of records that occurred in 1922 be mitigated? Many CSO records destroyed in 1922 were actually copies of original correspondence. During the early modern period, it was common practice for a lord lieutenant or chief secretary to retain his papers when his period in office came to an end. This practice was so common that in 1702 a state paper office was created, tasked with keeping duplicates of the records created by the Dublin Castle administration.[99] Thus, duplicates of many records destroyed in the Four Courts can be found in the private papers of the men who filled these key roles. These proxy CSO archives can be found in repositories such as the British Library or the various English county record offices.[100] An especially rich concentration of such records

---

[97] For the medieval origins of these offices, see H. G. Richardson and G. O. Sayles, *The Administration of Ireland, 1172–1377* (Dublin, 1963); J. P. Casey, *The Irish Law Officers* (Dublin, 1996); A. R. Hart, *A History of the King's Serjeants at Law in Ireland* (Dublin, 2000).

[98] A good example can be found in the career of John Fitzgibbon, Earl of Clare, who served as Irish attorney general from 1783 to 1789, and then as lord chancellor of Ireland from 1789 to 1802. For Fitzgibbon's role as advisor to the CSO, see D. A. Fleming and A. P. W. Malcomson (eds.), *'A Volley of Execrations': The Letters and Papers of John Fitzgibbon: Earl of Clare, 1772–1802* (Dublin, 2005), *passim*.

[99] H. Wood, 'The Destruction of the Public Records: The Loss to Irish History', *Studies: An Irish Quarterly Review*, 11:43 (1922), 371–2.

[100] Examples include the papers of Thomas Pelham (chief secretary, 1782–83, 1795–98), BL, Add. MS 33100–03; papers of Sir Robert Peel (chief secretary, 1812–18) BL, Add. MS

may be found at the Public Record Office of Northern Ireland (PRONI). For instance, PRONI holds the papers of Sir George Macartney (1737–1806), who served as chief secretary during the viceroyalty of George Townshend in the years 1768–1772.[101] This was a pivotal moment in the evolution of the CSO, as Townshend and Macartney oversaw the reorganisation of the office as well as increasing the influence of the chief secretary within the Irish parliament. Macartney's Irish papers effectively provide a substitute CSO archive for this key period.[102] A similar resource can be found in the papers of Robert Stewart, Viscount Castlereagh (1769–1822), who served as chief secretary at the time of the 1798 Rebellion, as well as during the negotiations and passage of the Act of Union in 1800.[103] PRONI also holds the papers of another influential lord lieutenant, Henry Paget, first marquis of Anglesey (1768–1854), who held the office between 1828 and 1833.[104] A liberal who supported reform and was sympathetic to the pro-Catholic campaigns of Daniel O'Connell, Anglesey's correspondence with his several chief secretaries are a key source for historians.[105]

However, the single largest source of replacement materials for the CSO are the collections of state papers held by The National Archives (UK). During the eighteenth century, the lord lieutenant regularly sent public dispatches, such as formal acknowledgements or requests, to the Secretary of State for the Southern Department, who was responsible for Irish affairs. After 1782, Irish affairs became the responsibility of the British Home Office. The bulk of correspondence between the CSO and the Home Office is located in a series in The National Archives (UK), known as the Home Office 100 series.[106] This 264-volume series, dating

---

40181–40613. See also papers of William Wickham (chief secretary, 1802–4), Hampshire Archives & Local Studies, MS 38M49/C; papers of Henry Goulburn (chief secretary, 1821–27), Surrey History Centre, SHC 304/1.

[101] T. Bartlett, 'Macartney, George (1737–1806), Earl Macartney, Diplomat, Chief Secretary and Colonial Governor', *DIB*.

[102] PRONI, D572, 'Macartney Papers', accessed on VRTI.

[103] P. M. Geoghegan, 'Stewart, Robert (1769–1822), Viscount Castlereagh and 2nd Marquess of Londonderry, Chief Secretary for Ireland, Politician', *DIB*. For his papers: PRONI, D3030, 'Castlereagh Papers', accessed on VRTI.

[104] V. Crossman, 'Paget, Henry William (1768–1844), 1st Marquis of Anglesey, Lord Lieutenant of Ireland', *DIB*.

[105] PRONI, D619/31, 'Correspondence of Anglesey with His Successive Chief Secretaries', accessed on VRTI.

[106] To browse the HO 100 series, see TNA Discovery catalogue (https://discovery .nationalarchives.gov.uk/browse/r/h/C8964).

from 1782 to 1851, contains a multitude of direct replacement and substitute materials for CSO series, both civil and military, destroyed in 1922. HO 100 contains additional papers on special subjects, such as Catholic emancipation, poor law reform, policing and 'outrages', and various special commissions.[107] For the period after 1852, equivalent materials can be found within a sub-division of the Colonial Office papers, also held in The National Archives (UK).[108]

In addition to collections in the above repositories, a considerable number of CSO records now in the National Archives of Ireland (NAI) avoided destruction in 1922 because they had not been transferred to the PROI from the Castle by the time of the fire. During the eighteenth and nineteenth centuries, the records produced by the CSO were stored in the Record Tower at the Castle, under the superintendence of the master of the rolls. Under sections 10–11 of the Public Records (Ireland) Act 1867, the State Paper Office remained as a discrete entity. The 1867 Act required the CSO to transfer records to the State Paper Office (SPO) on a regular basis, usually ten years after creation. These remained in the SPO until they were fifty years old, at which point they would be transferred to the PROI. However, this transfer to the PROI was dependent on the documents being properly arranged and indexed by the SPO: there were often lapses in this transfer schedule. Indeed, some of the most significant surviving CSO collections currently held in NAI arise from these very delays in calendaring and indexing. The most significant collection is the 'Chief Secretary Office Registered Papers' (CSORP), which consist of two main archival series covering the years 1818–1924, together with a number of sub-series within this date span.[109] In addition to CSORP, NAI also holds the 'Rebellion Papers', a collection dating from 1790 to 1808, being mainly letters to the government concerning the activities of the United Irishmen and the Rebellion of 1798.[110] There are also two other smaller collections of letters to Dublin Castle from this same period, listed separately as the 'State of the Country Papers', first and second series, dating from 1790 to 1831. In addition to

---

[107] A select calendar of seventy-eight volumes from HO 100 collection (HO 100/37-114), covering the years 1792–1803, is now accessible through VRTI (http://virtualtreasury.ie/curated-collections/home-office-and-ireland).

[108] TNA Discovery catalogue (https://discovery.nationalarchives.gov.uk/details/r/C5093).

[109] T. Quinlan, 'The Registered Papers of the Chief Secretary's Office', *Irish Archives* (Autumn 1994).

[110] D. Lindsay, 'The Rebellion Papers: An Introduction to the Rebellion Papers in the National Archives, Bishop Street, Dublin', *Ulster Local Studies*, 18:2 (1997), 28–36.

these survivals, NAI also holds a number of calendars of CSO materials. Even so, a considerable portion of the CSO papers had been transferred to the Public Record Office by 1919 and were lost in 1922.

The majority of Irish people did not encounter the legal system through the centralised courts in Dublin, but through the assizes and quarter or petty sessions. These were institutions for which the CSO had a duty of oversight, and it is in the records of the CSO that we most clearly see their functioning and shortcomings. The majority of the country's justices of the peace being untrained amateurs, accusations of bias and partiality were rife in the eighteenth century. This was aggravated by the fact that, for most of the century, there was only one state solicitor for the whole of Ireland. After 1787, however, the lord lieutenant was able to appoint 'assistant barristers' to assist magistrates at the quarter sessions.[111] While it was not customary for the crown to prosecute at assize, after 1801 crown solicitors responsible for crown prosecutions at the assize were appointed for each of the then six assize circuits. As the circuits were divided from 1846 onwards, crown solicitors proliferated, with twenty appointed by 1880. The CSO was responsible for transmitting the orders of the attorney general to crown solicitors, while also corresponding with justices of the peace on numerous matters.[112]

In certain circumstances, the CSO could exercise direct control in matters of justice. The lord lieutenant possessed power of pardon, sometimes using it to amend harsh sentences handed down by the courts. Under the Irish Convention Act 1793, extended by later insurrection acts, the lord lieutenant could assume direct jurisdiction over disturbed regions of the country. While this was rare, the lord lieutenant was also enabled by an 1814 Act to appoint stipendiary magistrates (known as 'resident magistrates' or 'RMs') in 'disturbed' districts, extended in 1822 to include any area where local magistrates requested a stipendiary magistrate. The use of stipendiary magistrates, paid by central government and professionally trained, expanded in the 1830s; they were more often appointed as a substitute for, than as a complement to, unpaid local magistrates. The central supervision of justice was further enhanced in the second half of the 1830s, when proceedings of petty sessions, quarter sessions and assizes came under increased surveillance by the CSO, as the

---

[111] The title of 'assistant barrister' changed to county court judge in 1877.

[112] For a guide to surviving papers of the chief crown solicitor held in NAI, see B. Griffin, *Sources for the Study of Crime in Ireland, 1801–1921* (Dublin, 2005), 20, 38.

compilation of jury lists and protection of witnesses fell under new regulations imposed by Dublin Castle. Additionally, stipendiary magistrates kept the Castle informed about conditions in the districts they visited, providing a vital source of intelligence. The CSO, in turn, relayed this information to London, serving as the 'window through which the Home Secretary and the cabinet viewed the Irish landscape'.[113]

A parallel development occurred in the realm of policing, an area which quickly became one of the core responsibilities of the CSO after 1800. While historians debate the extent to which Ireland was 'a laboratory for empire', there is little question that innovations in British policing first took place in Ireland. One might start with the innovative 'Peace Preservation Force' created by Chief Secretary Robert Peel in 1814. Soon known as 'the Peelers' (the same nickname was later bestowed on the London Metropolitan Police), this force was replaced in 1822 by the Irish Constabulary (after 1867, the Royal Irish Constabulary). From the outset, these new agencies of law enforcement had unique characteristics in a United Kingdom context. They were centralised forces, responsive to the will of the CSO which kept in close contact through an inspector general. The Irish Constabulary was an armed force responsible for the peace of the whole country except for Dublin, where a concurrent evolution in local law enforcement led in 1836 to the creation of an unarmed Dublin Metropolitan Police, a force similarly under the direct supervision of the CSO.[114]

While these innovations do not necessarily justify any idea of Irish legal exceptionalism, they do reflect a larger divergence in English and Irish legal process, especially criminal process. As one recent study of the subject has pointed out: 'habeas corpus was suspended or a coercion act of some form or another in place in Ireland for all but 16 years of the nineteenth century'.[115] In contrast, habeas corpus was only suspended in England on very few occasions during the nineteenth century: for eleven months in 1817, and briefly during 1866 in reaction to unrest produced by the Irish Fenian movement. The notion that Ireland could not be ruled under English common law was a persistent idea among administrators in both London and Dublin. The recurrent outbreaks of 'outrages', usually the

---

[113] G. Ó Tuathaigh, *Ireland before the Famine, 1798–1848* (Dublin, 1972), 80.
[114] Dublin Police Act 1836, 6 & 7 Will. IV, c. 29. See S. H. Palmer, *Police and Protest in England and Ireland, 1780–1850* (Cambridge, 1988), 184–5, 224–5, 267.
[115] K. Hughes and D. MacRaild, 'Introduction', in K. Hughes and D. MacRaild (eds.), *Crime, Violence, and the Irish in the Nineteenth Century* (Liverpool, 2017), 6.

work of the agrarian redresser groups which seemed to be an endemic part of Irish society, were used to justify exemplary policing measures, as well as prompting a seemingly endless sequence of select committees and royal commission on Irish 'disturbances'.[116]

This growing responsibility for 'law and order' was reflected in the CSO's involvement in Victorian Ireland's carceral state, as a result of reforms of the prison system. At the beginning of the nineteenth century, central government had only tangential authority over the country's network of 41 gaols and county prisons, along with another 112 bridewells, which for the most part were under the control of the county grand juries. The CSO only had direct control over Dublin's Four Courts Marshalsea, as well as responsibility for convicts awaiting transportation. The lord lieutenant had statutory power to appoint one, later two inspectors general of prisons, who regularly reported to parliament. The wide-ranging Prisons (Ireland) Act 1826 further enhanced oversight, providing for the establishment of new, and the improvement of existing, prisons.[117] This legislation generated a tidal wave of correspondence to the CSO, which had long been the recipient of petitions from prisoners or convicted individuals claiming mercy, leniency or a miscarriage of justice. Since the eighteenth century, it also had special responsibility for transportation of convicts, including the regulation of the prison ships or 'hulks' in which they were held before their journey to a penal colony. While the last transportation of convicts to Australia from Ireland occurred in 1853, the CSO nonetheless remained the main supervisory agency for Irish prisons until the end of British rule in Dublin.

The Land Question and the Law

The CSO was often caught up in debates over how Ireland was to be governed. As a recent survey of nineteenth-century Ireland has argued, the debates could often be reduced to a single question: would Ireland be governed like any other part of the United Kingdom, or did it require special treatment?[118] Even those who wished to assimilate Ireland to

---

[116] J. F. McEldowney, 'Some Aspects of Law and Policy in the Administration of Criminal Justice in Nineteenth-Century Ireland', in J. F. McEldowney and P. O'Higgins (eds.), *The Common Law Tradition: Essays in Irish Legal History* (Dublin, 1990), 117–56.

[117] Prisons (Ireland) Act 1826, 7 Geo. IV, c. 74.

[118] K. T. Hoppen, *Governing Hibernia: British Politicians and Ireland, 1800–1822* (Oxford, 2016), *passim*.

British norms had to recognise differences in the two countries' social conditions, not least in regard to the ownership and occupation of land. If the Act of Union was to transform Ireland into 'West Britain', then the island's agrarian economy and rural social structure had to be transformed, to make way for a modern, capitalist society along English lines. In the second half of the nineteenth century, a series of special courts were created to deal with Irish land ownership.[119] Given the central and emotive role that land ownership has played in Irish public life, this is another instance where legal records serve to illuminate a deeper social history.[120]

Even before the Great Famine of 1845–1850, many Irish landlords were heavily in debt, with mortgages on their properties frequently accumulating far beyond the value of the land used as collateral. Claims by creditors on the indebted landlord's estate were known as 'encumbrances' (sometimes 'incumbrances'). As estates were often the subject of multiple 'encumbrances' from several creditors, multiple parties had a claim to the property. This resulted in the land having a 'defective title', so that it could not be legally transferred to a buyer until all the encumbrances were discharged. However, in the majority of cases the cost of legal proceedings against a landlord would exceed the amount owed. By the 1840s, the Irish courts were overwhelmed with land cases involving title issues. In 1843, a Royal Commission – the 'Devon Commission', named for its chair – was established to examine the state of law relating to Irish land.[121] The inquiry identified serious delays in the Courts of Chancery and Exchequer as a major problem. The idea was floated that an independent tribunal should be established to handle these problematic cases, expediting the sale of insolvent estates. As a result, two Incumbered Estates Acts were passed in 1848 and 1849, designed to facilitate the sale of such lands through the creation of a new court, the Incumbered Estates Court (IEC). The IEC was a mechanism by which the state took ownership of heavily mortgaged properties to which title was disputed. Avoiding lengthy legal proceedings, these estates could then be sold on with an unassailable 'parliamentary' title.[122]

---

[119] The most notable example is the collection entitled 'Incumbered and Landed Estates and Land Judges' Courts' (PRO ILE).

[120] The classic study remains P. Bew, *Land and the National Question in Ireland, 1858–82* (Dublin, 1978).

[121] *Report from Her Majesty's Commissioners of Inquiry into the State of Law and Practice in Respect to the Occupation of Land in Ireland*, pt. II. 685: HC 1845 [C. 616] xx 1.

[122] The most extensive account to date is J. A. Crowley, '"The Five-Year Experiment": The Incumbered Estates Court, 1849–54' (unpublished PhD thesis, NUI Maynooth, 2017).

In 1858, the IEC was replaced by the Landed Estates Court (LEC), like its predecessor, a court of record with power to grant parliamentary titles but with broader jurisdiction to resolve all disputes under the provisions of the Settled Estates Act 1856, and not just those relating to title to incumbered estates. Nevertheless, the LEC's primary business remained the sale and transfer of incumbered estates. Under the Supreme Court of Judicature Act 1877, the LEC was replaced by the Land Judges Court (LJC), which was part of the Chancery Division of the newly established High Court. However, the rules and practice of the Landed Estates Court continued.[23] The LJC was soon joined by another entity: the Irish Land Commission (ILC). Not to be confused with the Devon Commission, which is colloquially referred to as 'the Irish Land Commission' in Wood's *Guide* and elsewhere, the Irish Land Commission established in 1881 was a departure from preceding land courts.[124] Although its primary focus was not on title issues but the adjudication of 'fair rent' under the Land Law (Ireland) Act 1881, nevertheless, from the outset, the Commission had a role in facilitating tenant purchase of the freehold estate, a role which developed under subsequent 'land purchase' legislation. Unlike the IEC, LEC and LJC, the ILC's records were never transferred to the PROI and thus escaped destruction in 1922.[125]

The volume of records produced by these special land courts was immense. One barrister, familiar with the workings of the Incumbered Estates Commissioners, estimated that they had transferred upwards of 250,000 documents and muniments of title to the PROI.[126] While this estimate seems high, the scale of land records lost in 1922 was undoubtedly considerable. Among the documents destroyed were petitions presented to the land courts, deeds of sale, notices, objections, schedules of incumbrances, commissioners' books, as well as minutes and

---

[123] J. A. Dowling 'The Landed Estates Court, Ireland', *Journal of Legal History*, 26 (2005), 143–76; F. Fitzsimmons, 'Records of the Irish Land Commission', *History Ireland*, 22:1 (2014), 49.

[124] See note 123 above, and Wood, *Guide*, 275.

[125] Following the partition of Ireland, the Irish Land Commission continued to function in the Irish Free State, and was part of the legal machinery of land ownership in Ireland until its formal abolition in 1999.

[126] A. M. Sullivan, *New Ireland*, 2 vols. (London, 1877), vol. 1, 296. Sullivan provided a number of 2,395 boxes of documents transferred to the Record Office. The figure of 250,000 documents was simply his best estimate.

correspondence of the court.[127] While such losses are disheartening, some strong replacement and substitute sources are available, for example, British Parliamentary Papers associated with the workings of the land courts described above. The IEC, for example, reported to parliament on the business of the court, providing general statistics and information on its internal workings.[128]

Many of the records of the IEC were printed and can be reconstructed from contemporary publications. One of the destroyed series was the official set of IEC rentals. These were published as part of estate sales supervised by the court. Several sets of rentals survive in private collections as well as in reference sets held by lesser courts. The most complete set are the 75,000 rentals collected as the 'O'Brien Rentals', held by NAI. This set had been preserved by Sir Peter O'Brien (1842–1914), who served as lord chief justice of Ireland from 1889 to 1913. It was probably a duplicate set created by the IEC and the successor bodies until 1881.[129] The O'Brien Rentals are complemented by two other sets held by the National Library of Ireland (NLI). While not as complete as the O'Brien Rentals, the NLI sets nonetheless contain a number of rentals not found elsewhere.[130] *Allnutt's Irish Land Schedule and Incumbered Estates Advertiser*, which appeared between 1850 and 1871, published the particulars of each sale that came before the court, providing the names of the owner, the location (both parish and townland), the annual rental, the conditions of tenure and date of sale. However, elements of the sale such as the petitioner's name and degree of incumbrance were not typically published. A complete set of *Allnutt's Irish Land Schedule* is not held in any Irish repository, although a complete set is available in the Bodleian Library, Oxford.[131]

---

[127] A number of boxes of LEC deeds and instruments of title survived the 1922 fire, due to their location in the basement of the PROI. A guide to these surviving materials is available in the reading room of NAI.

[128] E.g. *Report of Her Majesty's Commissioners Appointed to Inquire into the Incumbered Estates Court*, HC 1854–55 (1938), xix, 527.

[129] For an overview of the different sets of rentals, see T. Dooley, *The Big Houses and Landed Estates: A Research Guide* (Dublin, 2007), 99–101. The archival history of the O'Brien Rentals remains obscure, and the exact sequence of events that led to their deposit with the PROI after 1922 is unclear.

[130] NLI – 2M 1 and 2. The first set was maintained by the Irish Land Commission as a reference tool, while the second set is in the private collection of Joseph Burke. Yet another set of rentals, numbering 178 bound volumes, is also held by the King's Inns.

[131] It is also accessible in the British Newspaper Archive. For a full discussion of these potential replacement sources, see Crowley, 'The Five-Year Experiment', 15–18.

By the end of the nineteenth century, successive British governments had sought to counter Irish nationalist separatism by setting up agencies responsible for the development of Ireland's economy.[132] The IEC, LEC and ILC must be counted among these, having few parallels in other jurisdictions within the United Kingdom. The records of these courts do more than illustrate Irish legal exceptionalism; they chart the breaking up of the large landed estates and the creation of a new class of independent freehold-owning farmers in the process. While the events of the years 1916–1923 constituted Ireland's political revolution, the country's *social* revolution had occurred in the preceding decades, under the oversight and influence of these courts. What can be found in their various records is no less than an account of the remaking of the country's social structure. In reconstructing such records, the historian is presented with a clear view of how legal bodies touched the lives of everyday people, from the large estate owner to the poorest tenant farmer.

***

'Masses of records from all parts of the country, and of very various kinds, have been accumulated there during the last fifty years, and have been extensively used by historians, lawyers, genealogists and the general public.' Such was the warning given to the Provisional Government of Ireland on 29 May 1922, a mere month before the disaster that was to befall the PROI on 30 June: 'the loss of any of these records would be irreparable'.[133] The conjunction here of the PROI's principal classes of researchers – beginning with 'historians' and 'lawyers' – is striking. This chapter has explored the PROI both as a repository of legal records and as a store-house for legal history. We have emphasised the interaction of society and the law over many centuries. The PROI's archival collections documented the law through Irish history and, equally, enabled history to emerge from the study of legal records. While lawyers on legal business may have formed the largest group consulting the PROI's

---

[132] L. P. Curtis, *Coercion and Conciliation in Ireland, 1880–1892* (Princeton, NJ, 1963); A. Gailey, 'Unionist Rhetoric and Irish Local Government Reform, 1895–9', *Irish Historical Studies*, 24 (1984), 52–68.

[133] NLI, McEnery Papers, MS 22,432: M. J. McEnery, President of the Royal Society of Antiquaries of Ireland, to Mr De Valera, political leader of the anti-Treaty republicans, and to the Commandant Four Courts 29 May 1922, and their replies of 30 May and 6 June 1922; in C. Wallace (ed.), '"Their Loss Would Be Irreparable": The RSAI's Campaign to Protect the Public Record Office of Ireland, April to June 1922', *Journal of the Royal Society of Antiquaries of Ireland* (in press).

records – looking to inspect court records or order certified copies – they were by no means the sole category of readers, even in the nineteenth century. The PROI also welcomed a wider public of 'Literary Searchers' pursuing interests in Irish history and genealogy. Literary searchers were permitted to access the records free of charge, once the deputy keeper was satisfied that their investigations were for 'an exclusively literary purpose', that is, not part of a legal case. This was, in a sense, the birth not merely of the historical profession, but of legal history as an applied discipline.

The chapter has sought to demonstrate the benefit of understanding the archival provenance and arrangement of the PROI's destroyed collections, as well as the latent potential of so much material that either survived the fire or can be used to mitigate losses. The historian James C. Scott coined the phrase 'seeing like a state', imploring scholars to be aware of the ways in which their view of the past is moderated and shaped by the attitudes of those in power, whose documents historians frequently analyse.[134] We might modify Scott's dictum and implore researchers of the need to 'see like a state archive'. Historians from a variety of fields are increasingly concerned with what is dubbed 'the archival turn', with a fresh emphasis on how archives reflect the development of institutions, in all their messy changes, compromises and rationalisations, as well as how these documents must be read 'against the grain' to reveal wider social histories.[135] Court archives allow us to undertake an 'archaeology' of legal institutions and practices, but we should never forget that these archives are themselves institutions of social memory. In this way, the reconstruction of PROI's legal archives proves to be a powerful method of historical reappraisal in its own right. A key part of VRTI's work has been to construct an 'inventory of loss', the better to understand the extent and nature of what was destroyed in the flames in 1922. The investigation of the lost archive reveals the story of how courts were created, evolved and disappeared over several centuries of legal development and change. It has shown how Ireland's legal institutions both conformed with and departed from British precedents, and the ways in which this was reflected in broader political and constitutional debates. But more than all this, we see how the law, in all its various manifestations, touched the everyday lives of ordinary men and women.

---

[134] J. C. Scott, *Seeing Like a State: How Certain Schemes to Improve the Human Condition Have Failed* (New Haven, CT, 1998).

[135] A. Walsham, 'The Social History of the Archive: Record-Keeping in Early Modern Europe', *Past & Present*, 230, *Supplement Issue* 11 (November 2016), 9–48; A. L. Stoler, *Along the Archival Grain: Epistemic Anxieties and Colonial Common Sense* (Princeton, NJ, 2009).

INDEX

For EU product safety concerns, contact us at Calle de José Abascal, 56–1°, 28003 Madrid, Spain or eugpsr@cambridge.org.

www.ingramcontent.com/pod-product-compliance
Ingram Content Group UK Ltd.
Pitfield, Milton Keynes, MK11 3LW, UK
UKHW021947101025
463821UK00008B/143